Secret of the Vajra World

The Tantric Buddhism of Tibet

THE WORLD OF TIBETAN BUDDHISM
Volume Two

REGINALD A. RAY

Foreword by Tulku Thondup

SHAMBHALA · BOSTON & LONDON · 2002

SHAMBHALA PUBLICATIONS, INC.
HORTICULTURAL HALL
300 MASSACHUSETTS AVENUE
BOSTON, MASSACHUSETTS 02115
www.shambhala.com

©2001 by Reginald A. Ray

Excerpts from *The Tibetan Book of Living and Dying,* by Sogyal Rinpoche and edited by Patrick Gaffney and Andrew Harvey, copyright ©1993 by Rigpa Fellowship, are reprinted by permission of HarperCollins Publishers, Inc.

Further copyright information appears in the Credits, page 509.

9 8 7 6 5 4 3 2 1

FIRST PAPERBACK EDITION
Printed in the United States of America
⊚ *This edition is printed on acid-free paper that meets the American National Standards Institute Z39.48 Standard.*

Distributed in the United States by Random House, Inc., and in Canada by Random House of Canada Ltd

LIBRARY OF CONGRESS CATALOGING-IN-PUBLICATION DATA

RAY, REGINALD A.
SECRET OF THE VAJRA WORLD: THE TANTRIC BUDDHISM OF TIBET / REGINALD A. RAY.—1ST ED.
P. CM.—(THE WORLD OF TIBETAN BUDDHISM; V. 2)
INCLUDES BIBLIOGRAPHICAL REFERENCES AND INDEX.
ISBN 1-57062-772-X (ALK. PAPER)
ISBN 1-57062-917-X (PBK.)
1. TANTRIC BUDDHISM—CHINA—TIBET 2. SPIRITUAL LIFE—TANTRIC BUDDHISM. I. TITLE.
BQ7604 .R39   2002 VOL. 2
[BQ8912.9]
294.3′923 S—DC21
[294.3/925/095
2002007342

SECRET OF THE VAJRA WORLD

Mahakala

Contents

Foreword

Secret of the Vajra World is a comprehensive survey of the profound and vast teachings of the Vajrayana, focusing especially on the Kagyü and Nyingma lineages. Acharya Ray's mastery of the subject and devotion to the tradition—an inspiring combination of gifts—permeate the entire book. Streams of nectarlike quotations from the warm breath of many great masters and an abundance of illuminating stories produce a book that is meaningful, enchanting, and easy to understand. Taken together with the author's earlier work, *Indestructible Truth,* it provides an in-depth treatment of Tibetan Buddhism, including both its exoteric (Hinayana and Mahayana) and esoteric (Vajrayana) vehicles, illuminating its philosophical basis, meditation practices, goal of enlightenment, cultural context, and historical background.

Buddhism offers multiple approaches to awaken the enlightened nature of the mind. The true nature of the mind is enlightened, the utmost peace, openness, and omniscience. Conceptual notions of forms, words, and feelings are mere designations created and felt by the dualistic mind, all rooted in grasping at a "self," perceived as a truly existing entity. Therefore, when the enlightened nature of the mind is awakened, our grasping mentality dissolves and all the mental objects—the whole universe—are awakened as the Buddhafield, the qualities of the enlightened nature. Jetsun Milarepa said:

> Don't you know that all the appearances are the nature of your
>   mind?
> Don't you know that [the nature of] your mind is Buddha?
> Don't you know that Buddha is the ultimate body (*dharmakaya*)?
> Don't you know that ultimate body is the ultimate nature
>   (*dharmata*)?

If you know them, then all the appearances are your own
    mind.*

For us unawakened beings, the enlightened nature of our mind has
been obscured because of our own dualistic concepts and emotional afflictions rooted in grasping at "self." The mind's true nature has become
unknown to us, like a treasure buried under layers of earth. But when
the true nature is uncovered through the right Buddhist training that
suits us, we become the Fully Awakened One, the Buddha. Buddha
said:

Beings are Buddha in their nature.
But their nature has been obscured by adventitious defilements.
When the defilements are cleared,
They themselves are the very Buddhas.†

Buddhist trainings start with taming the mind, because the mind is
the source of all our mental events and physical actions. If our mind is
peaceful and kind, all our thoughts and efforts will benefit ourselves
and others. Buddhist trainings lead us directly to, or at least toward, the
goal—the realization of Buddhahood, the true nature of the mind and
the whole universe.

Buddhist trainings comprise a wide range of approaches, each
adapted to the particular needs of different kinds of trainees. Nevertheless, all can be distilled into three major vehicles, or *yanas*.

Fundamental Buddhism (Hinayana): In this training, practitioners
avoid encountering the sources of negative mentalities and emotions by,
for instance, living in solitary places and observing celibacy. This approach is like walking around a poisonous tree to avoid its afflictions.
This is the path of *pratimoksha* (individual liberation), which primarily
emphasizes adhering to a set of physical disciplines and refraining from
harming others.

*rJe bTsun Mi La Ras Pa'i rNam Thar rGyas Par Phye Ba mGur'Bum (India: Chitra
Monastery), folio 57b/6.
†Kyer rDo rJe Zhes Bya Ba [brTags Pa gNyis Pa]. Kanjur, rGyud. Vol. Nga (Tibet:
Dege Edition), folio 22a/2.

Progressive Buddhism (Mahayana): In this training, practitioners face negative concepts and emotions and their sources, and conquer them through the use of the right antidotes, such as conquering anger through compassion and tolerance. This approach is like talking to the poisonous tree and cutting it with an ax. This is the path of the bodhisattva (adherent of enlightenment), which emphasizes observing *bodhichitta* (the mind of enlightenment), a mental attitude of taking responsibility for bringing happiness and enlightenment to all mother-beings with love, compassion, joy, and equanimity, and putting those thoughts into practice through the application of the "six perfections." Practitioners here do not just refrain from harming others; they also dedicate themselves to serving others.

Esoteric Buddhism (Vajrayana): In this training, practitioners accept negative concepts and emotions and their sources and transmute them as enlightened wisdom and wisdom power. This approach is like transforming the poison of the tree into a medicinal potion. This is the path of tantra (esoteric continuum) that mainly emphasizes realizing and perfecting the union of wisdom and skillful means and accomplishing the goal of benefits for both oneself and others simultaneously.

Tibetan Buddhism is the major living Buddhist tradition that preserves and practices all three vehicles of Buddhism. The stream of lower vehicles merges into the higher vehicles The higher vehicles embody all the merits of the lower ones.

All Tibetan Buddhists are, at least in theory, initiated into tantra and are thus practitioners of all three vehicles. In their daily practices, though, some Tibetan Buddhists may stress one vehicle over the others. An ideal practitioner, however, practices all three paths simultaneously. Physically, they live according to the moral codes embodied in the *pratimoksha* disciplines. Mentally, they maintain bodhisattva aspirations and practices. At the wisdom level, they take everything as the path of pure nature and qualities as taught in tantra. Kunkhyen Longchen Rabjam writes:

According to the three disciplines of
Shravaka, bodhisattva, and vidyadhara—

You tame your mind-stream, provide benefits for others,
And transform every appearance into the path of pure (nature).*

Tulku Thondup
The Buddhayana Foundation

*Drimed Odzer (Longchen Rabjam), *rDzogs Pa Ch'en Po bSam gTan Ngal-gSo* (Tibet: Adzom Edition), folio 4b/2.

Preface

This is the companion volume to my earlier book, *Indestructible Truth: The Living Spirituality of Tibetan Buddhism*. While that book focuses on the more public, exoteric side of Tibetan Buddhism (known in Tibet as the Hinayana and Mahayana), this work treats its lesser-known, esoteric or tantric aspects as they take shape in the Vajrayana, or "Adamantine Vehicle." Taken together, these two volumes provide a broad introduction to the major facets and traditions of Tibetan Buddhism.

The two books may be read with profit independently of one another. For those who have not read my earlier book, I would like to summarize the approach that I am taking in both books. For many years, I have taught an introductory course at Naropa University and at the University of Colorado on Tibetan Buddhism for students with little or no background in either Buddhism or matters Tibetan. During this time, I have sought an introductory text that would (1) provide an outline to the subject in relatively short compass; (2) not be overly technical or burdened with the myriad details of Tibetan Buddhist history; (3) address the spirituality or "practice" of the tradition, rather than focus primarily on philosophy, dogma, institutional life, or political history; (4) give due attention to the Practice Lineage" traditions such as the Nyingma and the Kagyü, which are often underplayed in the story; and (5) try to strike a balance between my own Western perspective and that of Tibetans speaking about their tradition in their own voices. There are, indeed, several excellent introductions to Tibetan Buddhism on the market, yet none quite addresses these needs. I have thus written *Indestructible Truth* and *Secret of the Vajra World* for my students and also for others wishing a circumscribed, nontechnical introduction to Tibetan Buddhism.

Secret of the Vajra World is divided into four major parts. The first, "Foundations of the Vajrayana," provides a brief overview of the history, philosophy, and pretantric training that stand behind Tibetan Vajrayana Buddhism. Those who have read *Indestructible Truth* have already been exposed to much of this material and will find this part a summary of many of the major themes of that work; thus they may wish to begin their reading with part two. At the same time, the topics in part one are treated in terms of their bearing on the practice of the Vajrayana and include perspectives and material not covered in the earlier book.

Part two, "Entering the Vajra World," describes the unique tantric view of human nature and the external world; the special role of the "guru" or tantric mentor; the preliminary practices that prepare one for full initiation; and the major dimensions of Vajrayana practice, including the visualizations, liturgies, and inner yogas that form the main substance of the tantric way. Part three, "Meeting the Essence of Mind," consists of two chapters, one on mahamudra, the "great symbol" and the other on dzokchen, the "great perfection," the culminating practices of Tibetan Buddhism. Part four, "Tantric Applications," explores the tradition of the *tülku*, or "incarnate lama," the lore surrounding the death of ordinary people and of saints, and the practice of solitary retreat, the epitome of traditional Tibetan Buddhism.

My emphasis on the "spirituality" of Tibetan Buddhism in both *Indestructible Truth* and *Secret of the Vajra World* deserves some comment. By spirituality, I mean those kinds of activities that directly serve the inspiration for maturation, transformation, and, ultimately, realization. In this process, for Tibetans and also for Westerner practitioners of Tibetan Buddhism, meditation obviously occupies a central position, but further engagements also have critical roles to play, such as other contemplative practices, tantric liturgy, service and devotion to one's teacher, study of the dharma, and the sacred arts, to mention a few.

Indestructible Truth and *Secret of the Vajra World*, then, are not broad surveys of Tibetan Buddhism as such, but rather descriptions of the spirituality of the tradition, as practiced in Tibet, as conveyed by Tibetan masters teaching in the West, and as received by their Western students. In taking this approach, a great deal has been left aside, including the complex histories of the individual sects and subsects, the myriad details of the various philosophical schools, the subtleties of scholastic training, practice, and debate, and the intricacies of institutionalized, monastic life. But by leaving aside any effort to be comprehensive, in this and my previous book, I have been able to focus on what is most essential about Tibetan Buddhism, namely its attention to the dynamics of the spiritual life, and on that which is of greatest interest and perhaps most importance to modern readers.

Acknowledgments

I want to express my gratitude to the Naropa University community, which provided sabbatical leave and research grants to facilitate this work. Thanks to my friend Peter Goldfarb and the Goldfarb Foundation for underwriting some of the expenses involved in my research. Particular appreciation goes to Sakyong Mipham Rinpoche and Dzigar Kongtrul Rinpoche as well as the other Tibetan teachers who have allowed me to quote from their published and unpublished teachings. My thanks to Tulku Thondup and Matthieu Ricard, both of whom read the manuscript and provided useful suggestions. Special thanks to Diana J. Mukpo for permission to quote from her late husband's (Chögyam Trungpa's) published and unpublished works. Once again, I owe a special debt to my longtime friend and respected colleague Larry Mermelstein, Director of the Nālandā Translation Committee, who read the manuscript closely and offered many useful perspectives, insights, and suggestions. Thanks to others who contributed in various ways to this work, including Dr. Mitchell Levy for the remarkable interview that appears in chapter 18; to Jenny Bondurant for her fine account of retreat experience in chapter 17; to Irini Rockwell and Giovannina Jobson for the outlines of the five buddha family chart found in chapter 7; and to John Rockwell for discussions on the six yogas of Naropa. My appreciation goes, again, to my Shambhala editor Kendra Crossen Burroughs, whose assistance with this book has been invaluable; and to Hazel Bercholz and Lora Zorian for bringing the design of this and my previous book into such elegant alignment with its subject matter. Thanks to Emily Bower and Liz Monson, Sakyong Mipham Rinpoche's editors; Vern Mizner, editor for Dzigar Kongtrul Rinpoche; and L. S. Summer, who prepared the index. Thanks to my students at Naropa University and the University of Colorado who read and critiqued early drafts of this book. I am particularly grateful to Sam Bercholz, founder and publisher of Shambhala Publications, for inviting me to write *Indestructible Truth* and *Secret of the Vajra World,* and for his encouragement and support of me and my writing. Finally, I wish to express my gratitude to my wife, Lee, for her sharp eye and her unfailing wisdom in helping me bring the book to completion from initial draft to the final proofing.

SECRET OF THE VAJRA WORLD

Introduction

"VAJRA WORLD" TRANSLATES A TECHNICAL TERM IN SANskrit, *vajradhatu,* meaning "realm of indestructibility." It refers to that level of reality which is beyond all thought and imagination, all impermanence and change. It is a realm that is described as colorful, vivid, and filled with unexpected beauty and meaning. It is this vajra world, according to Tibetan Buddhism, that a fully realized person knows and inhabits.

In the title of this book, I use "vajra world" metaphorically to refer to the traditional culture of Tibet. In many respects, Tibet was like any other human society with its share of foibles and miscreants. But in another sense, not only for many modern people but also—poignantly enough—for the Tibetans themselves, Tibet came as close as perhaps a human culture may to being a vajra world. The shocking splendor and magnificence of its landscape; the warm and earthy character of its people; their seeming wholeness and rootedness in their lives; the brilliance of Tibetan philosophy and ethics; and the color, vividness, and drama of its religion—all communicate a life lived close to reality and drawing on its deep springs.

Of course, to call Tibet a "vajra world" is ironic, for old Tibet—like so many other premodern cultures—has shown itself to be anything but indestructible. As is too well known and all too painful to bear repeating, traditional Tibet has been overrun and nearly obliterated by the tidal wave of modernity.

Nevertheless, there is something of Tibet that lives on, something that has survived the mortal assault on the place and its people. This living quality of Tibet continues to fascinate and compel us modern people, and to fuel our imagination and inspiration. One may wonder, then, just what this enduring quality of Tibet might be. What is the secret of Tibet? What is the secret of this vajra world?

I believe that the attraction that Tibet continues to hold for modern people is not based purely on naive romanticism and the exoticism that surrounds such a far-off and different culture. It seems to me that there bleeds through Tibet something else, something more basic and universally understood—an evident commitment to life; a fullness of embodiment; a warmth toward others; a depth of experience; a joy in the most simple and ordinary experiences of life; and an ability to include and incorporate both happiness and the intense suffering and grief that have lately been the fate of Tibet. But what, one may ask, is the source of these profoundly human qualities that one finds so vividly embodied among Tibetans? What is the secret of the world that was traditional Tibet?

In this book, I propose that the secret of this vajra world lies in something that transcends Tibet itself, namely its spiritual traditions, and particularly the Tantric or Vajrayana Buddhism that provided the foundation of Tibetan culture for some twelve hundred years. As a tradition, far from being otherworldly, the Vajrayana directs attention to this world of sensory experience, of happiness and sorrow, of life and death, as the place where ultimate revelation occurs. The practice of tantra opens up an appreciation for ordinary life as the fount of inspiration, wisdom, and liberation. I suggest to the reader that the color, energy, and vivacity of Tibet are owing, in some significant way, to its tantric foundations.

From the tantric viewpoint, the vajra world—now in the sense of the *ultimate nature of reality*—is like a fiery ocean, an experiential intensity, that underlies all human cultures and human life. This flaming substrate—which is none other than the fire of primordial wisdom—continually gives rise to sparks and plumes and occasionally to conflagrations of incandescence. In the modern era, most people and most cultures preoccupy themselves with trying to blanket these expressions, to ignore and deny them, in order to maintain their habitual "business as usual." The Vajrayana, however, provides a means to open to the burning, turbulent wisdom of reality and to allow it expression in cultural forms and human creativity. It was Tibet's good fortune to encounter the Vajrayana at a critical moment and to assimilate its perspectives. The result is a culture that has, to a large extent, been born and shaped from the unending inspiration of ordinary life itself, experienced without shadows. Old Tibet, unlike most contemporary cultures, lay close upon the incandescent sea and was particularly transparent to it. It is ultimately this quality, I think, that people sense and that so many find engaging and compelling about Tibet.

Buddhism flourished in India from the time of the Buddha in the sixth century BCE to the Muslim invasions that destroyed institutionalized Buddhism in North India, culminating about 1200 CE. During the course of this seventeen-hundred-year history, three major Indian orientations developed. First to appear, following the passing of the Buddha, was that of the Eighteen Schools (sometimes called *nikaya* Buddhism). Some centuries later—around the first century BCE, the Mahayana, or Great Vehicle, entered upon the Indian scene. And finally, in the seventh century CE, the Vajrayana, the "tantric vehicle,"* made its appearance upon the stage of Indian history. Each of these three represents a distinctive approach to the practice of the dharma: the Eighteen Schools stresses the four noble truths and individual nirvana; the Mahayana places its emphasis on the compassionate ideal of the bodhisattva along with the altruistic practices of the six *paramitas*, or perfections; and the Vajrayana is a colorful and intensely practice oriented yogic tradition calling for the attainment of enlightenment in this life.

During its long existence in India, Buddhism spread from the Indian subcontinent throughout Asia. In most of the cultures to which it traveled, all three of these orientations were taught and propagated. Nevertheless, for historical and cultural reasons, in each culture one or another

---

*In this book, for the sake of simplicity and because of the general level of the discussion, I use "Vajrayana" and "Tantric Buddhism," as interchangeable terms. When employing these designations, then, I intend them to be inclusive, comprehending the teachings contained in the liturgical texts known as tantras as well as the formless practices associated in Tibet with mahamudra and dzokchen.

of the three orientations tended to predominate. For example, in Southeast Asia, in Sri Lanka, Burma, Thailand, and elsewhere, although the Mahayana and Vajrayana were known, the Theravada, one of the early Eighteen Schools, came to be the dominant force. Similarly, in China, Korea, and Japan, it was Mahayana Buddhism that provided the predominant Buddhist orientation. Tibet is unique in the Asian world, for it was here and here alone that the Vajrayana reigned supreme.*

Although at one time the Vajrayana was known throughout Asia, owing to its radical and unconventional approach it was not tolerated for long in most cultures to which it went. Tibet, however, proved a remarkable exception, and thus if one wants to know something of Vajrayana Buddhism, one must look to Tibet. The Vajrayana was not only transplanted into Tibetan soil but flourished there, continuing to grow and develop over some twelve hundred years. Tibet provided a uniquely welcoming environment for the practice of tantra owing to several factors—including the particular historical period during which the Tibetans were adopting Buddhism (the Vajrayana was prominent in India during this time); the indigenous shamanistic religion of Tibet (with its many elements in common with the Vajrayana); and the rugged character of the Tibetans (with their uncompromising sense of personal dignity, individuality, and independence, echoing the concept of "vajra pride" in the Vajrayana). Also critical to the survival of the tantra in Tibet was the social and political decentralization of the country, which inhibited attempts to standardize Buddhism along more politically and socially conventional lines.[1]

In Tibet prior to the Chinese occupation, the Vajrayana was not only the supreme and culminating Buddhist vehicle; in addition, to a large extent, it gave shape and color to the whole of Tibetan Buddhism. For example, it provided an overarching dharmic framework including within its folds both early Buddhist teachings of the pre-Mahayana

*The Vajrayana was also practiced among the Mongols, but in the vehicle of Tibetan Buddhism, which the Mongols adopted. Elements of Tantric Buddhism also survive in Japan (in Shingon and Tendai, which are based on the practice of Kriya and Charya tantras, understood in Tibet as the "lower" or more conventional tantras).

4

Eighteen Schools as well as the full range of Mahayana traditions. In addition, many of the most vivid aspects of Tibetan religious life have their roots in the Vajrayana, including its colorful temples, vivid iconography, and striking deities; the liturgies performed in every monastery and home; its theater and dances, and the esoteric yogas; its rich tradition of hagiographies and lineages of "mad saints"; the practices surrounding the incarnate lamas; and its many ways of working with death and dying. In fact, it was the special role of Tibet to provide a place where the multitude of Indian Vajrayana traditions could find safe haven.

Beyond this, however, the very culture of Tibet itself was permeated by the Vajrayana. Even the social, political, and religious institutions in Tibet were, to a large extent, expressions of a Vajrayana Buddhist outlook. It is true, then, that one needs to study Tibet in order to find out about the Vajrayana; but it is equally true that, as mentioned, one needs to study the Vajrayana in order to understand the Tibetans and their culture.

Tibet, as is well known, was occupied by the Chinese communists beginning with incursions into Tibet in 1949 and culminating in a complete takeover within a decade. In spite of the Tibetans' intense love of their country and the remarkable distinctiveness of their culture—or perhaps because of these—over the past half a century the Chinese have continued to wear away and destroy the face of Tibet. As each year goes by, this magnificent and wonderfully rich culture is coming more and more to assume the appearance of a mere economic and social appurtenance of China. The tradition does survive in various places in Tibet, but it is hard pressed. Within this context, one wonders how Buddhism—and especially the Vajrayana—will be able to survive in Tibet in any integral form.

Tibetan Buddhism also continues to exist in Asia, in pockets in which Tibetan culture still survives, outside of Chinese control. It exists in diaspora in other places in Asia, in India and elsewhere, in monasteries and refugee settlements that have been built. But the last generation of teachers trained in old Tibet has nearly disappeared. New generations of monks and nuns, who never knew Tibet, are receiving training, but it is a training that is severely strained by the brutal economic and political realities of refugee life. How much of the integral tradition will survive in these contexts, to be passed on?

At this fateful moment, the Vajrayana has appeared in the West. Ironically, it has come from the crucible of the conservative, medieval culture of Tibet, in a remarkably vigorous, engaging, and creative form. Beginning in the 1950s, first a small trickle, then an increasing flow of Tibetan teachers came to Europe and North America, teaching the Vajrayana in ever more open and accessible ways. In this context, it is an interesting question to what extent the integral Vajrayana will be able to take root in the West. One of the purposes of this book is to begin to explore this question.

PART ONE

Foundations of Vajrayana

1
The Indian Prelude[1]

In the eleventh century, a renowned Buddhist scholar named Naropa was sitting in the sun at the famed Nalanda monastic university in northeast India, studying his texts. Suddenly, in a revelation that broke open his life, an old hag appeared out of empty space and confronted him with the truth that in spite of his surpassing intellectual knowledge of the dharma, he had no idea of what it actually meant on a human level. She declared that to acquire genuine wisdom he must cast away his books, leave his comfortable and prestigious monastic lifestyle, and abandon what most people in his Indian context identified as the epitome of the dharmic life. His only hope, so he was informed, was to set out into trackless jungle wastes "to the east," in search of a Vajrayana master named Tilopa, who alone could show him the path to awakening.

Naropa saw no other option but to follow these rather imprecise instructions. As days turned into weeks and weeks into months, however, he was unable to find this tantric teacher. One day, coming to a certain small monastery, he was admitted and apparently invited to join the monks in their noonday meal. After the doors had been locked from the inside, as was the custom, Naropa happened to be in the cooking area. Suddenly, there appeared out of nowhere a dark-complexioned and very filthy beggar. This strange individual then began to roast live fish over the cooking fire. Naropa, scandalized that anyone would so blatantly contravene monastic procedure, attempted to restrain him but was unsuccessful. Given the Buddhist prohibition against the taking of life, the monks of the place were horrified because of the disrepute such

FIGURE 1.1 *Tilopa, Indian founder of the Kagyü lineage.*
Drawing by Chris Bannigan (Namkha Tashi).

actions would bring upon their establishment. The dark man responded, "If you find this displeasing, I will put the fish back in the water again." He then went outside and threw the roasted fish back into the adjoining river and, springing to life, they swam happily away.

Apparently none of the monks was particularly impressed by this peculiar series of events, and they returned to their usual business. Naropa, on the other hand, realized that something noteworthy had just occurred. In fact, he suspected that this filthy miscreant was a *siddha*, an enlightened tantric teacher. Perhaps, indeed, this was the long-sought-after Tilopa. Naropa forgot about his meal and followed after the beggar, going so far as to prostrate himself and plead for instruction.

Abruptly, the beggar turned on him and began to beat him, meanwhile speaking not a single word. However, when Naropa then began to think, "Is this Tilopa? Is this Tilopa?" The beggar replied out loud, "I am. I am." Then, when Naropa began to think, "No, this couldn't be Tilopa," the beggar replied, "I am not. I am not." His mind swimming with confusion and disorientation, Naropa realized that this must be the master he sought, and he began to follow him as his guru. Although now Tilopa—for it was indeed he—sometimes acted like an accomplished yogin and at others like a madman, Naropa entertained no more doubts. Attending Tilopa for many years, through the most harrowing of circumstances, having sacrificed literally everything he had in body and soul, the erstwhile scholar eventually attained the genuine realization he sought.[2]

Naropa's dates (1016–1100) put him at far remove indeed from the lifetime of Buddha Shakyamuni some fifteen hundred years earlier. More than this, however, the strange interactions between Naropa and Tilopa would seem to have little to do with the Buddha's dharma. In fact, the tantric way espoused by the siddha Tilopa might well seem to represent, by any and all accounts, a different religious universe altogether.

From the Tibetan point of view, however, Tantric or Vajrayana Buddhism represents Buddha Shakyamuni's most essential and ultimate teaching. If much of what is ascribed to him by tradition seems decidedly nontantric, this is only an appearance. In fact, for Tibetans, the

FIGURE 1.2 *Naropa, disciple of Tilopa and guru of Marpa;*
the Tibetan founder of the Kagyü lineage. Drawing by Robert Beer.

Vajrayana is the essential heart of the entire Indian dharma. If all of the apparently nontantric teachings of Indian tradition are boiled down to one point, that point is the essential nature of mind that is articulated most purely, explicitly, and directly in the Vajrayana. If the nontantric teachings of the Buddha appear so far removed from this essential, tantric heart, it is because they provide more gradual and accessible avenues of approach to this inner citadel of the Buddha's ultimate instruction.

Tibetans hold that human beings are generally not capable of seeing the whole of reality all at once. Rather, spiritual awakening must proceed in stages. Even if the fullness of reality were to be displayed, people could only see what their current level of maturity would allow. In consideration of this quality of human nature, the Buddha gave a vast array of teachings and practices, each of which addresses a particular stage on the path to enlightenment.

Tibetans believe that the Buddha, as a realized being, manifests himself on many different levels. Following Indian tradition, they divide these levels into three primary "bodies." First is the *nirmanakaya*, emanation body, the Buddha's physical, human form in which—as described in his early biographies—he appears as a prince, renounces the world, and follows the path to enlightenment. Second, the Buddha appears as the *sambhogakaya*, body of enjoyment, his brilliant, transfigured, nonphysical form of light. In this body he journeys to the heavens, teaches the gods, and reveals himself to highly attained people. Finally there is the Buddha's *dharmakaya*, the body of reality itself, without specific, delimited form, wherein the Buddha is identified with the spiritually charged nature of everything that is.

THE BUDDHA'S LEGACY

The Three Yanas and the Three Turnings of the Wheel of Dharma

For Tibetans, Buddha Shakyamuni's enlightenment at Bodhgaya in India can be viewed from the perspective of each of these three bodies.

As the dharmakaya, the Buddha has always been enlightened and his mind has never departed from that complete and perfect realization. On the sambhogakaya level, his enlightenment was essentially a tantric one, the union of male and female aspects of reality. According to one account, he experienced tantric initiations at the hands of celestial buddhas and realized *mahamudra*, the "great symbol," enlightenment as described in the Vajrayana. Yet, out of respect for the limitations of ordinary people, the Buddha showed to most people only his nirmanakaya form, that of a person, sitting alone underneath a tree, meditating, and achieving enlightenment as a human being.

For the same reasons, when the Buddha rose from his enlightenment experience, he refrained from talking about the full measure of his realization. Instead, he taught more exoteric doctrines, such as the four noble truths, as most immediately accessible and appropriate for the people of his day. Throughout the course of his life, however, the Buddha gave progressively deeper and more sophisticated teachings, sometimes in his human, nirmanakaya form, at other times in the "spiritual body" of the sambhogakaya. By the time of his passing at the age of eighty, he had presented an enormous array of discourses, including "84,000 dharmas," or types of instruction—in other words, a nearly limitless collection of different teachings to address the various types of situations and levels of maturity experienced by sentient beings. Nevertheless, at the center of all these, so the Tibetans hold, was the Vajrayana, with all the other innumerable instructions being understood as more or less provisional approximations, leading in the direction of this most profound of the Buddha's dharma.

During the time when the Tibetans were studying in India, Indian scholars were in the process of organizing the wealth of the Buddha's legacy into the system known as the "three yanas." In this system, the early traditions of the Eighteen Schools were loosely designated by the term Hinayana, the "lesser vehicle," while the second yana was called Mahayana, "the great vehicle," and the third the Vajrayana, or "adamantine vehicle."[3] The Tibetans, following Indian tradition, adopted this system and its way of viewing Indian Buddhist history. According to this interpretation, shortly after his enlightenment, at the Deer Park in Benares the Buddha presented the first yana, the Hinayana. Here he promulgated the "first turning of the wheel of dharma," consisting of the four noble truths. This teaching spread quickly to multitudes of people throughout India and became the foundational teachings of early Buddhism. Later, in Tibet, the Hinayana teachings provided Buddhist tradition both with important practices (the Vinaya, or monastic discipline) and teachings (the Abhidharma, or advanced Buddhist psychology).

Later in his life, to a more select audience, the Buddha presented the second yana, the Mahayana. The Mahayana included a second and a third turning of the wheel of dharma, outlining the basic view and philosophy of the great vehicle. The second turning of the wheel presented "emptiness," while the third outlined the doctrine of buddhanature. On the occasions upon which the Buddha gave the second and third turnings, he deemed that the world was not ready for these more advanced teachings, and so they were kept hidden until such time as people were able to receive them. Some centuries later, through the work of Nagarjuna and others, the Mahayana did begin to make its way in the human world—around 100 BCE, according to modern historians.

Subsequently, the Mahayana sutras originally preached by the Buddha were commented on by successive generations of scholars and meditation masters, producing a textual tradition of great richness and diversity. Standing at the forefront of this tradition were masters such as Nagarjuna, the founder of Madhyamaka, and Asanga, the initiator of Yogachara. The Indian Mahayana sutras and commentaries provide the basis of Buddhist philosophy in Tibet: the great scholars rely on them in their teaching and writing, and the most important texts are studied in the monastic colleges and universities.

Subsequently, in a sambhogakaya form, the Buddha presented the final and culminating yana, the Vajrayana, to a very small audience of his most advanced disciples. Like the Mahayana promulgations, these teachings were kept hidden until such time as the larger human world was able to receive them. Modern scholars date the public appearance of the Buddhist tantra at around the end of the seventh century CE. Between the eighth and the twelfth centuries CE, the Vajrayana

FIGURE 1.3 *Shakyamuni Buddha.*

flourished in India, becoming quite popular and receiving considerable financial support, with many hundreds of tantric texts (*tantras*) and commentaries being written down. Many of these were brought to Tibet and provided the basis of Vajrayana practice there.

Each yana contains characteristic doctrines and also practices tailored to that level of spiritual understanding. From the Tibetan viewpoint, the individual practitioner, in his or her own process of spiritual maturation, follows the three-yana unfolding of the Buddha's teaching, first practicing the Hinayana, next the Mahayana, and finally the Vajrayana. Table 1.1 (reproduced from *Indestructible Truth*) summarizes the essential elements of this Tibetan way of looking at the great variety of teachings given by the Buddha. The three-yana scheme will be discussed in chapter 3 of this book, while the three turnings of the wheel of dharma will be examined in chapter 4.

The Three Lifeways

In addition to the three yanas and the three turnings of the wheel of dharma, Tibetans understand the Buddha also to have taught three lifeways that still provide the basic options for Tibetan Buddhists. The first two of these require renunciation of the world, and the third provides a path for the laity. In terms of the renunciant options, then, one may abandon the world to become either (1) a monastic living in a settled monastery or (2) a yogin meditating in solitude in the wilds—"in the forest," as the Indian texts put it. Or, without renouncing the world, one may remain (3) a layperson and practice Buddhism in the context of ordinary household life. The most ancient of these three ways is the path of the yogin meditating in retreat, the very same path that the Buddha himself pursued and which he taught to his most gifted and advanced disciples. This is a path of radical renunciation in which one leaves all conventional comforts and security behind and lives in solitude, perhaps under a tree, in a cave, or in the open, subsisting on small quantities of food, and meditating day and night.

However, this radical path is difficult and demanding in the extreme, and it is only for the most ardent and dedicated. There are others who

TABLE 1.1

THE THREE YANAS
AS TAUGHT BY BUDDHA SHAKYAMUNI

YANA	VEHICLE	OCCASION OF TEACHING	LOCATION	CONTENT OF THE TEACHING	MAIN TEXTS
Hinayana	Lesser Vehicle	First Turning of the Wheel of Dharma	Deer Park in Benares, NE India	Four Noble Truths: 1) suffering 2) the origin of suffering 3) the cessation of suffering 4) the path	Tripitaka Vinaya sutras Abhidharma
Mahayana	Great Vehicle	Second Turning of the Wheel of Dharma	Vulture Peak Mountain and other locales	Emptiness: All phenomena are without self-nature	Mahayana sutras Prajnaparamita sutras
		Third Turning of the Wheel of Dharma	Vaishali, NE India	Buddha-nature: All sentient beings possess the buddha-nature within. *The Three Natures (svabhava)* Reality may be understood as exhibiting the imaginary, the dependent, and the fully perfected natures.	Buddha-nature sutras *Sandhinirmochana Sutra* *Lankavatara Sutra*
Vajrayana	Adamantine Vehicle	Revelation of the Vajrayana	Dhanya-kataka, Andhra Pradesh, SE India, and other locales	Skillful means of Vajrayana, including visualization and resting in the nature of mind	Tantras

are inspired to renounce the world but for whom the rigors of forest renunciation are beyond reach. In order to meet the needs of such people, a second renunciant option developed, that of settled monasticism. According to this second lifeway, a person may renounce the world and, as a monk or a nun, take up residence in a monastery, thus ensuring a roof over one's head, daily sustenance, and a community of which one is a part. Whereas the forest renunciant spends all of his or her time meditating, monastics typically engage in a variety of activities, revolving around a path of virtuous behavior in accordance with the monastic Vinaya, the study of the sacred texts, maintenance of the monastery, teaching and counseling the laity, caring for the sick, and so on.

The third lifeway is that of the layperson, who venerates renunciants, looks after their material support, and follows an ethical life defined by the well-known five precepts (*pancha-shila*). These include abstention from killing, stealing, lying, sexual misconduct, and intoxicants, and participating in the ritual life of their local monasteries. Through following this path, laypeople are able to receive the Buddhist teachings and accumulate the necessary good karma to advance them along their paths, directing their lives toward the eventual goal of enlightenment in a future life.

In Tibetan Buddhism as previously in India, these three lifeways are closely interconnected. For one thing, the same person, at different times in his or her life, might experience each of these three paths. One might begin as a layperson, renounce the world and become a monk or a nun, later be inspired to enter the forest for a period—perhaps of many years—of solitary meditation, and finally as an aged person return to the monastery to live and teach.

Tibetans view these three lifeways as each performing important and necessary functions within the overall spiritual economy of the dharma. In traditional Tibet, the way of the mountain hermit, the "forest renunciant" in Indian terminology, provided an arena where the teachings of dharma could be carried to their utmost fruition, for here people were able to focus their attention exclusively on meditation. Through this, they were able to attain, in their lifetimes, the realization of enlightenment, the supreme and ultimate goal of Buddhism. Monastic people provided the institutional continuity of the tradition, maintaining monasteries that were Tibet's primary religious centers; acting as paragons of virtue for the lay folk; copying and studying the sacred texts; through study and debate clarifying and refining the teachings; developing distinctive "schools" of interpretation; engaging in religious dialogue with other traditions; and passing their way of life and their understanding on through the training of new monastics. The way of the laity was equally important, for Tibetan laypeople venerated and supported the great saints and teachers; provided material sustenance to the monasteries and their inhabitants; through having children enter the monasteries, thus ensured their continuation; and through bringing the dharma into the many activities of their lives, made Buddhism the core around which Tibetan culture revolved.[4]

THE FURTHER HISTORY OF INDIAN BUDDHISM

From Forest to Monastery: Classical Patterns

The dharma of Buddha Shakyamuni was originally one of forest renunciation, subsequently developing the lifeways of both monastic and layperson. Mahayana Buddhism, in its earliest days, was also largely a forest tradition,[5] held by men and women practitioners meditating in solitude. These yogins and yoginis had devoted lay practitioners who revered them and supported them materially. We first see the "forest Mahayana" about 100 BCE in the earliest Mahayana text we know of, the *Collection of Precious Qualities.*[6] Many centuries later, perhaps around the fourth or fifth century CE, the Mahayana, like the traditions before it, gave rise to a monastic wing. During its full flowering in India, the Mahayana thus also came to possess three lifeways—those of forest meditator, settled monastic, and lay devotee.

Like earliest Buddhism and the Mahayana, the Vajrayana in India was also originally a forest tradition. According to the Tibetan historian Lama Taranatha, its lineages were passed down from one teacher to one or at most a very few disciples, and kept secret and hidden from outside view for centuries.[7] At the end of the seventh century, however, it began to become visible within Indian history as a vigorous and dynamic religious movement defined by its unconventionality and its intense focus on meditation and personal transformation.

From reading the earlier tantric texts, it is clear that the Vajrayana came forward in India at this time partly owing to a diminishing spirituality among the Eighteen Schools and the Mahayana. In the centuries prior to the appearance of the Vajrayana, these traditions had undergone a process of institutionalization. Originally forest lineages, they had largely moved into monastic environments and attained a high level of cultural esteem and material well-being. As part of this process, the monastic traditions underwent a certain amount of adaptation to the prevailing values of the Indian social context. Behavioral purity had become a primary desideratum among the monastic population and the mastery of texts the principal occupation of its elite. In this context, the learning and intellectual accomplishment of a monastery's scholars were crucial: the material well-being and even the survival of the Buddhist monastic lineages and schools depended to a large extent on the renown of their scholars and their success in scholarly debate.

By the time of the appearance of the Vajrayana in India, the dharma seems to have become largely identified with a monasticism in which the practice of meditation, originally the heart of Buddhist spirituality, played a generally quite peripheral role. In any case, this is the picture given in the earlier tantric texts and particularly the hagiographies of the tantric siddhas, the enlightened ideal of the Vajrayana. Here one finds a critique of the conventionality and scholasticism of monastic Buddhism and a call for a return to the primary values of radical renunciation, meditation, and realization.

Tantric Yogins, Monastics, and Lay Practitioners

The siddhas were men and women who came from all social stations and walks of life, from beggars, criminals, and menial workers at the lower end, to kings, queens, and brahmins at the upper. In spite of their great social differences, they were joined together in the intensity of their spiritual aspiration and devotion to their practice. Each in his or her own way had met a personal crisis that they were powerless to resolve through ordinary means. At this critical juncture, they typically met an accomplished tantric master, a siddha, who initiated them into one of the Vajrayana cycles and then set them to meditating. Many of these disciples carried out their practice in solitary retreat, as forest renunciants, but others remained in the world and carried out their meditation in that context.

After many years of practice, the disciples reached enlightenment and themselves became siddhas. Henceforth, they lived in the world, often continuing to follow their given caste occupations, converting others, teaching widely, and training disciples. In their hagiographies, they are depicted as often quite unconventional men and women of extraordinary insight, compassion, and power, and an abundance of miracles and magical feats is a standard feature of their lives. Sometimes, they behaved as if demented or insane, camouflaging their attainment to all but their closest disciples. Owing to their nonmonastic roots, their personal unconventionality, and the tantric practice they followed, the siddhas—at least as depicted in their standard Indian biographies—seem to have lived and practiced in more or less completely nonmonastic contexts.

The Vajrayana remained a mainly nonmonastic tradition until probably sometime in the ninth century, when it began to appear within contexts of Indian monastic life, like the Eighteen Schools and the Mahayana before it. In the ninth through the twelfth century CE, monasteries that were being built gave evidence of Vajrayana influence; Vajrayana texts were being studied in those monasteries; and scholars emerged from them "schooled in the three yanas," meaning that they were learned in Hinayana, Mahayana, and Vajrayana matters. Thus it was that the Vajrayana—like the Eighteen Schools and Mahayana— came to have adherents belonging to all three of the lifeways mentioned above, those of yogin, layperson, and settled monastic.

In addition, a fourth lifeway emerged at this time, which we may term the "householder yogin." This fourth ideal derived from the fact

FIGURE 1.4 *Some of the eighty-four mahasiddhas. From upper left to right:*
Shavaripa, Saraha, Luyipa, Lalipa, Ghantapa, Krishnacharya,
Naropa, Tilopa, Maitripa.

that among the siddhas, as mentioned, were not only forest renunciants
but also elite lay practitioners. These latter, the householder yogins,
lived what seemed ordinary lay lives, marrying, raising families, and
working at various occupations for their livelihood. At the same time,
however, they received tantric initiation, spent periods of time in retreat,

and carried out their Vajrayana practice in secret in their lay contexts, meditating at night and even in the midst of their daily activities, eventually attaining full realization. Typical is the housewife Manibhadra, who, having received initiation, meditated while her Hindu husband and the other members of her family were sleeping. Only years later did her tantric commitments become known, when she attained realization and herself became a siddha. This tradition of the householder yogin became important in Tibet, where many laypeople were able to practice and attain realization in the midst of an ordinary life in the world. The Nyingma lineage, in particular, continues this important development in the tradition of the "married lamas," among whom in each generation are accomplished scholars and teachers, and realized practitioners.

The movement of the Vajrayana into a monastic environment thus replicates the pattern by which both Hinayana and Mahayana similarly developed monastic wings. At the same time, the process and the results of this tantric "monasticization" were somewhat different. However dominant Vajrayana texts, concepts, and symbolism became in many Indian monasteries of the day, institutionalized Vajrayana was never able fully to replace the nonmonastic traditions. In fact, even after the Vajrayana came to reign supreme in much of Indian monastic life, it was an accepted fact that the most serious Vajrayana practice could only occur in the trackless wilderness of the "forest." As we have seen, even as late at the eleventh century Naropa was able to train in the tantra only by abandoning the Buddhist civilization of Nalanda University and setting off into the unknown in search of the elusive Tilopa.

One sees the same kind of pattern in the following story about the great scholar Abhayakaragupta (fig. 1.5), who also lived in the eleventh century.[8] This brahmin was a learned monk who resided at a monastery in North India. He had become a Buddhist in the first place because of a vision of the tantric *yidam* (personal deity), Vajrayogini, a female buddha who embodies one's own innermost being. However, after this vision, instead of entering the practice of Vajrayana, Abhayakaragupta elected to become a monk and follow the inclination, typical of his caste, to pursue the scholarly study of the Vajrayana instead.

FIGURE 1.5 *Abhayakaragupta, eleventh-century tantric scholar and practitioner.*

Nevertheless, he was not to be left alone, for Vajrayogini appeared to him repeatedly, enjoining him to abandon the mere study of the Vajra-yana and engage in the practice. Each time, the decorous monk de-murred, claiming that the practice was too risky to his identity as a monk and a brahmin. On the occasion of her last visit, Vajrayogini said to him, "You know three hundred tantras and have received the very best oral instructions on them. How can you possibly have doubts about the actual practice?" Yet the proud and stubborn monk would not be swayed, even by this stunning embodiment of buddhahood right in front of him. Hearing his refusal, the "Mistress of the Three Worlds"—as she is called—disappeared for the last time. To Abhaya-karagupta's credit, he eventually realized what he had cast away and rejected, and spent the rest of his life in search of the divine maiden, longing for nothing so much as to prostrate himself and offer all of his accomplishments to her wondrous cosmic form.

The stories of both Naropa and Abhayakaragupta make the point that whatever foothold the Vajrayana may have had in the monasteries, the real tradition and the real practice was to be found elsewhere, some-where in the outback where books, scholarship, and decorous behavior, where prestige, honors, and renown, have no meaning.

In Tibet, the model of the three yanas provided a framework for Tibetan Buddhism as a whole. The Hinayana and Mahayana defined conventional, institutionalized Buddhism. The Hinayana provided the Vinaya, which regulated both individual monastic behavior and collec-tive monastic affairs. It was also the source of the Abhidharma, one of the more advanced topics of Buddhist scholastic study and the basis of Buddhist psychology. The Mahayana articulated the all-important no-tion of "emptiness" (shunyata), the basis of Buddhist philosophy in Tibet as well as the ideal of the bodhisattva followed by all Tibetans, monks and nuns, yogins, and laypeople alike. And the Mahayana scholastic traditions, particularly the various Madhyamaka and Yogachara schools, defined the intellectual culture in Tibetan monasteries.

While the Hinayana and Mahayana defined conventional Buddhism in Tibet, the Vajrayana gave voice to its unconventional, forest side. Although Vajrayana ideas, symbolism, and liturgies were certainly prevalent within Tibetan monasteries, in order to engage in serious tantric practice, one would normally enter retreat. Furthermore, the most respected practitioners within Tibetan tradition were the yogins who devoted much or all of their lives to solitary meditation. It was these yogins who, when they attained realization, were understood as siddhas, virtually equivalent to the enlightened ideal of the Indian Vajrayana. These Tibetan siddhas often followed their Indian progenitors in their unconventional behavior, their critique of the religious establishment, and their unpredictable and sometimes fearsome demeanor. In the next two chapters, we shall examine the way in which the Vajrayana, as the centerpiece of this three-yana synthesis, gradually made its way to Tibet and became the defining orientation of Tibetan Buddhism.

2

How the Vajrayana Came to Tibet

THE EARLY SPREADING OF THE DHARMA

THE VAJRAYANA CAME TO TIBET AS PART OF THE LARGER enterprise of the transplantation of Buddhism to the Land of Snow. In order to understand how the Vajrayana came to play the role it does within Tibetan tradition, we need to gain some understanding of the tantric transmissions within this larger context.

Tibetans divide the nearly six centuries during which Indian Buddhism was making its way to Tibet (seventh through the twelfth centuries CE) into two major periods: the "early spreading of the dharma," from the seventh to middle of the ninth century, and the "later spreading," from the late tenth to the end of the twelfth century. During the seventh and eighth centuries in India, but later as well, Buddhists following the different trends often inhabited quite different worlds. Proponents of one or another of the Eighteen Schools (what Tibetans called the "Hinayana"), rejected the Mahayana sutras as inauthentic, not to speak of the tantras. Those following the Mahayana sutras, while perhaps acknowledging the tantras, saw the conventional bodhisattva ideal, defined by compassion and the six paramitas ("perfections") as the epitome of the Buddha's teaching. Even within the conventional Mahayana, there was a considerable amount of debate and disagreement over which philosophical traditions were most desirable. Tantric practitioners often ignored the monastic world altogether as a waste of time, and devoted themselves to their own esoteric practices as the essential heart of the Buddha's way. And through the period of the seventh to the twelfth centuries, there was always a tension, which could sometimes be considerable, between those pursuing the way of virtue and knowledge in the great monasteries and those unconventional yogins carrying out their esoteric practices in the dangerous precincts of cremation ground and jungle.

During the five centuries when the dharma was being transplanted to Tibet, the Tibetans were exposed to the full range of diversity of Indian Buddhism. To make matters more complex, beginning before the eighth century and continuing thereafter, Central and Far Eastern forms of Buddhism were known in Tibet and were being advanced, sometimes quite vigorously. The broad range of types and forms of Buddhism that were transplanted to Tibet may be viewed as positive in two respects: first, it allowed a great array of Buddhist traditions to undergo transplantation and to develop and flourish in Tibet; and second, it produced a Tibetan tradition that was uncommonly diverse, vigorous, and creative.

THE EARLY SPREADING OF THE DHARMA
(SEVENTH TO MID-NINTH CENTURY)

During the period of the early spreading, traditional histories identify three Tibetan kings as principally responsible for the successful transit of the Indian dharma: in the seventh century Songtsen Gampo (609– 649?), in the eighth, Trisong Detsen (754–797), and in the ninth, Ralpachen (815–836).

During the early spreading, it appears that the conventional Mahayana and the unconventional Vajrayana were transmitted by different sorts of Indians, came to Tibet in distinctive ways, and were welcomed into somewhat different environments. Tradition reports that in the seventh century Songtsen Gampo married a Chinese princess and a Nepalese princess, both of whom were Buddhists. Through them, Buddhism gained entry to the royal court. This ruler also sent one of his ministers to India to bring back an alphabet so that the Tibetan language could, for the first time, be committed to writing. Indications are that the Buddhism brought to the court was of the conventional Mahayana variety.

In the eighth century, the second religious king, Trisong Detsen, invited the Indian monk Shantarakshita to Tibet, a respected Mahayana scholar whose synthesis of Madhyamaka and Yogachara set the standard for the day. The king's plan was to have Shantarakshita supervise the building of the first major monastery in Tibet, oversee the ordination of a group of Tibetan monks (something that had not yet occurred), and establish conventional Mahayana study and practice at the monastery. Shantarakshita arrived but, so we read, the local spirits were offended at the prospect of the new Buddhist religion being given such a firm foothold in their domain, with the result that a number of natural calamities occurred and the Indian monk was forced to withdraw.

Before he left, however, Shantarakshita advised the king that tantric methods were needed to overcome the recalcitrant forces and that he, as a monk, was not competent in these matters. He further suggested that the king invite an accomplished tantric yogin named Padmasambhava (known as Guru Rinpoche or Padmakara in Tibet) to carry out the necessary taming of the indigenous deities. The invitation was drawn up by the king and relayed to the siddha.

Padmasambhava was a siddha whose life and person reflect the unconventional, nonmonastic environment of Vajrayana Buddhism during the eighth century in India. His biography reveals a life entirely devoted to spiritual realization. He was born, it is said, in no ordinary human way, but in a lotus in the middle of a sacred lake. Having no earthly mother and father, he arrived in this world with no hope of an identity, at least in conventional terms. Having been discovered, the foundling was taken to the palace of a local king, Indrabhuti, who, without a son, was delighted to bring the child up as crown prince.

From the beginning, the enlightenment within the child was pure and strong, and he would not or could not conform to normal human limitations. In time, the boundlessness of his inner realization proved too much for the royal court, and he was sent away into exile. Barred from the human world, Padmasambhava took up residence in a cremation ground, outside the bounds of the conventional society, inhabited by the dying and the dead, by criminals and the insane, by wild animals and marauding spirits. In this place, deemed an ideal location for tantric

FIGURE 2.1 *Guru Rinpoche (Padmasambhava) in "lotus-born" aspect.*

yogins bent on liberation, Padmasambhava took up the practice of meditation. He carried out his yogic endeavors for many years in this and similar locales, exploring the limitless realms of enlightenment. Eventually, he began to bring his realization into the world, and his biography is filled with the many encounters and experiences that now came to him. In due course, he married an Indian princess named Mandarava, who received tantric initiation and instruction from him. Living now mostly in caves in the mountains, Padmasambhava and Mandarava practiced together.

Padmasambhava accepted King Trisong Detsen's invitation. Once in Tibet, he made a connection with the indigenous deities and tamed them, thus rendering the building of Samye possible. Through Padmasambhava's "taming" activity at Samye and elsewhere, many indigenous spirits were brought to the dharma and enlisted as its protectors. Many of the most important "protectors" in classical Tibetan Buddhism trace their origins back to him. Shantarakshita, who had been gone from Tibet for several years, was now able to return. With Shantarakshita and Padmasambhava working together, Samye was built, being completed about 779. Now the first group of Tibetans underwent monastic ordination and took up residence in the monastery. During his time in Tibet, Padmasambhava accepted a Tibetan woman, Yeshe Tsogyal, as his principal disciple. She became his tantric consort (wife) and was responsible for the preservation of much of his teachings. Subsequently, the master traveled around the country giving extensive tantric instruction. In his work of spreading the dharma, Padmasambhava was joined by other tantric masters, such as Vimalamitra and Vairochana.

In the royal court and its entourage, and in Samye monastery, the conventional Mahayana now had found a solid foothold in Tibet. But into what environment could the Vajrayana come and who might be its recipients? In India, the tantric siddhas were unaffiliated yogins who, like Padmasambhava, wandered forth alone or in small groups. They roamed about giving tantric teachings and initiations, spending much of their time in retreat, and training disciples met in their travels. During the early spreading (and, as we shall see, also in the later), such yogins passed their lineages on to Tibetans in India and also in their own journeys to Tibet. It appears that, during the early spreading, these lineages were generally not passed on in monastic environments. Rather, as in India, transmission occurred in retreat settings where disciples were trained and in contexts of teaching among the laity.

So it was that during the early spreading of Buddhism in Tibet, alongside the conventional Mahayana traditions established in the royal court and maintained at Samye, tantric lineages were being transmitted in nonmonastic contexts, particularly to yogins and laypeople. By the end of the early spreading, a great variety of these tantric lineages had taken root among various families of the laity and were being practiced individually and in small retreat communities by male and female yogins.

This does not mean that the world of court and monastery on the one hand, and of the Vajrayana on the other, were entirely separate. In fact, the building of Samye shows how the conventional Mahayana and the unconventional Vajrayana, while distinctive, could cooperate in the development of the dharma in Tibet. Shantarakshita embodied a socially laudable and institutionally stable form of Buddhism. Padmasambhava embodied a more radical path that produced realization, miraculous powers, and the ability to handle problems outside of the normal ken of most laypeople and monks. Together, these two were able to bring about not only the foundation of Samye but the establishment of Tibetan monasticism, and the rooting of Buddhism itself in Tibetan soil.

The interface between Mahayana and Vajrayana in Tibet is also seen in other ways. For example, Trisong Detsen established support for both monks and yogins. Thus records indicate specific kinds and amounts of material support for the monks residing at Samye; and they also specify similar support for yogins living in the caves in the Samye vicinity. In addition, King Trisong Detsen provided the material resources necessary for the translation of both sutras and tantras into Tibetan, indicating his belief in the integrity and importance of both orientations.

Under Trisong Detsen, then, both Mahayana and Vajrayana Buddhism were included as having valuable and distinctive roles within the overall Tibetan Buddhist framework. The king realized that Buddhism would not survive without the strong institutional foundation provided by monasticism and without the comprehensive textual resources of the Tripitaka. His providing for the financial support of monastics and the translation of texts reflects this point of view. At the same time, the king saw that the practice of tantra lent legitimacy to the institutionalized side of Buddhism by providing an arena where people could follow the path to the end and attain enlightenment. This explains his own practice as a lay tantric practitioner and his interest in providing for support of the yogins meditating in caves around Samye.

The early spreading of Buddhism came to an end in the ninth century with King Ralpachen. Although by this time Buddhism had become established in Tibet as the religion of the land, far from everyone had accepted it. In fact, throughout the entire early spreading, one finds opposition in various places, including even the extended royal family, the government, and the nobility. The old shamanic traditions of pre-Buddhist Tibet continued to play an important role in Tibetans' way of life, and even in the ninth century there were clearly many who felt that the adoption of Buddhism was not in the best interests of the country.

Ralpachen took the opposite view, however, and was ardently and passionately devoted to the dharma. He even went so far as to become a monk, something that must have been considered a strange thing for a Tibetan king to do, and expressed his submission by tying ribbons to his braids and having monks sit on them. This evidently was going too far for some, and in 836 he was murdered. His non-Buddhist elder brother, Langdarma, was placed on the throne, and royal support of Buddhism was brought to an end, with an era of persecution being set in motion.

THE NYINGMA, OR "ANCIENT SCHOOL"

Tibetan Buddhism today is defined primarily by four schools: the Nyingma, Sakya, Kagyü, and Kadam/Geluk. Among these, the Nyingma, or "Ancient School," is unique in that it takes its foundation in the early spreading of the dharma. The Sakya, Kagyü, and Kadam/Geluk, on the other hand, all trace their origins back to the later spreading. These later-spreading lineages are collectively known as Sarma, "New Schools," to set them in contrast to the "ancient" transmissions of the Nyingma. Prior to the later spreading, however, while the bulk of the various traditions later understood as Nyingma were in existence, there was no self-conscious school by that name. All of these traditions were simply known as *chö*, Tibetan for the Sanskrit term *dharma*.

It was only during the later spreading, between the end of the ninth century and the end of the eleventh, that the lineages deriving from the early spreading came to be collectively understood as Nyingma, the Ancient School, in contrast to the new transmissions that were then occurring. It was thus during the later spreading that the Nyingma school took shape and found its identity as preserving the body of teaching that survives from the early spreading. While important monastic and scholarly transmissions are included in the Nyingma, it is probably fair to say that its primary and most distinctive heritage is the abundance of tantric lineages that have been passed down to the present day.

At the heart of this tantric inheritance are the many teachings ascribed to Padmasambhava, Yeshe Tsogyal, and their tantric associates. These consist of two sorts: (1) Kama, instructions given to disciples who passed these along through an unbroken lineage of human teachers and disciples, and (2) Terma, texts and other religious artifacts hidden by Padmasambhava and Yeshe Tsogyal in various places for later discovery by *tertöns*, yogins and yoginis through whom the hidden teaching can be revealed in subsequent ages. While the Kama contain dharma that is universally applicable, the Terma were tailored to meet the specific needs of the particular ages in which they were to be discovered. Terma continue to be revealed by tertöns even today, and great contemporary masters such as Dudjom Rinpoche and Khyentse Rinpoche have brought forth important teachings in this way for modern-day practitioners.

As a tradition with a particularly strong tantric identity, the Nyingma lineage has been characterized, since its inception, by an intense commitment to the spiritual life and an especially strong emphasis on meditation. It remained relatively decentralized through the period of the later spreading and afterward, thus providing a marked contrast with the schools of the later spreading, which developed more in the direction of centralization, institutionalization, and the building of large monasteries. It was not until the seventeenth century that the Nyingmapas began to build some larger monasteries of their own, to facilitate the continuity and survival of their tradition at a time when Tibet was becoming politically more centralized and bureaucratic.

Owing to the tremendous diversity of dharma—and particularly the rich tantric inheritance—that had come to Tibet during the early spreading, the Nyingmapas were faced with a steep challenge. How could they include and understand these various teachings in a systematic way and to appreciate their specific places on the path to realization? In response to this need, apparently drawing on Indian prototypes, they developed a system of nine yanas, the main features of which are summarized in table 2.1. Their philosophical orientation is discussed in chapter 5, "The View of Vajrayana." In chapter 10, we will examine the most distinctive meditation teaching of the Nyingma, dzokchen or the "great perfection."

Within Indian tradition, the Vajrayana was understood and assimilated in a variety of ways, depending on one's sectarian affiliation, one's specific lineage, and one's individual inclination. At one end of the spectrum were siddhas who spent their entire lives in the jungles, meditating and training disciples. Such people never saw the inside of a monastery and eschewed the pursuit of scholarly learning as an unnecessary, unprofitable tangent on the path to liberation. At the other extreme were monastic scholars who, like Abhayakaragupta prior to his encounter with Vajrayogini, were content to know the Vajrayana strictly as a subject for academic study.

In Tibet, among individual practitioners, one finds both of these extremes and every gradient in between. However, the four major schools of Tibetan Buddhism all take a more moderate approach, in which the Vajrayana is integrated into monastic life but is also the subject of serious practice in retreat. At the same time, however, even among the schools, there are marked differences in the interpretation of just what

TABLE 2.1

THE NINE YANAS OF THE NYINGMA TRADITION

Yanas of Cause	Yana	Main Teachings	Relation to the Deity
Hinayana	1. Shravaka-yana	Four noble truths	
	2. Pratyekabuddha-yana	Karma or causality	
Mahayana	3. Bodhisattva-yana	Emptiness and compassion	
Yanas of Result			
Vajrayana			
Outer yanas	In the Outer Tantras, the distinction between the two truths is maintained, divinities are not visualized with their female consorts, the five meats are not taken, and one does not attain the final result in this lifetime.[1]		
	4. Upayoga-yana	Purification of the practitioners' body, speech, and mind. Within absolute truth, all things are equal; within relative truth, deity is master, practitioner is servant.	The deity is visualized as exterior to oneself and is worshiped. Deity as master, practitioner as servant.
	5. Charyayoga-yana	Same view as Kriyayogayana.	The deity is still external, but more nearly on a level with the practitioner, as friend and helper.
	6. Yoga-yana	Absolute truth: all phenomena are free of concept, empty, and luminous. Relative truth: all phenomena are the mandala of deities.	One visualizes oneself as the deity. Deity is seen in conventional way without consorts and nonwrathful. Rituals are performed as offerings to the deity.

TABLE 2.1 (continued)

Yanas of Result	Yana	Main Teachings	Relation to the Deity
Inner yanas	In the Inner Tantras the two truths are held to be inseparable, all phenomena are equal, the five meats and the five nectars are taken, the divinities are visualized with their consorts, and the final result can be attained in this lifetime. The tantras of these yanas are the special and distinctive Nyingma practices.[2]		
	7. Mahayoga-yana (masculine principle)	"Within absolute truth all things are accepted as the essence of the mind and the Dharmakaya. All manifestation, thoughts, and appearances are considered to be the sacred aspects of the divinities within relative truth."[3]	Emphasis on the visualization of oneself as the deity with female consort. All phenomena are seen as the essence of the deities.
	8. Anuyoga-yana (feminine principle)	Emphasis on the "dissolution phase" of meditation; emphasis on the perfection of bliss, clarity, and nonthought. Practice of the "inner yogas" of the winds (prana), channels (nadi), and drops (bindu).	The visualization of the deities is not so much emphasized in this yana.
	9. Atiyoga-yana (nonduality of masculine and feminine principles)	"All appearances or apparent phenomena are illusions of the deluded mind. They are false because in reality their nature is free from conceptualizations. In nature all existents are the same and they are pure in the Dharmakaya. In practice there is no acceptance or rejection, rather all existents are accepted as manifestations of the nature, Dharmata."[4]	

role the Vajrayana should play on the Buddhist path and what its relation to institutionalized monasticism should be.

For the Nyingmapas, who represent one classical approach, the practice of the Vajrayana is the centerpiece of the spiritual life. As we have seen, the core transmission of the Nyingma lineage is the tantric teaching of Padmasambhava, Yeshe Tsogyal, and people like Vimalamitra and Vairochana. From them derive the rich array of tantric lineages that were carried through the period after Ralpachen and into the time of the later spreading and beyond by individual yogins, small communities of hermits, and families of lay practitioners. A distinctive aspect of the Nyingma heritage has been the importance of women teachers, a trend one sees in the women siddhas of India, the female gurus of Padmasambhava, human and otherwise;[5] Yeshe Tsogyal, his primary disciple; the women among his other major disciples; and the many accomplished yoginis down through Nyingma history.

The ongoing discovery of terma points to another feature of the Nyingma, namely its living spirituality and its orientation to the present. The Terma tradition reveals a fervent desire to maintain an intimate and immediate connection to Padmasambhava and his inspiration, such that the present is continually being nourished by fresh revelations from him. Although the Nyingmapas have certainly had their great monks and scholars over the course of Tibetan history, conventional monasticism and institutionalized Buddhism have tended to play a more limited role in the Nyingma than in the other schools. Particularly in recent times classical monaticism and Buddhist scholarship have increasingly gained importance.

3

How the Vajrayana Came to Tibet

THE LATER SPREADING AND BEYOND

THE LATER SPREADING OF BUDDHISM IN TIBET BEGAN IN the late tenth century and lasted until about 1200 CE.[1] During this period, Indian teachers made their way to Tibet, and Tibetans traveled to India. From these interchanges, a number of new lineages sprang up, including the other three (besides the Nyingma) of the four major schools of Tibetan Buddhism, the Kadam, later to become the Geluk, and the Sakya and Kagyü.

Since the time of the early spreading, the situation in India had changed, particularly in the way in which Vajrayana Buddhism was viewed. By the time of the later spreading, the tantric vehicle had become rather thoroughly integrated into the curricula of many of the great North Indian monasteries. Although Nalanda, where Naropa studied, seems to have remained a bastion of the conventional Mahayana, other monasteries, such as Vikramashila, Odantapuri, and Somapuri were much more explicitly tantric. The accomplished monastic scholar Abhayakaragupta was probably typical in his mastery of the texts of all three yanas. It is characteristic of this period that Atisha, the paradigmatic Indian monastic scholar, was also well trained in the study and practice of tantra.

While Buddhism in Tibet had flourished during the early spreading largely thanks to support from the royal court and powerful families, during the later spreading the pattern shifted. Now monastic centers of the new lineages began to appear, supported by an ever-growing per-

FIGURE 3.1 *Atisha, Indian scholar and tantric master, founder of the Kadam school. Drawing by Konchok Lhadrepa.*

centage of the Tibetan population. Moreover, through the accumulation of wealth and donations of land, the monasteries began to become power centers in their own right. Even the choice of new abbots, controlled by powerful families in the early spreading, now passed into the hands of the monasteries through the institution of the tülku, or incarnate lama, discussed in chapters 15 and 16.

This created a very strong situation for institutionalized Buddhism in Tibet. Owing to their power and their growing wealth, the monasteries became the centers of Tibetan culture. The propagation of Buddhist learning, the study of other religious and secular subjects, cultivation of the arts, the practice of medicine, the exercise of political power, the management of lands, the resolution of disputes, and even the protection of the weak in times of political turmoil all became activities of the monasteries. In addition, with mixed results, the later spreading lineages assumed political control of Tibet, a role that began with the Sakyapas in the thirteenth century, then passed to the Kagyüpas in the fourteenth and finally and decisively to the Gelukpas in the seventeenth century. Only the Nyingmapas stood apart from the fray, owing probably in part to the decentralization that marked their development as a tradition, and in part to their emphasis on noninstitutionalized spiritual practice.

Because of the shift in the Indian situation, the Vajrayana that came to Tibet during the later spreading was assumed to be compatible—at least up to a certain point—with monastic Buddhism. Thus, many of Tibetans active in the early days of the later spreading were trained in both monastic tradition and the Vajrayana. However, it still remained the case that serious tantric practice occurred outside of the monastic context, in solitary retreat settings. Moreover, although monks in some of the traditions now received tantric training, most of the really accomplished masters had spent much of their lives not in monasteries but in retreat and the nonmonastic settings of the lay yogin or household-practitioner.

MAJOR SCHOOLS OF THE LATER SPREADING

The Kadam school owes its inception to Atisha, who arrived in Tibet in 1042. As mentioned, Atisha, like most well-trained monks in India at

FIGURE 3.2 *Green Tara: the goddess in one of her more active aspects.*

this time, was schooled in all three yanas: he followed the monastic Vinaya (Hinayana); he was accomplished in his study of the Mahayana dharma and particularly of Madhyamaka philosophy; and he was well trained in the Vajrayana and was a devotee of the beloved female bodhi-sattva Tara.

Atisha embodied the best of Mahayana monasticism as it existed then

FIGURE 3.3 *White Tara: the goddess in her most inward and subtle manifestation, particularly associated with healing and long life.*

in India. Surveying the Tibetan situation, he found that the integrity of the monastic way as well as the rigor of the scholarly traditions was in decline. Atisha aspired to get the dharma in Tibet back on course and, though he was already sixty years old when he arrived, he set himself with vigor to that task. He accepted and trained monastic disciples, and he composed works on the Buddhist path, including the famed *Bodhi-patha-pradipa*, a text that guided many generations of Kadam monks and had great influence on the Geluk founder, Tsongkhapa.

Based on his training, his inclinations, and his vision, Atisha felt that the centerpiece of Buddhist spiritual life should be the conventional monastic way of the Mahayanist monk. He taught that living as a monastic renunciant, adhering to the rules of monastic restraint (Vinaya), studying and meditating, and working for the welfare of others constituted the best vehicle to enlightenment. He taught this lifeway to his close disciples, and in time his tradition became known for its integrity and for the gentleness and humility of its members. Atisha did not exclude the Vajrayana from his system, but he did view it as an optional, later involvement for his disciples.

Atisha's approach, derived from his training in India, is important because it established another of the major ways in which the Vajrayana was understood and practiced in Tibet. In this interpretation, the Mahayana dharma was the central teaching of the Buddha, and the focus was on monastic life and study. Though certainly not required or even necessarily recommended, the option of serious tantric practice was open, but only for monks who had proved themselves with many years of training in ethics and philosophy. This approach was later adopted, refined, and made more explicit by the Geluk founder Tsongkhapa.

The Sakya school arose from rather different origins, taking its inception from the Indian mahasiddha Virupa, who lived probably in the ninth or tenth century CE. Virupa was originally a monk who had received Vajrayana initiation and attempted to carry out his practice in secret, at night, while continuing to live in the monastery. In time, however, he was discovered and expelled from the monastic community. Thenceforth, he became a wandering yogin, meditating, teaching, and training disciples.

Virupa's tantric lineage was joined with the Mahayana monastic lineage in the person of Shantipa (eleventh century), a renowned Mahayanist monk who in later life practiced Vajrayana and attained enlightenment himself becoming a renowned siddha.[2] A Tibetan by the name of Drogmi (993–1077), who had journeyed to India in search of the Buddhist teachings, become a student of Shantipa's, and received from him both the conventional Mahayanist and unconventional Vajrayana lineages, the latter of which was deepened by Drogmi's study with the tantric master Viravajra. It was this unification of Mahayana monasticism and tantric practice that Drogmi brought back to Tibet and transmitted to his disciples there. In this approach, which became the standard one for the Sakyapas, one first lays a solid foundation through the study of the Hinayana and Mahayana, and the life of conventional monasticism. Only after this foundation has been well laid does one move on to practice the more elite, inner, and esoteric Vajrayana.

FIGURE 3.4 *Sakya lineage figures.*

This approach to the Buddhist path is embodied in the distinctive Sakya teachings of the lamdre, the "path and the fruition." The lamdre teachings are divided into two broad sections: the first section, the "three visions," contains teaching common to Hinayana and Mahayana; the second section, the "three tantras," based on the root tantra of the Sakya, the *Hevajra Tantra*, outlines the stages and practices of the Vajrayana section of the path. Taken together, the lamdre provides a comprehensive approach to the journey to enlightenment including the texts, teachings, and practices of all three yanas.

We can see this approach in Könchok Gyalpo (1034–1102), a disciple of Drogmi, a member of the Khön family of hereditary lamas, and the actual founder of the Sakya. From Drogmi, Könchok Gyalpo received a very thorough education in the sutras and commentarial literature, and also in the tantras, such that he was considered one of the most brilliant and learned Buddhist scholars of his day. In 1073 he built a monastery in southern Tibet known as "Gray Earth," *sakya* in Tibetan, and from this time Sakya monastery became the institutional focus of the school and a leading center for the scholarly study of Buddhism. The lineal succession of the Sakya hierarchs continued through members of the Khön family down to the present day.

The Sakyapas represent a third way, alongside those of the Nyingmapas and the Kadampas, in which the Vajrayana came to be understood and practiced in Tibet. Its ideal is the proper balancing of Sutra (Hinayana and Mahayana) and Tantra in study and practice. Like the Kadampas, the Sakyapas emphasize the importance of the monastic life and scholarly training. But, this accomplished, one is encouraged to move on, to complete one's Buddhist life in the practice of the core Sakya tantric traditions. The scholarly traditions of the Sakyapa have remained exemplary and have produced many generations of eminent scholars, while through their tantric training they have produced many realized masters.

The Kagyü school, like the Sakya, originated among the unconventional, yogic traditions of the eighty-four Indian mahasiddhas; and also like the Sakya, in time it came to include a monastic and scholarly element. The human founder of the lineage was Tilopa, the eleventh-century saint mentioned in chapter 1. Tilopa's entire life was devoted to meditation in the jungles of northeastern India. After studying with many teachers, he finally met face to face with Vajradhara, for the Sarma schools the ultimate embodiment of buddhahood. From this encounter, Tilopa's lineage began and was passed on to his disciple Naropa, whose meeting with his guru is recounted in chapter 1. Naropa consolidated Tilopa's teachings in the well-known six yogas of Naropa (see chapter 11), a particularly important and distinctive part of the Kagyü heritage. In this way, the Kagyü lineage took its inception from the intense spiritual calling and the rigorous commitment to meditation of the Indian siddhas.

Naropa transmitted his lineage to Marpa (1012–1096), a Tibetan householder who had come to India in search of the dharma. Naropa and a master named Maitripa (eleventh century) trained Marpa well, and he returned to Tibet, marrying, undertaking a life of farming, and training disciples. Through his work, Marpa became the Tibetan founder of the Kagyü lineage. Marpa's primary disciple was Milarepa (1040–1123), a person who began life as what we would call an "abused child," having had his inheritance torn away from him and his family by a rapacious uncle and having been subsequently starved, beaten, and treated like a slave. Milarepa in retaliation subsequently killed a number of people through black magic thus inheriting karma that, unless purified through the extreme measures of the Vajrayana, would certainly land him in the depths of a hellish rebirth in his next life. Milarepa met and trained under Marpa, eventually entering into retreat in the mountains as a yogin and spending the rest of his life in that way. Up until this point, the Kagyü lineage had been entirely nonmonastic, being composed of yogins (Tilopa, Naropa, Milarepa) and a householder (Marpa).

In the next generation, however, the strictly nonmonastic character of the Kagyüpas changed, and the new configuration enabled the lineage to play a role in the developing of monasticism in Tibet. One of Milarepa's primary disciples was the Kadam monk Gampopa. This person, well trained as a monk but in search of a more profound and personal understanding of the teachings, sought out Milarepa where he was in retreat in an isolated cave in the mountains. Gampopa was accepted by the master as a disciple, trained under him, and eventually attained realization. Gampopa's disciples included Tüsum Khyenpa, who also followed the monastic path, like his teacher. Tüsum Khyenpa was retroactively recognized as the first Karmapa and thus began a line of successive incarnations (see chapters 15 and 18) that extends down to the

FIGURE 3.5 *Vajradhara, the ultimate form of buddhahood among the Later Translation schools.*

FIGURE 3.6 *Kagyü lineage figures, including Vajradhara, Tilopa, Naropa, Marpa, Milarepa, and Tüsum Khyenpa (first Karmapa).*

present, seventeenth Karmapa, now in residence in India. The Karmapa's tradition is known as the Karma Kagyü.

The Kagyü tradition came to include a number of other lineages. One of the most interesting is the Shangpa Kagyü, founded by a student

50

FIGURE 3.7 *Marpa, Tibetan founder of the Kagyü lineage.*

of Naropa's tantric consort Niguma, a person known as Khyungpo Naljorpa, the Yogi of Kungpo (978–1079).[3] Other principal Kagyü lineages included three in particular, the Drigung Kagyü, Taglung Kagyü, and Drukpa Kagyü, all deriving as sub-branches from the Phaktru Kagyü founded by one of Gampopa's disciples.

The Kagyü represent yet another, fourth way in which the Vajrayana was understood and practiced in Tibet. Like the Nyingma, the Vajrayana stands at the forefront of its heritage. Even after the introduction

FIGURE 3.8 *Milarepa, Marpa's primary disciple and the prototype of Tibetan hermit saints.*

of institutionalized monasticism, the theme of intensive meditation, whether practiced as a hermit in retreat or as a householder-yogin, has continued to form the basic inspiration of the Kagyü lineage. Those considered accomplished in the Kagyü dharma are expected to have completed the major tantric cycles of the Kagyü, to have spent substan-

FIGURE 3.9 *Scenes from Milarepa's life.*

tial time in retreat, and particularly, to have carried out the six yogas of Naropa. At the same time, as indicated, settled monasticism has played a relatively more important role among the Kagyüpas than among the Nyingmapas. After the time of Tüsum Khyenpa, most of the great tül-kus and teachers have been celibate monks.

FIGURE 3.10 *Gampopa, Milarepa's principal disciple and the first monastic Kagyü lineage holder.*

FIGURE 3.11 *Tsongkhapa flanked by Shakyamuni Buddha (left) and Avalokiteshvara (right).*

The tantric style of the Kagyüpas also shows some contrast with that of the Nyingmapas. Recall that for the Nyingma, the paradigmatic saint is the siddha Padmasambhava, a person who, while originally a meditating yogin, is depicted in his biography as subsequently fully engaged in the world, traveling about, encountering those hostile to the dharma, and wielding his magical power to subdue, tame, and convert across two cultures. By contrast, for the Kagyüpa, the paradigmatic realized person is Milarepa, the gentle and retiring hermit who spent his life in caves, meditating and training like-minded disciples.

Like the Nyingma before them, the later-spreading schools confronted a large array of Buddhist points of view, teachings, and methods of practice belonging to all three yanas. Deriving from a period in India several centuries after the Indian Buddhism received by the Nyingmapas, the later-spreading transmissions were distinct and, like the teachings of the early spreading, also needed to be put into some kind of order. The later-spreading schools, basing themselves on Indian models, developed the scheme of the four tantras. Table 3.1 lists these and correlates them with the nine-yanas system of the Nyingmapas.

CLASSICAL TRADITIONS: THE GELUK AND RI-ME

Tibetan Buddhism, as it existed in modern times, was defined by two large and relatively distinct syntheses, the Geluk and the Ri-me, that included the various schools and traditions of the early and later spreading, described above.[4] In terms of their understandings and approaches to the Vajrayana, both the Geluk and the Ri-me draw on earlier trends: the Geluk represent a well-organized, monastically oriented school that, with refinements, follows the Kadam model set forth by Atisha, while the Ri-me represents a loose synthesis of the approaches particularly of the Nyingma and the Kagyü. The Sakya acts as a kind of bridge between these two, for Sakya masters participated in the Ri-me, while the lineage as a whole shows aspects both of the monastic and scholarly focus of the Geluk and also the tantric commitments of the Ri-me.

The Geluk and Ri-me syntheses, then, represent two quite different orientations to the practice and understanding of the Vajrayana. The Geluk, "Virtuous Order," represents a monastic synthesis, drawing mainly on the classical traditions of the great North Indian monasteries and, more proximately, the Kadam lineage, while also including tantric elements. The Ri-me, "Nonsectarian Order," represents a yogic synthesis, inspired primarily by the renunciant and householder-yogin models of Indian tantric tradition and, in Tibet, the Nyingma and Kagyü approaches, at the same time incorporating within it both scholarly and monastic trends.

The Geluk

The Geluk founder, Tsongkhapa (1357–1419), was a Kadam monk who sought to reinvigorate the tradition of Atisha. Following in the footsteps of Atisha, Tsongkhapa felt that the monastic way of life was the most

TABLE 3.1

THE FOUR TANTRAS AND THE NINE YANAS COMPARED

Sarma: The New Translation Schools	Nyingma: The Ancient School
Hinayana	**Hinayana**
Shravaka-yana	1. same
Pratyekabuddha-yana	2. same
Mahayana	*Mahayana*
Bodhisattva-yana	3. same
Vajrayana The Four Orders of Tantra *Lower or Outer Tantras*	**Vajrayana**
1. Kriya Tantra	4. Kriyayoga-yana
2. Charya Tantra	5. Upayoga-yana
3. Yoga Tantra	6. Yoga-yana
4. Anuttarayoga Tantra	*Higher or Inner Tantras*
a. Father Tantra b. Mother Tantra	7. Mahayoga-yana 8. Anuyoga-yana
c. Nondual Tantra	9. Atiyoga-yana (= dzokchen)
Realization: mahamudra	Realization: dzokchen

noble Buddhist calling, and he championed this approach widely, working for the revitalization of monastic discipline and scholarship and the strengthening of institutionalized Buddhism.

Tsongkhapa showed extraordinary scholarly abilities, even as a young monk. He traveled widely, studying with some of the most eminent masters of his day. As he matured, his remarkable talents showed themselves in a prodigious ability to memorize texts, an incisive intellectual understanding of whatever he read, and great skill and power as a debater. Tsongkhapa was clearly on his way to become one of Tibet's greatest scholars.

However, at the age of thirty-three, over the objections of his primary tutor, Tsongkhapa put aside his studies and entered into retreat in order to practice the Vajrayana. During many years of practice, he had a number of visions of the celestial bodhisattva of wisdom, Manjushri, of whom he was later held to be an embodiment. After eight years, following a dream of the Indian Prasangika master Buddhapalita, Tsongkhapa attained realization. The fact that, on this momentous occasion, he dreamt of one of India's greatest philosophical minds is indicative, for it shows the depth of Tsongkhapa's connection with Buddhist scholarship and prefigures his later life, which exhibits such stunning scholarly virtuosity. Subsequently, the master left retreat and undertook his project of reformation with vigor and skill, training disciples, studying, teaching, and composing over two hundred texts, many of which still stand as classics.

Tsongkhapa's synthesis incorporates both Sutra (Hinayana and Mahayana) and Tantra (Vajrayana). On the one hand, the way of settled monasticism was clearly the centerpiece of Tsongkhapa's vision of the ideal Buddhist life. Central to this were his efforts to reestablish the purity and integrity of Buddhist monastic discipline, the Vinaya. Equally important, Tsongkhapa sought to rectify a sloppiness and lack of precision that he felt had crept into Buddhist scholarship of his era. He put forward a curriculum of Buddhist studies consisting of the classical topics of study and debate, including epistemology and logic, the Prajnaparamita, Madhyamaka philosophy, Vinaya, and Abhidharma. He laid out a scholarly path that, in its maturity, would take a student two to three decades to complete. So far, Tsongkhapa was drawing on the conventional Hinayana and Mahayana of Indian and earlier Tibetan tradition.

At the same time, however, Tsongkhapa also included the practice of Vajrayana within his system. Concerned with what he deemed excesses and misadventures in the practice of tantra in his day, he sought to place the practice within a context of greater safety and integrity.

Therefore, following in the footsteps of Atisha, he instituted a system whereby only fully ordained monks were eligible for the practice. Among these, only those who had successfully passed through the long Geluk course of study would be permitted to enter into tantric study and practice. It was Tsongkhapa's view that when a person had lived for such a long time as a monk and had been trained so rigorously and thoroughly in Buddhist philosophy, the maximum assurance was present that he would neither misunderstand nor pervert the practice of tantra. This approach has characterized the Geluk since Tsongkhapa's time.

Although the tantric aspect of Tsongkhapa and his legacy is usually downplayed in public presentations of the Gelukpas, it plays a central role in the Geluk tradition. This point needs to be made because, in the West, Tsongkhapa is known primarily for his scholarly brilliance and philosohical achievements. However, in Tibet and particularly among the Gelukpas, Tsongkhapa is revered as a person who attained and manifested full tantric realization. Lama Thubten Yeshe remarks that "Western academics do not seem to recognize him as a great yogi, a great tantric practitioner, a mahasiddha. Actually, Lama Tsongkhapa taught and wrote more on tantra than on sutra; but because he did not publicly show his mahasiddha aspect, Westerners have the impression that he was merely an intellectual. . . . But you should understand that Lama Tsongkhapa's principal field was tantra."[5] One of two main disciples, Lama Khedrub Je, weeping with despair after the death of the master, experienced a vision that is indicative. Tsongkhapa suddenly appeared in the midst of space, sitting on a jeweled throne surrounded by celestial beings. He declared to the disciple, "My son, you shouldn't cry. My principal message is to practice the tantric path. Do this and then transmit the teachings to qualified disciples. [Then] you will make me very happy."[6]

The Ri-me Movement

The Ri-me movement, which developed during the nineteenth century, represents a modern embodiment of the ancient ideals of yogic practice and realization in this life. In Tibet, it is the Ri-me that has most strongly and purely continued the Vajrayana heritage originally deriving from India.

The term *Ri-me* means "without boundaries" and may be glossed as "nonsectarian." Instead of being a specific "school" in the sense of the Geluk, it is a particular outlook and orientation held in common by practitioners and teachers belonging to a variety of different lineages and schools, including principally the Nyingma, the Kagyü, and the Sakya.

Rather than being defined by any single "essence," the Ri-me is best understood as a movement characterized by certain typical features. First, its proponents understood the essence of Buddhism to lie in the practice of Vajrayana. In addition, they celebrated the fact that the Buddha gave many different instructions and set in motion a variety of contemplative traditions—that is, lineages in which meditative practice is paramount. It was their understanding that each tradition had its own particular genius and its own strengths. The Ri-me masters considered the diversity of contemplative traditions not just a good thing but essential to the survival and health of the dharma, for in their view each approach could supplement, complement, and deepen the practice of the others. The recognition of the value, power, and particular gifts of other lineages also provided a powerful antidote against pride, self-satisfaction, and sectarianism among one's own group.

The Ri-me masters put their ideas into practice in several ways. For one thing, they studied with one another, taking initiations and oral instructions from each other, and carrying out practice together. In addition, they sent their own disciples to study with masters from other schools and lineages. Finally, they engaged in a project of preservation of contemplative traditions. They viewed this project as necessary because they lived at a time when sectarianism and persecution were on the rise in Tibet. In their own day, they saw unique and powerful lineages, perhaps held by a single monastery or a single family of householder-yogins, beginning to disappear under pressure from some of the larger and more powerful schools. By receiving initiations from these lineages, by making written copies of their texts, and by passing these initiations on to their own students, they tried to see to it that these contemplative traditions would not be lost.

While the Ri-me masters were, in one way, remarkably open, interested in, and accommodating of the wealth of practice instructions and lineages available in their own day, they were nevertheless far from indiscriminate. The traditions they sought out to study, preserve, and transmit were only those they found to have genuine profundity in meditation and realization. It is also interesting that throughout this work they remained fully loyal to their own training: they stood firmly grounded in their own lineal traditions and maintained primary allegiance to their own monasteries, orders, and schools. They reflect the idea that it is only from the foundation of rootedness in one's own lineage that authentic encounter and appreciation of others become possible.

Although Ri-me origins are not so focused on one personality as those of the Geluk, there are nevertheless certain figures who played a critical role in its development and reveal the particular way in which Ri-me masters tended to view the Vajrayana. Standing in the background is the great fourteenth-century Nyingma scholar and yogin Longchenpa, who, for the first time, brought together the various doctrines and practices of the Ancient School into one grand and comprehensive synthesis. The Ri-me movement per se, however, looks more immediately back to Jigme Lingpa (1730–1798), also a Nyingma yogin and scholar. While Jigme Lingpa himself precedes the actual Ri-me movement and is therefore not considered a Ri-me master, we may touch briefly on his life because it exemplifies in a rather complete form the principal themes of what became Ri-me in the century following his lifetime.

Jigme Lingpa was a boy of humble origins who, having entered monastic life, owing to his family's inability to provide support for him, had to function as the servant of others. Although his economic status deprived him of either a tutor or any formal opportunity to study, he had deep devotion to Guru Rinpoche (Padmasambhava), received whatever initiations he could, and learned from listening to his more educated peers and from reading whatever texts he could obtain. As he matured, he met the teacher Thekchok Dorje, who became his root guru and beloved spiritual father. In time, Jigme Lingpa's intelligence, devotion, and genuine accomplishments began to be recognized, and more opportunities became available to him. He continued his study, particularly of Longchenpa, and began a series of multiyear retreats. During this time, he had a number of visions of deities and of departed teachers, including Guru Rinpoche and his Tibetan consort and disciple, Yeshe Tsogyal. In time, Jigme Lingpa abandoned his monastic identity and took up the lifestyle of a wandering yogin.

When he was twenty-eight, Jigme Lingpa had a monumental revelation in which Longchenpa came to him and transmitted the Longchen Nyingthik, the innermost essence of his teachings. This revelation constituted a terma, a spiritual treasure, hidden in an earlier time and now made available as the essence of the dharma for Jigme Lingpa's own time. During the next seven years, Jigme Lingpa did not reveal the revelation to anyone but continued to practice, receiving further visions of Longchenpa and experiencing an ever-deepening identification with him. At the end of this period, he began to teach and to give empowerments in the Longchen Nyingthik. As word spread of these extraordinary teachings, people came from near and far to receive them. Soon they had spread throughout the Nyingma world and came to be considered the essence of Nyingma spirituality.

The themes of Jigme Lingpa's life provided a kind of immediate inspiration and set of hallmarks for the Ri-me movement that arose in earnest in the nineteenth century. These include his fervent meditation practice and emphasis on retreat; his reverence for the Vajrayana dharma; his devotion to Guru Rinpoche and Longchenpa and his love for his own guru; the primacy of visions and revelations in his life; his role as a tertön (discoverer of spiritual treasures) and, in particular, his miraculous reception of the Longchen Nyingthik; and his simple, unaffected nature and lack of interest in institutionalizing his lineage.

The themes of Jigme Lingpa's life and teachings were carried forward by his personal disciples, those later recognized as his incarnations, and others who were inspired by his example and by what he taught.

FIGURE 3.12 *Jamgön Kongtrül Lodrö Thaye, one of the leaders of the nineteenth-century Ri-me movement. Thangka painting by Cynthia Moku.*

Foremost among these were people such as Paltrül Rinpoche (1808–1887), Jamyang Khyentse Wangpo (1820–1892), and Jamgön Kongtrül the Great (1813–1899). Today, the Ri-me tradition continues to inspire the practice of the Vajrayana in much of Tibetan Buddhism. It provides the kind of solid foundation upon which the tradition can continue in its integrity but also reap the rewards of mutual openness and interchange, not only with other Tibetan schools but also with the other forms of Buddhism that are important in the modern world, including Zen, Theravada, and Pure Land.

CONCLUSION: THE POSITION OF THE VAJRAYANA IN TIBET

The Vajrayana came to Tibet from an Indian Buddhist situation characterized by vigor and diversity. Many streams of tantra entered Tibet during the early spreading and another whole series of transmissions occurred during the later spreading. Wandering yogins who had never known monastic life, ascetics who had previously been monastics, monks and nuns, lay yogins, and ordinary laypeople all received Vajrayana transmissions and kept them alive in their particular environments. Thus the many strands of Vajrayana in Tibet were multiplied by the different kinds of people, with their different lifeways, who practiced them and passed them on. This diversity was further multiplied by the different regions and subcultures of Tibet to which the tantric teachings traveled.

Over time, as we have seen, the Vajrayana in Tibet began to crystallize into certain dominant schools and lineages. At one end of the spectrum were the Nyingmapas, who retained many of the tantric traditions of the early spreading. These they practiced in a great variety of lifeways and settings, remaining the most institutionally decentralized of all the schools. At the other end of the gradient were the Gelukpas, for whom the practice of Vajrayana was understood in a much more restrictive sense, appropriate only as the culmination of a life of monasticism and scholarly study. The Kagyüpas and the Sakyapas stand in between these two extremes, the Kagyüpas perhaps more toward the Nyingma end and the Sakyapas more toward the Geluk approach. Yet, within the sects and subsects, it would be a mistake to draw such distinctions too sharply, for there are many accomplished yogins among the

Gelukpas and, particularly during the past two centuries, many highly trained and accomplished scholars among the Nyingmapas. Among all the schools with their divisions and subdivisions, the Vajrayana has continued to be considered the ultimate teaching of the Buddha and has acted as the basic inspiration of Tibetan Buddhism as a whole.

4

The Vajrayana in the Context
of the Three-Yana Journey

WITHIN BUDDHISM, THE SPIRITUAL LIFE IS DEFINED AS A
journey of progressive maturation. As one travels along the path, one's
understanding becomes more subtle and more profound. Buddhist tradition has found it useful to divide the path into specific stages, for truth
appears differently depending on one's degree of maturity, and a practice that works at one level may be ineffective at another.

The various Buddhist traditions handle this need to separate out
stages on the path in different ways. Within Tibetan Buddhism, following the practice of late Indian tradition, the graduated journey to awakening is divided, as mentioned, into three successive yanas, or vehicles.
In the Tibetan context, a yana is a specific and comprehensive convey-
ance or methodology by which a person works with his or her mind at
any given point. In Tibet, one is first to practice the Hinayana, then the
Mahayana, and finally the Vajrayana. Each subsequent yana rests on the
preceding ones: the Hinayana acts as the foundation for the two higher
yanas, while the Mahayana is understood as the necessary precondition
for the practice of the Vajrayana.*

*As we have seen, the idea of the three yanas originated in India. During the
course of its long history, Indian Buddhism produced a tremendous variety of
schools, orientations, and lineages. Questions naturally arose: Are these all doing
the same thing? Are they entirely different? Are some authentic and some not
authentic? How are all these related to one another? Out of this creative ferment,
answers to these questions began to appear early on. When the Mahayana arose, its
proponents were well aware of the many schools already in existence. In defining

In this system, as we saw in chapter 1, the Hinayana, or lesser vehicle, consists of taking refuge, thereby entering the path, and following a course of training in ethics, meditation, and wisdom. The second yana, the Mahayana, the great vehicle, involves taking the bodhisattva vow to liberate suffering beings and engaging in the six *paramitas*, or "transcendent actions," altruistic practices devoted to developing both compassion for all beings and the wisdom to see true reality. Both the Hinayana and Mahayana are thought of as "conventional vehicles" in the sense that they can be fully practiced in the ordinary social contexts of home, temple, and monastery.

---

their relation to these earlier schools, they determined that these earlier schools were all "lesser" in that they promoted "individual salvation" and did not proclaim the ideal of the bodhisattva, who aspires to become a fully enlightened buddha for the sake of all beings. The term for "lesser" in Sanskrit is *hina*, and so all of these pre-Mahayana schools became known as "Hinayana," "Lesser Vehicle," in the Mahayana way of speaking. In this solution to the problem of Buddhist diversity, the Mahayana did not reject the Hinayana as invalid. Instead, it held that it was the first stage on the path to awakening and that, at a certain point in his or her maturation, the practitioner needed to leave the Hinayana behind and enter the Mahayana.

When the Vajrayana developed in India, there is evidence that it was originally practiced as a self-sufficient form of Buddhism and that it was not set in relation to either Hinayana or Mahayana. However, as the Vajrayana became more popular in the eighth century and after, the question arose in people's minds, "But how is this related to those forms of Buddhism that we already know about, the Hinayana and the Mahayana?" The answer patterned itself on the existing model of the Hinayana as the first stage on the path and the Mahayana as the second, more advanced stage. Now the Vajrayana was seen as even more advanced than the Mahayana, and it was believed that having practiced first the initial two yanas, the Hinayana and then the Mahayana, one would then need to practice the third and culminating yana, the Vajrayana. In this system, the Vajrayana was seen as more advanced not in its ultimate realization—for there could be no higher goal than the buddhahood described in the Mahayana—but rather in its spiritual methodology. The distinctiveness of the Vajrayana, then, was that it provided methods enabling the practitioner to attain buddhahood in a single lifetime, rather than only after innumerable lifetimes outlined in the conventional Mahayana.

The three-yana scheme is mentioned in the early tantras. In the *Hevajra Tantra*, for example, it said that prior to entering the Vajrayana, a person should first train in the Hinayana, then practice the Mahayana. Following this lead, between the

The third and culminating yana is known as the Vajrayana, the "indestructible vehicle." Like the Mahayana, the Vajrayana is also a bodhisattva vehicle, but at a more advanced level. Having attained some fruition in the Hinayana and having trained in the Mahayana through taking the bodhisattva vow and practicing the paramitas, the tantric practitioner aims to fulfill his or her bodhisattva commitment through a path of yoga, meditation, and retreat practice. Because of this yogic emphasis and particular tantric methods, the Vajrayana is understood as the "unconventional vehicle." Because its methods were considered unsurpassed, it is known as the "supreme yana" and is compared to the golden roof of the temple of enlightenment that has the Hinayana as foundation and the Mahayana as its superstructure.

Vajrayana Buddhism, as practiced in Tibet, presupposes that the yogin has practiced and attained some measure of competence in both the Hinayana and the Mahayana. It is assumed that the tantric yogin has assimilated the Hinayana view of suffering, has trained in its basic meditation techniques, and has attained some measure of renunciation. Likewise, one's understanding of emptiness as well as one's Mahayana motivation and commitment are taken for granted, as is practice of the paramitas and other Mahayana disciplines. In order to understand the spirituality of the Vajrayana and how its path unfolds, then, we need to make some acquaintance with the Hinayana and Mahayana as preliminary stages to tantric practice. (For a detailed discussion of the Hinayana

---

eighth and twelfth centuries in India, the Indian Buddhist commentators synthesized the various traditions of the Eighteen Schools or Hinayana, the Mahayana, and the Vajrayana into one comprehensive system, within an overarching framework of levels and stages. Their final product was known as the "three yanas" or "three vehicles." It was this scheme that the Tibetans who came to India in search of Buddhism found, and it was this that they took back to Tibet.

Ultimately, the three-yana scheme is not a historical model but rather, as mentioned, a way of understanding the distinctive stages of the Vajrayana path. It is true that this model did arise out of contact with other schools, the Eighteen Schools and the Mahayana. However, from the beginning, the three-yana idea defines three levels of spiritual maturity and should not be taken to tell us very much about the schools labeled as "Hinayana" or even necessarily those labeled as "Mahayana."

and Mahayana stages on the path, see *Indestructible Truth*, chapters 10–13.)

THE HINAYANA

There are many ways to analyze and understand the three yanas. One of the most useful is to divide each into view, practice, and result. *View* refers to the philosophical standpoint toward reality that one holds at any point. In Buddhism, it is believed that a correct "view" is the necessary foundation of any successful practice. If one does not know what to think about what is real and unreal, and what is relatively good and bad, then one will have no sense of direction and no set of criteria to determine whether one is on the path or has strayed off. *Practice* refers to the actual methodologies that are used in each of the yanas to advance one along the way. Traditionally, practice includes behavioral norms—ethics, morality, discipline—as well as specific meditation practices of all sorts. And *result* indicates the fruition of that particular yana, in other words, the end point toward which that yana is heading.

Hinayana View: The First Turning of the Wheel of Dharma

Tibetan tradition holds that, as mentioned, Buddha Shakyamuni gave three major promulgations of teaching known as the three turnings of the wheel of dharma. In Tibet, the *view* of Hinayana is associated with the first turning wherein the Buddha expounded the four noble truths: the truth of suffering; the truth of the cause of suffering; the truth of the cessation of suffering; and the truth of the path. The specific view of Hinayana is associated with the first two truths, while the fourth truth concerns the path of Hinayana and the third truth its goal of cessation. Simple as these truths appear, there is a great wealth of instruction contained in each. In fact, the entirety of the teachings of Hinayana, as found in the dozens of volumes in the Tibetan canon devoted to the Hinayana, can be classified according to the four noble truths.

The first noble truth, that of suffering, declares that imperfection, unsatisfactoriness, and incompletion mark every moment of samsaric existence. Suffering covers everything from the subtle sense that things are not quite perfect all the way to the most hellish physical and mental pain that can be experienced. There is no safe haven, no oasis of escape from the fact of suffering. Within the human realm, the out-and-out suffering of disease, injury, famine, war, old age, and death are blatant facts of life that confront us all. But it is also true that in moments when we seem to have attained some transient pleasure or security, we are still haunted by their unavoidable impermanence. Finally, on the most subtle level, even the very nature of our conceptualizing process, the very way we narrow down experience to recognize and "own" it, is riddled with tension. The more aware we become, the more we realize that pain is an inescapable element of human life as such.

The second noble truth points to the cause of our suffering, the reason why our experiences as human beings always seem incomplete and insufficient. This cause is explained as *trishna*, thirst, our basic hunger or underlying search for physical, emotional, and mental satisfaction. Trishna expresses itself in our continual desire for comfort and security, for status and approval, for a view of the world that can provide a reliable reference point, and even, on the most subtle level, for freedom from the struggles of existence. Thirst rests upon a more fundamental root cause, namely our ignorance of the true state of affairs: that our notion of an "I" that has to be aggrandized and protected is a made-up idea.

The second noble truth also provides a detailed view of karma and how it works. It explains how every aspect of our current existence is the fruition of causes laid down in the past. And it shows how the way in which we respond to the givenness of our lives will create the karma for our future, both in this life and in subsequent births. Meritorious actions of gentleness, kindness, and understanding will generate positive karma toward the future, while demeritorious actions such as anger, aggression, and enmity will create negative karma that we will one day inherit.

As it is presented in the Hinayana texts, the teaching on karma examines the various destinies that occur as the result of one's actions. Thus, there are six realms of being within samsara, and beings are repeatedly born into each of these six as they cycle among the realms. These realms include from the lowest and most painful to the highest and least painful: the hell realm; the hungry ghost realm; the animal realm; the human realm; the jealous god realm; and the god realm. Greater pain and lesser pain (what we may call pleasure) alternate, based on causes and conditions. Sometimes one is in a relative state of woe; at other times one finds oneself in a relative state of happiness. The important point is that each of these realms leads to another of the six; in and of themselves, there is never any escape.

Hinayana Practice

In Tibetan Buddhism, a person enters the Hinayana by taking refuge and becoming a Buddhist. This means going through the "refuge vow ceremony," in which one takes refuge in the "three jewels"—the Buddha (the founder), the dharma (the teachings), and the sangha (the community). In this context, one takes refuge in the Buddha as the example of what a human being can attain; it is a refuge equally in one's own potentiality for enlightenment. Refuge in the dharma involves relying upon the teachings the Buddha gave, both in the textual corpus, and in the oral teachings of authentic masters. Finally, refuge in the sangha means that one joins the community of practitioners of dharma; this membership implies both that one provides assistance to others and that one is willing to receive their feedback and help.

Having become a Buddhist, one now sets out on the Hinayana path, the fourth noble truth, which is divided into *shila*, ethical behavior; *samadhi*, meditation; and *prajna*, wisdom or insight into the nature of things. In one sense, these three are progressive: one must first cultivate a life that is marked by kindness and good intentions towards others, a life that is ethically well grounded. On this basis, one may then enter the practice of meditation. And, having developed a sound meditation practice, insight begins to arise. In another sense, however, shila, samadhi, and prajna may occur in any order and mutually reinforce each other in a variety of ways. For example, from one point of view they unfold in reverse order: it is insight (prajna) into suffering that often motivates people to enter the dharma in the first place. Then they practice a little meditation (samadhi) and realize, perhaps for the first time, how self-centered and unkind they are to others. Based on this, they may attempt to be more ethical in their behavior (shila).

Shila (Ethical Behavior)

Shila is a general principle within Tibetan Buddhism and also a set of specific ethical or behavioral guidelines that include precepts for laypeople, rules of monastic restraint, and codes of conduct for yogis and yoginis.

In terms of its role as a general principle, the functions of shila are several. In the beginning, shila provides a way to address the important question of how one is with others. A relationship to others characterized by selfishness, aggression, and antipathy provides serious obstacles to spiritual development. In the present, such behavior creates a mind that is anxious, turbulent, and obsessively discursive. Toward the future, it produces karmic retribution in which we suffer the painful physical, psychological, and social consequences of our negative behavior.

In addition, shila is also helpful as one progresses along the path. In Buddhism, the different codes of conduct are not imposed upon practitioners but are rather taken voluntarily. Take, for example, the precept to refrain from false speech or lying. Most of us continually present situations as different from what they actually are, but we tend to block out our awareness of this fact. As a famous Tibetan saying goes, "We see others' faults, be they as fine as a mustard seed; our own faults, which may be like a mountain, we ignore." This kind of approach is readily reflected in our speech. We often sense quite easily when others are being deceptive, but we remain conveniently unaware of our own duplicity.

As we attempt to carry out the commitment to abstain from false speech in our lives, we begin to see just how continual and extensive our misrepresentation is, how we are always verbally reshaping things to suit our own purposes. The self-knowledge gained in this way is painful and hard to take—but it is also purifying. Once the light of awareness is shed into the dark corners of our self-deception, it becomes much harder to speak untruth. In this way, the various dimensions of shila further our awareness and, in that way, complement the practice of meditation.

Finally, shila functions as a portrait of the spontaneous behavior of a realized person. On account of his realization, a buddha, for example, is said to exemplify all of the shilas in a complete and perfect way.

Shila not only is a general principle but also comprises various sets of precepts for laypeople, monastics, and yogins. For example, in Tibet laypeople most commonly take the "five lay precepts," including, as mentioned, abstention from taking life (killing), from taking what is not given (stealing), from false speech (lying), from sexual misconduct (adultery, etc.), and from intoxicants as tending to cloud the mind. These five precepts become greatly elaborated and supplemented in the *pratimokṣha*, the several hundred rules of monastic restraint for monks and nuns. Finally, yogins take vows specific to their lifestyle, such as the vow to remain in retreat for a certain period of time, to eat only one meal a day, and to meditate throughout the night, not lying down to sleep even at night, and so on.

In their classical formulations, shila usually tells us what should *not* be done, what one is to refrain from doing. But, in addition, it shows us what *should* be done, what actions one should engage in. For example, the first lay precept, and a precept also for monastics and yogins, is to refrain from killing any living being. In Tibet, this precept points to the importance of reverence for life and saving it whenever possible. In parts of India, for example, animals to be slaughtered are kept alive by the butcher until he is ready to sell the meat, at which time they are killed. One of the sixteenth Karmapa's favorite activities was the traditional Mahayana practice of buying animals slated for slaughter and setting them free. Those who witnessed the Karmapa engaged in this action could hardly resist participating in his love for these poor creatures, and his delight and joy at wresting them from the hand of their killer.

It is important to realize that shila does not involve "being good" as if one were trying to win approval from some human authority or from an external deity. Rather, in Tibetan Buddhism, one follows the codes of shila because of their positive impact on oneself and others. We see here the eminent practicality of the Tibetan dharma: you behave well, you act in a kind and helpful way to others, because it enables you to mature spiritually and because it is beneficial to them. Our actions are judged at death, according to the Tibetans, but the judgment is wrought by ourselves. Once we have passed beyond, we stand face to face with everything we have done, down to the last detail. Stripped of all distraction, posturing, and deception, the virtuous and nonvirtuous character of our actions is laid bare, for us and the buddhas and bodhisattvas to see. To stand naked in this way in the face of what we have done is surely the most complete judgment that we could ever experience.

SAMADHI (MEDITATION)

The centerpiece of the Hinayana path, as indeed of Tibetan Buddhism itself, is the practice of meditation. This is generally divided into *shamatha*, mindfulness, and *vipashyana*, insight. In our ordinary state, our minds are restless, unstable, and overrun with discursive thoughts of all kinds. People are often subliminally aware that they think incessantly, but most have no idea of just how wild and untamed their minds really are.

The rabid mind poses a serious problem for the practice of spirituality. The reason is that spirituality involves seeing, and too much thinking gets in the way of seeing. In order to see, we need to clear some space amid the rampant discursive overgrowth of our thinking mind.

It sometimes happens in life that some occurrence will bring about this kind of space naturally. For example, it is likely that if we experience the death of someone close to us, this will have a profound impact. Feelings of grief now break through our usual thought process; we can no longer think in the same way; many of our old mental preoccupations no longer have meaning; we may slow down and simplify our lives; and we may become more reflective. Within such a state of mind, painful though it may be, there is much more room for seeing. If a person undergoes grave illness, or is tending another who is ill or dying, he or she may experience a similar slowing down, quieting, and opening up of inner territory.

The purpose of shamatha is, in a deliberate and methodical way, to bring about this same effect. The practice could not be more simple. One takes a specific "object of meditation" and rests one's attention upon it. When the mind drifts away into thoughts and fantasies, one simply brings it back to the object. The meditation object most commonly used in Tibetan Buddhism, as in most other Buddhist traditions, is the breath. In the basic practice, one rests the attention on the breath, attending to both the in-breath and the out-breath. When the mind wanders away, as it inevitably will do, one brings it gently back to the breathing. The practice of shamatha leads to two important results. First, the sheer speed and volume of one's thinking process begins to diminish. Second, one begins to become acquainted with one's tendency toward distraction and also with the various ways in which one gets pulled away, whether by sense perceptions, thoughts, feelings, or other distractions.

The lessening of discursiveness is usually experienced with great relief. However, the growing awareness of the level of chaos in one's mind is sometimes extraordinarily painful. It is as if the anesthetic of our habitual ignorance is beginning to wear off and we begin to feel the actual disease more acutely. Painful though it may be, however, such growing awareness shows us what we are actually working with in the practice and represents the beginning of sanity.

There are many styles, methods, and levels of shamatha, even just in terms of working with the breath. Put in a simple way, these can be graded from techniques that require a great deal of effort to those that seem almost effortless. Thus, at one end of the spectrum, one may be instructed to focus 100 percent of one's attention on the sensation at the tip of one's nose, feeling the coolness of the air as it enters and its warmness as it departs. One is to hold one's awareness exactly at that point, attempting to maintain complete and total presence, without the least wandering or even the least flicker of inattention. When one's mind wanders away, one simply and gently, but firmly brings it back.

A more subtle technique involves the same basic method, but this time resting one's attention in a much lighter way, with, say, only 25 percent of one's attention on the breath and the other 75 percent on the environment, the room in which one is sitting, the space, the temperature of the air, the quality of the light, and so on. At the other end of the spectrum, one might be instructed to maintain only the very slightest attention on the breath and to rest nearly all of one's awareness on the space of the environment.

These various techniques are designed for specific situations and not for haphazard application. Many Western practitioners of meditation have heard of these and other methods, and will try out different techniques in different meditation sessions, and even within the same meditation session. Not infrequently, one's choice of the moment is governed by what feels "most comfortable." Unfortunately, all too often one is not employing any further criterion of what technique to use. The problem with this approach is twofold: at best, it may not be based on any real understanding of what the immediate challenge is in the person's state of mind and of what approach might most effectively address it; and, at worst, it uses meditation to avoid confronting painful dimensions of experience and thus to maintain one's obstacles and blind spots. This is why every meditator needs a mentor who is experienced in the practice.

The most important point in the practice of shamatha is this: the level of heavy-handedness of the technique must match the level of grossness of one's conceptual activity; the technique, in the degree of effort required, must be commensurate with the degree of conceptuality that one is experiencing. A light technique applied to heavy conceptuality will get nowhere. A heavy technique applied to very little conceptuality will itself generate more conceptuality than was there in the first place. The adjustment must be appropriate and skillfully applied. Dialogue with a spiritual friend skilled in meditation is the best way to find the technique appropriate for one's current situation. Eventually, through good training and sustained practice, one becomes able to judge for oneself what is needed. At this point, without abandoning the need for occasional outside guidance, as Sakyong Mipham Rinpoche says, "one can begin to function as one's own meditation instructor."[1]

Prajna (Knowledge)

As the conceptual process begins to slow down through the practice of shamatha, the meditator begins to see that his or her thinking is not as solid as it had first appeared. In fact, there are many gaps in one's thoughts, and through these gaps insight, vipashyana, begins to dawn. The nature of this awareness is evident from the etymology of this Sanskrit word. *Pash* means "to see," while *vi* means away, out, as in "out of the ordinary" or "extraordinary." Thus *vipash*yana means to see in a way that is not ordinary, that is, in short, from outside of the reference point and territory of ego. To experience vipashyana is to see situations from the viewpoint of non-ego.

Vipashyana is an experience of prajna, knowledge, the third and final stage on the Hinayana path. In the Hinayana, *prajna* means knowledge on two different levels, the first corresponding to "view" and the second, as here, to the culmination of the path. On the level of view, *prajna* means "right knowledge" in an abstract and intellectual sense. It means having the right conceptual understanding of the dharma. In its role as the fruition of the path, however, *prajna* refers to the nonconceptual knowledge that sees things as they are. At this level, then, prajna is seeing the truth of the four noble truths—but *seeing* their truth, not just holding the intellectual conviction of it. Thus suffering is seen in its all-pervasive extent; one gains a clear view of how one creates it through thirst; one experiences glimpses of the cessation of ego; and one clearly sees the necessity and logic of the path.

Prajna reveals that the solid and continuous "self" that we think we are is actually composed of nothing more than a series of impersonal, momentary events. A lot of things go on in our experience—thoughts, feelings, sense perceptions, emotions, and so on. These momentary events that make up our experience are known in the Hinayana as *dharmas*. Because they are momentary, dharmas are impermanent: they appear and disappear instant by instant. They have a face or an identity, which is how they appear. A moment of pride, anger, or jealousy would be an example of a dharma, as would instants of faith, modesty, or joy. What governs which dharmas appear in our lives? Each moment of our experience is linked by karma to the moment preceding and the moment following. Within this never-ending cascade of karmically determined experience of dharmas, no "self" is given, no "I" is present. Our "self" derives from attaching a personalistic label of "I" to the impersonal flow of these dharmas. It is nothing more than a mistaken idea.

The dharmas that make up our supposed "person" may be conveniently divided into five groups or types, known as *skandhas* in Sanskrit, translated as "aggregates." "Form," *rupa,* refers to experiences of physicality, including the five senses and their five sense objects, colored according to the four elements of earth, water, fire, and air. "Feeling," *vedana*, refers to our primitive positive, negative, or neutral sensation that accompanies each moment of experience. "Perception," *samjna,* represents our perceptual identification—which occurs prior to thinking—of the content of our experiences as, for example, big or small, long or short, black or white, familiar or unfamiliar. "Karmic formations," *samskaras*, are the collection of fifty-one concepts, labels, ideas, and judgments that we use to further locate what arises in our experience. Finally, "consciousness," *vijnana*, is the territorial field of awareness that reflects our experience, but always with a self-serving intention and twist.

These five skandhas, seen by the eye of Hinayana prajna, are extremely important for the Vajrayana in two ways. First, they reveal that there is no solid or identifiable "self" that could become the object of grasping or territoriality on the part of the practitioner; second they demonstrate that, even when no "I" or "self" is present, reality "on the other side of egolessness"—in the Hinayana described as the five skandhas—continues to manifest and to display itself to awareness. In the Mahayana, in the second turning of the wheel of dharma, the nonexistence of the self is deepened in the discussion of emptiness (shunyata), and in the Vajrayana it is explored further in the notion of "vajra being." In the Mahayana, in the third turning of the wheel, the display of reality beyond thought is extended in the idea of buddha-nature, while in the Vajrayana it is given further refinement in the idea of "vajra world" (see chapter 7).

The Result of Hinayana

The third noble truth articulates the teaching on "cessation." The first two noble truths, suffering and its cause, describe a repetitive and conditioned but unnecessary way of being called samsara, one's endless cycling through the various realms. The third noble truth maintains that when the causes and conditions that maintain samsara are removed, then samsara in and of itself ceases. This cessation marks the individual's attainment of liberation and his or her exit from future rebirths. In the early Buddhist schools, a person who attains this kind of liberation is known as an *arhant,* sometimes rendered as "foe" (*ari*) "destroyer" (*hant*).

In Tibetan tradition, owing to its Mahayana character, there is no question of attaining complete cessation in this sense. Indeed, to do so would be to break one's bodhisattva vow to continue to be reborn within samsara to benefit others. Instead, the practical and more Mahayana-related "result" of Hinayana practice is called in Tibetan *soso tharpa* (Skt. *pratimoksha*), "individual liberation." This liberation involves realizing that the game of ego is a battle that can never be won. The practitioner comes to see that no matter how hard he or she tries, the image of the self carried around in one's head will never be actualized. In short, one will never achieve samsaric happiness.

Soso tharpa is an experience of certainty: one sees and one knows beyond a shadow of a doubt that suffering touches every moment of phenomenal experience and that no amount of struggle is going to change that fact. This realization is devastating, at least to the ego. One sees, truly, that there is no way out.

At this moment, one gives up the battle and gives in to the excruciating truth. One realizes that there is no hope but to abandon the struggle to exist, in the way of ego. One surrenders one's thirst, in the same way that in the Old West one might surrender firearms at the door of a tavern. For, it is now discovered, thirst is not an inevitable thing; it is rather our primary weapon in the struggle to convince ourselves of our own existence. We continually manufacture thirst, pretending that this is "just the way things are," without seeing its contrived nature. Now that the deceiver has been exposed and his powerlessness revealed, there is no choice but to abandon him. When the inevitability of suffering is experienced, when thirst is surrendered, then one experiences true renunciation. The allures of samsara no longer have any power over the practitioner. This is an experience of "cessation," the goal of the first yana on the Tibetan Buddhist path.

THE MAHAYANA

In Tibetan Buddhism, the Hinayana is seen as providing the preliminary step on the way to the Mahayana, and one remains on the Hinayana level of practice only until this foundation has been sufficiently well laid. Once this has occurred, it is believed that in order to develop further, one must enter the Mahayana and take up the way of life of the bodhisattva.

When a person steps onto the Mahayana path, the Hinayana foundation is by no means discarded. Quite to the contrary, it serves as the basis without which one could never follow the bodhisattva's way. That means not only that the Hinayana dimension of a person's path must have reached some level of maturity prior to engaging the Mahayana; in addition, while one carries out the bodhisattva practices, the Hinayana disciplines must be kept fresh and constantly revitalized. A direct and open relation to suffering, the ongoing exploration of karma and how it works, the continual effort toward one's shila, the practice of meditation, and the sense of renunciation continue, for a bodhisattva, to provide the foundations of dharmic life.

Like the Hinayana, the Mahayana may be understood according to view, practice, and result. The view of Mahayana is defined by the notions of shunyata and buddha-nature. These teachings are understood to have been given in a second and a third turning of the wheel of dharma emphasizing, respectively, the vacant and the present qualities of shunyata. The practice element of Mahayana consists of the six paramitas and various types of meditation, contemplation, and action that derive from them. Finally, the result of the Mahayana is the perfected state of a completely enlightened buddha.

The View of Mahayana

Understanding fully the Hinayana view of suffering, its cause, and its cessation tears asunder one of the primary veils obscuring reality. In spite of the majesty and profundity of such a realization, from the Mahayana point of view it is limited. For the Hinayana is focused on the personal attainment of a longed-for goal. Moreover, this goal is exclusionary. It factors out everything considered "samsara" and represents an attainment of "nirvana." In order to abandon one thing and attain another, there must be someone engaged in these actions. It may be asked: Who longs for such a goal and who attains it? From the Mahayana viewpoint, the Hinayana has not met with the full attainment of egolessness.

The Mahayana takes the view of the Hinayana several steps further in the second and the third turnings of the wheel of dharma. These two turnings provide the view of Vajrayana. This is a critical point: the Vajrayana does not possess its own distinctive philosophical position but articulates its view in terms of the second and third turnings of the wheel. Since these two turnings provide the view of Vajrayana, they will be discussed in detail in the next chapter. At this point, however, a brief indication of their primary elements is in order.

In the second turning of the wheel of dharma, the Buddha preached the doctrine of shunyata, or emptiness. In the second-turning discourses, he taught that, not only is the individual "I" or self devoid of any enduring and substantial being, but indeed all aspects of reality whatsoever are empty of any essential nature. The entire world that we think we see and experience is fundamentally empty of anything solid or definitive. Not only are ordinary things like tables and chairs "empty," but even our most subtle and fleeting experiences—the dharmas—the five skandhas—are also empty of any abiding or objectifiable nature. Even samsara and nirvana, the most basic categories of our spiritual life, are finally nothing more than our projections; even they are empty of any essential being. Through these teachings, the Buddha sought to clear away the last vestige of our mental projections. Only on the basis of such a thorough mental housecleaning is Vajrayana practice possible.

In the Third Turning of the Wheel of Dharma, the Buddha preached the doctrine of the "three natures" and of the buddha-nature. The "three natures" teaching says that reality is not just nonexistent; in addition, it has a kind of ineffable being that arises dependent on causes and conditions. The buddha-nature doctrine points to an enlightened essence that is present in the heart of all sentient beings. Through these teachings, the Buddha sought to point to a world that, while utterly beyond thought, is not utterly nonexistent. It is this world that is the object of Vajrayana practice.

The Practice of Mahayana

The first step in entering the Mahayana and engaging its path is the taking of the bodhisattva vow. In a ceremony conducted by a preceptor, the aspirant announces his or her intention not to strive for personal liberation but to continue to be reborn in samsara for others' sake. One vows to continue in this process for three incalculable eons until one has attained the state of a fully enlightened buddha. One declares further that during all of this time, one will train in wisdom and compassion for sentient beings, helping them in every way possible to grow and mature in their own paths, so that they may also attain enlightenment.

In practical terms, the bodhisattva vow means that one will work to become more and more sensitive and aware of the situation and needs of other people. In all activities, one will try to incorporate them into one's thinking. It is no longer possible to approach life asking only "What is best for me?" Now one has to include the question of what may be best for other people as well. Raising this question obviously makes life much more complicated and demanding. It is the difference between the relative simplicity of a single person and that same person who wakes up one morning and finds him- or herself the parent of a houseful of small children that need continual care. Yet this is the way of the bodhisattva. Now one is being asked to truly see and find sympathy for the others that one may meet. Eventually, when reaching the stage of a fully enlightened buddha, one will be asked to see and find sympathy for all sentient beings.

The bodhisattva vow is fulfilled through a variety of practical means, foremost among which are the six paramitas or "transcendent actions." These are both contemplative and active practices that serve the dual purpose of helping other beings and developing one's own spiritual maturity. At first glance, the six paramitas do not seem very much different from the virtues and practices that we have seen in the Hinayana: (1) *dana*, generosity; (2) *shila*, ethical behavior; (3) *virya*, exertion; (4) *kshanti*, patience; (5) *dhyana,* meditation; and (6) *prajna*, wisdom.

However, there are some important differences between the six paramitas and their Hinayana counterparts. Most important, the "ultimate" or sixth paramita, *prajnaparamita,* the perfection of wisdom or "transcendent knowledge," is direct perception of shunyata, emptiness. This permeates the other five, "relative" paramitas. Prajnaparamita grounds each of the other paramitas in two mutually interdependent ways: first, it makes possible an understanding of the ultimate emptiness and thus openness of all categories and fixations; and second, emerging from this, it provides access to an understanding of the exact situation and needs of the sentient being one is trying to help. This latter understanding is possible because, if one is not preoccupied by the validity of one's own ideas (groundlessness, emptiness), one is that much more able to discern what a particular sentient being needs. It is the emptiness or inseparability with prajnaparamita of, for example, generosity, that makes it a "perfection" rather than an ordinary virtue. To say that generosity is "open" in this way means that it is not governed by external criteria; the way the generosity is enacted depends entirely on the specific, ever-changing needs of the sentient being in question; to practice the paramita of generosity, the bodhisattva must be free of any and all fixed concepts of self and other. It is similar with the other relative paramitas.

The "prajna" element within each paramita also ensures the purity of the practice. Whatever action is performed, however great its apparent benefit, one sees that it is ultimately ineffable and cannot become an object of one's own sense of accomplishment or pride. This is formalized in the well-known "threefold purity": one realizes that, ultimately, no actor can be located who is "generous"; no recipient can be identified who receives the "act of generosity"; and there is no action that can be objectified as "generosity." To be sure, on the relative plane, great benefit may be accomplished. But when one looks closely enough at the elements of "generosity," one finds that they are beyond our projections, that they exist in an indefinable and ungraspable way in the *dharmakaya*, the true being of this world. As with generosity, so it is with the other relative paramitas.

Generosity, ethical conduct, and patience represent ways in which the bodhisattva is with sentient beings. Generosity involves giving whatever is needed for the other to be able to move ahead, whether that is material goods, healing, freedom from oppression, dharma instruction, or anything else. Shila never wavers from one's commitment to others. Patience means holding sentient beings in one's heart, no matter how difficult they may turn out to be, and waiting, until the end of the world if need be, to provide needed assistance. Exertion involves diligence in meditation. Meditation includes shamatha and vipashyana, carried out on the Mahayana level. Here shamatha attends to emptiness and vipashyana discloses its very nature. Prajna is the flavor of emptiness that runs through the other five paramitas.

Along with the paramitas, and as expressions of them, are many other practices designed to soften one's heart and develop sympathy, kindness, and love for others. Various contemplative practices help us overcome the idea that "I" and "other" are fixed, separate entities. For example, in a famous Mahayana text known as the *Bodhicharyavatara*, one is instructed to select an acquaintance and then visualize him or her (1) as superior to oneself; (2) as inferior to oneself; and (3) as equal to oneself. One observes in each case how an entirely different set of projections and attitudes arises. One sees that much of how we see others, including our envy, our paranoia, and our disdain, is a projection of our own minds and depends on where we think that other person stands in relation to ourselves. This insight tends toward a desolidification of one-self and the birth of sympathy for the other.

Tonglen, "sending and taking," is another powerful and extremely effective bodhisattva practice. The practitioner selects a person who is suffering, whom he or she would like to help. One employs the in-breath and out-breath as the medium of the contemplation: on the in-breath one visualizes the suffering of the other coming to oneself; on the out-breath one visualizes all the goodness that one possesses going to relieve the other. Like the "exchange," this practice dissolves the apparent duality of self and other, and the resistance we all feel toward taking the welfare of another person truly to heart.

All of the Mahayana practices continually mix wisdom and compassion. Wisdom desolidifies our rigid, conceptual versions of ourselves and others; compassion is the natural, intelligent, appropriate outflow of this desolidification. Once one no longer sees oneself as separate, it is natural to feel sympathy for others' suffering and a desire to help in some way. This fundamentally altruistic attitude is considered the only proper motivation for a person to undertake Vajrayana practice.

The Result of Mahayana

The result of the Mahayana is the attainment of the full and perfect enlightenment of a world-redeeming buddha. From the time of taking the bodhisattva vow, as mentioned, it is said to take three incalculable eons for a practitioner to attain this goal. During this immeasurable span of time, the bodhisattva is born millions upon millions of times not only into the human realm, in all of its conditions of misery and woe, but also into the other five realms as well. As he progresses along his path, increasingly he takes rebirth not out of karmic necessity but rather in fulfillment of his bodhisattva vow. For it is only through this interminable series of rebirths, undergone without karmic compulsion, that he can develop the wisdom and ripen the compassion that he must eventually have as a buddha. For the practitioner, this seemingly endless vista of future rebirths has the effect of taking all investment out of the eventual goal. The final attainment is so far in the future that one is led to relinquish any fixation on the ultimate fruition and to focus on the task at hand of trying to attend properly to the suffering of each person one encounters.

CONCLUSION

The three yanas are three phases of understanding and practice along one unbroken continuity of development. The Hinayana establishes the basic tools and perspectives for the entire Buddhist path, while the Mahayana and Vajrayana provide refinements. In a very real sense, the Vajrayana is not fundamentally different from the earlier yanas, except that it wants to take the journey to a more subtle level and develops language and practices necessary to that end.

View

The Hinayana "view" establishes the "reality orientation" of Buddhism, that the dharma is not about some other world, but rather about this world and how we perceive and understand it. The first two noble truths thus talk about our concrete, earthy experience of reality—that it is most basically characterized by suffering and that this, in turn, is driven by our thirst.

The Mahayana deepens the "this-worldly" orientation of the Hinayana in an interesting way. Through the teaching of emptiness, it reveals that even our most subtle thoughts about what is real get in the way of direct experience of our lives. Emptiness shows that whatever we think about ourselves and our world is ultimately inapplicable. Even the notion of a spiritual goal to be attained, nirvana, is a projection that must be abandoned. Wherever we may imagine we are going, even in a spiritual sense, is another projection of ego. Understanding emptiness thus leaves us, in a deeper way, with nothing other than this world and the immediacy of the present.

The Vajrayana continues the Hinayana interest in laying bare the actual, tangible reality of our experience as human beings. But it has passed through the Mahayana fire and assumes a present reality that is empty—that is, beyond objectifiability and in essence ineffable. The Vajrayana now goes a step further. It declares that once emptiness is recognized, we are by no means done with the world. Having seen that what we think about it is inapplicable, having given up on our version of how things are, we are still left with the question of what the world beyond emptiness may be like and how we are to be in it. For although the world may be empty, it continues to appear and to operate.

The Vajrayana examines the nature of this reality "beyond emptiness." Moreover, this examination is done in fulfillment of the bodhisattva vow. In spite of emptiness, one is still—perhaps even more—obliged to engage the world, for the welfare of all beings. Again, this leads to *the* tantric question: what is the world, beyond emptiness, like? The tantric vehicle is a way of finding out more about this ordinary world that we live in, in all of its profundity and sacredness, and how it can be used to help others on their spiritual paths.

Practice

SHILA

The prospect of exploring reality beyond thought obviously carries with it certain dangers, and the shila developed in the Hinayana and Mahayana provides important protections. The cultivation of shila leads one to practice restraint so that one does not need to indulge every urge and emotional upheaval that passes through one's mind. Through training in shila, one learns to wait through the assault of an impulse until the point where a transmutation can occur, resulting in insight and thoughtfulness. This kind of psychological distance between one's impulses and one's actions is particularly important in the Mahayana, where activity is directed toward benefiting others. Attempting to work closely with other people can provoke strong reactions and, without restraint, one would be led to all kinds of ill-considered responses that might end up harming those one is trying to assist.

The kind of discipline implicit in shila is particularly critical to the practice tradition of the Vajrayana because, in the tantric vehicle, one is engaging the depths of one's mind and perceiving the world in a naked manner. One is exploring realms of ego and of egolessness, including the depths of passion, aggression, pride, ignorance, and paranoia as well as the open space, clarity, bliss, and nonthought of the awakened state. Such a naked inquiry naturally brings with it strong experiences that are hard to handle. Without the Hinayana and Mahayana training in shila, one would be more likely either to repress what occurs or to try to act it out, either of which would cause one to veer off the bodhisattva path.

The Hinayana teaching on suffering provides a particularly important protection for the tantric practitioner. Through Hinayana practice, one has come to realize that any attempts to build up and fortify ego will inevitably lead to further suffering. Without this understanding, one will still believe that egoic happiness can be attained. Vajrayana practice will then be seen as a way to serve oneself in some way. In such a case, the tantric disciplines will be used to try to build up and fortify one's ego. Such is the way of the demon Rudra, a mythical being in Tibetan Buddhism who symbolizes the tantric egomaniac, a possibility that remains active within every tantric practitioner.

SAMADHI

In the Vajrayana, the question of what the world may be like beyond emptiness is addressed through the practice of meditation. Vajrayana meditation aims to fathom the depth and color, the subtlety and dynamics, of a world that is empty yet continues to manifest itself in all kinds of ways. In order to explore the world in the tantric way, an extraordinary degree of mental calm and settledness is required. The techniques of Hinayana and Mahayana meditation provide the basic tools for this enterprise. Shamatha develops mental stability so that one is able to hold the attention in a steady and one-pointed way, a necessity when carrying out the tantric visualizations. The steadiness of mind developed in shamatha also develops the mental evenness and strength so that one is not shaken by the rough winds of emotional upheavals or "religious" experiences. Vipashyana opens the mind and clarifies insight, so that one sees and understands in an increasingly accurate manner one's practice and experiences along the way.

If the tantric practitioner were not well grounded in shamatha and vipashyana, he or she might well become a victim of the ups and downs of the path. Such a person might be led to wild imaginings of all kinds; he or she might get lost in the "implications" and possibilities of spiritual experiences. One might feel that one has finally become solid, definite, and real, or has even attained some high state, drifting toward some sort of religious megalomania. However, shamatha and vipashyana training enables one to notice such thoughts, to realize that they are nothing more than inflated fantasies, and to let them go, simply returning to the breath.

The Mahayana meditation on emptiness undermines the attempt to convert tantric practice into the currency of ego from another direction. The teachings on shunyata reveal that whatever may occur in our state of mind, it is "empty" in the sense that we cannot take hold of it with thought, build on it, or make anything out of it. If we are not familiar with the teachings on emptiness, we might try to convert what occurs in our practice into a reference point for ego; to take our experiences as "real" in some substantial sense.

Beyond this, through the bodhisattva vow and associated practices, we are continually reminded that the only legitimate motivation for Vajrayana practice is to help others. In the Mahayana, we train in surrendering personal territory and dedicating ourselves to others' welfare. Without some maturation in Mahayana practice, there is the danger that we will forget others and begin to practice for our own benefit alone. This is, of course, problematic, because any thought of using Vajrayana practice in a self-serving way involves breaking our bodhisattva vow. Again, the specter of Rudra looms on the horizon.

Result

The Hinayana teachings on cessation, and also the Mahayana restatement, provide final, critical foundations for tantric practice. The Hinayana teaches that a cessation of the ego mechanism, of samsara, can be attained. Through the teachings on emptiness, the Mahayana points to a place in our experience not only where samsara ceases, but where any conceptual distinctions whatsoever, even those of samsara and nirvana themselves, are inoperative. In the buddha-nature doctrine, the Mahayana says further that this "cessation" is constantly with us, as a background awareness, untainted by ego, that accompanies every moment. The Vajrayana brings this "cessation" more explicitly into the foreground, deepening and extending it. When one visualizes oneself as a buddha, one is learning to abide in the representation of the most inward essence. In fact, the sole purpose of the Vajrayana path is to train practitioners to rest in the "inherent nature" so that the abundant compassion contained therein can flow forth freely to the world.

5

The View of Vajrayana

In Tibet, it is said that the Vajrayana does not have its own distinctive philosophical position or "view." Instead, the view of Vajrayana is provided by the Mahayana, including both the second and third turnings of the wheel of dharma comprising the teachings on emptiness of the second turning and the teachings on the three natures and the buddha-nature of the third turning. This is not to say that the Vajrayana does not have its own way of articulating Mahayana philosophy. In fact, the teachings of the second and third turnings appear in a distinctive way in the Vajrayana, in the context and the idiom of tantric meditation. Nevertheless, the basic understanding of reality present in the Vajrayana is essentially Mahayanist, and to have a correct understanding of the Vajrayana, one needs some grounding in Mahayana philosophy.

The fact that the Vajrayana does not possess its own distinctive philosophical view makes sense when we consider that this tradition is essentially meditative in nature, containing various practices for attaining enlightenment in one lifetime. In fact, in Tibet, the Vajrayana is sometimes known as *upaya yana*, meaning the yana of skillful means (*upaya*). This refers to the rich array of methods contained in the Vajrayana by which practitioners may advance toward the goal of realization.

THE SECOND TURNING AND THE
VIEW OF EMPTINESS

Subsequent to the first turning of the wheel of dharma, in order to lead his followers deeper into the nature of reality, the Buddha gave a second turning near Rajagriha, at Vulture Peak Mountain, in which he presented the teachings on emptiness. These are most quintessentially set out in the Prajnaparamita, a genre of sutra with many different extant versions, and also in the Madhyamaka, a philosophical tradition providing commentary on the Prajnaparamita Sutras. The teachings on emptiness as found in the Prajnaparamita, other sutras, and the various Madhyamaka schools are referred to in Tibet as the "doctrines of the second turning."

As we saw in the last chapter, the teachings on emptiness are critical for the Vajrayana practitioner, because they establish the ultimately open and nonobjectifiable nature of reality. This means that the *subject*—the practitioner—is ultimately nonexistent in any solid or definitive sense; he or she is a process that can never be pinned down or solidified. The *object* of the practice, such as the deities encountered in tantric ritual, are equally empty and beyond any thought or characterization. And the various *practices* themselves are beyond objectification or quantification. Without such a view of the world of practice as empty in this sense, the practitioner would quickly fall prey to the enticements of spiritual power and gain. This, as mentioned, would lead to the religious megalomania of Rudra.

According to the view expressed in the Prajnaparamita Sutras, there are three basic levels possible to human beings in the perception of reality. First is the ordinary samsaric view that takes conventional reality at face value, believing that "I" really exist as a substantial, continuing entity. The second, deeper level is that of the Hinayana, in which one realizes that the apparently solid and enduring "I" is an illusion and is actually a superficial label attached to the endless flow of experiential moments, the dharmas mentioned in the last chapter, classified according to the five skandhas.

The third and most profound perception of reality is that of the Mahayana. Here, not only does one realize that the superficial, conventional world is illusory; in addition, one sees that the more fundamental substrate of dharmas, identified by Hinayana, that make up our experience, is also illusory and contrived. In other words, just as we project the concept of "I" upon a reality that does not accord with this notion, so at the Hinayana level we also project the ideas of dharmas, of the skandhas, of samsara and nirvana, onto a reality that is quite beyond such designations.

What is this ultimate reality that does not correspond to the Hinayana ideas of samsara and nirvana and so on? This is just the point: that reality cannot be put into any words or concepts. In fact, from the Mahayana viewpoint, that was where the Hinayana went wrong, in trying to set up a definitive problem (samsara), a definitive reality (that of the dharmas), and a definitive answer (nirvana).

The short Prajnaparamita text known as the *Heart Sutra* responds to the Hinayana analysis by looking at the experience of the first skandha, form, the experience of matter or physicality.[1] The text says, "Form is emptiness." Emptiness in this context means devoid of any objectifiable essence or defining characteristic. When we say "form," in other words, there is nothing in reality corresponding to our idea. The *Heart Sutra* is saying, in essence, "What form really is, is actually empty of whatever it is we may think of when we say 'form.'" There is no such substantial and definitive thing as "form." We may think that form exists in some substantial and objectifiable way, but this is a false projection upon reality; this is no different from the way in which we may imagine the existence of the "self," which also is a fallacious and finally empty projection.

The text continues, "Emptiness also is form." This is to say that emptiness, the absence of objectifiability, is encountered within, in the very midst of our experience of what we think of as form. Further, "Emptiness is no other than form." In the Prajnaparamita, as the primary sutras of the second turning of the wheel of dharma, emptiness is said to be the nature of ultimate reality. The text now makes reference to the ultimacy of emptiness. It is saying, "If you are looking for emptiness, this ultimate, where will you find it? You will find it nowhere else but only *as form*." In other words, in looking at form, we sense its insubstantiality. In this way, we sense emptiness. It is not that this "ultimate reality" called emptiness exists in some other place as a thing. No. It exists as the final nature of form, the first skandha.

Someone may object that his or her experience of form certainly seems solid and defined by certain definite characteristics. The Prajna-paramita contends, however, that the seeming solidity of form is a trick we play on ourselves. If we look deeply into our experience of form, we will begin to see that there is something fluid and ungraspable about it, and that we react to this intangible nature of form by labeling it "form" and thinking of it in a certain solid and definite way.

The text then says, ". . . and form is no other than emptiness." In other words, it is not that there are some forms that are empty of any "essence" and other forms that are not empty. No. Form, any form whatever, is fundamentally empty of any essence or own being. It is the very nature of form to be empty in this way.

The text continues, "In the same way, feeling, perception, formation, and consciousness are emptiness." In other words, what was just said about the first skandha is also true of the other four skandhas: they are emptiness; emptiness itself is they; emptiness is no other than they; and they are no other than emptiness. Then we read: "Thus all the dharmas are emptiness. . . ."

This statement makes the point that whatever experiences we may have, they are all marked by emptiness. This applies even to the rather solid and definitive readings of the dharma given in Hinayana. The *Heart Sutra*: "There is no suffering; no origin of suffering; no cessation of suffering; no path; no wisdom; no attainment and no nonattainment." The text is not denying the Hinayana experience; it is not saying that at the Hinayana level, one does not experience these things. Of course, at that level of spiritual maturity, one does experience these things, and they do exist as stated.

However, according to the *Heart Sutra*, there is a deeper level to which we need to go. We need to look more closely at our experience. Take the example of suffering. If we bring the actual phenomenal experience that we label "suffering" before our eyes and contemplate it with a still mind, we will find in that experience nothing that corresponds to what we think of when we say "suffering." Suffering is a gross and inaccurate label that is applied to reality that is . . . is what? That is the point. Nothing can be attributed to it.

The text continues: "Therefore, since the bodhisattvas have no attainment, they abide by means of prajnaparamita; since there is no obscuration of mind, there is no fear. They transcend falsity and attain complete nirvana. All the buddhas of the three times, by means of prajnaparamita, fully awaken to unsurpassable, true, complete enlightenment." In other words, the teachings on emptiness are the vehicle by which the buddhas have journeyed to realization, and the full recognition of emptiness represents their awakening.

The *Heart Sutra*, then, like the other Prajnaparamita Sutras, outlines a view of reality consisting of two truths. Ordinary people live on the level of relative truth where "form"—as a metaphor for what we normally experience—is taken as self-evident and real. When one sees, however, that form is in fact empty of any characteristic of "form," that its essential nature is emptiness, then one has come face to face with ultimate truth, the truth of emptiness.

The teachings on emptiness are subtle and challenging to follow, and they sometimes appear to be little more than abstract philosophizing. Particularly to most Westerners, it is not immediately clear what, if anything, these teachings have to do with the practical spiritual life. In fact, the teachings on emptiness make the bodhisattva path possible. This is so because the bodhisattva is asked to return again and again to samsara, to work for the welfare of sentient beings in all of their conditions of suffering. This is no small commitment, for one is vowing to take repeated rebirth not only in the human realm and the other "higher realms" of the gods and jealous gods, but also in the "lower realms" of the animals, hungry ghosts, and hell-beings. The bodhisattva's commitment is to spend three incalculable eons exploring every nook and cranny of samsara, learning about the suffering of sentient beings by being reborn in every situation and condition of their misery. For it is only through such a heroic journey that one can finally attain the realization of a fully enlightened buddha and know every iota of the pain and confusion of those whom he wishes to save.

The daunting prospect of the bodhisattva's commitment is possible only because he or she realizes that, however solid and eternal the various samsaric worlds may appear to be, that solidity and permanency are only a projection. Moreover, even one's "suffering," "confusion," and "unenlightenment" are again projections upon a reality that is beyond characterization and beyond thought. It is only thus that the bodhisattva can cycle through samsara endlessly, not as a victim of its illusions, but as one who sees the essentially empty nature of the entire phenomenal display. And it is only because of this insight that he or she can be of genuine assistance to those still trapped in ignorance.

The recognition of the emptiness of one's projections leads to a feeling, as Trungpa Rinpoche says, of an empty heart. This empty heart has nothing to say for itself, nothing to assert, nothing even to hope for or—as the *Heart Sutra* says—to fear. However, such an empty heart is one that is ever available to others. It is one without agenda, but with a ready tenderness and responsiveness to another person's suffering and confusion. A realization of emptiness, then, is the precondition for genuine compassion. And such an empty heart, though desolate from ego's standpoint, is an expression of the wisdom that sees the utter and unbreachable freedom of our essential being.

For the Vajrayana practitioner, the teachings on emptiness provide the indispensable foundation of the tantric path. For example, as we saw in the last chapter, it is part of the spiritual journey that one sees more deeply into one's own confusion and egotism and also that one attains moments of unexpected freedom and joy. Coming face to face with one's darkness can lead one to become disheartened. The teachings on emptiness say, "Look closely into your discouragement or depression; see what is really there. If you look deeply enough, you will pass beyond the concept that you are holding and will behold that which you are labeling face to face." Invariably, what one finds is not what one thought was there; it is not something that can be pinned down in any way. It is open, unbounded, and inseparable from the ultimate, emptiness.

In a similar fashion, again as mentioned, insights and feelings of clarity and bliss may lead one to feel very happy. One may well take this as some kind of attainment and try to incorporate it into one's "view" of one self. At this moment, pride and arrogance will arise. The teachings on emptiness remind the practitioner that his or her belief that something has been gained is equally a projection and is empty in essence. In other words, one was becoming inflated over literally nothing. Realizing this fact acts as a pin puncturing the balloon of one's puffed-up "spiritual" ego.

In this way, the teachings on emptiness call into question every painful and depressing experience, as well as every pleasurable and inflating experience. These teachings are saying, "Things are not what you think; if you think things are a certain way, take a closer look. You cannot make anything out of your experience." The reason is that to make something out of your experience, you have to have some idea of what your experience is. Only then can it be of service to your ego. However, your experience is, really and truly, beyond words and concepts; it is empty. Therefore, you are left with nothing to make anything out of. Only when you remain in this open and indefinable space can the tantric journey continue.

The teachings on emptiness are expounded, as noted, in the sutras that belong to the second turning of the wheel of dharma, principally the Prajnaparamita Sutras. These teachings in India and Tibet became the source of a rich, sophisticated, and extensive philosophical tradition known as Madhyamaka. Whereas the Prajnaparamita texts are known as *buddha-vachana*, buddha word, because they are held to have been spoken by the Buddha, the texts of the Madhyamaka are commentaries on the Prajnaparamita composed by scholars and practitioners on the path. The founder of Madhyamaka, as mentioned in chapter 1, was the great sage Nagarjuna (ca. second century CE), who composed a number of texts considered the root texts of Madhyamaka, including the *Mula-madhyamaka-karikas*, verses on the root teachings of Madhyamaka. Nagarjuna was followed by a series of Indian Buddhist scholars, who appeared over the course of one thousand years, and by an equally illustrious succession of Tibetan scholars belonging to all four schools of Tibetan Buddhism.

The importance of Madhyamaka is that it takes the teachings of the second turning as its foundation. While in the Prajnaparamita, these teachings on emptiness are given without argument or comment, in the Madhyamaka they are presented in the form of logical arguments and philosophical reflections that reveal how the opposite of emptiness, namely substantial existence, cannot be maintained. In the course of the vast Madhyamaka corpus, every conceivable human opinion about reality is made the subject of philosophical scrutiny, and none can stand up to the light of wisdom. Each human concept about reality is like a building that begins to waver, then crack, and finally collapse as a result of the earthquake of emptiness.

In Tibetan monasteries, and particularly those of the Gelukpas and the Sakyapas, the teachings of the second turning of the wheel of dharma, both sutras and the shastras of the commentarial tradition, are the centerpiece of scholarly training. Monks undergoing the academic training will typically spend many years studying the various arguments and positions of Madhyamaka, memorizing hundreds and even thousands of pages of texts in the course of their work. In addition to memorization, they hear lectures by masters and hone their skills of logic and reasoning in the ancient tradition of monastic debate.

While all of this study may seem far removed from the cave of the tantric yogin, in fact it is not. In all four schools of Tibetan Buddhism, it is believed that by training the mind thoroughly in the Madhyamaka, one is laying a foundation that is essential for successful Vajrayana practice. This is why, as we saw in chapter 3, Geluk monks wishing to undertake tantric practice must first complete the many years of scholarly training in which the Madhyamaka forms the essential core.

THE THIRD TURNING: YOGACHARA AND BUDDHA-NATURE

According to Tibetan tradition, later in his life, in the North Indian town of Shravasti, Buddha Shakyamuni turned the wheel of dharma for a third time. The content of the third turning is twofold, including both those teachings associated with the classical Indian Yogachara school and those concerning the buddha-nature. Although in Indian Buddhism, these two streams of thought had somewhat distinct histories, in Tibet they are understood as aspects of one unified teaching.

According to the *Sandhinirmochana Sutra*, where the third turning is first articulated, when the Buddha turned the wheel of dharma this third time, he presented the ultimate, definitive "view" of the Mahayana. We read in the *Sandhinirmochana Sutra* that the first turning concerns the Hinayana, deals with relative truth, and is provisional and surpassable. The second turning presents the Mahayana teaching on emptiness, articulates the view of the ultimate, but is also not complete. The third turning brings the Buddha's promulgation of the "view" to completion, in which the relative and the ultimate are seen in proper relation to one another.

Why did the Buddha feel the need to give a third turning of the wheel of dharma, when the second, as we have seen, presents the view of ultimate reality, emptiness? According to the *Sandhinirmochana Sutra*, the commentaries of Asanga and his school, and the buddha-nature texts, the Buddha gave the teachings of the third turning because the very presentation of the second turning on emptiness, by virtue of its relentless and single-minded propagation of shunyata, could too easily be misunderstood by practitioners as nihilism.

The teachings on emptiness, as we have seen, are designed to dissolve fixations so that one may come face to face with reality. However, that dissolution can itself all too readily turn into a project. And, in order to have a project, one has to have an end point or goal that one is projecting. In every situation, then, one can begin to look for emptiness. But to look for emptiness, one has to have an idea of what emptiness is. Thus, one can fall into the trap of using one's concept of emptiness to address, to try to handle, one's experience.

The concept of emptiness—although certainly not the reality of it— can be taken as nihilistic. This is so because as it appears in the texts, emptiness is the absence of any characteristic or essential nature. Nothing that we conceive through the apparatus of the skandhas has any inherent existence. In its essential nature, it does not exist. Holding this as a view, and using it as a tool or technique to relate with one's life, can lead to a nihilistic denial of the relative world.

If we hold emptiness as a concept and take this view of the relative, then we will have no interest in it. In psychological terms, our libido will have been disconnected from the relative world. This means that we will be unwilling to connect with it and feel no obligation to relate with it. We may treat karma as utterly nonexistent and see its operation as not worth respecting. And we will regard the suffering of sentient beings as unimportant and not to be taken seriously, since it does not exist.

Worse than this, emptiness can be viewed as a panacea. It can be used as a weapon against relativity. One may ask, what is wrong with this? For an unenlightened person, judgments about relativity are always being made: this is comfortable, this is not; this I like, this I don't like. If one has only the second turning of the wheel of dharma as a reference point, it is all too easy to use one's concept of emptiness to minimize and discredit those aspects of relativity that one does not like. This may be carried out under a guise of "spirituality." For example, when one experiences certain emotions or states of mind as "nonspiritual," one may try to remove their sting through applying emptiness.

But what if, karmically, this is something that we need to live through? What if this leg of our journey requires us to face and fully experience something very painful? In that case, we have cut off our progress and repressed that unwanted state of mind once again, thus creating more negative karma for ourselves.

In this case, emptiness has become a way of avoiding and dismissing—on "spiritual grounds"—the first noble truth, the truth of suffering. Emptiness does not mean that suffering is utterly nonexistent, only that its energy cannot be objectified or definitively pinned down in any way. Such a point of view does not remove the "charge" of suffering, but leaves it in the realm of the ungraspable.

The Three Natures

In the Tibetan view, the Buddha addressed this problem by giving the third turning of the wheel of dharma, with its twofold teachings on the "three natures" and on the "buddha-nature." In the Yogachara texts, the Buddha expands on the second-turning teachings of the two truths, ultimate (in which emptiness is seen) and relative (in which phenomena are thought to be substantial). Now the Buddha speaks of three natures.

First is *parikalpita*, the "imaginary nature," conceptualized reality, which is illusory and empty, like the "relative truth" of the second turning. Then there is *parinishpanna*, the "perfected nature," the mind that is resting in the ultimate, which is analogous to the "ultimate truth" of emptiness of the second turning. In addition, however, the Buddha also speaks of *paratantra*, the "dependent nature," which is not so explicitly designated in the second turning. Each of these three natures has a particular ontological status. The imaginary nature (parikalpita), conceptualized reality, is utterly nonexistent because what it claims exists, essential natures, in fact is purely an illusion. The dependent nature (paratantra) is dependently existent, a notion presently to be explained. And the perfected nature (parinishpanna) is completely existent in the sense that the emptiness of realization is beyond birth and death, and indestructible.

If the imaginary nature corresponds to relative truth in the second turning and the perfected nature is analogous to ultimate truth, then how is the dependent nature to be understood? The great Indian commentator on the third turning, the master Asanga, explains the dependent nature by asking an interesting question. When we project a relative world made up of truly existing things—which are utterly nonexistent—are we merely making this up, based on nothing? Are we just projecting our concepts into a vacuum? Or might there be some substrate that is serving as a basis of our projections? Asanga says that there is indeed such a substrate, although it is not one that can be labeled or conceptualized, because in that case we would be right back into the imaginary nature, which is utterly nonexistent. However, there is a substrate that is ineffable. This is the world of appearances that arise in accordance with the operation of karma. According to Asanga, there is the attribution of "form," which in itself does not exist. But there is a karmic situation, beyond our thinking process, that gives birth to a complex of causes and conditions that we are then led to label "form."

For Asanga, there are two kinds of relativity, that of the conceptualized imaginary nature, which we might call impure relativity, and the nonconceptualized world of karma, the dependent nature, which we might call pure relative truth. It is this latter that the Buddha saw at the moment of his enlightenment: he saw the causes and conditions according to which the entire wheel of samsara revolves. In other words, when the Buddha had passed utterly beyond the illusory, conceptualized reality of the imaginary nature, he attained the perfected state, the perfected nature. In the moment of his enlightenment, the Buddha did not see nothing. His experience of enlightenment had content, as it were: the entire realm of causes and conditions, as it truly is, with nothing left out.

Based on this way of looking at things, we could describe samsara and nirvana in the following way. Samsara is viewing the pure relative world, the dependent nature, through the filter of concepts in which we attribute self-nature to things. This is the imaginary nature. Nirvana consists in seeing the pure relative world, the dependent nature, as the Buddha did on the night of his enlightenment, devoid of the imaginary nature. This is the perfected nature.

The teachings of the three natures have important implications for the path. They indicate that phenomenal experience is actually composed of two elements. On the one hand, there is the conceptualized overlay, the imaginary nature, which needs to be abandoned. But on the other, there is the substrate of karma, the dependent nature, that exists relatively and needs to be acknowledged and respected. Through taking the ineffable substrate seriously, through being willing to travel through it as a walkway, there can be a path and there can be transformation. This is so because until enlightenment, life consists in the arising and resolving of karma; this can only occur if one is willing to relate to that arising—which is inherently ineffable—but to do so without conceptualizing it. If, by contrast, one either takes the imaginary nature as real or seeks to dismiss the dependent nature as utterly nonexistent, there can no longer be any journey. Then, as one sometimes finds among spiritual practitioners, the process of the path is frozen and one abides in a wasteland of emptiness.

In the Vajrayana, as we shall see, the process of tantric meditation brings the pure relative truth of the world into view. On the one hand, through meditation on emptiness, one abandons one's own defiled, conceptual versions of reality. On the other, through visualizing the world as the pure abode of the tantric deities, one realizes the splendor of manifestation beyond ego. The process is progressive: through the visualization, one continually calls up the relative world in its nonconceptual purity. This brings about a process of gradual "purification" (*vishuddhi*) in which one is gradually disabused of one's view of reality as impure and laden with the conceptual dirt of ego. One's perception grows into "sacred outlook" (*tag-nang*), in which the truth of the pure dependent nature and its inseparability from the perfected nature are realized on a tantric level, as the inseparability of appearance and emptiness.

Buddha-nature

The second major teaching given by the Buddha in the third turning of the wheel concerns buddha-nature and is contained in a number of important sutras on this topic. In Tibet, the most important text on buddha-nature is the *Uttara-tantra Shastra*, a commentary attributed to the future buddha Maitreya. This shastra contains quotations from many of the most important buddha-nature sutras, arranged to highlight the most important aspects of this doctrine. In the *Uttara Tantra*, the root verses by Maitreya are accompanied by Asanga's verse and prose commentary. The text was brought to Tibet during the second spreading and has become the subject of a number of important traditions of interpretation.

According to the *Uttara Tantra*, within each sentient being is the actual nature of a buddha. This is not a seed that will one day grow into the full nature of a buddha; rather, it is, at this moment, that very nature. The nature of a buddha is the dharmakaya, the "body of reality," the mind of enlightenment itself. What is this buddha-nature like? Its essence is emptiness; its nature is complete clarity and cognizance; and it manifests as compassion. It is this dharmakaya, this enlightenment, already in itself mature and complete, that exists within the heart of all sentient beings.

If we human beings possess this enlightened core as our very basis, then why are we so confused and why do we suffer? The reason, according to the *Uttara Tantra*, is that the buddha-nature is covered over by defilements of all sorts. These defilements are adventitious—that is, they are not essential. They in no way actually damage or blemish the buddha-nature, they merely hide it from our view. Thus we go about our lives, feeling beleaguered and lost, unaware that this jewel of inestimable worth resides in our very heart.

In the *Uttara Tantra*, many analogies are given to illustrate how the buddha-nature is covered over and hidden yet never compromised or damaged. For example, the buddha-nature is said to be like an image of the buddha wrapped in some dirty, tattered rags lying by the side of the road. The rags represent one's phenomenal personality, how one views oneself. When you first see it, it may seem like a worthless pile of garbage—which is certainly how we sometimes feel about ourselves. Yet, when we look closely into this seemingly worthless rubbish, when we take the trouble to unwrap the rags around it—and we do this through the practice of meditation—we make the miraculous discovery of the resplendent buddha within.

There is a tendency among Western Buddhists to identify the buddha-nature with a mind that is open, clear, and expansive, that is untroubled by the chaos of experience. This certainly is one basic way in which the buddha-nature can show itself, particularly in our meditation practice. Many meditators are always looking for the buddha-nature as this untrammeled clarity, which brings with it a settled and peaceful feeling.

But there is far more to the buddha-nature than this, and it manifests in our lives in countless other ways. In order to understand some of these other ways, let us personify the buddha-nature for a moment, and ask some questions. For example, what is the "intention" of the buddha-nature? It is to lead us to—or push us in the direction of—full and perfect enlightenment. What is this enlightenment? It is our full presence to ourselves, our unbroken awareness of the fullness of our being, in which our compassion can flow forth spontaneously, in whatever way it will given our karma and our gifts.

What stands in the way of this goal of spiritual maturation? Only our mistaken concepts of ourselves, our rigid and defensive ego structures. What is an example of where the buddha-nature is at work? In fact, the buddha-nature operates in all people, all of the time. It is said that the universal experience of suffering is a manifestation of the buddha-nature. It is the message that our egoic versions of reality are inadequate and cannot bring about lasting satisfaction or comfort. How does the buddha-nature move us forward? Through revealing to us the shabbiness and hollowness of the ego that we are trying to maintain, through showing us the inadequacy of the ways in which we try to allay pain and control our lives.

Meditation practice is the primary Buddhist way for softening and relaxing the rigidity of ego and for providing space for awareness outside of the ego mechanism to grow. Yet the path of meditation is challenging, for it mostly consists of seeing through our own posturing and pride, unraveling our self-deception, and recovering dimensions of our person that—because of the pain cloaking them—we ignore and repress. Those who devote themselves to a life of meditation often find themselves face to face with the most difficult of emotional upheavals and egoic inflations and deflations as their awareness grows and they integrate more of what they are in their totality. This vivid and often excruciating process is itself a manifestation of the buddha-nature.

The buddha-nature works also in other ways. For example, it may often be said to be "behind" certain dramatic occurrences, such as when a relationship collapses, we lose a job, we fall gravely ill, someone close to us dies, or some other catastrophe befalls us. At that moment, our carefully constructed and maintained world falls to pieces. At such a time, when everything else is more or less in complete disarray, the buddha-nature is there, as openness, tenderness, and intelligence that transcends the ups and downs. Practitioners can take very great advantage of such "catastrophes" and use them to deepen their own sense of being.*

The buddha-nature obviously exists in all people, whether they are Buddhists or not, and regardless of the level of their commitment to a spiritual path. Though human beings try to ignore it, the buddha-nature

---

*Occasionally, it may also be a positive occurrence that shatters our habitual world, the most notable example being when one "falls in love."

is always in the background, trying to break through the walls of ego, to lead us to a deeper and fuller way of being. It is at the basis of who we are as human beings. Nevertheless, it sometimes happens that we try to hold on to a very narrow way of being, some adaptation that we bring from earlier in our lives. In this event, we sometimes find that the harder we try to hang on to some old, constricted way of being, the more pressure the buddha-nature exerts. Often, the buddha-nature will break through in the most surprising and unexpected ways, causing temporary demolition of aspects of our adaptation. If people absolutely resist the inner imperative to grow, the buddha-nature can manifest itself in even more drastic ways and the consequences can be calamitous, at least from ego's viewpoint.

The tantric journey is directed to uncovering the buddha-nature within, and this is not an easy or painless process. It has been said that, in the journey to awakening, the buddha-nature does not particularly care what our personalities have to go through or how difficult the process may be. Our deepest nature is uncompromising and will not let any of us stray very far from the path. It will ultimately put up with nothing short of enlightenment. Meditation is a way of "sacrificing to the gods," of making a positive relationship with the buddha-nature so that the journey, while painful and challenging, at least continues in the direction of awakening and takes advantage of each turn in the road.

In the Vajrayana Buddhism of Tibet, the teachings on buddha-nature are considered a source of unbounded confidence, certainty, and joy. One may wonder, particularly in light of the more daunting aspects of the buddha-nature, how this could be so. The reason is simple: the buddha-nature doctrine shows us that the seemingly problematic aspects of our lives are gateways to a deeper and fuller mode of being. Suffering, deflation, and life's other difficulties are all manifestations of our basic, enlightened being, calling us forward. Moreover, the unending stream of ego-defeats that characterize the life of even the most "successful" person represent continual opportunities to wake up, to soften up, to expand our awareness, to see more. The teachings on buddha-nature represent a kind of unconditional positivity—that whatever occurs in life, and particularly the more difficult situations, provides a tangible opportunity to come closer to who we are.

As we shall see, in the Vajrayana one visualizes oneself as a fully enlightened buddha. This visualization gives imaginative representation to our own buddha-nature within, which is otherwise inaccessible. Through enacting the tantric liturgies, one's own sense of being a separate, egoic self gradually dissolves and is replaced by the buddha-nature. This is not a new identity and has nothing in common with the old egoic identity that is being released. Rather, it represents the ability to rest in the open, empty, cognizant nature that is the very core of our being. In the Vajrayana, one thus trains to live in terms of the buddha-nature, not thinking of oneself as a solid and discrete entity, and to act, but without need for the deliberate and self-referential strategies of the self-conscious "I." In this way, then, the Vajrayana, based on the second-turning teachings of emptiness, represents the actualization of the teachings of the third turning of the wheel of dharma.

PART TWO

Entering the Vajra World

6

Some Initial Vajrayana Perspectives

THE VEHICLE OF CAUSE AND THE VEHICLE OF RESULT

The two lower yanas, the Hinayana and the Mahayana, are termed *hetu-yana*, yanas or vehicles of cause. They are so called because of their basic method of working toward the enlightened state from the outside in. They do this by generating, through their specific practices, the various "causes" of enlightenment. It is true that the awakened state is itself beyond causality. Nevertheless, from the viewpoint of the lower yanas, it can only appear within the human stream of consciousness when the appropriate conditions are present. The Hinayana and the Mahayana both work in a gradual way with ethical behavior, study, and meditation to bring about these conditions.[1]

The Vajrayana is called the *phala-yana*, or yana of result, because it attempts to bring practitioners to a state of realization working from the inside out. In the Vajrayana, a person is brought into direct contact with the awakened state through one of two methods. Most commonly, one undergoes the *abhisheka* ritual (empowerment initiation), which gives one authorization to practice one of the deity cycles or mandalas, sets of meditations connected with a particular deity. Through this method, one visualizes oneself as a fully awakened one and accomplishes a certain number of mantras of the deity. In addition, a person may be introduced directly to the buddha-mind within—a Vajrayana way of speaking of the buddha-nature—and then receive instruction on how to meditate upon this. In usual practice, these two methods are used in tandem: one receives abhisheka and the "pointing out" of the nature of mind as part of the same initiatory process. Through these methods—both visualizing oneself as a buddha and receiving pointing-out instructions—one's inner nature is empowered and enlivened so that it begins to dissolve the armor of ego from the inside, so to speak.

WHAT IS INCLUDED IN VAJRAYANA BUDDHISM?

Vajrayana Buddhism as practiced in Tibet includes a considerable array of different traditions and practices. These may be grouped loosely into those traditions and practices that belong to the Nyingma, or Old Translation School, and those that belong to the New Translation schools, the Sarma lineages, although there are many overlaps and shared traditions.[2] As we have seen, the Nyingmapas divide their path into nine yanas, six of which are tantric in nature; the final three—Mahayoga-yana, Anuyoga-yana, and Atiyoga-yana—are the ones that are most commonly practiced. The Kagyüpas, Sakyapas, and Gelukpas, again as noted, divide their traditions into the four tantras, with the Anuttara-yoga Tantras—including father, mother, and nondual—being the ones that are generally practiced. With the exception of the practices of formless meditation, to be discussed, all of these involve *yidam* practice, the carrying out of *sadhanas* (practices given in texts of ritualized meditation) in which one visualizes oneself as a deity and meditates in that way. Associated with these cycles of teachings are practices of "inner yoga" in which one visualizes one's body as an inner mandala, composed of the *chakras* ("wheels" or psychic centers), *nadis* ("channels" or psychic pathways), *prana* ("wind/breath" or energy), and *bindu* ("drop/sphere"). The yogas are discussed in detail in chapter 11.

The Vajrayana also includes "formless practices" known among the Nyingmapas as dzokchen, the "great perfection," and among the New Translation schools as mahamudra, the "great seal" or "symbol." Although these traditions of formless practice possess different lineages, different ways of speaking, and different authoritative texts, they are closely similar if not identical on most points. One reason for this comparability is that they derive from many of the same sources; another is that over the course of Tibetan history, many of the most accomplished and influential mahamudra teachers studied with dzokchen teachers and vice versa.

Dzokchen and mahamudra are considered the most advanced realizations, respectively, of the Nyingma and the New Translation schools. Generally, one traverses the path to these realizations through a certain amount of yidam practice. At a certain point, when one's teacher deems the time appropriate, one is given mahamudra or dzokchen instruction and then sent into retreat. Occasionally, in the case of extraordinarily "ripened" disciples, a person may be set to practicing the formless meditations directly, with little or no preliminaries.

THE SECRECY OF VAJRAYANA

Unlike the Hinayana and the Mahayana, which in Tibet are exoteric traditions, the Vajrayana is an esoteric tradition in which secrecy plays an important role.* The Vajrayana is secret first, on a literal level, in that one must receive initiation or *abhisheka* before being given the permission, texts, and instructions to practice it. The *abhisheka* is a serious event, requiring often many years of preparation on the part of the disciple and rigorous commitments to the lama and to the practices that one has received. As part of the initiation process, one makes a commitment to keep secret both the nature of the *abhisheka* itself as well as the instructions that one receives in connection with it. This secrecy is necessary not only in the case of non-Vajrayanists, but also of Vajrayana practitioners who have not received the same abhishekas. According to the tantric vows taken in an abhisheka, one is permitted to discuss the practice, as well as one's understanding, and experiences, only with those who have been entered into the same mandala.

*Originally, as mentioned above, much of what we now call Hinayana and Mahayana also seem to have been esoteric, secret traditions.

This situation has been somewhat confused by another approach to such ritual occasions, such as public abhishekas that are quite different from the methods of preparing for, receiving, and understanding abhishekas just described. This other "abhisheka" is a public ceremony given by lamas to large numbers of people, sometimes even running into the thousands, with no prerequisites or preparation whatever required. Often those turning up for this initiation have never even met the presiding lama and some may have no particular connection with Buddhism and no interest in meditation. Kalu Rinpoche, who gave many such abhishekas during his lifetime, commented that these should be thought of as ceremonial blessings that would sow positive karmic seeds for the future.

The secrecy surrounding the Vajrayana acts as a protection both for oneself and also for non-initiates. Secrecy protects the tantric practitioner and his practice in several ways. It is said that the power and efficacy of the Vajrayana is dependent upon the devotion and respect of its practitioners. If one were to disclose to non-initiates one's practices and experiences, these would be met with misunderstanding and lack of appreciation, at the very least. As in Native American traditions where it is believed that the telling of a visionary dream diminishes its power, so in the Vajrayana, to disclose the inner essence of the teachings would severely compromise and weaken them. In addition, maintaining secrecy discourages the tantric practitioner from using his spiritual knowledge and insights to advance personal, ego-oriented agendas. This is particularly important in the West where the educated public tends to be intrigued by "tantra" and where one's involvement could all too easily become a topic for titillating cocktail party conversation. In general, one needs to maintain secrecy in order to keep the spiritual vessel closed, to contain the energy, and to let it work its transformations.

Secrecy also protects non-initiates, and this in two ways. First, it protects those who will one day receive abhisheka. In general, when Tibetan teachers give students a new practice, while they may explain the actual practice in detail, they will generally say very little about what to expect. This is because ideas and expectations about a practice that one is engaged in create obstacles and impediments to understanding. In addition, each person has a unique entry into any practice and will make discoveries that are more or less unique to him or herself. In the case of the Vajrayana, then, the less preconceptions one has, the better.

Secrecy also protects non-initiates from inherent dangers in Vajrayana practice. The Vajrayana provides methods, as mentioned, that open the mind to a deep level. All of us walk around with many layers of armor over our sense perceptions and our experience of the world. We do this because the world in its naked rawness and reality is vast, vivid, and shocking, and we prefer to keep to our small, safe, insentient versions. Yet, in our numbness, all of us long for the openness and the intensity of experience that is our birthright. The Vajrayana is a method to progressively remove our defensive coverings so that we may once again experience the colorful, surprising, magical world that stands beyond thought and beyond ego. Yet removing one's armor is not without its dangers. In relation to this, Trungpa Rinpoche remarks:

> The world is so magical that it gives us a direct shock. It is not like sitting back in our theater chair and being entertained by the fabulous world happening on the screen. It does not work that way. Instead it is a *mutual* process of opening between the practitioner and the world. Therefore tantra is very dangerous. It is electric and at the same time extremely naked. There is no place for our suit of armor. There is no time to insulate ourselves. Everything is too immediate. Our suit of armor is punctured from both outside and inside at once. Such nakedness and such openness reveal the cosmos in an entirely different way. It may be fantastic, but at the same time it is very dangerous.[3]

The Hinayana and Mahayana, and the Vajrayana preliminaries, as well as the relation of teacher and student, provide the ground, the context, and the stability for this opening. But without these preparations and safeguards, the Vajrayana methods would almost certainly be beyond our capacity to handle. Even with them, the journey is risk-filled enough. Hence it is an act of decency and kindness to keep the specific teachings and methods of the tradition secret from non-initiates.

Secrecy also appears in the Vajrayana in what is called the "self-secrecy" of the tradition. Even if Vajrayana truths are spoken, they can only be "heard"—that is, understood—by those who are ready to hear and understand them. The most profound truths can be shown, yet if one is not at a level where one can receive them, it will be as if nothing has happened. One may recall the famous story from Zen Buddhist tradition in which the Buddha conveyed his teaching by holding up a flower. Although there was a large crowd gathered, only one person, Mahakashyapa, understood what the Buddha meant to reveal.

LAMA TARANATHA'S ACCOUNT OF VAJRAYANA ORIGINS

Tibetan tradition, as noted in chapter 1, identifies a number of points of origin within Indian Buddhist history. Each of the three turnings of the wheel represents a kind of new beginning for the dharma, and the Buddha's preaching of the Vajrayana represents another fresh revelation. In the revelatory process, all three bodies of the Buddha are involved, including his two "form bodies" (*rupakaya*), that is, his pure physical form (*nirmanakaya*) and his subtle, nonphysical body (*sambhogakaya*), as well as his ultimate body, identified with reality itself (*dharmakaya*).

According to Indian Buddhism, while the dharma ultimately derives from the *dharmakaya*, in order to be apprehended by human beings, it must be mediated by the form bodies. As we saw in chapter 1, the Buddha is understood to have taught in his two rupakayas, either his nirmanakaya or his sambhogakaya. The Vajrayana, in particular, was taught by the Buddha in his sambhogakaya, or nonphysical, body of light. For many modern people, the idea that a person could present spiritual teachings while in a nonmaterial form is implausible. Thinking that "such things cannot happen," one might dismiss the traditional accounts and look elsewhere for explanations. However, within the traditional Asian and particularly Buddhist context, it is taken for granted that such things can and do happen. It is routinely assumed that accomplished meditators can move about in an ethereal or subtle body and interact with other, similarly disembodied beings. It is also considered a matter of fact that one can teach dharma in such a form, and that to do so one need not be a buddha, or even a follower of the Mahayana or Vajrayana, where such things are more commonly talked about. In this context, one may consider the example of Acharn Mun, a revered and realized Thai saint of the forest who lived earlier in this century. The Acharn's biography, which was composed from experiences that he himself related to his closest disciples, devotes considerable attention to dharma teaching that he gave, at night and in his subtle body, to various divinities inhabiting the god realms who came to him for instruction.[4]

In the Vajrayana, following earlier tradition, the Buddha's teachings are understood to derive ultimately from his dharmakaya, the unoriginated "body" of reality depicted as Samantabhadra in Nyingma tradition and Vajradhara in the New Translation schools. Yet, for human beings in general, the dharmakaya is inaccessible; therefore, out of compassion, the primordial dharmakaya buddha takes shape in sambhogakaya and nirmanakaya forms. Tulku Thondup clarifies the doctrine of the three buddha bodies for an understanding of Vajrayana.

> The doctrine of the three bodies of the Buddha is important for all aspects of tantric teachings. The transmission comes from the ultimate body, the formless absolute, empty aspect of Buddhahood, the *dharmakaya*, to the body of enjoyment, the *sambhogakaya*. The latter is the first of the two form-bodies. Its radiant, transcendent form, endowed with the major and minor marks of buddhahood, can be perceived only by enlightened or highly attained beings. The Buddhas of the *sambhogakaya* level dwell in inconceivably vast pure lands or Buddha-fields, whereas the other expression of the form-body, the *nirmanakaya*, enters samsara and manifests in various ways in order to free beings from suffering.[5]

These themes come to life in the following account, told by Lama Taranatha, of the first time that the Vajrayana was taught by the Buddha to human beings. In this rendering, the Buddha gives the tantric teachings for the first time to King Indrabhuti, ruler of the land of

Uddiyana. In the story, recounted here with commentary, the Buddha first appears in his *nirmanakaya* form and then, when he wishes to reveal the tantric teachings, manifests himself as the *sambhogakaya* Buddha at the center of a vast mandala.[6]

King Indrabhuti, who rules over the tantric country of Uddiyana (in present day Pakistan) is one day sitting on his palace veranda looking out over the plains. In the far distance, he notices what appears to be a flock of reddish birds flying across the sky. When he asks his courtiers what these are, they reply, "Oh, that is Buddha Shakyamuni, together with this five hundred arhants."

> *Commentary*: One of the qualities of enlightenment is that the realized person has gained various miraculous powers, including the ability to fly. Thus the Buddha and his arhants, as realized people, are credited with this ability. They appear in the distance as reddish birds because of the saffron robes that the Buddha's disciples wore.

Indrabhuti expresses his wish that an invitation be extended to the Buddha and his disciples to come to the palace for a noonday meal. Although the king's attendants express doubts that the Buddha will come because he is so far away, nevertheless, the next day he and his five hundred arhants arrive for the meal.

> *Commentary*: In Indian Buddhism, it was customary to make offerings of food to wandering holy men and women. On such occasions, the layperson could expect to gain merit, proportionate to the sanctity of the recipient. In addition, it was common for the donor, after the meal was finished, to request teachings. Indian kings were not only political rulers but also the ritual leaders of their kingdoms. The well-being of the kingdom was thought to be dependent upon the king's purity and store of merit. As part of his royal role, a king like Indrabhuti would frequently invite noted holy people along with their renunciant disciples to partake of a noonday meal, which might be quite lavish indeed. It was thought that the great merit accrued by

the king on such occasions would be enjoyed by the lands under his protection.

After the meal is concluded, the king asks the Buddha for teachings. In particular, he requests teachings on the means of attaining buddhahood. The Buddha responds, "O king, abandon sense pleasures, keep to the three trainings, and practice the six paramitas."

> *Commentary:* The Buddha is giving the king the teachings of the conventional Hinayana and Mahayana. The king is advised to abandon sense pleasures—in other words, to renounce the world, in the "Hinayana" way. He is next told to keep the three trainings, which include *shila* (ethical conduct), *samadhi* (meditation), and *prajna*, (wisdom). Shila would involve for the king, as a layperson, the five lay precepts; meditation would be *shamatha-vipashyana*; and prajna would refer to study. Finally, the king is advised to practice the six *paramitas* of the conventional Mahayana path.

The king, however, is not satisfied with this instruction and responds: "I request a method of attaining buddhahood through the enjoyment of the five senses with my retinue of ladies." Then the king composes a brief spontaneous poem:

> In the Rose Apple Grove so joyful to experience,
> Even if I were to become a fox in my next life,
> A liberation that abandons the sense pleasures
> I could never desire, O Gautama.

> *Commentary:* The king is saying that in the Rose Apple Grove, referring to our human world, he cannot renounce the basic experience of human life, oriented as it is to the pleasures of the five senses. Seen from the point of view of the lower yanas, the king's hesitation is a sign of his weakness: an indication that he is so self-indulgent that he cannot give up sensual gratification to follow a spiritual path. From the Vajrayana point of view, however, something else is in motion here. The king senses the

sacredness of human experience in its full range and depth, and he affirms that he will not turn his back on this even were it to land him in the low birth of a fox in his next existence. The king desires a path to liberation that makes use of, rather than rejects, the naked experience of human existence.

The following comments by Trungpa Rinpoche about the tantric practitioner describe King Indrabhuti's inspiration: "Some people are tantric by nature. They are inspired in their lives; they realize that some reality is taking place in the true sense, and they feel that the experience of energy is relevant to them. They may feel threatened by energy or they may feel a lack of energy, but they have a personal interest in the world: the visual world, the auditory world, the world of the senses altogether. They are interested in how things work and how things are perceived. That sense of enormous interest, that interest in perceptions, is tantric by nature."[7]

Then abruptly the assembly of shravakas disappears. At that point, a voice resounds from the sky saying, "None of the eight classes of holy persons are here. There are not even any shravakas or pratyekabuddhas. The bodhisattvas, whose magical power is great, are manifesting their forms."

> *Commentary:* Buddha Shakyamuni is evidently going to grant Indrabhuti's request, because the area is being cleared of those who are not prepared or authorized to hear the secret Vajrayana. Those who depart are all "Hinayanists," including the five hundred arhant disciples of the Buddha (the shravakas), along with the pratyekabuddhas, the solitary saints who dwell alone in the forest meditating. In fact, it seems to be only the high-level bodhisattvas, those of great magical power who can manifest various forms, that are able to remain.

Then the Buddha produces a great, vast mandala. He grants the king initiation, abhisheka, and at that very moment King Indrabhuti attains the body of unification (*yuganaddha*).

Commentary: The abhisheka is the ritual of initiation through which the king is "shown" the secrets of the Vajrayana, in the form of the deities of the mandala. Although appearing in external form, these deities have both inner and outer dimensions: they represent the underlying, substructure of external reality, the essential, inner body of the yogin, and the full form of the buddha-nature of a person. Having been granted this empowerment, the king instantly attains the body of unification, which is, according to Trungpa Rinpoche, the coemergence of wisdom and skillful means, and the *svabhavikakaya*, which is the union of the three kayas or buddha-bodies. It is the experience of reality, without an experiencer or subject. The king's immediate attainment of this realized state marks him as a fully ripened person and appropriate for the introduction of the Vajrayana into the human world.

Following the abhisheka and King Indrabhuti's attainment, the Buddha bestows on him all of the tantras. Then the king teaches extensively to all the people in his kingdom of Uddiyana and also writes the tantras down in text form. Finally, together with his retinue of royal consorts, he disappears and they all become sambhogakaya beings. Indrabhuti subsequently travels from one buddha-field to another, and acts as a collector and holder of the entire Mantrayana.

Commentary: This story, which reflects the view of the New Translation schools on the appearance of the Vajrayana in the human world, sees King Indrabhuti as the progenitor of the various tantras that make up the tradition. It depicts him as a person of great inspiration and attainment, so much so that after receiving tantric teachings from the Buddha, he, along with his consorts, leaves his human body behind altogether and becomes a sambhogakaya being, travelling from one pure land to another.

At that time, not only the king and his retinue, but also all the people of the land of Uddiyana, plus its spirits (*bhutas*) and its animals all the way down to the insects, attain *siddhi* by the path of *mahasukha* and achieve the rainbow body.

> *Commentary*: The path of mahasukha ("great bliss") is a way of speaking about the Vajrayana in which liberation is attained by means of experiencing the "pleasure" of the five senses. A master of great attainment is said to have the ability to enable his close disciples, students, and lay devotees, to participate in his realization. In this story, even the insects of Uddiyana attain the rainbow body, the highest attainment of Vajrayana that can be gained on earth. This attainment, another way of talking about the realization of the sambhogakaya, will be discussed in chapter 11.

Taranatha's account illustrates the Tibetan perspective that people other than buddhas can be pure incarnations—nirmanakayas—and that they may also manifest on the sambhogakaya level. We have already seen in the story how King Indrabhuti became a sambhogakaya being. In addition, Taranatha tells us that the king is the human incarnation of the sambhogakaya deity Vajrapani, the Lord of Secret, whose role is to disclose the tantras to human beings.

Subsequent Tantric Origins

In the Tibetan view, the primordial, dharmakaya buddha exists beyond time and space, and can give forth teachings at any time. While the teachings contained in the early, Hinayana canons represent one occasion on which the dharma was transmitted to the human world from the primeval state, it is by no means the only one. In the Mahayana, as noted, the second and third turnings of the wheel of dharma also constitute fresh promulgations. Beyond this, the individual Mahayana sutras are often equally presented as unprecedented expressions of the Buddha's teaching. The Vajrayana, in particular, has from its inception been characterized by a more or less continuous stream of revelations, seen most vividly in the Terma tradition. From the Tibetan viewpoint, this is to be explained by the intense practice orientation of the tantric vehicle.

Vajrayana practitioners who spend a great deal of time in meditation will, by virtue of their practice, draw near to the primal, sacred sources of the dharma. They will be able to receive fresh teachings in a way that others, more preoccupied with books and past tradition, will not.

Thus it is that throughout the history of Tantric Buddhism in both India and Tibet, one observes the continual appearance of new revelations, understood as originating from the Buddha himself in his ultimate, dharmakaya aspect. Sometimes these teachings are mediated by a sambhogakaya buddha to the nirmanakaya. At other times, a realized human being, understood as a nirmanakaya, can journey in his or her subtle body to receive teachings directly from the dharmakaya.

We may see an example of this latter approach in the life of Tilopa, the guru of Naropa, mentioned in chapter 1. Tilopa had pursued a long journey that included renouncing the world, spending some time as a monk, and then entering the Vajrayana. At this point, after studying with many tantric masters, Tilopa felt that he still remained within the realm of the conditioned, that he had not yet broken through to the ultimate. He therefore went to Bengal and took up residence in a cremation ground. There he planted himself in a tiny grass hut, barely big enough for his body upright in meditation, and remained there. To ordinary people, Tilopa appeared to be sitting immobile in his little shelter, in a state of samadhi. However, at this very same time, he was traveling to a celestial realm in his ethereal body and was receiving transmissions directly from the dharmakaya buddha Vajradhara. In this instance, it was Tilopa himself who made the link with the dharmakaya through his own subtle body and brought these teachings back to the world, where he, himself understood as a nirmanakaya, transmitted what he had received to his human disciples. It was Tilopa's extraordinary ability to find his way to this ultimate, original dharmakaya source that enabled him to become the human progenitor of the Kagyü lineage. (For a summary of Tilopa's hagiography, see *Indestructible Truth*.)

Tulku Thondup articulates the Nyingma explanation of the process of the Three Lineages, by which new revelations originate from the dharmakaya buddha and are mediated by the sambhogakaya buddha to the nirmanakaya beings of the human realm. Thus, the dharmakaya

Buddha—Samantabhadra in the Ancient School—is the original source for the Vajrayana.[8] He transmits these teachings to his disciples, the sambhogakaya buddhas, through direct mind transmission, known as the Thought Lineage of the Victorious Ones, without the use of signs or words. The sambhogakaya divinities then transmit them to the nirmanakaya emanations through the use of signs and symbols, termed the Sign Lineage of the Vidyadharas. These nirmanakayas are the masters who stand at the origins of the various tantras, such as Garab Dorje for atiyoga or dzokchen, and King Ja for mahayoga and anuyoga teachings (see chapter 2).* The nirmanakayas teach other human beings with words and concepts, called the Hearing Lineage of the Individuals. These teachings came to Padmasambhava, Yeshe Tsogyal, Vimalamitra, Vairochana, and others who either propagated them in Tibet to be passed on from one generation to another (the Nyingma Kama lineages) or hid them for later discovery (the Terma lineages). (See chapter 2.) (For a discussion of the Three Lineages, see *Indestructible Truth*.)

The informed reader may find the Tibetan Vajrayana approach to origins—particularly the notion of the three *kayas* and of people other than the Buddha engaging these levels of spiritual reality—to be far removed indeed from the Buddhism of the early canons of the Eighteen Schools. However, as the scholar Edward Conze noted a half century ago, the notion of the three kayas is quite present in early tradition, if under different names.[9] For example, in the early texts, the Buddha is quoted as observing that the realm of dharma exists beyond time, whether or not there is an awakened person to proclaim it. In other words, the "realm" of reality—structurally equivalent to the dharmakaya—abides eternally, there needing only someone to give it expression. If the prototype of the dharmakaya is in pre-Mahayana tradition, so is the sambhogakaya, for Buddha Shakyamuni is depicted one rainy season as journeying in his subtle body to the Tushita heaven (the god realm where a buddha-to-be awaits his final birth and blessed individuals may take rebirth), when he gives teachings to his deceased mother.[10]

*Dudjom Rinpoche suggests that King Ja is King Indrabhuti or perhaps his son. Dudjom Rinpoche, *The Nyingma School of Tibetan Buddhism*, vol. 1, 458–59.

It is also interesting that in pre-Mahayana tradition it is not only the Buddha who can speak "buddha word" (buddha-vachana), i.e., speak with the wisdom and authority of a buddha. In the Sarvastivada, a member of the group of early Eighteen Schools and the one whose traditions are most important to the Tibetans, the texts of the *Abhidharma Pitaka*, understood as buddha word, are each attributed to human authors who, by virtue of their realization, can speak the dharma in a pure form as did Buddha Shakyamuni. All three kayas, then, are prefigured in early Buddhism. This suggests that there is some truth to the Tibetan view that the continually appearing revelations found in tantric tradition are simply the intensification of a process that is present in all the schools of Buddhism, going back to the earliest appearance of the dharma in our world.

7

The World beyond Thought

FOR TIBETANS, AS WE HAVE SEEN, THE THREE TURNINGS of the wheel of dharma outline the basic *view* of Tibetan Buddhism, while the three *yanas* articulate the stages according to which that view is realized. The three turnings present the philosophical orientation taken for granted by the Vajrayana. Among these, the two Mahayana turnings on emptiness and buddha-nature provide the view of Vajrayana, with somewhat more emphasis on the third turning. Although the Vajrayana is a yogic tradition aimed at actualizing Mahayana philosophy, its tantras and commentaries nevertheless have distinctive ways in which they give voice to those teachings. In the texts, one finds a Vajrayana language that is characterized by a strong experiential rather than a philosophical tone. Thus, while particularly the second- and especially third-turning ideas are articulated in the Vajrayana, they are presented in a tantric idiom. In this chapter we examine the way the Vajrayana speaks about reality from the viewpoint of its essential nonexistence (second turning) and, beyond that, its quality of purity (third turning).

In Vajrayana, the term "vajra being" refers to that which we are seeking to uncover, the buddha-nature within. Vajra being is nothing other than awareness of our own nonexistence. It is the experience of ourselves as being without solidity or objectifiability, as an open, uncertain, mysterious process; it is the experience of ourselves without any conception of who we are or could be, without self-reference, literally without a thought. One is even without the concept of one's own nonexistence. It is an experience of ourselves completely without territory, even the territory of egolessness.

Vajra being takes its root in the Hinayana, where the absence in one-self of a substantial "I" is discovered. It is deepened in the Mahayana in the second turning, wherein one realizes that even the skandhas are illusory projections. And it is given full expression in the third turning, where the indestructibility of one's nonexistence is expressed in the terminology of buddha-nature. It is left for the Vajrayana to show the way to full realization of this vajra being.

In the Vajrayana, vajra being is said to be open, free, and—most important—indestructible. It is indestructible because if we are wholly without any conception of ourselves that we are trying to maintain, fortify, or promote, then we have nothing to lose. If we are without any agenda, then we cannot be hindered or obstructed. And if we are truly without any territory to defend, then we cannot be defeated. Of vajra being, Trungpa Rinpoche comments, "It brings an experience of complete indestructibility that is unchallengeable, immovable, and completely solid. The experience of indestructibility can only occur when we realize that nonexistence is possible. . . . Such indestructibility can only come out of the state of nothingness, egolessness, or nonexistence . . . [out of] a basic attitude of trust in the nonexistence of our being. . . . In the tantric notion of indestructibility, there is no ground, no basic premise, and no particular philosophy except one's own experience."[1]

A second important notion in Vajrayana is that of the "vajra world." While *vajra being* refers to our own indestructible nonexistence, *vajra world* refers to the nonexistence and hence indestructibility of whatever arises, of that which appears within experience. The notion of vajra world takes its foundation in the Hinayana, where it is said that there is a reality that manifests itself, once the projections of the "I" are discarded. This is the reality of dharmas, organized according to the five skandhas, which reveals itself to the eye of Hinayana realization. This notion is taken another step in the second turning, in which even the dharmas are said to be projections. And it is given further expression in the third turning, where the notion of appearance beyond emptiness is articulated in the idea of the dependent nature.

As long as we cling to ideas about what reality is, then we have not understood emptiness and there can be no question of Vajrayana.

However, once we have had some taste of shunyata, once we realize that our ideas about what exists are merely our own projections, then another kind of experience can arise. This is the experience of reality as ineffable appearance, manifestation that is beyond language, beyond thoughts, beyond any kind of fixation. It is an experience of the world as ultimately mysterious and beyond any attempt to pin it down or know it in a conceptual sense. The vajra world is empty because it stands completely free of all thoughts. It is egoless because it has no "essence" or "nature" that can be objectified. And it is indestructible because, since it is beyond fixation, it is exactly how it presents itself to be in each instant. Because it has no objectifiable essence, it never comes into definite existence and it never leaves any trace—therefore there is never anything that could be destroyed. In the Vajrayana, then, this reality is referred to as "apparent yet empty," the tantric way of speaking of the dependent nature, free of concept.

THE MANDALA: HOW REALITY APPEARS

Our samsaric version of reality, then, is finally the imaginary nature, an illusory projection of our own hopes and fears. It is this that is empty, without substance or truth. While apparently true and accurate from our ego-centered viewpoint, samsara is essentially conceptual; there is nothing that actually corresponds to its images, ideas, and pictures. This raises the all-important question, addressed theoretically in the third turning and practically in the Vajrayana: is there then nothing beyond our own samsaric fantasy? The answer, as we have seen, is that reality is not utterly nonexistent.

Let us recall that, from the traditional Tibetan viewpoint, the samsaric reality known through abstraction is a second-order reality. For example, the world as we view it through modern scientific description is part of this second order. The world conceived in terms of models, maps, classifications, measurements, and other conceptual abstractions is not the world that we contact in our direct experience. It is a world that, however much we may think of it as the real one, has in fact never been seen or directly experienced by anyone. This is because it does not exist. It is a world that, for all of its apparent objectivity, is ultimately ego-driven and tainted by our collective human intentions. This second order is a world in which, to use Gerard Manley Hopkins's wonderful phraseology, "all is seared with trade; bleared, smeared with toil; / And wears man's smudge and shares man's smell."[2]

In contrast to this second-order reality is first-order reality, that which is known to us directly, in the unmediated experience of selfless intuition. Thus one can speak, as in the third-turning teachings, of the ultimate truth of the emptiness or nonsubstantiality of phenomena, and of pure relative truth, pure appearance, ineffable phenomena, arising in a relational mode, based on causes and conditions. It is this unspeakable reality beyond mind that we wrongly conceptualize and misconstrue as samsara. It is this ineffable reality that forms the "basis," in third-turning language, of our samsaric ideation.

This, in turn, raises another question. Given that the phenomenal world of pure appearance is beyond thought, is there any meaningful way in which we can point toward it or evoke it? In Vajrayana Buddhism, we are directed toward pure relative truth through the language of symbol. The symbolic language that is used in the Vajrayana to suggest the actual way in which the world appears is that of the *mandala*, "sacred circle."

The basic principle of the mandala is that there is an order or a pattern to reality that stands apart from our samsaric thinking. "Reality" in this context does not refer to something fixed and eternal. Rather it points to the continually fresh, unanticipated way in which the actual relative world arises in experience. Attributing an "order" or "pattern" to this reality does not mean that it is something static that stays the same from one moment to the next and that can be abstracted into a theory. Rather, it points to the possibility of discovering a "sense" or a logic in the way things happen—a sense or logic that comes to us, that bursts upon us, rather than being something that we manufacture based on our own preconceptions and expectations.

In the Vajrayana perspective, there are certain fundamental energies that circulate in the ocean of being. These energies are, as we shall presently see, rooted in the buddha-nature. They can be pointed to, implied, and even called into manifestation with the language of symbols. In the Vajrayana, the most important symbolic language is that of the mandala. While the symbolism of the mandala is schematic in the telling, it is essential to realize that what it points to can only be discovered when the mind is free from theory. Nevertheless, the theory of the mandala can sensitize us to that which cannot be spoken and cannot be thought.

The mandala is the central symbol in Vajrayana Buddhism because it represents the buddha-nature. While the buddha-nature itself is beyond "one and many," like a diamond held in the sunlight that gives off a variety of colors, so the buddha-nature manifests itself in various aspects. In tantric tradition, the primordial wisdom of enlightenment is said to refract itself into five primary aspects, known as the "five wisdoms." Each of these is associated with one of the "five buddha families" of which it is held to be the foundation.

Each human being is said to embody a particular configuration of the five wisdoms. Depending on which wisdom is most prominent, that person is said to belong to the corresponding buddha family. This family defines an individual's primary energy and the way he or she perceives and interacts with reality. In addition, a person may manifest qualities of the other families, as secondary functions.

In the realized state of buddhahood, the wisdoms will be expressed in an open, selfless, and unobstructed way. However, while we are still within samsara, we cover the wisdoms over and twist them into perverted, sometimes grotesque ego versions. These ego distortions manifest as the display of the primary defilements—aggression, pride, passion, jealousy, and ignorance. Thus the relation between the fully manifest wisdom and its samsaric version could not be more intimate: it is through an egoic reaction against the outrageous openness of the deep core of wisdom within us that we develop our afflicted samsaric personalities.

It is important to realize that the five buddha families are more than a way of understanding the human person. In addition, they provide a means to view manifest reality as a whole, for all phenomena are seen as an expression of the five families. The symbolism of the mandala reveals the living wisdom of enlightenment that is equally present as the basis both in people and in the very being of the world.

In terms of the application of the mandala theory, Chögyam Trungpa Rinpoche explains:

> The buddha family or families associated with a person describe his or her fundamental style, that person's intrinsic perspective or stance in perceiving the world and working with it. Each family is associated with both a neurotic and an enlightened style. The neurotic expression of any buddha family can be transmuted into its wisdom or enlightened aspect. As well as describing people's styles, the buddha families are also associated with colors, elements, landscapes, directions, seasons—with any aspect of the phenomenal world.[3]

In Trungpa Rinpoche's description, then, the "neurosis" of any buddha family is its covered-over, defiled ego distortion.

Thus the symbolism of the mandala reveals the pure energies or wisdoms of enlightenment, which are the basis of samsara and nirvana. The mandala is an esoteric symbol in the sense that the underpinning of ourselves and our world is generally not seen by ordinary people. This substructure is a hidden one. Perhaps rather than "substructure" one should say "subenergy," for, as mentioned, the mandala points to something that is alive, fluid, and ever in motion, manifesting as the energetic upsurge that continually threatens to destabilize our attempts to find solid and secure ground.

THE SYMBOLISM OF THE MANDALA

The mandala symbolism is complex, illustrating as it does both immaculate reality and the defiled reality of our samsaric versions of things. The following represents a simple schematic picture of the most important dimensions of this symbolism, along with summaries by Trungpa Rinpoche, who has written extensively on this topic.

FIGURE 7.1 *The Five Buddhas of the Mandala, by Sanje Elliot.*

Center: Buddha (Tathagata) Family

Trungpa Rinpoche:

> The first is the buddha principle of the buddha family, which is basically being even, not reacting. Being steady, not reacting to excitement, being basically solid yet open at the same time. Basically sound and earthy, steady, but somewhat dull. Not particularly enterprising.
>
> Buddha neurosis is the quality of being "spaced-out" rather than spacious. It is often associated with an unwillingness to express ourselves . . . Another quality of buddha neurosis is that we couldn't be bothered. Our dirty laundry is piled up in a corner of our room . . . As time goes on, our dirty socks become unbearable, but we just sit there.[4]

When the ignoring quality of buddha neurosis is transmuted into wisdom, it becomes an environment of all-pervasive spaciousness. This enlightened aspect is called the Wisdom of All-Encompassing Space. In itself, it might still have a somewhat desolate and empty quality, but at the same time, it is a quality of completely open potential. It can accommodate anything. It is spacious and vast like the sky.

Buddha energy is the foundation or the basic space. It is the environment or oxygen that makes it possible for the other [buddha family] principles to function. It has a sedate, solid quality. Persons in this family have a strong sense of contemplative experience and are highly meditative.[5]

Each of the five families is embodied in a particular buddha. The buddha of the buddha family is Vairochana ("Brilliant"). (In some arrangements, the Buddha Akshobhya stands in this position, in which case Vairochana is associated with the vajra family in the east.) His color is white, said to be the color of basic space. His *mudra*, or hand gesture, is the mudra of teaching dharma, indicative of the moment when Buddha Shakyamuni taught the dharma to his first disciples (see figure 7.2). His symbol is the *dharmachakra*, or dharma wheel, again pointing to the preaching of dharma. Each of the five buddhas also has a consort. Vairochana's consort is Dharmadhatvishvari, Lady of Space.

The wisdom of the buddha family is *dharmadhatu* wisdom—openness that is without center or periphery, that is vast and timeless. The defilement (*klesha*) that represents the egoic version of this wisdom is delusion—actively blocking out awareness of the full and unimpeded reality of things as they are, the "space" of things seen free from concept, the *dharmadhatu*. It is precisely because one possesses a vast awareness without boundaries that one's ego can develop solid ground only by setting up a massive pattern of shutting down and ignoring this awareness. People predominating in this energy tend to have an ego style that is "spacey," unconnected, uninterested in "relating," and tuned out. In its purified form, vajra ignorance manifests in ignoring the samsaric upheavals in oneself or others. One knows Tibetan teachers who exemplify this beautifully—when one approaches them with some neurotic expression or ego "game-playing," they will not cooperate and act

Mudra of Teaching Dharma (dharmachakra mudra)

Earth-touching mudra (bhumisparsha mudra)

Mudra of generosity (varada mudra)

Meditation mudra (dhyana mudra)

Mudra of fearlessness (abhaya mudra)

FIGURE 7.2 *Mudras.*

as if nothing is happening. They just ignore what one is presenting entirely. They are unwilling to depart from the basic vastness of space to engage the tiny world of one's ego.

Each buddha has further associations, aspects that are different modes of the wisdom he embodies. For example, each is associated with one of the skandhas, and his consort is the expression of a particular element. Vairochana is associated with the skandha of form, while Dharmadhat-vishvari is associated with element of space. The buddha families are also associated with particular seasons, times of day, and emotional temperatures. In the case of the Buddha family, there is no particular season or time of day, and the characteristic emotional temperature is neutral.

In attempting to follow the complexities of the symbolism of the mandala, it is important to remember that what is being articulated is not an abstract, scholastic model. It is rather a description of how the world shows itself to be, how it coheres and works, when one looks at it from a viewpoint of non-ego, of no self-reference. In terms of this first buddha family, if you look at ignorance deeply enough, you will gradually uncover the vastness of dharmadhatu wisdom. In terms of the external world, if you contemplate the element of space, you will similarly find the dharmadhatu wisdom as its essential energy.

East: Vajra (Adamantine or Diamond) Family

Trungpa Rinpoche:

> The vajra buddha family . . . is extremely sharp, intellectual, analytical. You can relate with things precisely, and you can also see the disadvantages of various involvements. You can see the holes in things or the challenges that might occur. Precisely open and clear, analytically cool, cold, possibly unfriendly, but always on the dot. Seeing all the highlights of things as they are. Very precise, very direct, very sharp. Reactivity is very high. You are ready to jump, ready to pursue and criticize.[6]

> Intellectually, vajra is very sharp. . . . A person in the vajra family knows how to evaluate logically the arguments that are

used to explain experience. He can tell whether the logic is true or false. Vajra family intellect also has a sense of constant openness and perspective.

The neurotic expression of vajra is associated with anger and intellectual fixation. If we become fixated on a particular logic, the sharpness of vajra can become rigidity. We become possessive of our insight, rather than having a sense of open perspective. The anger of vajra neurosis could be pure aggression or also a sense of uptightness.[7]

The buddha of the vajra family is Akshobhya (Immovable), and his color is dark blue. His mudra is the earth-touching mudra, indicating the moment of enlightenment when Buddha Shakyamuni put his right hand down and touched the earth, calling her to witness of the reality and unshakability of his realization. The symbol of Akshobhya is the *vajra* (Tibetan, *dorje*), used in Vajrayana practice (see figure 10.5, page 215). His consort is Mamaki.

The wisdom of the vajra family is mirror-like wisdom, reflecting all things clearly, exactly and precisely as they are. In a person, it is an energy, a drive to see, an inherent fascination with the myriad details of reality. The defilement is anger or aggression.

The tremendous brilliance and clarity of this wisdom is so overwhelming that ego tries to create ground by solidifying and freezing what it sees into concepts; these concepts then become personal territory that ego tries to maintain. Eventually, they become a prison. When things do not go according to plan, according to one's conception of how they should be, one becomes angry and aggressive. People predominating in this energy tend to be very conceptual and heady, disconnected from the body and physical reality. In their preoccupation with concepts and ideas, they typically have ready answers for everyone else's problems; they live in a world of "rules" they make up for themselves and others. They tend to be arrogant, rigid, and inflexible. In purified form, vajra anger will see with utmost clarity samsaric games and deceptions in oneself and others, and will respond in an uncompromising way to these, sometimes by pacifying (that is, calming the waters so that the

FIGURE 7.3 *Akshobhya Buddha, one of the five buddhas
of the mandala, lord of the vajra family.*

reality of things can stand forth), sometimes wrathfully, by destroying the obstacles to clear vision.

Akshobhya is associated with the skandha of consciousness. Mamaki is associated with the element of water. In terms of time of day, the vajra family is associated with the clarity and freshness of dawn; its season is winter, as in a sun-drenched winter morning after snow has fallen, with the sharpness and vividness of brilliant light and dark, stark shadows. In Trungpa Rinpoche's words, "it is a winter morning, crystal clear, icicles sharp and glittering."[8] The emotional temperature of the vajra family is cool.

The skandha of consciousness and the element of water each appear to our ordinary awareness as relatively distinct and solid realities. However, what we samsaric beings call consciousness is essentially mirror-like wisdom, narrowed down to become manageable; likewise, when we see water, apart from our concepts and projections, it is in its true being mirror-like wisdom, "as though the sky had melted."[9] The natural associations are equally indicative—the energy of both dawn and a crystalline winter morning, seen in their essence, is mirror-like wisdom.

South: Ratna (Jewel) Family

Trungpa Rinpoche:

> Ratna is a personal and real sense of expanding ourselves and enriching our environment. It is expansion, enrichment, plentifulness. . . . The enlightened expression of ratna is called the Wisdom of Equanimity, because ratna can include everything in its expansive environment. . . . Such plentifulness could also have problems and weaknesses. In the neurotic sense, the richness of ratna manifests in being completely fat, or extraordinarily ostentatious, beyond the limits of our sanity. We expand constantly, open heedlessly, and indulge ourselves to the level of insanity.[10]

The buddha of the ratna family is Ratnasambhava, "Born from a Jewel." His color is yellow, the color of golden fields at harvest time, signifying richness and abundance. His mudra is the gesture of generosity, the right hand held outward, palm out, and fingers pointing downward, dispensing abundance to others. The symbol of Ratnasambhava is the jewel. His consort is Lochana.

The wisdom of the ratna family is the wisdom of equanimity, which is all-accommodating because it recognizes the goodness and rightness of everything that appears in the world. It manifests as appreciation for the richness and resourcefulness of every situation, even those which seem the most depleted and poverty-stricken. One always sees the abundance implicit in what is, whatever it may be, and realizes that dignity and workability of whatever exists. The defilement of the ratna family is pride. The equal goodness and rightness of everything is so all-pervasive that ego loses all sense of "specialness" and all reference points. Thus it frantically attempts to secure its ground by taking possession of all this goodness and turning it into personal territory. People predominating in this energy tend to be very warm and generous, but do so exacting a price in return, expecting praise, loyalty, and confirmation of their own existence, importance, and grandeur. In purified form, vajra pride is the immovability and dignity of one who knows that ego does not exist and that the world is an inexhaustible treasure house of sacredness and richness.

The skandha of the ratna family is feeling and the element is earth. The season is autumn— in Trungpa Rinpoche's rendering, "fertility, richness in the sense of continual generosity. When the fruit is ripe, it automatically falls to the ground, asking to be eaten up."[11] The time of day is midmorning, and the emotional temperature is warm.

In a way similar to the preceding examples, here the wisdom of equanimity manifests itself as the essential energy of pride, in the skandha of feeling, in the element of earth, the autumn, and so on. Through this symbolism, we can see clearly what is meant when the Vajrayana texts say that one must not reject one's defilements, that one must not abandon one's sense experience. One's defilements—ignorance, anger, pride, and so on—are, in essence, the corresponding buddha wisdoms. Moreover, they provide an avenue to that wisdom. Meditation on anger, as mentioned, opens a pathway to mirror-like wisdom. In a similar manner, one's ordinary sense experience, defined by the elements—space, earth, fire, water, and wind— is essentially a reflection of enlightened wisdom. This is the esoteric meaning behind King Indrabhuti's request to be given a dharma that does not involve rejection of the senses. The king realized that the sense perceptions are fundamentally transcendent wisdom, and he wanted a teaching that would open that transcendence to him.

West: Padma (Lotus) Family

Trungpa Rinpoche:

> The symbol of the enlightened padma family is the lotus, which grows and blooms in the mud, yet still comes out pure and clean, virginal and clear. Padma neurosis is connected with passion, a grasping quality and a desire to possess. We are completely wrapped in desire and want only to seduce the world, without concern for real communication. We could be a hustler or an advertiser, but basically, we are like a peacock. . . . In the awakened state, the heat of passion is transmuted into the warmth of compassion. When padma neurosis is transmuted, it becomes fantastically precise and aware; it turns into tremendous interest and inquisitiveness. Everything is seen in its own distinct way, with its own particular qualities and characteristics. Thus the wisdom of padma is called Discriminating Awareness Wisdom.[12]

The buddha of the padma family is Amitabha, Limitless Light. His color is red, the color of fire, passion, and heat. His mudra is the meditation mudra, the two hands held at the navel, open and facing upward, right hand resting in left, thumbs touching. This mudra conveys the feeling of resting with a completely open and receptive mind. The symbol of the padma family is the lotus. Amitabha's consort is Pandaravasini.

The wisdom of the padma family is discriminating awareness, which appreciates the ultimate beauty and sacredness of each "other" encountered. There is a sense of the inestimable value of every "other" that one meets, no matter how ugly or valueless from a conventional viewpoint. The padma defilement is passion, in the sense of hunger or grasping. The beauty and value of the other are so overwhelming that there is no room for ego; ego reacts by trying to grasp onto the other and own it. People predominating in this energy are very warm and loving, and sometimes tend toward dependency on the beloved. In purified form, vajra passion manifests as passion without grasping, tremendous appreciation and love for all beings.

The skandha of the padma family is perception, and the element is fire. The season is early spring. As Trungpa Rinpoche says, "The harshness of winter is just about to soften. Ice begins to melt, snowflakes become soggy."[13] The time of day is sunset, and the emotional temperature is hot.

North: Karma (Action) Family

Trungpa Rinpoche:

> Karma in this case simply means action. The neurotic quality of action or activity is connected with jealousy, comparison, and envy. . . . We would like to make everything very efficient, pure, and absolutely clean. However, if we do achieve cleanliness, then that cleanliness itself becomes a further problem: we feel insecure because there is nothing to administer, nothing to work on. We constantly try to check every loose end. Being very keen on efficiency, we get hung up on it. . . . The enlightened aspect of karma is called the Wisdom of All-Accomplishing Action. It is the transcendental sense of complete fulfillment of action without being hassled or pushed into neurosis. It is natural fulfillment in how we relate with our world. In either case, whether we relate to karma family on the transcendental level or the neurotic level, karma is the energy of efficiency.[14]

The buddha of the karma family is Amoghasiddhi, Infallible Accomplishment. His color is green, the color of life, growth, and movement.

His mudra is the mudra of fearlessness, the right hand held up, fingers extended and palm turned outward. His symbol is the sword of all-accomplishing action. His consort is Samayatara.

The wisdom of the karma family is all-accomplishing wisdom. This has nothing to do with the self-conscious and intentional accomplishment of predetermined aims. It manifests in people as a heightened awareness of the momentum and unfolding of events, to the naturally ripening potential of situations—it always sees the "next step" implicit in every occurrence and knows how to bring everything toward its natural completion. This wisdom knows the winds of karma, where they are heading and what their fruition is. It is the tremendous intelligence of knowing how to accomplish things; it is egoless efficiency and effectiveness. The defilement of the karma family is jealousy, excessive and compulsive ambition, or paranoia in the sense of fear of failure or of being surpassed by someone else (*irshya*). The wisdom of all-accomplishing action is relentless like the wind, moving from one situation to another, accomplishing in each whatever needs to be accomplished. This relentless activity leaves no room for ego. The ego reacts by trying to turn accomplishments into personal territory. Thus karma people tend to define themselves by what they do. They take pride in what they have accomplished, are filled with anxiety that they are not doing enough, and are jealous of anyone who seems to accomplish more than they. People predominating in this energy tend to be very active, efficient, and "speedy"; they are often very competent people and "successful" in the world; they are competitive and constantly on the alert lest someone else do more or get ahead of them. In purified form, karma wisdom is sensitive to the unfolding of situations, can "see around corners," and is always prepared to lend a hand in the most intelligent and selfless way.

The skandha of the karma family is karmic formations, and its element is wind. The season of the karma family is high summer, when all things are at their most vital stage of growth. Trungpa Rinpoche remarks that in summer things are "active, growing, fulfilling their functions. Millions of interconnected actions take place: living things grow, plants, insects, animals . . . you are never left to enjoy the summer because something is always moving in order to maintain itself."¹⁵ Its time of day is after sunset, dusk, late day, early night. The emotional temperature of this family is cold, in that everything is and can be sacrificed for victory—as in the case of a general who willingly commits multitudes of soldiers to certain death in order to win the day.

SOME QUESTIONS OF APPLICATION

The question "To what buddha family do I belong?" or "To what buddha family does so-and-so belong?" can be difficult to answer. One way to determine buddha family is to look at the predominating neurotic style of the person, which is ego's way of trying to "handle" the primary wisdom. Sometimes, however, the neurotic style is a complex mix of habitual patterns relating with several buddha families, which can be hard to sort out. In some people, one of the five buddha family styles is so pronounced as to be self-evident. In many people, however, there may be two or even three energies visible. A person with one energy predominant will tend to rely on this approach in every situation. People with more than one energy will tend to shift gears, depending on what is called for. Thus a ratna-karma person might be very warm, accommodating, and loving at home, but cold, active and competitive in the work environment.

The situation is further complicated by a person's "exit," a term coined by Trungpa Rinpoche to refer to the protective coloration that someone may adapt in order to survive in the world. This "exit" may be quite different from the predominant family or families. For example, parents may place extreme demands on a child to conform to a different kind of buddha-family energy than his or her actual nature. Suppose that softness, warmth, gentleness, and sweetness are predominating values in a family. A young child who is actually vajra and karma may be forced to exhibit padma or ratna qualities to win approval and love. Yet, underneath, the cooler, more efficient, and cut-and-dried energies will remain. Or suppose that a padma-buddha child is born into a situation of great poverty and material distress. This person may be required to work from dawn until dusk for the survival of the fam-

TABLE 7.1

THE FIVE BUDDHA FAMILIES[16]

Buddha Family	Buddha	Vajra	Ratna	Padma	Karma
Direction	center	east	south	west	north
Presiding buddha	Vairochana[17]	Akshobya	Ratnasambhava	Amitabha	Amoghasiddhi
Consort	Dharmadhat-vishvari	Mamaki	Lochana	Pandaravasini	Tara
Mudra	teaching dharma	earth-touching	generosity	meditation	fearlessness
Color	white	dark blue	yellow	red	green
Symbol	wheel	vajra	jewel	lotus	sword
Skandha	form	consciousness	feeling	perception	karmic formations
Element	space	water	earth	fire	wind
Temperature	neutral	cool	warm	hot	cold
Wisdom	wisdom of all-encompassing space	mirror-like wisdom	wisdom of equanimity	discriminating awareness wisdom	all-accomplishing wisdom
Enlightened style	spaciousness, accommodation	clarity, precision	generosity, richness	selfless appreciation and love	efficiency without ambition
Defilement	ignorance	anger	pride	passion	envy/paranoia
Neurotic style	spaced-out, stupid	aggressive, irritable	territorial, suffocating	clingy, grasping, poverty-stricken	competitive, pugnacious
Time of day	no time	early morning	midmorning	sunset	after sunset, dusk, late day, early night
Season	none	winter	fall	springtime	high summer
Association with part of body	none	eyes	stomach	throat	limbs, genitals
Realm	god, animal	hell	hungry ghost	human	jealous god
Primary function	being	thinking	consuming	relating	doing
Type of suffering	insentient, no feeling	freezing	suffocating	wishful thinking	struggling

ily, exhibiting karma-family traits, while all the time containing a soft and "live and let live" approach underneath. The more discrepancy between a person's "exit" and his or her actual energy, the more conflicted that person is likely to be.

It was mentioned that the five wisdoms are inherent in the buddha-nature of each person. If only one or a few of these energies predominate in each of us, what is the status of the rest of them? These non-predominant wisdoms are still present in the buddha-nature, but they are not visible or functional in our conscious personalities. The non-predominant energies fall into two categories: each of us has one or more wisdoms that we can draw upon in a pinch; and there are always one or perhaps two energies that are completely buried, that we cannot access at our present level of development.

This leads to an important question: if the five wisdoms are inherent in the buddha-nature of each one of us, then why do we differ in the energies that we manifest? The answer has to do with our karma, with the particular way in which we, as sentient beings, have evolved. But why this way and not another? Karma, as understood in Buddhism, is both past-oriented and future-oriented; it is individual and also connected with all other sentient beings. Thus we could say, "I am the way I am because of what has happened to me in the past." But this is only part of the answer. We also need to say, "I am the way I am because of what I need to be in the future, and this is related to all other sentient beings and to what the world needs of me down the road." Seen from this viewpoint, each of us has a particular gift to bring to the limitless realm of being, and this gift is reflected in our primary buddha family or families, and in our particular configuration of the five wisdoms altogether.

THE FOUR KARMAS

As one travels along the path, engaging in the Vajrayana practices, one is in the process of developing all five wisdoms. A fully enlightened person, though manifesting one or two energies predominantly, will have developed all five wisdoms to their height and will be able to draw on all five at will. How he or she manifests them at any point will depend on what is called for by the particular needs of the situation at hand.

As they express themselves in fully realized people, the wisdoms constitute "buddha activity"—actions that reflect a natural, unpremeditated, and spontaneous response to the suffering of samsaric beings. In Vajrayana Buddhism, this buddha activity of the wisdoms is articulated in terms of the four karmas. As we have seen, dharmadhatu wisdom, located at the center of the mandala, is basic, all-pervading enlightenment, of which the four other wisdoms, at the four cardinal directions of the mandala, are more active manifestations.

The four karmas represent the ways in which these four active wisdoms manifest in fully realized people, as they express their enlightenment in the world. As we shall see, the karmas are not ways of overriding the natural processes of the world, but rather embody the power that emerges once these are fully seen and understood. Once this occurs, as it does in enlightenment, then the realized person becomes a transparent vehicle for the wisdom and compassion of the universe, and this expresses itself in terms of the four karmas.

The four karmas include pacifying, enriching, magnetizing, and destroying: pacifying actualizes mirror-like wisdom; enriching sets in motion the wisdom of equanimity; magnetizing implements discriminating awareness wisdom; and destroying brings forth all-accomplishing wisdom. The fifth wisdom, dharmadhatu wisdom, provides the basic ground within which the four karmas operate. In order to carry our understanding of the wisdoms a little further, let us briefly consider the four karmas in two perspectives, first as they are expressed by enlightened people and, second, as they are perverted through the mechanism of ego.

The Four Karmas as Enlightened Activity

PACIFYING

From an enlightened perspective, things, as they operate in the world, work in an inherently peaceful way. This means that there is room for everything to occur in its own manner, apart from judgments or evaluations. The karma of pacifying accommodates everything, understands its appropriateness, and acknowledges its right to be—as an expression of karma. The karma of pacifying reveals that there is actually no such thing as problems, obstacles, or enemies, and that the aggression of ego against such supposed negativities is entirely beside the point and unnecessary.

ENRICHING

Having begun with pacifying, the attitude of "for and against" in conventional thinking has been overcome, and things are seen and related to on their own terms. Out of this comes the karma of enriching, which involves bringing to light the spontaneous processes of growth, maturation, and enrichment that occur as natural expressions of reality, left to its own devices. As we saw above, situations are always abundant with resources, no matter how poverty-stricken they may seem from a conventional viewpoint. In the karma of enriching, realized beings show the perfection of the artless and effortless unfolding of these resources.

MAGNETIZING

In conventional reality, we continually try to draw desired situations and people toward ourselves and to fend off undesirable ones. We find ourselves "lonely" or "disappointed" when we do not have what we desire, and "fulfilled" when we do. The karma of magnetizing bypasses this logic entirely: when a realized person simply remains as he or she is, then what is actually needed is naturally and spontaneously attracted, without any need for egoic intervention whatsoever.[18]

DESTROYING

The karma of destroying is connected with compassion in the sense that it destroys what needs to be destroyed. The targets of this karma are the accretions of ego that have occurred. Through the operation of destroying, the ego overlay in any situation is eliminated, leaving the basic energy. The karma of destroying is also connected with creativity be-cause the ego is the ultimate anticreative force. It continually seeks safety and permanence by trying to freeze the spontaneous, creative processes of life. It wants to cut off the uncontrived flow of energy of the other three karmas. So the karma of destroying is directed specifically at ego's manipulations. It is thus not rampantly and indiscriminately destructive but rather highly intelligent and apt in terms of what it destroys.

The Distortions of Ego: The Four Maras

As we have seen, each of the wisdoms can be distorted by the machina-tions of ego and then appears in a distorted, self-centered form. In this case the four karmas appear in a perverted, samsaric form, known as the "four *maras*," four types of activity directed to building up and forti-fying our concept of "self."

The karma of pacifying, for example, appears as *devaputra mara*. It represents the attempt to make peace into a reference point of pleasure and security and to eliminate what is unpleasant. It is an imitation of genuine pacifying, which is beyond any self-serving strategy.

The mara connected with enriching is *skandha mara*, the mara of accumulating. In this case, the ego takes the natural growing and en-riching quality of reality and attempts to turn it into its own ground. It attempts to accumulate that richness, to grasp on to it and possess it. Now one preys upon the world's abundance and process of growth, and converts it into *my* wealth and *my* possessions.

The mara related to magnetizing is *klesha mara*. One attempts to use attraction—one's own natural power of attraction as a human being—to feed one's ego with what is considered desirable. Based on that, possessiveness, jealousy, anger, pride and the other kleshas develop.

Yama mara represents the perversion of the karma of destroying. Yama is the Lord of Death and destroys indiscriminately. Yama mara, instead of destroying what needs to be destroyed, obliterates everything, not only the dead leaves of the tree but also its branches, trunk, and roots. Yama Mara, in Trungpa Rinpoche's words, "begins to get inspired in the wrong way of uprooting whole trees. . . . And that is the karmic quality of destruction gone wild, unnecessarily."[19]

CONCLUSION

Enlightenment and the World

The mandala, then, points to reality as it is experienced beyond thought. It reveals that, fundamentally, reality is nothing other than wisdom. It is important to realize that this statement does not imply a dichotomy of any sort, with a "false world" of our life on this earth being set in opposition to a "real world" of wisdom existing someplace else. This kind of dualism is completely alien to the Vajrayana. Rather we are being asked to look closely at the world that we actually inhabit and to contemplate our most ordinary experience. If we do so, if we let go of what we think and simply let the true being of this world show itself to us and work on us, we will discover that it is nothing other than primordial, immaculate wisdom.

Mundane reality, then, which usually seems so solid, monolithic, and impenetrable, is actually an open, ever-changing manifestation of primordial wisdom. Through connecting with the wisdom inherent in the most ordinary experiences of our lives, we can find liberation. The wind, taken in and of itself and from its own side, breaks open our ego world, and so do earth, fire, water, and space. The arising of perception, feeling, or any of the other skandhas within us likewise sets us free, if we can simply let them manifest without mental interference. This perspective again helps us understand King Indrabhuti's apparent desire to indulge himself in the sense perceptions. It was not that Indrabhuti wanted to gratify his egoic thirst for pleasure and comfort, but that he wanted to partake of the liberating wisdom that inheres in our most elemental experience of the world.

The Mandala and the Yidam

In previous chapters, mention has been made of the yidam, the male or female buddha that acts as a representation of one's own fundamental nature. Chapter 10 will explore the way in which the yidam or meditation buddha forms the basis of Vajrayana liturgy and meditation. In preparation for that discussion, it is important to understand the relationship of the mandala to the yidam. In brief, the mandala and the yidam are different expressions of the same reality. A mandala is always the mandala of a particular deity. It shows the deity in his or her full form, with a central buddha and four divinities at the four directions, representing emanations of the central figure. In the further symbolism of the mandala, there are other beings and these also are understood as the emanations of the central buddha. Thus one might say that the mandala is a depiction of the complete form of the yidam, showing his or her central manifestation and various other "faces."

The mandala thus helps us understand that the yidam is nothing other than the manifestation of wisdom, in fact the five wisdoms of enlightenment. This view counteracts any tendency to see the yidam as a solid and enduring deity with which one could be in a theistic relationship. Like a tongue of flame that appears but is ungraspable and gone in an instant, wisdom is fleeting, the impact of a moment that can never be held. This is the "empty" nature of the yidam, which appears but cannot be in any way objectified or pinned down.

Tantric Realization, Individualism, and Individuality

Sometimes it is thought that an Asian tradition such as the Vajrayana represents the loss or destruction of a person's individuality. We can now see how this is a serious misunderstanding. The variety of particular configurations of the five wisdoms and corresponding egoic distortions that human beings possess are potentially infinite. Thus the buddha-family manifestation that each of us presents to the world is also finally individual and unique. It is the purpose of the tantric path to fully realize one's unique configuration of enlightened wisdoms. In this respect, Trungpa Rinpoche remarks:

> Those five principles of buddha-nature, traditionally known as the buddha families, are the basic working basis that tantra has

to offer. In the tantric tradition, there are different deities, different approaches to your action, that are related with those five styles. . . . In tantra, there are all kinds of variations you can get into, based on the five different perspectives. There are five different kinds of relationships with things, and you can identify yourself with all or one of these, or partially with any of them. You could have one leading aspect and a suggestion of something else. You might have a vajra quality along with a padma quality and maybe a touch of karma as well, and so forth.

Basically, psychologically, vajrayana permits the openness to work on all kinds of elements that you have in you. You don't have to tune yourself in to one basic thing. You can take pride in what you are, what you have, your basic nature. . . . I think that is the basic core of understanding of tantra. Tantra permits different aspects of you to shine through, rather than your having to be channeled into one set of characteristics. It allows your basic nature to come through.[20]

The "ego" is the root of "individualism," and it is this that the path overcomes. But individualism and individuality are opposing categories. Individualism is the tendency to think of oneself in a fixed way as such-and-such a person, separate from others, cut off from the rest of the world, responsible only for oneself, independent and autonomous. The idea of individualism, so dominant in the West, is a collective ideology of the most pernicious nature. By seeming to insist on the worth and dignity of the individual, it invites rampant confusion among those who sense that their uniqueness is being sacrificed to some kind of "group think" or ideology but are told all the time that this is not the case. By contrast, individuality is the unique person that we actually are, complete with the vast web of interconnected relationships of which we are a part, entirely apart from who we think we are or should be. Individuality in Vajrayana Buddhism is defined through the configuration of the five wisdoms and reflected in one's karma.

The World as Mandala

As we have seen, the buddha families describe the energies active not only within each person but also in the world at large. An important distinction needs to be made between the five wisdoms as they are dimly reflected in the samsaric world of defiled relative truth, and their naked appearance as pure relative truth. For example, there is the color red, as we normally and habitually see it through our conceptual filters. But there is also the pure energy of the color red that underlies the conceptual version. As long as we stay within our samsaric, mediated experience of the color red, we are not in direct contact with its wisdom. But if we see the color red without filters, then it is none other than discriminating awareness wisdom.

This is an important point that we shall need to explore below: when the doors of our sense perceptions are cleansed, when we experience phenomena directly and not through the medium of concepts, we know our sense perceptions as the play of the five wisdoms. In what we see, hear, smell, taste, and touch, we encounter directly the awakened play of the universe. The mandala, then, is the underlying structure of the world that is already there, energizing and empowering all sentient beings, but hidden from view. All that is needed is for us to tune ourselves in to it and realize that our lives are nothing other than an expression of enlightened energy.

8

The Vajra Master

MOST OF US LIVE MORE OR LESS ENTIRELY IN A REALITY defined by concepts. The immaculate wisdom of the "world beyond thought," expressed in the symbolism of the mandala, is generally hidden and inaccessible. Many people live and die without suspecting that there is another, deeper, and more true way to experience the world. In order to rediscover this hidden depth, we need a mentor to show us the way. For this reason, it is commonly said that in order to practice the Vajrayana, a teacher is indispensable.

In explaining the great importance of the lama or guru, Kalu Rinpoche remarks:

> For the disciple, the source lama [one's primary tantric mentor] is more important than all the Buddhas. If you rely on the Buddhas to reach Awakening, this requires much time. On the other hand, it is said that if one prays to the lama from the depths of the heart, one will very quickly attain Awakening. The grace of Buddhas and bodhisattvas resembles the radiance of the sun. Even in the hot season, the sun cannot make a piece of paper on the ground catch fire, but if you have a magnifying glass, the paper will easily burst into flames. The Vajrayana consists of inserting the magnifying glass of the lama between the grace of the Buddhas and bodhisattvas and the mind of the disciples.[1]

Kalu Rinpoche says, "We need someone who can guide us on the path, teach us, direct us, help us, and show us the dangers and the right way."[2] Following the tantric path, because it is so intensely practice-oriented, is one of the most challenging things a person can do. Virtually all the mountains and valleys that we come upon we have never seen before, and the passages and defiles can seem impassable. When the fog descends, it is easy to become disoriented and lost. We are ultimately alone in this journey. For that very reason, to have any hope of success, we need the help of someone in possession of the collective wisdom of the many generations of previous travelers.

FINDING A TEACHER

Examine the Teacher

Chagdud Tulku says it is vital that before we come to rely on a spiritual teacher "we carefully research that teacher's qualities." It is somewhat like when we are ill and need to be certain that the doctor we consult is informed and skilled. In a way, however, the selection of a spiritual guide is weightier, because

> if we didn't investigate a doctor, it wouldn't be such a big deal, because mistreatment might cause us to lose only this life. But if we place our faith in a spiritual teacher who isn't qualified, we might develop counterproductive habits that could remain with us for lifetimes to come and create tremendous obstacles on the path to enlightenment.[3]

How is one to find a qualified teacher? What, in particular, should one look for? Kalu Rinpoche emphasizes the qualities of wisdom and compassion:

> The master must have good knowledge of the three Vehicles (Hinayana, Mahayana, and Vajrayana). In the context of the Vajrayana, the master must have received scripture empowerments and transmissions, and must have accomplished at least some practice.
> The master must have great compassion. Whether in the presence of a vast gathering or in a small group, when the mas-

ter teaches, it is always with the motivation of helping those students on the path of Awakening.

Knowing Dharma and motivated by compassion, the master must care only about benefitting the disciple and never pursue his or her own interest. The given instructions must not have any other function than guiding the disciples on the inner path.[4]

Paltrül Rinpoche, writing in the formal, traditional style of nineteenth-century Tibet, adds to the qualities of wisdom and compassion those of moral purity and of personal attainment.

He should be pure, never having contravened any of the commitments or prohibitions related to the three types of vow—the external vows of the Pratimoksha, the inner vows of the Bodhisattva and the secret vows of the Secret Mantrayana. He should be learned, and not lacking in knowledge of the tantras, sutras and shastras. Toward the vast multitude of beings, his heart should be so suffused with compassion that he loves each one like his only child. He should be well versed in the practices—outwardly, of the Tripitaka and, inwardly, of the four sections of tantras. He should have actualized all the extraordinary qualities of liberation and realization in himself by experiencing the meaning of the teachings.[5]

Tulku Urgyen Rinpoche includes knowledge, compassion, and moral purity among the qualities we should look for in a teacher, but he particularly emphasizes that person's realization:

We should be seeking the kind of teacher who can surely lead us to [the awakened] state. The most qualified teacher is called a "vajra-holder possessing the three precepts." He or she should possess the perfect qualities of being outwardly endowed with the vows of individual liberation, called *pratimokṣha*, while inwardly possessing the trainings of a bodhisattva. On the innermost level, the qualified master must be competent in the true state of *samadhi*. . . . A true vajra master should have already liberated his own stream of being through realization. This means actualizing the authentic state of *samadhi*. Furthermore, he or she should be able to liberate others through compassion and loving kindness; that is the second essential quality.[6]

People are often impressed by a teacher's learning or eloquence. If a teacher seems to know a great deal and can speak in an interesting and entertaining manner, they may think that this is a worthy guide. In the modern world, if a teacher has written popular books, has achieved fame, or has a large following, people may be impressed and willing to follow him or her. However, according to Chagdud Tulku:

> Eloquence is not the most important quality of a dharma teacher, for it's not so difficult to deliver a nice lecture; what's crucial is that, through a genuine and profound practice of meditation, he or she maintains a direct, personal experience of the teachings. Otherwise the teacher might be like a parrot who repeats again and again, "Practice virtue, don't practice nonvirtue," but who devours an insect as soon as it enters the cage.[7]

In attempting to find a qualified mentor, one can and should ascertain from others his or her qualities. Most important, however, one should rely on one's own observations. Does the teacher show kindness and compassion in his or her actions? Is that teacher beyond self-interest and devoted to the welfare of others? Does he or she exhibit wisdom and accuracy in dealing with situations? Has that teacher integrated the teachings into his or her life, and does he or she truly live them? When near the teacher, does one feel his or her mental stability, openness of mind, and realization?

Chagdud Tulku observes that it would be hard to find a completely faultless teacher, and even if we did, we probably wouldn't realize it. Nevertheless, "we can rely on a lama who, through meditation practice, has removed some of the mind's obscurations, attained some degree of realization, and developed great compassion. Teachers with a good heart have your interest, not theirs, in mind."[8] This last point is particularly important. A genuine teacher is there to speak for our essential nature and to act on its behalf, until we can learn to do so for ourselves.

Trust Your Heart

Nevertheless, particularly in relation to the Vajrayana, there can be something unreasonable, irresistible, and miraculous in the process of finding a teacher. Much depends on the student's own initial motivation and the genuineness of his or her longing. Important also is the student's patience to avoid latching on to the first teacher who appears on the horizon. One needs to look for a teacher with whom one feels a strong karmic connection, a person to whom one feels drawn from one's inner being. In stories of the great masters of the different Tibetan schools, one frequently finds examples of this kind of feeling of linkage—in some cases merely upon the student's hearing the name of his or her future teacher. In terms of the Kagyü lineage, when Marpa heard of the siddha Naropa, "a connection from a former life was reawakened in Marpa and he felt immeasurable yearning."[9] Likewise Milarepa tells us, "Hardly had I heard the name of Marpa the Translator than I was filled with ineffable happiness. In my joy every hair on my body vibrated. I sobbed with fervent adoration. Locking my whole mind on a single thought, I set out with provisions and a book. Without being distracted by any other thoughts, I ceaselessly repeated to myself, 'When? When will I see the lama face to face?'"[10] And when Gampopa heard mention of Milarepa, he was overcome by longing and set out at once to find him.[11]

Lest we think that these kinds of examples belong only to the past, I relate the story of a friend concerning her meeting with Trungpa Rinpoche, who subsequently became her guru. What is interesting is that in talking with students of this or other Tibetan teachers, one discovers that this kind of story is not particularly unusual.

> I had been looking for a spiritual guide for about ten years and, although I met quite a number of legitimate teachers, I had not found a particular connection with any of them or felt that any of them could provide what I needed. One day, in about 1968, two years before Trungpa Rinpoche came to the U.S., I happened to come upon his autobiography, *Born in Tibet*. After reading this, somehow I knew instinctively that he was my

teacher, although I didn't know where he was or how I would ever be able to meet him. It so happened that two years later, by a series of circumstances, I made my way to Karmê Chöling, then called Tail of the Tiger, a farmhouse in northern Vermont that had been donated to Trungpa Rinpoche for a meditation center. He had literally just arrived in the U.S. He received me in a small front room, over the stairs, with a low, slanted ceiling. The day was dark and completely overcast and yet, as I sat down opposite him, the clouds parted and a burst of brilliant sunshine filled the room, falling on him. We talked, and he articulated for me thoughts about my own life and path that I had not yet had the courage to think but that were there, waiting on the edge of my consciousness and insistently wanting to come through. To me, these events confirmed what I had been thinking all along about him. Later, I remember sitting on the floor of a big room listening to a talk by Rinpoche on the bodhisattva path, weeping uncontrollably at the sorrow, the pain, and the joy of the incredibly strong connection I felt with him.

This sense of connection deepened and matured over the next seventeen years, until Trungpa Rinpoche's death in 1987.

This young woman, through having read Trungpa Rinpoche's autobiography, was informed about his training and stature in Tibet, and this gave her a sense of confidence in him from the very beginning. In contrast to this is the following account of an American man who became a student of His Holiness the sixteenth Karmapa. This individual had made his way to Sikkim in the early 1970s before the Karmapa had visited the West and before he was at all known in the United States. On the advice of a friend, he went to Rumtek, the Karmapa's monastery, to meet His Holiness, although he had no idea who the Karmapa was or why he should meet him. His account:

"My wife and I took the bus to the bottom of the mountain on which Rumtek is located. Having no idea how far up it was, we started to walk. It was a very long hike, and by the time we arrived at the monastery, we were exhausted and famished. At that time, there were no shops or stalls, and we asked if there was any food available. A dish of not very savory vegetables was brought, along with rice that was filled with gravel. If the rice was inedible, the vegetables were even more so, and we had brought no food with us. At this point, our mutual and growing frustration boiled over, and my wife and I got into a terrible argument. Oblivious that we were in the middle of a monastery, we stood there glaring at each other and shouting at the top of our voices.

"At this moment, the person who had brought the food returned in a state of considerable excitement. He kept pointing to the temple up the hill, saying, 'You come, you come.' His arrival brought our shouting match to a quick end and, compelled by his insistence, we followed him up the hill to the temple. There we were motioned to wait on the porch. Then followed a series of events for which I was completely unprepared.

"Almost immediately, we heard the blaring of Tibetan trumpets, indicating that something important was about to happen. Then around the corner of the temple came a small procession of monks, led by two men playing the trumpets, followed by a person walking slowly and with great dignity. At the first glimpse of him, I felt as if I had been hit by a bolt of lightning. I was immediately overcome with emotion, my eyes were flooded with tears so that I couldn't see, and I actually doubled over. His Holiness Karmapa—for it was he—walked slowly into the main shrine hall, and the handful of those gathered followed him in, with me coming last of all, with difficulty.

"His Holiness then performed—as I learned later—the black crown ceremony, a ritual for which he was well known and loved. In this rite, sitting on the high teaching throne, he placed the traditional black hat of the Karmapa incarnations on his head and assumed the aspect of the Bodhisattva of Compassion, Avalokiteshvara, an incarnation of which he is held to be.

"During the Karmapa's procession into the shrine hall and throughout the ritual, I was completely unable to look at His Holiness. It was as if he were emitting a light that was so brilliant it was blinding, and I literally could not raise my eyes. It wasn't that I didn't want to look, but I just couldn't. I kept my head bowed, and by now my shirt was soaking

FIGURE 8.1 *Avalokiteshvara (or Chenrezig in Tibetan), the Bodhisattva of Compassion. The Dalai Lama and the Karmapa are both held to be incarnations of Avalokiteshvara.*

wet with my tears. Even with my head down, however, I could feel, in a most intense and tangible manner, the energy and power of His Holiness, his compassion as well as his magnificence and splendor.

"During the ceremony, we went up twice to receive a blessing from His Holiness. The first time, I was still in a state of overwhelming feeling, longing, and devotion for this person, whoever he was. When His Holiness blessed me this first time, his hand lingered on my head, and I felt the most unbelievable tenderness and love from him. I sat back down, and the ceremony concluded.

"I now began pulling myself together. I realized something very extraordinary had happened. I knew that I wanted His Holiness to be my teacher, and I wanted some indication and confirmation from him of what had just occurred. Now the time came for the final blessing, and I approached his throne with my wants and expectations in full force. Now the touch of his hand was quick, sharp, and perfunctory, as if to say, 'There is nothing to hang on to *here*!' Whereas before I was unmade by who His Holiness was, now I was devastated that—in spite of the intensity of my experience—there was nothing I could turn into a source of security or a reference point. I was amazed that His Holiness was able to respond to my state of mind and to what I needed in such a perfectly precise and accurate way.

"I am not prone to 'experiences,' and in religious matters I tend to be more on the skeptical side. Certainly nothing like this had ever happened to me before. It still surprises me how all of this came like a bolt out of the blue. As I have said, I had no previous idea who His Holiness was and had never heard of the black crown ceremony.

"I learned later how different teachers are renowned for different qualities. His Holiness the sixteenth Karmapa, for example, was known for the magnificence and splendor of his person and it was said that simply upon seeing him, beings were tamed. As you can see, this was precisely my own experience. It was quite eye-opening for me to see the way that traditional attributes like that—which could be taken as pro forma kinds of statements—can be so vividly rooted in people's most intimate experience of a master like His Holiness.

"Now that His Holiness has been dead some twenty years [since

1981], people still talk about what a glorious, magnificent person he was. Certainly much of what is said must sound like gross exaggeration to those who never met him. But based on the experiences I had of him, it is all an understatement."

(See the account of the passing of H.H. the sixteenth Karmapa in chapter 18.)

THE ROLE OF THE VAJRA MASTER

The essence of the student-teacher relationship in Tibetan Buddhism is communication and friendship. Trungpa Rinpoche: "The teachings emphasize a mutual meeting of two minds. It is a matter of mutual communication, rather than a master-servant relationship between a highly evolved being and a miserable, confused one. . . . A guru should be a spiritual friend who communicates and presents his qualities to us."[12] The prospective disciple also must present him or herself straight-forwardly, without deception. Trungpa Rinpoche illustrates this point with the following account:

> There is an interesting story of a group of people who decided to go and study under a great Tibetan teacher. They had already studied somewhat with other teachers, but had decided to concentrate on trying to learn from this particular person. They were all very anxious to become his students . . . but this great teacher would not accept any of them. "Under one condition only will I accept you," he said: "if you are willing to renounce your previous teachers." They all pleaded with him, telling him how much they were devoted to him, how great his reputation was, and how much they would like to study with him. But he would not accept any of them unless they would meet his condition. Finally all except one person in the party decided to renounce their previous teachers, from whom they had in fact learned a great deal. The guru seemed to be quite happy when they did so and told them all to come back the next day.
>
> But when they returned he said to them, "I understand your

hypocrisy. The next time you go to another teacher, you will renounce me. So get out." And he chased them all out except for the one person who valued what he had already learned previously. The person he accepted was not willing to play any more lying games, was not willing to try to please a guru by pretending to be different from what he was. If you are going to make friends with a spiritual master, you must make friends simply, openly, so that the communication takes place between equals, rather than trying to win the master over to you.[13]

Kalu Rinpoche points out that one's relationship with one's spiritual teacher evolves in gradual stages, beginning in the Hinayana, continuing through the Mahayana, and culminating in the Vajrayana. In each yana, one has a characteristic relationship with one's teacher, who plays the role that we need at that stage.

At the Hinayana level, we respect the teacher and have immense gratitude for his kindness in giving us the dharma. . . . In the Mahayana . . . he becomes a "spiritual friend," a counselor at the inner level. The Vajrayana places even more importance on the spiritual guide. At this level, he is the lama. The "root lama," or the lama who personally guides a Vajrayana practitioner, is regarded as Buddha Vajradhara, the essence and union of all the buddhas of the three times and the ten directions. . . . He is the Buddha's equal in his qualities, and even more esteemed than any other aspect of Buddha because of his kindness in transmitting the teachings to us. It is this essential relationship that allows the transmission of the blessing and provides the spiritual direction at the deepest level, the Vajrayana level.[14]

As Trungpa Rinpoche describes this evolving relationship, at the Hinayana stage, the teacher is like a doctor and we are like the patient. We are confused and without resources, and the teacher has advice and instructions that can help us. Therefore we tend to approach him as a higher being who can save us from our misery. At the Mahayana level, we have learned through study how to understand our mind and through meditation how to handle its rocky terrain. Now we are more settled and confident, and now the teacher becomes a "spiritual friend" (*kalyanamitra*) a person with whom we can share the ups and downs of our spiritual journey, and who always has useful insights.

> In the discipline of hinayana, we relate to the teacher as a wise man who gives us constant instruction and guides us precisely. The relationship between teacher and student is very simple and clear-cut. In the discipline of mahayana, we regard the teacher as a kalyanamitra, or spiritual friend, who works with us and relates to us as a friend. He guides us through the dangerous and the luxurious parts of the path; he tells us when to relax and when to exert ourselves, and he teaches the disciplines of helping others. In the discipline of vajrayana, the relationship between teacher and student is much more vigorous and highly meaningful. It is more personal and magical than consulting a sage or, for that matter, consulting a spiritual friend.[15]

At the Vajrayana level, the guru becomes a "vajra master," a person who introduces us to the mystery, the power, and the magic of the phenomenal world. We approach our teacher initially with only a dim awareness of a world beyond our samsaric version. Through our Hinayana and Mahayana practice, we begin to slow down, soften, and become more sensitive to the world beyond thought. When we enter the Vajrayana, we are being introduced to and reconnected with this true, naked, raw reality. If we begin to shy away from our path, if we lose our connection, the vajra master can spark a reconnection. The vajra master is like a magician, not in the sense of contravening the basic order of the universe, but rather in his ability to tap the self-existing magic that exists. He is a dangerous person for us to relate with because, if we begin to try to use our training for our own self-serving ends, he will intervene without mercy. Or rather, he will not hold back the response of the universe.

> Relating with the vajra master is extremely powerful and somewhat dangerous at this point. The vajra master is capable of

transmitting the vajra spiritual energy to us, but at the same time, he is also capable of destroying us if our direction is completely wrong. Tantra means continuity, but one of the principles of tantric discipline is that continuity can only exist if there is something genuine to continue. If we are not genuine, then our continuity can be cancelled by the vajra master.[16]

Throughout the Buddhist world, the teachings are passed on, not through books, but through the personal, direct, intimate communication of one person, the teacher, with another, the student. The teachings are so subtle and complex, and so situational, that someone must point to the reality that we live in and say, "Look! Do you see? This is it." The need for personal communication and exchange is all that much more critical in Vajrayana Buddhism. "The tantric system of working with the world and the energy of tantra have to be transmitted or handed down directly from teacher to student. In that way the teachings become real and obvious and precise."[17] "A direct relationship between teacher and student is essential to Vajrayana Buddhism. People cannot even begin to practice tantra without making some connection with their teacher. . . . Such a teacher cannot be some abstract cosmic figure. He has to be somebody who has gone through the whole process himself."[18]

Whereas on the Hinayana and Mahayana levels the teacher is doctor and friend, on the Vajrayana level he is a master warrior with whom we are in training.

It is a process of training the student as a warrior. At first, a warrior teacher does not use a sword on you. He uses a stick and makes you fight with him. Since the student's swordsmanship is not so good, he gets hurt more than he is able to hurt the master. But when the student gains confidence and begins to learn good swordsmanship, he is almost able to defeat his own teacher. Then instead of a stick it becomes a sword. Nobody really gets killed or hurt, because all the levels of communication take place within the realm of the rainbow or mirage anyway. But there is a training period. A learning process takes place. . . . On the vajrayana level, the student-teacher relationship is similar to that in the martial arts. You could get hurt severely if you are too tense. But you could also receive a tremendous—almost physical—message. The message is not verbal or intellectual. It is like a demonstration of putting tables and chairs together. The teachings come out of the world of form, the real world of form. The teachings consist of colors and forms and sounds rather than words or ideas. . . .

Each time we come closer to tantra in the journey through the yanas, the relationship to the teacher changes and becomes more and more personal. The teacher acts as his own spokesman but also as the spokesman of the vivid and colorful world that you are part of. If you don't have any experience of winter, you have to take off your clothes and lie in the snow at night. That way you will learn a very good lesson on what winter is all about that doesn't need words. You could read a book about it, but it doesn't mean very much unless you have that very immediate and direct experience—which is frightening, very powerful.[19]

Ultimately, the vajra master is the human person who will take us on a journey through the many realms of this universe and beyond, pointing out the wonders and the horrors, from the pure lands, where all experience is vibrant with the reality of dharma, to the depths of samsara, where beings are utterly lost; from the unbearable bliss of the god realms to the unspeakable pain of the hells. He leads us on this journey so that we will understand in our bones and our blood the boundless possibilities of being and know the sacredness of what is. Only from such experience, according to the Vajrayana, can we fulfill the bodhisattva's commitment to help beings no matter where they are or what condition they may be in. Only through our own fearless openness to what is, in its full extent, can we offer ourselves for the universal salvation of all who suffer.

At the level of Vajrayana, the more one works with one's teacher, the more one comes to realize that he is a vehicle for something that transcends the idiosyncrasies of his individual person. He is ultimately a person—we could almost say a principle or a force—speaking and acting on our behalf, not on behalf of the "us" that is the self-conscious ego, but rather our deeper self, our awakened nature. At the same time, the teacher is speaking and acting on behalf of the cosmos. This brings up an important point: ultimately, our deeper self and the cosmos are in league with each other. What we ultimately want and need to be and what the cosmos wants and needs from us are not two, but one single thing.

DEVOTION IN THE RELATION OF TEACHER AND DISCIPLE

It is often said in Tibetan Buddhism that devotion is the most fundamental and most important Vajrayana practice. Dzigar Kongtrül Rinpoche remarks that without devotion the Vajrayana teachings cannot be transmitted and without devotion they cannot be carried onto the path.[20] Tulku Urgyen Rinpoche remarks that "the method for realizing buddha-nature requires devotion from the core of our heart."[21] Rinpoche describes the logic behind this remark:

> The state of mind of all the buddhas is dharmakaya itself. The nature of our mind is also dharmakaya. The fact that we have the same essence serves as a direct link between us and all awakened beings. Lacking faith and devotion, it is as though the dharmakaya nature of our mind is encased in obscurations. But the very moment you open up in devotion, you receive the blessings of the buddhas.
>
> The dharmakaya of enlightened beings is like a butter lamp where the flame is burning brightly. The dharmakaya nature of a sentient being's mind is like a butter lamp where the wick has not yet been lit. Therefore, it is very important to allow compassion and blessings of enlightened beings to enter us. The link between us and the state of enlightenment is faith and devotion.[22]

As we have seen, the teacher is the representative of the buddhas, and therefore devotion to the buddhas largely comes down to devotion to one's personal guru. It is interesting that the more traditional explanations of devotion to one's teacher in Tibetan Buddhism can sometimes appear excessive and unreasonable to Western ears. For example, Kalu Rinpoche remarks, "From the moment one considers someone as a master and receives teachings, it is no longer possible to adopt a critical attitude. In case one eventually doubts the master's knowledge, capabilities, or behavior, it is necessary to think, 'These defects are without doubt not within the master, but in my own way of seeing.'"[23] Again, "in the Vajrayana . . . the disciple must conform precisely to the word of the master without having the least doubt. If the master says that fire is water, the disciple must think, 'I would say that this is a fire, but since the master says it is water, it must be water.'"[24] Indeed, "When one has received a single word of teaching of a master, if one does not respect the master, one will be reborn five hundred times as a dog, and then as a miserable human being."[25] There are several important ideas expressed in these quotations: (1) that one must respect one's teacher; (2) that one must give up any attitude of criticism toward the teacher; (3) that any doubts must be regarded as one's own mistaken projections; (4) that one must accept the master's version of reality; and (5) that failure to regard the master in the right way will result in generating very negative karma.

What is one to make of statements such as these? Asking any adult, and particularly a modern Westerner, to take up this kind of attitude toward another person would seem highly questionable. If anyone were to manage to adopt such an attitude, at least in a Western context, he or she would likely be regarded as emotionally impaired.

It is important to realize that in the traditional context, requirements such as the above were necessary for the kind of practice environment they created. It would be a mistake to assume that Tibetan students simply fell into line, without a second thought, with the demand for total, unwavering faith in their teacher. Milarepa, for example, struggled mightily in his relationship with his teacher, Marpa. At times he thought Marpa was acting out of drunkenness, or that he was actually insane. Milarepa tried to deceive his teacher on several occasions and at one point attempted to get the teachings he wanted from another guru, again through deception. He distrusted Marpa's insistence that the desired teachings would be forthcoming to the point that he decided to commit suicide. And yet, Milarepa is held up as the example of a person with perfect devotion.

The requirement of complete and total trust in one's teacher is not possible for any person with an ego, with any semblance of a self-concept. Yet the demand is articulated and it is an important one. At the very least, it acts as a mirror that reflects back to us exactly how little trust we have in anyone or anything. It shows us that even when our teacher is giving us teachings we may so fervently desire, we are of a mixed mind, we cannot open ourselves and surrender fully to what is occurring.

The requirement of complete faith in one's teacher thus puts the disciple in an impossible situation. He must surrender, but he cannot do so. The more he tries to relate to his teacher outside of the framework of his ambition, grasping, and paranoia, the more these very qualities are thrown back in his face. In such a situation, he finds himself with no alternative but to live with himself and with what he is, experiencing the torment of a seemingly unresolvable dilemma, continuing to relate with his teacher and carrying out the traditional practices for dissolving ego.

In attempting to understand the relation of teacher and student, it is important not to be put off by differences in traditional Tibetan and modern Western ways of speaking about mentor relationships. It is also necessary to probe the nature and functioning of the teacher-student relationship and not to remain at the superficial level of ideology. Most central, it is critical to realize that the role of the teacher is to mediate the selfless wisdom of the buddha-nature. In Tibet, teachers were rigorously trained to put aside personal intentions and motives when relating with students. A teacher who falls into self-serving patterns is no longer fulfilling his or her role.

It is also helpful to realize that the devotion of the teacher to the student is at least as important as the devotion of the student to the teacher. The well-trained teacher can see the confusion of the disciple and how he is constantly trying to be someone else, to live up to some inappropriate and maladroit concept of who he is. The teacher's devotion expresses itself in a clear and unwavering commitment to who the disciple is and to working with him or her to bring out that covered-over and obscured reality. In spite of horror stories of a teacher's abuse of power that one hears told and repeatedly recycled among Western Buddhists, in my own observation it is most often the teacher who ends up making the greatest effort, is the most vulnerable in the relationship, and pays the greatest price for any success that the disciple may find.

In a modern Western context, it can also be helpful to realize that devotion in the Vajrayana is not one thing nor is it static. It is similar to the relationship of marriage partners over a period of many years. During a long marriage, the relationship is in a continual state of evolution, and many stages are passed through along the way. In the same way, the relation of student and teacher evolves in a gradual manner. Even the dramatic meetings of master and disciple so often described in the tradition are only the beginning of the relationship, and all the work remains to be done.

In fact, it is possible to identify several stages in the evolution of the devotion of the disciple:[26]

1. *Attraction to the teacher.* In the beginning, one may feel instinctively drawn toward a certain teacher. One may be impressed by the intelligence, kindness, or dignity of that person and want to draw closer to him and find out more about him.

2. *Trust in the teachings.* Then the student may receive instructions from the teacher and discover that what is being taught helps one a great deal. At this level, one trusts the teachings as being true and beneficial.

3. *Faith in the teacher.* From this, the student may then begin to develop some faith in the person of the teacher, that this is a person who knows important things and is able to communicate them in a way that can be understood. At this juncture, equally important as the formal teachings being received are the student's personal experiences with the teacher and observations of how he conducts himself. One can see how

helpful the teacher has been to oneself. Beyond this, one observes the teacher in all kinds of situations, interacting with his other disciples. He may be seen in difficult straits, "pressed to the wall," so to speak. Then one can assess whether he is really kind, whether he is genuinely patient, insightful, and selfless with others. He may be observed continually sacrificing his comfort and security in order to help those who come to him. As one sees more and finds oneself with more and more faith in the trustworthiness of the teacher, one begins to discover greater and greater openness in him or her. One finds oneself expectant and receptive to what the teacher presents.

At this point, it is critical that the disciple begin to put the teachings into practice—and in the Practice Lineage this means that one must undertake meditation. Without meditation, it is unlikely that one's devotion will be able to develop much further. However, through meditation, the disciple begins to realize just how precious the instructions of the teacher are. Through the practice, as the superficial, inauthentic identifications of oneself begin to drop away, one begins to discover increasing depths of authentic being. The more one practices, then, the more one appreciates one's guru.

4. *Longing for the teacher*. This, in turn, leads to a desire to see more of the teacher, to receive more teachings, to be physically closer to him or her. It is often at this point that the teacher will say, "If you really want to be close to me, then look to your practice. It is through your meditation alone that you will be able to fulfill this longing." It is true that the more one practices and the nearer one draws to one's own buddha-nature, the closer one feels to one's teacher. One increasingly understands his teaching on deeper levels, begins to share his world, and sometimes even experiences moments of inseparability with him.

It is noteworthy that in the Vajrayana devotion of disciple to master is often expressed in absentia from the human guru. Milarepa stands as an early, classical example. Subsequent to receiving the long-sought-after instructions from Marpa, Milarepa went into retreat. After some period of time, he came out of retreat and prepared to visit the home where he grew up. At this time, Marpa told him, "You and I will never see each other again," and in fact this turned out to be the case. Milarepa spent the rest of his life in meditation, and in his songs he frequently calls Marpa to mind and addresses him; but it is not a Marpa of the flesh who hears and responds.

The life of Milarepa reflects another theme that is common in the Practice Lineage, namely that of the "unrequited love" of disciple for teacher. This is the notion that the more one's love and appreciation for the teacher grow, the less one is able to fulfill that love in any concrete way. The human teacher will not permit neurotic grasping and dependency, and one is more and more forced out on one's own, to find the teacher through one's practice.

At this point, one is experiencing genuine devotion, which is called *mögü* in Tibetan. Trungpa Rinpoche comments, "*Mö* means longing and *gü* means humbleness. So the idea is one of opening, like an open flower. When rain falls on a flower, if the flower is open already, it can receive the rain. But if the flower has no longing for the rain, it doesn't open. And if the flower doesn't open, there is no humbleness to receive the rain. So devotion is somewhat emotional; it is a longing to receive the truth that has been taught by the teacher, to receive it thoroughly. . . ."[27]

Tulku Urgyen provides a similar analogy: "The compassionate activity of the buddhas is like a hook that is just waiting to catch sentient beings who are ready and open and who are attuned to this compassion. If we have faith and devotion, we are like an iron ring that can be caught by the hook. But if we are closed and lack faith and devotion, we are like a solid iron ball. Not even the 'hooks' of the buddhas can catch an iron ball." [28]

5. *Complete surrender.* The final stage of devotion is a willingness to relinquish one's logical reference points and to trust the teacher wholeheartedly. This is a very advanced stage of devotion and not for beginners. At a beginner's level, this kind of surrender would be a regression to the dependency of a small child on its parent. If a person attempted—or was permitted—to move into this kind of devotion too early, his or her opportunity for spiritual growth would be cut off.

However, at a certain point, one realizes that one has experienced the wisdom, kindness, and selflessness of the teacher a thousand times over.

It may be that one has observed repeatedly how skillful the teacher is in working with oneself and others. Even on occasions when the teacher has acted in a way that made no sense, perhaps one was subsequently surprised to discover remarkable intelligence and skill in the teacher's action.

At a certain point, the disciple begins to realize that he or she could continue to hold on to reservations and suspicions, and could always wait until tomorrow to acquire further experiences and further proof of the teacher's authenticity and reliability. But then the question arises, how much information is enough? At what point will one be convinced? And then one realizes that no matter how much information is acquired, there is always the uncertain future that stretches out in front forever. The disciple realizes that, at some point, to go further he or she will have to make a leap.

One begins to realize at this point that what is at stake here is not mistrust of the teacher but fundamental paranoia and unwillingness to trust anything. One always wants to hold on to some shred of solid ground, some filament of self-reference, to make sure that one is all right. But the disciple sees now that that basic mistrust itself is the problem; it is preventing him or her from going deeper. It is necessary to abandon oneself to the good graces of the teacher. It is obvious that there is no other way to continue on the path. At that point, one needs to leap.

And so you leap . . . and suddenly find yourself alone—on the upper reaches of a lofty mountain. It is night, the air is crisp and clear, the stars are brilliant; and the majestic desolation of the place is overwhelming. You realize that you have been left on your own, dependent entirely on your own resources. But now those resources begin to appear, just as if your guru were still with you, by your side. And you can see that it is only now, having been abandoned by your teacher, just when you finally felt unreservedly open to him, that your real journey can begin.

In the beginning, we rely entirely on the guru to bring us to ourselves. Through our relationship, through the informal interactions, the teachings, and the rituals, the guru acts as the midwife of our own rebirth.

The guru's mediation brings us to the practice itself, through which we begin to make our own relationship with our deeper selves and with the cosmos. In the beginning, the human guru must give voice to these realities beyond ego, because we are as yet unable to hear them in any other way. But through our practice, it comes to be that our inner nature and the world beyond thought begin to speak for themselves. Through this process, we begin to discover that the voice of our human guru can be heard not just in his human speech or actions, but in and through our practice, and in and through our experience altogether. This may be termed the "universality of the guru" or the "cosmic guru," wherein the guru principle or force becomes more and more evident to us, wherever we may be and whatever we may be doing. The human guru, then, comes to be understood as the human representative and spokesperson for the living intelligence and sacredness of what is, the voice of reality itself in all its infinite ways of appearing.

The transition from seeing the guru as an external person to seeing him or her as a living force within us usually occurs gradually as the practitioner traverses the path. Sometimes, however, it is brought about abruptly by the death of the teacher. Tenzin Palmo, an Englishwoman who spent many years in retreat in India, provides an account of her own experience of the transformation that followed the unexpected death of her guru Khamtrül Rinpoche:

> [His death] was an incredible shock. He was only forty-eight years old, and we were not expecting it. At first it was really devastating. It was like being in a huge desert and suddenly losing your guide, this sense of being totally abandoned and the thought that I would never see him again. I remember crying and crying. I never realized I could cry so much.
>
> The pain in my heart was so intense that it was an excellent object of meditation, because it was very obvious. So I looked into the pain in my heart, and as I looked it was like layer after layer peeled away until in the end I reached this level of great peace and calm, almost bliss, and I realized that of course the Lama is always in your heart. You are never apart from your

Lama. The physical manifestation is the most gross level, and when you really think and contemplate the Lama, he's there right with you, in the most intimate part of yourself. So from feeling incredibly abandoned and despairing, I suddenly felt extremely happy.[29]

CONCLUSION

Many people are suspicious of Buddhism in general and particularly of the Vajrayana because of the intensity of the guru-disciple relationship. They are made uncomfortable by the level of projections that occur in the interaction of teacher and student. They do not like the lack of explicit restrictions, rules, and limitations on the relationship. They would prefer clear expectations and boundaries, without the uncertainty and intimacy that Vajrayana Buddhism implies.

Without denying the dangers in this as in all other intimate human relationships, and acknowledging that there can be no complete guarantee against mistakes and abuses, still there would appear something shortsighted in this point of view. As long as human beings live in the realm of samsaric duality, there is the inevitability of projection—in this case the positive projections of seeing something "out there" to which we are attracted and that we feel we need. What is sometimes not sufficiently realized is that no human beings are outside of this cycle.

Moreover, projection of this nature is not an inherently bad or undesirable thing. In fact, it is only because we are willing to project, willing to seek our dreams, that we can come up short and begin to integrate the part of ourselves that we had at first seen as outside. People do get "stuck," but usually not forever. This process always involves vulnerability and suffering, but only in a culture that abhors pain and equates it with evil can one fail to see the transformative element.

The Vajrayana operates by eliciting and provoking the projections of our own deepest nature, then forcing us back on ourselves so that we have to integrate and take possession of those projections. This process is seen no more clearly than in the relation of teacher and student that forms the backbone of the path. Trungpa Rinpoche comments that at the beginning of the path, the teacher is seen virtually as a demigod. In the middle, he is experienced as a friend and companion. And at the end, when we have attained the state of realization that we once saw uniquely in him, he becomes inseparable from the inborn, living wisdom within.

What is sad is not to see this process of projection in Buddhism, where it can lead to something dignified and noble, but to see the way that it operates in the contemporary "modern" world, where it so often leads to an utter dead end. Here, people project their deepest yearnings onto things that have little to do with the human spirit and its maturation—new cars, upscale houses, clothes, vacations, credentials, fame, wealth, and power. It is not surprising, for example, that it is often among those who have succeeded most fully in realizing the materialism of the American Dream that one can find the most emptiness, fear, and unacknowledged despair.

9

Entering the Vajrayana Path

THE HINAYANA AND MAHAYANA STAGES OF THE Tibetan Buddhist path provide the necessary ground for the Vajrayana. In the Hinayana, by means of shamatha, the practitioner has trained in the mindfulness practice of following the breath. Through this simple technique, one has overcome the wildness of discursive thought and is no longer blown here and there, distracted by every thought that arises. In possession of one's attention, one's awareness can be directed at will. The result of shamatha training is a certain collectedness and stillness and, most important, presence to one's experience. Vipashyana, as we saw in chapter 4, arises out of shamatha, and involves the experience of non-egoic awareness in which reality is seen from a viewpoint that transcends one's own narrow field of self-interest. More and more, things are experienced on their own terms. As the experience of vipashyana develops through practice, the world increasingly comes to be seen not as cold and mechanical, but as filled with warmth and intelligence that continually arise to correct one's balance and invite one into relationship with reality beyond ego.

Through the Mahayana, the practitioner's awareness extends out further and further, leading to relaxation and bringing all sentient beings into view. Through practices like tonglen, one trains in overcoming addiction to pleasure and aversion to pain, and thereby reverses the usual logic of ego. Through this, the meditator's heart becomes open and tender, and one's ability to sense and to feel existence develops new subtlety. In so doing, there develops a deeper availability to the world, in constantly extending oneself outward and making oneself available even in the face of threat or suffering. In so doing, one has come to the threshold of Vajrayana.

From the very first glimpse of vipashyana, we have been aware that there is a world beyond our own version that is real, vivid, and filled with intelligence. In the Mahayana, through extending ourselves to other sentient beings, and through ever-deeper realization of the "emptiness" of our own preconceptions about reality, we become more and more sensitized to this "real world" that exists beyond thought, the realm of "isness," or *dharmata*. As we continue to practice, we become more and more drawn to this level of being. A longing to know this world, to touch it, taste it, and experience it more fully, to enter into it completely, and finally to *become* it, with no residue of ego left over, marks the inspiration to enter Vajrayana. Indeed, as we approach the gate of Vajrayana, we realize that it is ultimately this inspiration that led us to the dharma in the first place; and it is this that underlies the devotion that we feel to the vajra master.

THE PRELIMINARY PRACTICES (NGÖNDRO)

In order to fully enter into Vajrayana practice, it is necessary to undergo *abhisheka*, Vajrayana initiation or empowerment. Before this can occur, however, one's state of being needs to be further softened, ripened, and opened. This is brought about through the *ngöndro,* or "preliminary practices," the four practices of prostrations, Vajrasattva mantra, mandala offering, and guru yoga, each of which is performed one hundred thousand times. Within Tibetan Buddhism, there are several different traditions of the ngöndro, although they agree in their essentials and have the same general function. To give an impression of the kinds of variations that exist, for example, in the Karma Kagyü tradition, the ngöndro are generally performed sequentially—one carries out first prostrations, then Vajrasattva mantra, and so on, in linear sequence. Not until prostrations are completed is it appropriate to enter into Vajrasattva practice. Among the Nyingmapas, practitioners typically carry out their ngöndro in a sequential way, as do the Kagyüpas, beginning with prostrations. However, unlike them, they are often encouraged to perform the liturgy of the entire ngöndro text. In this case, they only emphasize and count one of the practices, beginning with prostrations, and do a small amount of each of the other ngöndro in each session. Among the Nyingmapas, another ngöndro is typically added, that of one hundred thousand repetitions of a formula similar to refuge, making five in all.

The tradition summarized here is the one typically followed in the Karma Kagyü lineage. The general outline of the ngöndro, abhisheka, and sadhana practices discussed here are not particularly secret and are now found in books by both Western scholars and Tibetan teachers. The more detailed and experiential instruction is reserved for the personal relationship and mutual commitment between teacher and student. It can only be transmitted orally, and can never be given only in writing. For this reason, the following description is necessarily reticent in relation to the oral instructions for these and the inner experiences that they involve.

Prostrations

Like the other ngöndro, prostrations involve a simple practice that is repeated one hundred thousand times. Prostrations involve repeating some version of the refuge formula over and over and, while doing so, carrying out the physical act of prostrating. To begin with one places on a shrine a picture of the human teachers and realized beings who make up the lineage one is following. These are typically arranged in what is called a lineage tree, upon whose branches these figures are depicted as sitting. In the central position on the lower branches in front is Vajradhara (see figure 9.1), who is considered inseparable from one's own principal teacher. Vajradhara is blue in color, like the cloudless sky, and sits in cross-legged meditation posture. He holds a dorje (vajra) in his right hand and a bell (see figure 10.5 on page 215) in his left, symbolizing the union of wisdom and skillful means, emptiness and compassion, feminine and masculine, and indeed all dualities. Because Vajradhara and one's root guru are inseparable, the practitioner may visualize Vajradhara with the guru's face and demeanor. At the very top of the refuge tree is a smaller Vajradhara, in the Kagyü and other New Translation schools representing the ultimate dharmakaya. Below him and also smaller than the central figure of the guru as Vajradhara, are the human lineage masters seated in descending fashion, beginning with Tilopa, Naropa, and Marpa, while *dharmapalas* (guardian deities), yidams, and other figures are arranged around the main figure on the lower branches.

The inseparability of the guru and Vajradhara points to a critical theme in the Vajrayana. For whatever practice one is carrying out, the buddha or yidam is always seen as inseparable from one's own teacher. This is because it is only through the guru that one is able to encounter the dharmakaya buddhas and all the other transcendent realities met in tantric practice. It also serves to personalize Vajradhara, the other buddhas, and the yidams. Without this, the vajra world would be too cold, remote, and abstract. To see it in this way would be a fatal misunderstanding. The vajra world is, in fact, not indifferent. It *will* reveal itself to us, to help and heal, to liberate us. And the way it does so is through the human being who is our mentor. In a very real sense, then, the ultimate has a human face. Therefore, the inseparability of Vajradhara and one's guru is not a psychological trick—it expresses a fundamental aspect of reality itself.

The practitioner sits in front of his or her shrine and, using the detailed description given in the prostration liturgy, visualizes the lineage tree in as clear and complete a fashion as possible. One then begins doing prostrations, moving from a standing position, going down to one's knees, then putting one's hands on the floor and sliding them forward until one is lying face down, flat upon the floor. One then gets up and prostrates again. In the West where many homes are carpeted, practitioners often use a "prostration board" (such as a sheet of particle board), to make the process of sliding the hands out easier. During this, one recites a stanza of taking refuge, a variation of the formula "I take refuge in the Buddha, I take refuge in the dharma, I take refuge in the sangha."

For Westerners, with our ideology of equality and individualism,

FIGURE 9.1 *Kagyü lineage tree.*

prostrations can rouse a surprising amount of resistance and emotionality. It is one thing to bow to a teacher on a high seat and sit reverentially
listening to a lecture, as is common practice in Tibetan Buddhism in the
West. It is quite another to prostrate oneself over and over before a
Buddhist shrine and to a blue buddha called Vajradhara who is inseparable from one's human guru. The idea of prostrating to another per-

son, even if it is one's guru, and having to do this one hundred thousand times, can be hard to take. Moreover, the physical act of prostration is inherently humiliating, and we may find ourselves protesting in the most vigorous, energetic, and inventive ways. Many questions arise: Why am I doing this? What is this? What or whom am I really prostrating to? Why do I have to prostrate? Isn't there some other way to accomplish the same end? Moreover, prostrations are physically exhausting and time-consuming. In the Western mind if not in the traditional Tibetan, the thought frequently arises, "Surely there is something better I could be doing with my time and energy." Bringing these questions to one's teacher, one typically meets with the response: "Don't think too much; just do the practice, and your questions will be answered; we can talk about this after you have finished." Through the practice, in fact, questions do have a way of resolving themselves.

Prostrations, like the other Vajrayana practices, involve body (performing the physical action), speech (reciting the liturgical formula), and mind (visualizing). In this case, the visualization, the repetition of the refuge formula, and the physical prostrations work together to involve the body, speech and mind of the practitioner in the main intention of the practice, which is to invite surrender. Surrender to what? To the larger world—as it is variously expressed—of non-ego, things as they are, the buddha-nature, the lineage of awakened ones, and so on.

One might ask why the physical aspect in particular is necessary. Couldn't it be converted into a mental dimension? In Vajrayana Buddhism, the physical, as much as the vocal and the mental, are *symbols* in the special sense that they embody truth and reality in a way that cannot be converted to another idiom. As is said in the Vajrayana, "The symbol symbolizes nothing other than itself." Prostrating repeatedly on the ground before something has an immediate, visceral meaning before any interpretation is offered. It is, in and of itself, humbling and stirs up strong emotional ego responses. As mentioned, the physical is an inherent realm of meaning, a kind of language in and of itself, like speech and mind. The recognition of body, speech, and mind as distinct languages and symbolisms is part of this "skillful" aspect of the Vajrayana.

In order to understand prostrations properly, it is necessary to remember the nontheistic perspective within which the practice occurs. The object of prostration is the ultimate buddha, Vajradhara in the New Translation schools, inseparable from one's personal teacher. Vajradhara is an external representation of the selfless wisdom of our own basic nature, all-encompassing, all accommodating, and beyond change. He is sky-blue in color because the sky is experienced as similarly all-embracing and eternal. When we prostrate, it is thus ultimately our self-conscious ego that is prostrating to the inherent nature. This process may be illustrated by the following analogy. Suppose it happens that we have been less than honest with a friend and, to avoid poisoning the relationship, are faced with the necessity of having to acknowledge what we have done. Our deeper wisdom makes it crystal-clear that we acted in a wrongful manner and that we must openly admit our misdeed. But another part of us, the defensive, proud ego, does not want to be humiliated and brought down in this manner. At some point, our ego—the lower part of ourselves—has to surrender to the higher part—what we know to be right, true, and necessary. And this can be extraordinarily painful. Prostrations are a way of turning such a process into a formal spiritual practice.

Vajrasattva Mantra

The second of the four ngöndro, Vajrasattva mantra, is more inward and subtle. Prostration practice, through the commitment and surrender it involves, wears away the facade covering our ego, churns up its primitive emotions, and reveals its infantile emotionality. The emotional and egocentric underbelly that we have kept hidden from ourselves and others has finally been exposed. It is the purpose of the Varjasattva practice to purify this material. Here one visualizes the buddha Vajrasattva, the embodiment of our own fundamental purity, our buddha-nature. He is visualized on the top of the head as a white being, sitting in meditation posture, holding in his right hand a vajra (dorje) at his heart center and in his left at his hip, a bell. In Vajrasattva's heart center, there is the "seed syllable" HUM, embodying his essence.

Currently Tibetan teachers ask their Western students to visualize this and other syllables used in visualization practice in Tibetan characters. For those who are not familiar with the written Tibetan language, this can be challenging. Western practitioners sometimes point out that when Buddhism traveled to Tibet, Tibetans were permitted to visualize the seed syllables and mantras using the Tibetan script and therefore Westerners might perhaps be able to carry out these visualizations using their own alphabets. The inadvisability of this, for at least some Tibetan teachers, has to do with the fact that Sanskrit and Tibetan (the written alphabet of which was adapted from Sanskrit) are written syllabically: a single figure represents a complete syllable, containing the vowels and consonants of that syllable. This stands in obvious contrast to European languages in which a single syllable may contain many letters strung together. The former lends itself relatively easily to visualization, while the latter does not. In addition, the Tibetan approach, because its script is an adaptation of the Indian, is a virtual replication of the Indian Tantric Buddhist methods. Still, particularly among the younger Tibetan teachers, there are some who seem to be leaning toward allowing visualizations in English.

In the Vajrasattva practice a liturgical element is introduced that will be important throughout the Vajrayana journey, namely infusion of the *samayasattva* ("conventional being") by the *jnanasattva* ("wisdom being"). *Samayasattva* refers to the visualization, which we ourselves have generated, of Varjasattva on top of our heads. So far, this is just a product of our own imagination, as if, near lunchtime, we might visualize ourselves going out for a hamburger to allay our hunger. Our own imagined visualization of Vajrasattva needs to be ritually empowered, made real—"sanctified," in our Western terminology. It needs to take on the transcendent wisdom that it points to. To do this, one visualizes light rays streaming out from the heart center of Vajrasattva and inviting, from beyond samsara, the jnanasattva, the wisdom principle that will animate our visualization.

One may ask, where is "beyond samsara"? Theoretically, one could say that it is the buddha-nature within us. However, we do not have ready access to this level of our own inwardness, since we tend to see

ourselves as samsaric through and through. Therefore, saying that "beyond samsara" is within us would not be very helpful, at least at this
stage of practice. The realm beyond samsara can also be visualized "outside," beyond our known world, as in the case of the pure lands of the
buddhas (for discussion of this, see *Indestructible Truth*). In the beginning, this "location" is effective. Thus the jnanasattvas, the wisdom beings, come from all directions like snowflakes and dissolve into
Vajrasattva. Now he is an embodiment of nonconceptual wisdom and
animated with the power of vajra being. As devout Roman Catholics
will tell you in relation to the moment when, in Holy Communion, the
ordinary bread and wine become the very body and blood of Christ,
one can have the experience here of something more than just one's
own imagination.

The practitioner now begins to recite the hundred-syllable mantra of
Vajrasattva. In Tibet, owing to their sanctity and power, the Indian
mantras were not translated, but left in their original form. For this
reason, Westerners, like Tibetans, repeat the mantra in Sanskrit: OM
VAJRASATTVA SAMAYAM ANUPALAYA, VAJRASATTVA TVENOPA TISHTHA . . . ,"
a mantra that will be repeated one hundred thousand times. Although
many Sanskrit mantras do not have any particular literal meaning,
much of the Vajrasattva mantra does, and can be roughly translated
into English. The translation is often given to Western students to increase their sense of the significance of the practice: "O Vajrasattva,
please purify, please protect me. . . ." While reciting the mantra, one
visualizes *amrita* (elixir of immortality), the embodiment of the death-
less wisdom of realization in the form of a white liquid, flowing from
the HUM syllable (fig. 9.2) in Vajrasattva's heart center, filling his body,
then exuding from the lower part of his body and entering the top of
one's head. This liquid light—for that is what it is—then flows down
through one's body, down into the earth. First it comes as a tiny trickle,
then as a growing stream, finally a river of wisdom, purifying all of
one's evil deeds and obscurations. One visualizes that one is gradually
becoming cleansed and purified.

In the Vajrayana, it is often said that the fundamental impurity in
our state of being is our discursive thought, our misconceiving and dis-

FIGURE 9.2 *Tibetan syllable* HUM, *the primordial sound of emptiness.*

torting the basic sacred reality of what is.* We take our vajra being and the vajra world and defile their purity and sacredness with our thought process. Through Vajrasattva practice, we literally wash away that defilement. In the beginning, we may experience only fleeting moments

*It is always our impure discursive thought that underlies all our words and actions causing harm to others. This point of view is, of course, fundamental to Buddhism

when our discursive thought ceases and we experience things without the pollution of its distorting process. But the eventual goal is to learn to live out of that level of ourselves where our perception is indeed pure. This way of experiencing things is called in Tibetan *tag-nang,* which may be translated as "pure perception" or "sacred outlook." For Western practitioners, with a cultural heritage of ideas of original sin, evil, and inherent human imperfection, Vajrasattva practice represents a blatant challenge to fundamental ways of viewing self and world.

Mandala Offering

Vajrasattva practice may have left us with a sense of accomplishment. The usual samsaric approach is, of course, to view all of our attainments—material, social, psychological, and spiritual—as our property and key to the process of maintaining our personal identity. At this point, there is the danger that we will take our practices, including our prostrations and Vajrasattva mantra recitations, in the same way, converting them into subtle self-aggrandizement.

In true Mahayana fashion, these and all the spiritual and other riches that we may come upon must now be relinquished and given away. Particularly in relation to our Buddhist practice, any other approach would provide the ego ground to solidify and fortify itself as a "highly evolved and accomplished spiritual person," fostering pride and arrogance. In the mandala, ideally one would offer gold and silver. In the *Lives of the Eighty-four Mahasiddhas,* we read that when King Indrapala (later Darika) and his minister arrived before the siddha Luyipa to request abhisheka, having neglected to bring an appropriate gift, they found it necessary to offer themselves, and it took them each twelve years to discharge the debt.[1] In lieu of such extensive offerings, in the practice, one heaps gold-colored rice with one hand onto a "mandala plate," usually of copper or brass, that is held in the other hand. This

---

throughout its history, beginning with the early *Dhammapada,* but it is especially emphasized in the Vajrayana.

rice, often containing gems, semiprecious gems, coins, and other precious items to indicate wealth, represents all of the riches of whatever sort that we humans possess or enjoy, including even trees and animals, the earth and the sky, the sun, moon, and stars, as well as all our human possessions, both material and nonmaterial. All of this is to be offered to the buddhas and to the lineage, for the sake of our own accomplishment and for the sake of all other sentient beings. Having piled this wealth in the form of sand onto the plate, we offer it, reciting an accompanying verse. In doing so, we visualize everything that we may possess being offered.

It may be thought that this practice is "only" symbolic and involves "only" our minds. However, recall that most of the life we live is actually lived in, through, and by our minds—our minds are the generator of actions and their meaning, and the recipient as well. The physical part only has significance because of what we attribute to it and think about it. In addition, the mandala practice has an important physical dimension: one is holding golden rice and jewel representations, and to us humans these have meanings of richness and wealth. To hold in one's hand symbolizes possession. Moreover, with one's offering hand, one is physically offering this to the visualized lineage in front. Here, as elsewhere in the Vajrayana, the physical actions with their accompanying meanings give the practice its particular power. To engage ourselves in this kind of visualization and action, over and over, has its own profound and powerful effect.

In one way we are not "really" offering everything that we have, but in another way we actually are. Think how pleasurable it is to visualize ourselves winning the lottery, gaining a desired partner, or enjoying a delicious meal. Just in carrying out the imagination of these things, we are participating in the meaning of the event, although it has not physically occurred. Think how painful it is when we contemplate losing someone we love, being deprived of our material possessions, becoming ill with a dreaded disease, or dying. The same logic applies: when we go through something negative in our imagination, we experience much of the distress of the actual event. In fact, it sometimes happens that our anticipation of a painful event fills us with more suffering than the event itself when it finally transpires. In the same way, the offerings made in the mandala practice, though mostly imagined, have the stamp of reality. We do not want to give away whatever good things we have, and to imagine ourselves doing so can be difficult and painful.

The purpose of this practice is to give birth, in us, to a different attitude toward "our" possessions. Moreover, this new attitude is not an alien one—except to ego—for it expresses a kind of open-handedness and generosity that is natural to us, as qualities of our buddha-nature. To learn how to give freely, completely, and without reservation is, in the end, the only way to keep moving along the spiritual path. And giving without any demand or anticipation of recompense, even social or psychological, is the way to be most helpful to others, for it leaves them unencumbered in their own journeys by our own wants and ex-pectations.

Guru Yoga

The mandala practice leaves one in a rather empty place, having given away virtually everything thought of as one's own and as definitive of one's person. But emptiness is also openness, and the practice has left the practitioner as a "worthy vessel" to receive Vajrayana teachings. The image of the student as vessel is an important and often-used one in Vajrayana Buddhism. The disciple may be like a vessel turned upside down and unable to receive any teachings. This refers to people who are so full of opinions and so smug about their spirituality that they are not really able to receive what the teacher has to offer. Or the disciple may be like a vessel full of holes, wherein the water of instruction can be poured in, but then just runs out the bottom. This refers to a person who, while open enough, has no discipline to put the teachings into practice, and so the instructions just dissipate and produce no lasting benefit.

The purpose of the first three ngöndro, culminating in the mandala offering, is to render the disciple a fit vessel to actually receive the wis-dom of the lineage in the proper manner. In fact, from the first moment of meditation at the Hinayana level up to the beginning of guru yoga, the practitioner has been developing the openness to receive the dharma teachings in their full extent and also the discipline to engage in the contemplative practices that can bring these teachings to fruition in his or her being.

In the guru yoga, one visualizes the guru in the form of Vajradhara sitting on the top of the head. Rousing devotion for the teacher, one recites a particular mantra associated with the guru and visualizes the *amrita* of blessings flowing down and filling the empty vessel of one's body. Through guru yoga, literally "union with the teacher," the meditator seeks to unite with the wisdom mind of the guru.

All four of the ngöndro have implications that extend beyond the preliminary practices themselves. For example, as we shall see, each of the ngöndro appears in different contexts in the course of full Vajrayana practice. Thus, through the preliminaries one is not only preparing to receive abhisheka but also learning specific practices that will be useful as the subsequent path unfolds. For example, prostrations are offered when meeting a high lama, listening to tantric teaching, or receiving an abhisheka. In a similar manner, the Vajrasattva mantra is performed in the course of regular tantric practice and also at points when additional purification is called for. And both the mandala offering and guru yoga appear throughout the course of the tantric journey. Among these, the guru yoga is somewhat unique because, after one has taken abhisheka, it constitutes a practice in and of itself that may be carried out in retreat and as part of ongoing daily practice. Nyingmapas, for example, perform the guru yoga of Guru Rinpoche regularly. After Chögyam Trungpa died in 1987, H.H. Dilgo Khyentse Rinpoche composed a guru yoga to enable Trungpa Rinpoche's students to maintain contact with his realized energy and continue to receive his blessings.

The implications of the four ngöndro also extend beyond the abhisheka in another way, in that each of them embodies basic themes that run throughout the transformative process of the Vajrayana. For example, prostrations embody the surrender that is required at each step on one's tantric path. The Vajrasattva mantra entails the purification, the washing away of discursive thinking, that is the essence of the Vajrayana meditation. And the mandala offering represents the generosity and lack of territoriality that must accompany everything one does as a tantric practitioner, lest it be perverted in the direction of self-aggrandizement.

In a similar way, guru yoga embodies the openness and devotion without which Vajrayana practice is not possible. In this regard, Dzigar Kongtrül Rinpoche explains that guru yoga is not only the fourth and culminating member of the ngöndro but, in a very real sense, the essence of Vajrayana practice itself.

> The Vajrayana path is not something that you can learn and master like an art form; it is not a skill. It is the unbroken lineage of gurus passing down their blessings. And these blessings manifest as the realization that dawns in an individual's mind dependent solely on guru yoga and the practice of devotion. In fact, the practice of guru yoga and the practice of devotion in guru yoga represent the crucial point of Vajrayana. We talk about the importance of study and practice and, of course, these are needed and necessary. But without the practice of guru yoga, there can be no realization at all. And, in fact, even if one's study and practice are lacking, if one just does guru yoga with a whole heart, this can be enough.[2]

POINTING OUT THE NATURE OF MIND

At some point in one's Vajrayana training, particularly in the Kagyü and Nyingma lineages, the disciple is given the "pointing-out instructions or "introduction to the nature of mind" (*ngo-trö*) by the root guru. In some cases, the "pointing out" occurs after completion of the ngöndro, prior to receiving abhisheka. In other cases, it may be given at the very beginning of Vajrayana practice, before one undertakes ngöndro practice. In still other instances, the nature of mind may be introduced independently of where one is on the path, on rare occasions even before one has learned to meditate. Generally, though, it occurs somewhere in the context of the practice of the Vajrayana.

Until recent times, the pointing-out instructions were generally given in the individual meeting of guru and disciple. In addition, this was a secret event, not to be discussed with others. Trungpa Rinpoche commented that one of his own principal teachers, Khenpo Gangshar, was quite unusual in that he was able to give pointing-out instructions to large groups of disciples. This was a practice imparted to Trungpa Rinpoche, as one of two people empowered in this special tradition of ngotrö or pointing out, and Rinpoche followed it in his Vajrayana teaching in the West. At the three-month training programs given to his advanced students, preliminary Vajrayana teaching would sometimes be given to as many as three or four hundred people at one time, culminating in "pointing out," after which students would begin their ngöndro.

The pointing out of mind could be a seemingly low-key and unexceptional event. In his well-known book, the *Tibetan Book of Living and Dying*, Sogyal Rinpoche recounts two occasions in which his guru, Jamyang Khyentse Rinpoche, introduced him to the nature of mind.

> The first of these moments occurred when I was six or seven years old. It took place in that special room in which Jamyang Khyentse lived, in front of a large portrait statue of his previous incarnation, Jamyang Khyentse Wangpo. This was a solemn, awe-inspiring figure, made more so when the flame of the butter-lamp in front of it would flicker and light up its face. Before I knew what was happening, my master did something most unusual. He suddenly hugged me and lifted me off my feet. Then he gave me a huge kiss on the side of my face. For a long moment, my mind fell away completely and I was enveloped by a tremendous tenderness, warmth, confidence, and power.
>
> The next occasion was more formal, and it happened at Lhodrak Kharchu, in a cave in which the great saint and father of Tibetan Buddhism, Padmasambhava, had meditated. We had stopped there on our pilgrimage through southern Tibet. I was about nine at the time. My master sent for me and told me to sit in front of him. We were alone. He said, "Now I'm going to introduce you to the essential 'nature of mind.'" Picking up his bell and small hand-drum, he chanted the invocation of all the

masters of the lineage, from the Primordial Buddha down to his own master. Then he did the introduction. Suddenly he sprang on me a question with no answer: "What is mind?" and gazed intently deep into my eyes. I was taken totally by surprise. My mind shattered. No words, no names, no thought remained—no mind, in fact, at all.[3]

At the same time, the pointing out could be abrupt and dramatic. Such an occasion occurred in the life of Naropa when Tilopa opened his disciple's awareness by hitting him across the face with a shoe. Paltrül Rinpoche experienced something similar from the guru Do Khyentse, a highly realized and unconventional dzokchen master. Tulku Thondup provides the following account:

One day Do Khyentse, who was wandering while performing esoteric exercises, suddenly showed up outside Paltrul's tent. Do Khyentse shouted, "O Palge! If you are brave, come out!" When Paltrul respectfully came out, Do Khyentse grabbed him by his hair, threw him on the ground, and dragged him around. At that moment, Paltrul smelled alcohol on Do Khyentse's breath and thought, "The Buddha expounded on the dangers of alcohol, yet even a great adept like [Do Khyentse] could get drunk like this." At that instant, Do Khyentse freed Paltrul from his grip and shouted, "Alas, that you intellectual people could have such evil thoughts! You Old Dog!" Do Khyentse spat in his face, showed him his little finger (an insulting gesture), and departed. Paltrul realized, "Oh, I am deluded. He was performing an esoteric exercise to introduce me to my enlightened nature." Paltrul was torn by two conflicting feelings: shock over his own negative thoughts and amazement at Do Khyentse's clairvoyance. Sitting up, he immediately meditated on the enlightened nature of his mind, and a clear, skylike, open, intrinsic awareness awakened in him.[4]

The pointing out could often arouse intense devotion on the part of the disciple. Dilgo Khyentse Rinpoche recalls the pointing out he experienced from his guru, Gyaltsap Rinpoche:

I was often overwhelmed by the splendor and magnificence of
his expression and his eyes as, with a gesture pointing in my
direction, he introduced the nature of mind. I felt that, apart
from my own feeble devotion that made me see the teacher as
an ordinary man, this was in fact exactly the same as the great
Guru Padmasambhava himself giving [instruction] to the
twenty-five disciples. My confidence grew stronger and
stronger, and when again he would gaze and point at me, asking, "What is the nature of mind?," I would think with great
devotion, "This is truly a great yogi who can see the absolute
nature of reality!"[5]

What is the quality of that "moment" when the nature of mind is
pointed out? Sogyal Rinpoche, reflecting on his own experience at the
age of nine with Jamyang Khyentse, describes it as follows:

Past thoughts had died away; the future had not yet arisen; the
stream of my thoughts was cut right through. In that pure
shock a gap opened, and in that gap was laid bare a sheer, immediate awareness of the present, one that was free of any
clinging. It was simple, naked, and fundamental. And yet that
naked simplicity was also radiant with the warmth of immense
compassion.

How many things I could say about that moment! My master, apparently, was asking a question; yet I knew he did not
expect an answer. And before I could hunt for an answer, I
knew there was none to find. I sat thunderstruck in wonder,
and yet a deep and glowing certainty I have never known before
was welling up within me.[6]

The pointing out is a necessary analogue to Vajrayana practice because it provides a sense of direction and confidence to one's practice. It
is as if you were journeying through fog and mist, trying to find a
certain mountain that you had heard about, but you were not quite sure
where it lay, what it looked like, or whether it really existed at all.
Suppose suddenly that the fog lifted for a moment and you could see

that mountain clearly, in all its majesty and glory. You could take a compass reading at that moment and know in which direction to go. Furthermore, you could proceed with a confidence that was lacking before, for you had seen the actual thing and what it looked like. When the fog again descended, the lack of visibility would no longer derail your progress, because you would know precisely where the mountain lay and could keep advancing regardless of the weather. And you would be better fit to endure the dangers and struggles encountered along the way because you knew for certain that the goal was real.

In a similar way, before pointing-out instructions, the nature of realization—the inherent awakened awareness within—was only a matter of hearsay and speculation. After experiencing the nature of mind, one knows the end point of the path that one is traveling. This gives tremendous inspiration and trust. In addition, by having tasted the immaculate wisdom within, one is less apt to become confused and get lost in sidetracks. And one is less likely to take conditioned experiences and partial realizations for full awakening. As Sogyal Rinpoche says, the experience of pointing out leaves one with a deep inner certainty, relaxation, and joy.

ABHISHEKA

The purpose of ngöndro is to prepare the disciple for full entry into the Vajrayana. That entry occurs with the initiation ceremony known as abhisheka, literally empowerment. In India, the abhisheka was probably originally a ritual of coronation wherein a prince was invested and empowered as a king. The principle of the abhisheka is found in the conventional Mahayana literature dealing with the *bhumis*, or higher stages on the journey to buddhahood. There it is described as the empowerment that one receives when reaching the bhumi of buddhahood. At this bhumi, through the abhisheka ritual, a bodhisattva is invested and empowered as a dharma king—a fully enlightened buddha—and, by virtue of his enlightenment, reigns over the entire universe.

In Vajrayana Buddhism, the abhisheka is similarly a rite of coronation in which the disciple becomes a king or a queen in the dharmic sense. Through the ritual, he or she is connected with the dharma king or queen within, the buddha-nature, and experiences the power and dignity of that state. Having experienced this, one may then practice so that this condition of fruition becomes the foundation of the path, the basis upon which one meditates, the distinctive keynote of the Vajrayana.

Through the liturgy of the abhisheka, one is introduced to the nature of true reality. This nature has shape, color, sound—indeed it is the underlying and generally hidden "pure land" of which the conventional, conceptualized world is but a dim reflection.

The abhisheka leads us into a "vajra world" that is quite different from the habitual realm which we usually inhabit. This vajra world is none other than the domain of the mandala discussed in the previous chapter. In this world, there is no substance or permanence, but rather the continual and unceasing play of the energies of the five wisdoms. This world is shocking because within it there is no room for ego or its petty, self-serving perspectives. On the other hand, the vajra world opened up by the abhisheka is recognized as our true home, for it frees us from the deadly and claustrophobic prison of "I," "me," and "mine."

Prior to abhisheka, we perceived the fundamental power of reality as external to us, localized primarily in our teacher. Through the ritual, that power is now revealed to be within us and confirmed as our essential nature. One feels, indeed, that one has finally come into possession of one's true being.

The abhisheka is thus a central moment in one's relationship to the guru. It is said that in the ritual there is a "meeting of two minds," of the teacher and the disciple. This "meeting" can occur because we feel devotion and love to that which, seen initially in our teacher, is now seen to be the very same "nature of reality" that is growing and maturing in ourselves. In the abhisheka, an opening can occur so that we glimpse the inseparability of our selves and the guru: what he or she is and what we most fundamentally are embody one selfsame reality. Thus the abhisheka is a process by which the vast power of our own inner buddha-nature, is finally called to life.

Once the disciple has been introduced into the vajra world of the guru and his or her lineage, it becomes important to deepen the connection to that world. Each abhisheka is associated with a particular yidam, or "personal deity," and confers permission to engage in the various practices of that yidam cycle. Taking initiation and receiving the practices, as we shall see, also implies a commitment to a certain level of Vajrayana practice within that cycle.

The necessity of such a commitment is not far to seek. It is as if the abhisheka establishes an umbilical cord between ourselves as the fetus and the vajra world as the mother. In this situation, we cannot live without continual nourishment from the mother. It is the purpose of our practice to keep the umbilical cord fresh and wet, so that the nourishment of the vajra world can continue to flow to us and enliven us. Without following the abhisheka with regular, sustained practice, the umbilical cord dries up and we suffocate in the toxins and airlessness of our habitual patterns.

In Tibetan tradition, many different abhishekas are known. The particular abhisheka that one receives depends both upon the lineage of the teacher and upon one's specific karmic dispositions and needs as a disciple. In India and Tibet, teachers would recommend specific abhishekas and their associated practices as particularly appropriate to individuals at certain moments in their paths. At the same time, specific abhisheka cycles were the specialty of particular lineages and given to all Vajrayana students in that lineage. For example, in the Kagyü lineage, the abhishekas surrounding the yidams Vajrayogini and Chakrasamvara are considered important for all practitioners.

In the earlier days of the Vajrayana in India, it appears that tantric practitioners often received just one abhisheka—such as that of Guhyasamaja, Hevajra, Chakrasamvara, or Vajrayogini—and carried out that practice for many years until they attained realization. Most of the siddhas, after meeting their gurus, were given a particular abhisheka and then told to undertake the practice intensively, usually in retreat. The most typical period of time mentioned for these intensive practice periods is twelve years. The siddha would usually continue with the practice of that one yidam until the moment of realization.

By contrast, in recent times in Tibet and the West, people might receive dozens and sometimes even hundreds of "abhishekas" through large public ceremonial blessings (mentioned above) and other abhishekas to which they might win admittance. Trungpa Rinpoche remarked that it became common recently in Tibet, and now in the West, for people to go from one lama to another, taking as many abhishekas as possible. He said that this practice was not a particularly helpful one, for it generally led people to not take the abhisheka situation seriously. Such collecting could provide a kind of substitute spiritual life, giving people the false impression that they were moving ahead and diverting them from actually focusing upon one cycle and engaging in its intensive practice.

> Receiving abhishekas is not the same as collecting coins or stamps or the signatures of famous people. Receiving hundreds and hundreds of abhishekas and constantly collecting blessing after blessing as some kind of self-confirmation has at times become a fad, a popular thing to do. This was true in Tibet in the nineteenth century as well as more recently in the West. That attitude, which reflects the recent corruption in the presentation of the Vajrayana, has created an enormous misunderstanding. People who collect successive abhishekas in this manner regard them purely as a source of identity and as a further reference point. They collect abhishekas out of a need for security, which is a big problem.[7]

There is a middle ground between these two extremes of carrying out the practice of one abhisheka for life and taking a multitude of abhishekas while doing little or no practice at all. This middle ground, the mainline Vajrayana tradition in Tibet, was for a disciple to receive an abhisheka and carry out that practice for a set amount of time or until a certain number of mantra recitations were accomplished, as specified by the teacher. Then the teacher might either ask the disciple to repeat the process or give him or her directions to receive another empowerment and carry out the associated practices. Serious practitioners might still attend the large, general, public abhishekas, but they would understand that the commitments implied in doing so were entirely different from those made in the more serious, private abhishekas undergone at the specific instructions of their own teacher.

In Tibetan Buddhism, there has been a certain amount of latitude for practitioners to move between the various yidam practices they have been given. In this context, the ancient Indian model is worth pondering. Tulku Urgyen Rinpoche:

> An old saying has it that, "Tibetans ruin it for themselves by having too many deities." They think they have to practice one, then they have to practice another, then a third and a fourth. It goes on and on, and they end up not accomplishing anything, whereas in India a meditator would practice a single deity for his entire life and he would reach supreme accomplishment. It would be good if we were to take this attitude. If we practice [a certain yidam], it is perfectly complete to simply practice that single yidam. One doesn't have to be constantly shifting to different deities, afraid one will miss something, because there is absolutely nothing missing in the single yidam one practices. . . . Sometimes one feels tired with a particular practice, like "It's enough, practicing this one yidam!" Then you give up that one and try practicing another one, then after a while, another. . . . If you accomplish one buddha, then you accomplish all buddhas. If you attain the realization of one yidam, automatically you attain realization of all yidams at the same time.[8]

Preliminaries

WAITING PERIOD

Trungpa Rinpoche remarks that in ancient times, students might be notified half a year in advance of the abhisheka date.

> In that way students would have six months to prepare. Later the tantric tradition became extremely available, and some of the teachers in Tibet dropped that six-month rule—which

seems to have been a big mistake. If we do not have enough time to prepare ourselves for an abhisheka, then the message doesn't come across. There is no real experience. That suspense—knowing that we are just about to receive an abhisheka but that, at the same time, we are suspended for six months, is extremely important. We have no idea what we are going to do . . . we have no idea what we are going to experience.[9]

The waiting period was important because it separated disciples from their habitual, compulsive attachment to their ordinary lives—the great unknown of the abhisheka was looming—and it helped ripen the openness, humility, and daring needed to properly enter the ritual space of the abhisheka.

THE CHEMISTRY OF PARTICIPANTS

Trungpa Rinpoche remarks that the particular number and configuration of people to receive an abhisheka is critically important. It might be twenty-five people, or it might be three.

It is the discretion of the vajra master to decide on the number of students and to choose the particular students to be initiated, because he knows the students' development and their understanding. Receiving abhisheka is an extremely precious event. And the psychology that happens between people involved and the environment that such people create together are right at the heart of the matter.[10]

ATTITUDE OF THE DISCIPLE

The serious, nonpublic abhisheka is dealing with the deepest and most intimate part of the teacher and of ourselves. For this reason, an attitude of openness and trust between teacher and disciple is critical. This is partly a trust in the teacher, for we have come to know this person in many situations and have confidence in his or her insight, selflessness, and compassion. But at a deeper level, it is a trust in ourselves and our lives. We trust the journey we are on, and we have trust in our lives to the point where we are willing to open ourselves to the spiritual universe that beckons. We have come to realize that the more we try to hold on to life and control it, the more it slips away from us; and the more we open to it and surrender, the more we feel its abundance and find our rightful place within it. This rouses our longing to enter in more deeply, leads us to request abhisheka, and fuels the kind of radical openness that is necessary to receive the empowerment.

No genuine ritual space is ever "safe" for ego. When one invites the unseen powers to be present at the abhisheka, one is entering upon a process whose end result cannot be foreseen. That is why unconditioned trust and confidence are important. Anytime one opens oneself in such a fundamental and dramatic way, and to such a boundless source, part of the power of the situation is that there can be no guarantees. There is no such thing as a prenuptial agreement in Vajrayana Buddhism, any more than there can be any such guarantee anywhere in life, at least when one is dealing with reality.

In its earlier days in India, the nature of the abhisheka ritual probably varied considerably from one tantric tradition to another. In classical times in India and Tibet, however, a more or less standardized form came to be used in many lineages, and it is this form that one most often encounters today. In this standard form, the ceremony is divided into preparations and then "four abhishekas"—the vase, the secret, the prajna-jnana (knowledge-wisdom), and the "fourth" or "word" abhisheka. Each of these four is considered a separate empowerment because each conveys a different aspect of the awakened state.

PREPARATIONS

On the morning of the rite, the vajra master enters the ritual space and performs a ceremony of preparation. Here the intention of the forthcoming ritual is stated; the ground is purified of obstacles; and the mandala into which one will be ritually entered is laid out and empowered. The vajra master calls on the deities of the abhisheka and invites them to be present and participate in the rite. The various ritual implements and substances are also purified and empowered.

The Abhisheka Rite

The first of the four abhishekas, that of the vase, has five parts, corresponding to each of the five buddha families. In each, through the liturgy, one is connected with one of the five wisdoms. In (1) the vajra abhisheka, through being sprinkled from a ritual vase, one is symbolically bathed with water and thereby purified. In the vase abhisheka, the elements associated with the buddha families are not understood in the secular, ordinary sense. Rather here—once the conventional, conceptual obscuration has been dispelled through the ritual process—the elements are understood as wisdoms that naturally effect transformation. In this case, water is understood in the sense of its elemental nature to cleanse and purify. In (2) the ratna abhisheka, a crown is placed on one's head and connects one with the qualities of confidence, lack of threat, and richness of the ratna family. In (3) the padma abhisheka, a vajra is placed in one's hand. Trungpa Rinpoche says, "In this abhisheka you are acknowledged as a powerful person and at the same time you are told that you can make love [i.e., communicate genuinely] without destroying somebody else. Rather, you could create by making love. So holding the vajra brings a feeling of compassion, warmth, and hospitality."[11] In (4) the karma abhisheka, one is given a bell (ghanta) to hold, and one makes contact with the karma-family wisdom of all-accomplishing action: the bell's sound rings out as an imperative to perform whatever actions are called for by various situations. The ringing sounds out and fills the room: there is nowhere to hide from the command. In (5) the buddha abhisheka, a vajra and bell, tied together, are held over the head, and the bell is rung. This is also called the "name abhisheka" because here the disciple is given a Vajrayana name, the name he or she will have in the future as a tathagata, a fully enlightened buddha: "Now you are known as Shri So-and-So Tathagata." This name is secret and represents the innermost power of our person, the power that manifests itself in our most basic gift to the world, the inescapable and unthinking manifestation of our own energy, which—whether we like it or not— shows itself and effects transformation in our environment.

The second of the four abhishekas, the secret abhisheka, as well as the third and fourth, the prajna-jnana and "fourth" abhishekas, in a similar way introduce the recipient to aspects of the buddha-nature, the level of being that is found within and that is at the same time the elemental reality of the phenomenal world. The fourth abhisheka is particularly noteworthy, for it corresponds to the "pointing out" of the nature of mind discussed above and represents the place, in the ritual of the four abhishekas, where the essence of mind is directly disclosed.

The abhisheka ritual imparts a sense of well-being and settledness at a very deep level. One may feel that a fundamental shift has occurred in oneself. One has touched something profound and timeless, and this brings a sense of relaxation and joy. Trungpa Rinpoche comments that while many religious traditions point to the weaknesses and faults of the human being, the Vajrayana connects people with their sanity, compassion, and well-being. This experience is called the "ground of Vajrayana" and becomes the basis of further practice.

SAMAYA

It is understood ahead of time that receiving abhisheka implies a mutual commitment between teacher and student. This commitment is not something extrinsic or external to the ritual itself. It is rather a natural outcome of the process of the abhisheka. It is like when two people experience a moment of truth or reality together. Once something real or genuine has been experienced, as human beings we naturally feel the need to honor that experience as having occurred. It is only and always the sharing of reality that truly binds two people together. After such a shared experience, to pretend that it never occurred, to deny it, to try to revert to previous conventional ways of behaving, is inherently painful, undermining, and dehumanizing.

The idea of a mutual commitment, of course, did not appear on one's spiritual journey for the first time at the Vajrayana level. From the beginning of the Buddhist path, in receiving teachings on the four noble truths and in taking refuge, a link was formed with the teacher. At the level of the bodhisattva, that sense of connection was deepened. However, through the Vajrayana abhisheka, a bond has been forged between teacher and student that is said to be indestructible and indissoluble. It is as if in the abhisheka, one has entered into a permanent marriage. A permanent marriage with what? In a very real sense with the human guru, but in his aspect as representative, instrument, and guardian of reality itself.

In this Vajrayana marriage, then, one is not simply dealing with the human guru. The guru is inseparable from—and speaking and acting on behalf of—reality itself in its many manifestations, both inner and outer. Both within us and in our environment, ultimate reality manifests itself as the deities of the mandala. In some mysterious way, the guru is in league with these divine forces. He is not only in league with them, he is inseparable from them. In some sense, they are his agents. And, as the guru is the embodiment of our own inner enlightenment and the awakened wisdom of the world, so the yidams are another way of representing these inner and outer realities. In the abhisheka, then, one is entering into a marriage with the human guru that is a union of the inner and outer reality of vajra being and vajra world, of the mandala of the yidam as found within and without.

This marriage from which there can be no escape applies continual pressure on our self-concept. The inner yidam, as our vajra being, gnaws at the rotting flesh of ego—for the ego is, in fact, moribund—from the inside. This occurs in the form of inspiration, insight, and the feeling of being continually haunted by how paltry and posturing our ordinary "self" really is. And the yidam as the external, vajra world, gnaws from the outside in the form of situations and events that shock us into recognizing our own nonexistence. The shaky, dissolving sense of "I," then, is caught between two forces, the inner vajra being and the outer vajra world, and stands not a prayer of surviving.

This permanent marriage is reflected in the *samaya* vow, the basic

Vajrayana vow, which parallels the refuge vow in the Hinayana and the bodhisattva vow in the Mahayana. The samaya vow is taken at the time of abhisheka and, like the vows of the two lower yanas, it enters into one's system and becomes part of one's karmic situation from that time forward. However, the samaya vow itself is far more demanding than either the Hinayana or the Mahayana vow. This is because it includes the vow of the lower yanas within it and adds additional commitments, and also because it includes a more subtle dimension and allows less room for ego.

In the Hinayana vow of refuge, one is making a commitment primarily to oneself. One expresses that commitment in the various vows of shila, which concern the "body" or physical actions. The bodhisattva vow, which incorporates and includes the Hinayana vow, emphasizes one's commitment to the well-being of others. Because this vow concerns the way in which we communicate and interact with others, it is said to relate to "speech." The Vajrayana vow, incorporating the basic Hinayana disciplines and the bodhisattva vow, emphasizes "mind," how one holds one's mind and views reality. In the Vajrayana, as Tulku Urgyen Rinpoche remarks, one reviews and retakes each of these "three vows":

> As Vajrayana practitioners, we abide by all these three sets of principles. For instance, we take refuge at the very beginning of any empowerment, and have therefore received the refuge precepts of the shravakas. After that, we form the bodhicitta resolve and so also receive the bodhisattva precepts. As for Secret Mantra [the Vajrayana], the moment we drink the "samaya water," the drops of water from the conch given out before the actual empowerment, the water is transformed into Vajrasattva, who rests in the center of our hearts. When we keep the samayas we are never separate from Vajrasattva.[12]

The basic principle of samaya is to regard the world as sacred and to avoid falling into the degradation of conventional thoughts and judgments. This general samaya is articulated in dzokchen, for example, in the injunction to maintain the view of the nonexistence of all phenomena (that is, their lack of substantiality, their emptiness) and the ultimate, irrefutable sacredness of their appearance.[13] There are then specific samaya commitments and disciplines through which one can fulfill the basic samaya.

In one popular formulation, these specific samayas are set out as fourteen root and eight branch vows, the breaking of which causes the defeat of one's path. The first and most important samaya is not to disrespect or disparage one's guru. The guru is, as mentioned, the representative of reality, inseparable from the yidam and one's buddha-nature. To turn against this can lead only to spiritual self-destruction. The second samaya involves respecting and adhering to the teachings of the three vehicles and maintaining their vows, including particularly the bodhisattva vow. These vows all concern the teaching of egolessness and relating to others in a selfless way. The third vow calls for not becoming angry and aggressive toward one's Vajrayana brothers and sisters, particularly those who study under the same teacher as oneself and with whom one has taken abhisheka. Other samayas enjoin one to maintain loving-kindness to all beings, not to depart from the twofold bodhicitta (the emptiness of reality and compassion for others), to respect the secrecy of the Vajrayana, and not to harm others by revealing what should not be revealed. The last of the root samayas, one seemingly intended primarily for men, concerns women:

> If one disparages women who are of the nature of wisdom, that is the fourteenth root downfall. That is to say, women are the [embodiment] of wisdom and Sunyata [emptiness], showing both. It is therefore a root downfall to dispraise women in every possible way, saying that women are without spiritual merit and made of unclean things, not considering their good qualities.[14]

It is said that if one keeps samaya—if one maintains the view of the sacredness of reality—one will gain great accomplishment. But if one breaks samaya—if one falls back into habitual judgments—one will fall into great misery. A common analogy used in the Vajrayana to describe the nature of samaya is that of a snake in a bamboo tube: there are only two ways the snake can go, up or down. Tulku Urgyen Rinpoche explains:

> Going up describes what is called the "upward directness" which indicates we are ready to enter a buddha field. On the other hand, there is the "downward directness" which applies to those who break the samaya vows. I hate to mention this, but such a person can only go downward into the three lower realms. This is precisely what is meant by the tremendous benefit or the correspondingly huge risks involved in the Vajrayana samayas.[15]

> If you keep the samayas you gain supreme accomplishment. If not, then that which remained as Buddha Vajrasattva in the center of our heart as long as you observed the purity of samaya transforms itself into a 'fierce yaksha,' a force that shortens your life-span and 'consumes the vital essences of your heart blood.' This is the way to inescapably propel yourself into the 'downward directness' at the end of your life.[16]

Some people may be put off by the severity of this statement, claiming that it reminds them too much of the more distasteful aspects of our Western religious heritage. However, such a reaction does not take into account that the spiritual life, if lived fully and without reservation, is demanding and unavoidably dangerous. Exploring the realms of reality that lie beyond conventionality is dangerous because there is no guarantee that we will not turn around and try to use what we have seen and learned in the service of ego, to build a more secure and solid fortress for ourselves and to manipulate others to our own ends.

Seen in this light, the samaya vow in Vajrayana Buddhism represents a vital safeguard against the misuse of the teachings and the ultimate harm and destruction that this will inevitably bring. It is as if a fail-safe device has been implanted into our system so that if we go against the basically selfless intention of the dharma, we will be destroyed. The "we" here is, of course, our ego: our buddha-nature will not allow us to use the Vajrayana dharma for ego-centered ends. But if we have taken the path of the megalomaniacal demon Rudra (mentioned earlier), then what we experience is an utter destruction—the elixir of samaya in our system turns into molten lead. Yet this destruction is ultimately compassionate. It removes us from the possibility of creating any further negative karma for ourselves and prevents us from turning the power and understanding that we have accumulated against others.

10

Tantric Practice

MEDITATION ON THE YIDAM

A FURTHER SAMAYA TAKEN AT THE TIME OF ABHISHEKA
is the commitment to carry out the sadhana, or practices, associated with
it. In the abhisheka, we have been shown the sacred world of the guru
and been introduced into the mandala of the divine yidams. Yet we still
carry around our habitual ways of seeing and acting in the world. There
is a huge discrepancy here: we have seen reality, but we still have all of
our deep-seated mechanisms of avoidance and resistance. Having received abhisheka, we must now take up the practice that will progressively undermine and dissolve our small-minded versions of ourselves
and the world, leaving only our enlightened nature. This process may
be compared to a metal plate with an etching on it that is put in an acid
bath. The flat surface is our egos, while the etching of our enlightened
selves is invisible. Through the sadhana practice, which is the acid bath,
gradually the extraneous ego matter is dissolved. Finally, only the etching remains, which is our fully awakened being, manifesting in a selfless
way the enlightenment of our basic nature.

THE NATURE OF THE YIDAM

The yidam, or personal deity, is an embodiment of our own buddha-
nature. Practice of the yidam enables us to connect with that nature and
identify more and more fully with it. Yidams may be male, female, or
male and female in close embrace. Each also manifests a particular aspect, whether peaceful, semiwrathful, or wrathful. Associated with each
is an abhisheka and a series of sadhanas, or practice texts, that provide

FIGURE 10.1 *The mandala of Hevajra, a yidam important among the Sarma or Later Translation schools.*

a variety of means for identifying with the yidam. In Vajrayana Buddhism, many different yidams are known. In the New Translation schools, for example, primary yidams include Hevajra (fig. 10.1), Guhyasamaja (fig. 10.4), Chakrasamvara (fig. 10.3), Vajrayogini (figs. 10.2,

FIGURE 10.2 *Vajrayogini, female buddha, a central yidam of the Kagyüpas.*

10.3), Tara (figs. 3.2, 3.3), and Avalokiteshvara (fig. 8.1). Among the Nyingmapas, the principal yidams include Vajrakilaya and Vajrasattva. Also important in the Ancient School are the eight Herukas (wrathful yidams), practiced either together in one mandala or in separate manda-

FIGURE 10.3 *Vajrayogini and Chakrasamvara, important Kagyü yidams.*

las and sadhanas, as well as their peaceful forms (Manjushri, Avalok-iteshvara, etc.).

The yidams are known as *lha* (*deva* in Sanskrit), meaning "deity." This raises an important question: to what extent is the yidam an external deity like the deities of other religions? This is a particularly critical question in view of the avowed "nontheism" of Buddhism in Tibet as

FIGURE 10.4 *Guhyasamaja (Sangdu), a principal yidam of the Gelukpas.*

elsewhere. In one way, the yidam is very like our usual understanding of deity in the sense that it manifests to us as an external being coming from the "other world" who embodies reality itself. But in another, more basic sense, the yidam is clearly not a purely external being because, seen on a deeper level, it is a configuration of our own awareness.

In other words, the yidam is finally not external but is a representation of who we most essentially are. This marks an important difference between the Vajrayana notion and a "deity" in the conventional sense: here, the deity cannot be said to "exist" in an objective way. As a reflex of our own awareness, the yidam is "apparent yet empty"—that is, the yidam appears in a most vivid fashion but is utterly ungraspable, without an objectifiable, solidified, conceptualizable nature.

SADHANA PRACTICE AND ITS RITUAL STRUCTURE

A sadhana is a liturgical text that forms the basis of day-to-day Vajrayana practice. The sadhana that one performs is part of the abhisheka cycle that one has been initiated into. In fact, the sadhana contains the same symbolism and liturgical process as the abhisheka, except that instead of the vajra master enacting these for the disciples, one is now empowered to practice on one's own.

The sadhana may be understood as a kind of ritualized meditation, or meditation practices set within a ritual format. Tantric ritual provides a context within which one is able to experience various dimensions of the ego-mind as these give way and dissolve into larger, non-egoic awareness. Throughout the following rituals, the practitioner uses various ritual implements, foremost among which are the vajra, or dorje, held in the right hand, and the bell, or ghanta, held in the left hand and rung at various points, particularly when invocations, offerings, or praises are chanted.

Preliminaries

Sadhanas typically begin with some type of formless meditation such as shamatha-vipashyana. This formless practice acknowledges the inherent emptiness and purity out of which the yidam arises, in this sense reaffirming the nontheistic quality of deity practice in the Vajrayana. Its

FIGURE 10.5 (LEFT) *Bell* (ghanta) *and* (RIGHT) *vajra* (dorje),
ritual instruments used in tantric practice.

immediate, practical purpose is to enable the practitioner to let go of mental preoccupations and begin to tune his or her awareness into unconditioned space, in preparation for the practice and purifying its ground. Following this, one makes an offering of *torma* (usually a cake made of butter and flour, specially shaped and colored) to the various spirits in the environment. The idea of this short liturgy is to honor the local spirits (*lokapalas*), feed the hungry ghosts, and satisfy whatever forces may be lurking on the fringes of the environment that could disrupt one's practice. It is an open question to what extent these spirits represent fringe aspects of mind and to what extent they are external entities with their own journeys. After they are fed, satisfied, and pleased, they are then sent away.

Establishing Protective Boundaries

One next establishes the boundaries of the space in which one will carry out the practice. In order to do this, the particular guardian forces associated with this practice are invited and installed at the perimeter of the immediate room, meditation hut, or practice area. These protective deities defend against psychological disruption by heavy, more solidified energies, including potentially disruptive beings from the lower realms.

These guardians are ultimately not separate from our own inborn awareness. In fact, they are external representations of fundamental qualities of our inherent being, including clarity and strength. These aspects of the enlightened mind are now invoked because when they are activated, ego distortions and confusion cannot survive. The invitation of the guardian forces, then, represents a calling forth of these basic qualities and "installing" them at the periphery of our awareness.

It may be asked, again, are these protector beings nothing more than projections of interior aspects? Does this then mean that they do not really exist in the external world as discrete beings? To ask this question is to forget the basic nondual perspective of Vajrayana Buddhism. In the vajra realm, as we have seen, the reality of enlightened wisdom precedes the duality of subject and object. In the present instance, the protector forces are inherent aspects of reality before we dichotomize it into self and other. For this reason, the forces of protection can be invoked as external beings, although in fact the energy they represent lies beneath the subject-object split, and is found at the basis of ourselves just as much as of the external world.

Recapitulation of the Ngöndro

There follows a short refuge liturgy and a section in which one takes the bodhisattva vow. This is considered the first section of ngöndro, that of refuge and prostrations. This is followed by the other three ngöndro, a short Vajrasattva mantra practice, the mandala offering, and some form of guru yoga. In this way, from refuge up to guru yoga, one recapitulates the essence of the tantric path up to this point. This is not just a reference to past history: one is supposed to enter into each of these fully so that one taps into and freshly experiences their transformative power and their function on that path.

It might be asked whether it is possible to follow the ngöndro process, which is lengthy and arduous, so quickly and easily. In fact, in the ngöndro as in the other Vajrayana upayas, one internalizes the structure and the processes of the practices so that they become a part of one's being and readily available even after having completed the practice and moved on. In this way, it is possible to touch and reexperience each of the phases of the ngöndro, as one moves in the sadhana liturgy toward the main yidam practices. Of course, for any of this to work, one needs to be mentally present and not be thinking about something else; hence the importance of a proper grounding in shamatha.

The Main Practice

The preceding are all preliminaries to the central practice now to be undertaken. One visualizes oneself as the yidam, representing one's own vajra being. There then follows the visualization of the central yidam on the shrine in front, representing the vajra world. Often these two visualizations are divided into two sections of the liturgy. In this case one would first enact the visualization of oneself as the deity with associated liturgical and meditative elements and then the "front visualization" with the same components. The iconographic descriptions given in the texts are often quite detailed and thorough. One reads through the visualization and attempts to picture the deity, first as oneself, then in front. There will be a statue, *thangka* (painting) or other representation of the yidam on one's shrine, which provides help in the process of visualization. As in the case of the Vajrasattva practice, whether visualizing the yidam on the shrine in front or as oneself, one first produces a visualization that is the humanly created image, the samayasattva. Into this, one invokes the true or living wisdom being of the yidam, the jnanasattva.

An essential part of the visualization process entails recognition of the nonsolidity or "emptiness" of the deity. As the texts say, the deity is to be visualized as "empty yet apparent." But what does this mean in experiential terms? Certainly, on one level, it involves not falling into the fallacy of thinking that the yidam is a real, solid, objectively existing entity. On another level, however, the emptiness of the deity is perceptual. The visualization has the character of a mirage or a rainbow. The form of the deity is visualized as if it were nothing more tangible than light, as if one could pass one's hand through it without encountering anything solid. Indeed, in a very real sense, there is the appearance, the outer outline or shell of the deity as light, but it is as if the deity were hollow, with nothing inside. The yidam is just as empty as a drawing made in space.

Following the establishment of the visualization, the practitioner makes various imagined and real offerings to the deity. Then one chants various praises to him or her. These praises articulate the magnificence and glory of the yidam, and his or her salvific qualities. The offerings and praises are presented to both the deity as oneself and the deity as the essential being of the world. It may seem odd to offer praise to oneself, but here there is no question of oneself as an egoic entity but rather the selfless, all-compassionate being that one essentially is. It is reminiscent of the praise that Saint Paul feels compelled to offer to the indwelling Christ: "It is not me, but Christ within me."

The practitioner then begins to recite the particular mantra that is associated with the yidam. Just as the visualization represents the nature of the deity in its form aspect, the mantra embodies the nature of the deity in its sound aspect. In the same way that we habitually visualize ourselves in the form of a "self," likewise our speech represents our "self" in sound, and is habitually geared toward confirming, defending, and augmenting our ego. Like the practice of visualizing ourselves as a buddha, the recitation of the mantra reverses and undermines this trend. In mantra, we speak the language, the sound-nature, of the deity. In so doing, our mind is temporarily occupied with nonsamsaric, non-ego-oriented speech.

Kalu Rinpoche, in speaking of the power of the mantra of Avalok-iteshvara, provides a traditional explanation of the effectiveness of mantra recitation:

Mantras carry the power of purifying the mind from faults and veils and making its true nature obvious. . . . Let us take, for example, the mantra of Avalokita (Chenrezig), called the mantra of six syllables, *om mani padme hung*. To each syllable one attributes the following powers:

- They close the door of rebirth in the six classes of beings in samsara.
- They eliminate the six basic conflicting emotions: desire-attachment, hatred-aversion, blindness, possessiveness, jealousy, and pride.
- They allow one to achieve the six wisdoms.
- They lead to perfect practice of the six paramitas, and so on.[1]

It is typical for one's mantra recitation to aim for a million, a few million, up to ten or more million repetitions.

Sadhana practice includes, finally, the use of mudras, or physical hand gestures. As mentioned, human beings are composed of body, speech, and mind, and we use all three in the development, maintenence, and expression of our egos. Thus, just as we use samsaric visualizations and speech to bolster our sense of self, so we also use physical gestures. In sadhana practice, just as the activity of mind and speech can be used to call forth our enlightened nature, so may also the use of the body through mudras. These mudras are graceful and evocative gestures that convey various meanings. For example, in certain sadhanas one makes seven, eight, or ten offerings to the yidam. When consisting of seven, these include water for bathing, flowers, incense, light (a candle), perfumed water, food, and music. Each of these has its accompanying mudra that one makes with the hands while repeating the associated liturgical phrases. Often these phrases are in Sanskrit, such as OM VAJRA DHUPAM . . . ("I make the offering of incense"). Although most Tibetans, and Western practitioners, do not know Sanskrit, the translation of the phrases is usually given in a commentary. The offering verses are repeated so often in the course of practice that their meaning soon becomes second nature. The offering mudras make the act of offering a complete one: the practitioner visualizes the yidam and the offerings being made to him or her; recites the words that express the offering that is being made; and performs the mudra of that offering. In addition to the offering mudras, there are dozens of other mudras that accompany different aspects of the ritual and bring the meaning being expressed into physical embodiment.

The process of visualizing the deity and reciting the mantra is known as *utpattikrama*, or the development stage (Tibetan, *kyerim*). It is so called because one is mentally generating the form of a deity, imagining it to be the nature of oneself and one's world. When we are in our habitual samsaric mode, we also carry out visualizations, but in these we imagine ourselves to be a centralized self living in a threatening and degraded world, separate from others, needing protection and security. In contrast to this soiled visualization of ourselves and our world, in the development stage we are visualizing ourselves as having the form and the qualities of a realized buddha. From one point of view, we are imagining something that is not really the case, carrying out an act of imitation. However, this imitation is different from the samsaric one in that it is at least based on reality: we are visualizing ourselves as we really and truly are, beneath our conventional defilements. Our usual visualization of ourselves as substantial egos is also imagination and also an act of imitation. However, this samsaric visualization is not based on reality: there is nothing in actuality that corresponds to our visualization as an existent "self."

Through visualizing ourselves as an enlightened buddha, even at the level of imitation, we are accomplishing two things. First, we are temporarily taking our concept of ego "offline" and rendering it inactive. This disruption of our normal, habitual egoic visualizing makes room for something deeper and more genuine to emerge. Second, we are engaging in seeing ourselves as a selfless, compassionate being, and in the long term we find ourselves beginning to identify with this enlightened image. These two effects of visualization are referred to, in traditional terms, as the accumulation of merit. Tulku Urgyen explains:

> The development stage is not a real meeting with the actual deity but a facsimile, a likeness. We cultivate this likeness, be-

cause our minds have fallen under the power of habitual tendencies, delusions, various thought patterns and negative emotions. To remedy this, we engage in "white training"—we think about celestial palaces, pure deities, and so on. We are not emptying ourselves of impure thoughts, but we can temporarily stop them. Due to the kindness of the buddhas, we can purify an immense amount of bad karma by practicing development stage. . . .

When training in the development stage we attempt to manifest the semblance of enlightened qualities. These are not yet the real, authentic qualities; they are just a semblance. . . . Nevertheless, by imitating our intrinsic qualities we purify our habitual tendencies to perceive and fixate upon an ordinary solid reality. These obscurations are purified because the development stage engenders a simulation of our true, innate qualities.[2]

According to Tulku Urgyen, then, all the activities of the development stage, "are not merely superficial ways of spending our time: they are profound methods of purifying the habitual tendencies that obscure our buddha-nature."[3] This is the case even though, in our lives, we may spend a mere fraction of our time visualizing ourselves as a yidam, as compared with the time we spend seeing ourselves as a solid "self." The reason is that, as mentioned, the visualization of the development stage has a reality, truth, and power that the nonexistent ego of the samsaric visualization cannot have.

The development stage engages the practitioner's body, speech, and mind in another way. By visualizing the form of the deity, one identifies with the body of the deity; through the mantra practice, one unites with his or her speech; and through holding one's mind in the state of emptiness, one realizes one's mind as that of the deity. Tulku Urgyen gives the following analogy of how the process of visualizing replaces one's own body, speech, and mind with those of the yidam.

Take the example of our habitual idea of living in a solid house. To combat this, we try to grow used to the idea that our environment, our dwelling place, is a celestial palace made of rainbow light. Instead of perceiving our ordinary body, we try to perceive our body as the pure, insubstantial form of a deity. Instead of ordinary conversations, we try to perceive all communication as the praise of enlightened qualities. Instead of fixating on sense impressions, we present them as offerings to the awakened ones.[4]

There are various styles of visualization. One may follow a visualization text, building up the image of the deity in one's imagination, step by step. In the case of Vajrayogini, for example, one visualizes first her red body, then her face with three eyes, then her limbs in dancing posture, then her ornaments, and so on (figure 10.2). Another style, one that Tulku Urgyen tells us is the most profound, is that of "instantaneous recollection." "This means that the deity is already present in the mandala of our mind, so we do not need to make it present with our hands or intellect. We merely need to think that we are Buddha Samantabhadra, for instance, and that's enough.[5]

In each practice session, the meditator carries out the development stage along with its mantra recitation, for some period of time. Following this, one meditates in the completion stage (*sampannakrama*; Tibetan, *dzog-rim*). Whereas the development stage involves the vivid appearance of oneself as the form of the yidam, in the completion stage one dissolves the visualization and rests the mind in the ultimate emptiness of the primordial state. Thus, at the end of visualization practice, one dissolves the outer environment into the deity, the deity into the seed syllable at its heart center, the seed syllable into a dot (*bindu*), and that dot into emptiness. One then rests the mind in the luminous, empty expanse.

At higher levels of meditation, one practices the inseparability of the development and completion stages. Practice of the development and completion stages, and their unity, are the means for the realization of the inseparability of appearance and emptiness. Tulku Urgyen explains:

This unity of these two is exactly what is meant by the unity of development and completion. The stages of development and

FIGURE 10.6 *Vajrayogini mandala.*

completion are at the same time the very methods used to realize this essential principle. To attain stability in the manifest,
cognizant aspect we need the development stage. To attain stability in the empty aspect, we need the completion stage, samadhi. The ultimate fruition of these two stages is the "kayas and
wisdoms," which constitute the true buddha-nature. When our
ordinary body and the mind are refined they are the kayas and
wisdoms, the former supporting the latter.[6]

Tulku Urgyen mentions two ways in which the unity of the development and the completion stages may be attained. In the first, one gradually creates the image of the deity in one's imagination and subsequently rests in the completion stage. In the second, one rests one's mind in ultimate space of the true nature and allows the visualization to emerge of its own accord. The first is known as "following the development stage with the completion stage."

> First, you practice the development stage, for instance by thinking, "I am Padmasambhava; I'm wearing a crown on my head and such-and-such garments, and I'm holding these various attributes in my hands." After that, you look into, "Who is it that imagines all this?" At that moment, it is seen that that which imagines or visualizes all this is empty, and at the same time cognizant. This empty knowing is called completion stage.[7]

The second method of unification is to let the development stage unfold from within the completion stage.

> Here you start out by looking into mind essence, allowing the awakened state of mind to be an actuality. Without leaving this state of nondual awareness, you then allow the visualization to take place. The very expression of nondual awareness then takes the form of a celestial palace, the form of Padmasambhava and all the other details of the mandala. The nondual state of awareness is unimpeded, just like images being unimpededly reflected in a mirror.[8]

How does this process occur? How is it that when the mind is left open and empty, when one is resting in the natural state, the forms that arise are those of the deity and its environment?

"While unwholesome or egotistical thought-forms cannot arise as the expression of the awakened state, pure forms, such as the celestial palaces, deities, and so forth, can occur without leaving the state of *rigpa* [rikpa, the awakened mind]. This is because the duration of recognizing *rigpa* resembles a clear mirror that unobstructedly reflects everything."[9]

The view of oneself as "ego" and the world as impure and degraded is, as mentioned, not real, but purely a conceptual contrivance. When appearances are reflected in the awakened state, they appear as they are, as the pure, sacred, and divine mandala of the yidam.

Concluding the Liturgy

After some period of time resting in the completion stage, the practitioner arises again as the deity and performs the concluding parts of the liturgy. These may include a mandala offering of thanks for the blessings bestowed by the yidam, repetition of the Vajrasattva mantra to purify any inadvertencies or mistakes in the practice, and final offerings and praises.

Conclusion

One engages in the development stage, visualizing the deity and reciting his or her mantra, for some period of time, anywhere from perhaps ten or twenty minutes for a short practice session to two hours or more for a longer session. In daily practice, the shorter session would be more appropriate. When in retreat, the day is often divided into "four sessions," each customarily about three to four hours in length. In either case, the liturgical parts of the sadhana might take anywhere from around twenty minutes to an hour or more. It is difficult to generalize in these matters because sadhanas can vary a great deal from one cycle to the next. Nevertheless, these rough approximations indicate the level of commitment that is required to carry out the practice.

In Tibet, practitioners might carry out their sadhanas in retreat for many years, accumulating many millions of mantras over tens of thousands of hours of meditation. Westerners rarely have the opportunity to practice at that level—and Tibetan teachers circumspectly do not generally require them to do so (for some exceptions, see chapter 17). Nevertheless, what is typically asked of Western practitioners is often experienced as daunting. To people who are accustomed to thinking of religion in terms of spending an hour or two per week in church or synagogue, the kind of involvement required by Tibetan Buddhism can come as a shock. One often hears new practitioners stupefied by the prospect of an hour or two of daily practice and months of retreat to complete even the first phase of Vajrayana practice. Yet, even in the busy world of the modern West, people do somehow find the time to carry through their basic tantric commitments. And, perhaps surprisingly, they often claim that the practice opens up their lives, creates an environment of less stress, and seems to enable them to accomplish more than previously. Observations such as these point back to the tantric dictum that when you enter the practice in a serious manner, it effects a transformation not only in yourself but in the external world.

FEAST PRACTICE

An integral part of yidam practice is the ganachakra, or the practice of feast, carried out on the tenth and twenty-fifth day of the new moon. On this occasion, disciples of a certain teacher initiated into a particular abhisheka—"vajra brothers and sisters," as they are called—assemble to practice together. In fact, the Sanskrit term for the feast is composed of two words, *chakra*, which in this context means the "circle" of those assembled, and *gana*, which means the Vajrayana sangha.

Tantric feasts are occasions of liturgical celebration generally composed of three main elements:

1. *The practice of the sadhana of the yidam.* This is the same practice that individuals will carry out in retreat and in their daily practice.

2. *The performance of the "self-abhisheka."* This is the very same abhisheka liturgy that was performed by the teacher, initially empowering the students to enter into yidam practice. Having received the original abhisheka, practitioners become authorized from that time forward, as mentioned, to perform the abhisheka for themselves. The "self-abhisheka" may be carried out at any time but, owing to time constraints, is usually done only on feast days or during a solitary retreat. It is sometimes also enacted at the end of a period of extended group practice, such as a group retreat. The purpose of the self-abhisheka is to

reconnect with the special blessings that are available through the abhisheka rite. The buddhas and bodhisattvas are invited; one's body, speech, and mind are again purified in the ritual; and one is crowned again as a king or queen in the dharmic sense, having the opportunity to experience once more the dignity and majesty of one's enlightened being.

3. *The enactment of a specific feast liturgy.* The feast liturgy has it roots in ancient India, where those bound together through the tantric samayas would gather together at night in isolated places, usually cremation grounds, for the performance of the liturgy. In the feast, the buddhas and bodhisattvas, the yidams with their retinues, and the local helpful spirits were all invited to join in the celebration. On those occasions wine, symbolizing passion, and meat, symbolizing aggression, were ritually taken, and there was music and dancing, perhaps analogous to the sacred music and dance found in the temples of East India, in the state of Orissa, into the nineteenth century. As part of the feasting, spontaneous songs called *doha* or *vajra-giti* were composed.

Feast practice is based on the Vajrayana principle of not rejecting the world of sense experience, but rather enjoying it to the fullest extent. This enjoyment of life is, of course, quite different from the samsaric practice of attempting to use pleasure to comfort, fortify and satisfy the ego and to ward off discomfort and pain. The Vajrayana notion is "to take, but not take in." It is like enjoying the full pleasure of a gourmet dinner, the arrangement of the table, the disposition of the meal on the plate, the delicate and tantalizing aromas of the food, and the delectable tastes in one's mouth. The only part left out is the actual swallowing, the glutting of oneself and stuffing one's belly, and the anesthesia that comes with consumption. Through "taking but not taking in," one's intelligence and sensitivity are never dulled, but—for all the ego hunger that is never satisfied—actually heightened and refined. As an analogy, we may think of the wine-taster, who savors the rarest vintages but does not swallow them, lest the ability to taste and appreciate the wines be dulled.

In the ganachakra liturgy, one is invited to enjoy the "feast of experience," to take joy in whatever arises in one's state of being, whether pleasure or pain, whether hope or fear, whether passion, aggression, or ignorance. Indeed, our petty egos could never take such an approach. But through identifying with the yidam in the liturgy, one eats, drinks, and enjoys—not only food but "whatever arises"—in just the manner of the deity. All is fit meat, all is sacred fare for the tantric practitioner as deity. How would the deity behave? How would the deity feast? How would the deity interact with others? How would the deity enjoy? The answers to those questions are found in the feast practice. And, through feasting as the yidam would, all of the apparent negativities and obstacles of samsara become transmuted and transformed.

Through the feast, one is enjoined to regard all of reality within the Vajrayana perspective of "sacred outlook" (dag-nang). Sacred outlook involves seeing the inner and outer world as the mandala of the yidam, as perfect, pure, and sacred. Whatever one sees is the form of the deity, whatever one hears is mantra, whatever one thinks is marked with emptiness and luminosity. This injunction is really a metaphor for a certain way of taking the world—as brilliant, pure, and filled with wisdom. According to the Vajrayana, as we have seen, the world is already inherently this way. This is not seen, however, because ego—in the service of its own survival and self-aggrandizement—insists on taking this sacred world as ordinary, impure, and marked with defilement. Through Vajrayana practice and culminating in the feast, one sheds the habitual distortions of ego and regains the inherent purity of what is.

In Tibet, while the ancient practice of feasting in charnel grounds at night was occasionally carried out, it was far more usual to feast in temples, shrine rooms, and homes on the appointed days. While in the early days of the Vajrayana in India, the liturgies were most likely not written down and were probably adjusted from occasion to occasion, in Tibet the feast practice of a certain deity was generally standardized and fixed in a written text that was performed in the same manner on every occasion. Nevertheless, the essential elements of the original Indian feast practice have been retained.

Feast practice, always an essential component of tantric practice in traditional Tibet, remains so among modern Western practitioners. In my own community, performance of the feast on the tenth and twenty-fifth days of the moon is an important part of fulfilling one's samaya.

The full feasts of Vajrayogini or Chakrasamvara take six or seven hours to carry out, no mean commitment for people with jobs and families. In recent times, abbreviated feasts have been introduced for busy, modern people who find it difficult to carry out the longer feast liturgies on weeknights.

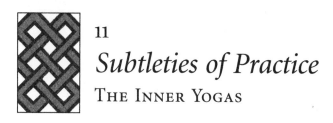

11

Subtleties of Practice
THE INNER YOGAS

THE INNER YOGAS

There are three distinctive arenas of Vajrayana practice: (1) the visualization of oneself as the yidam and the practice of the various sadhanas, discussed in the chapter 10; (2) the practice of the inner yogas, which work with the subtle body, to be examined in this chapter; and (3) "formless" meditation, in which one rests directly in the nature of mind, to be explored in chapters 12 and 13. These three types of practice may be correlated with the two basic phases of Vajrayana meditation, utpattikrama, the development stage, and sampannakrama, the completion stage. While yidam practice is particularly associated with utpattikrama, the development stage, the other two phases of Vajrayana practice are associated with sampannakrama, the completion stage: the inner yogas are known as sampannakrama with signs—that is, with some subtle form—and the "formless practice" of resting directly in the nature of mind is known as sampannakrama without signs.

The General Principle of Inner Yoga

Through the sadhana practices outlined above, one engages the outer aspect of the deity, in oneself and the external world. Connected with these practices and complementing them are the various practices of inner yoga. The inner yogas involve working with the subtle, energetic dimension of the body. This subtle aspect of ourselves is known as the "illusory body" because it is not physical in the normal, gross sense but

TABLE 11.1

THREE TYPES OF VAJRAYANA PRACTICE

Yidam practice	utpattikrama	development stage	practice with form
Inner yogas	sampannakrama with signs	completion stage with signs	practice with subtle form
Resting in the nature of mind	sampannakrama without signs	completion stage without signs	formless practice

rather energetic or psychic in nature. This body is configured according to various *chakras,* or "psychic centers"; *nadis,* the "channels" or "pathways" along which one's energy flows; *prana,* "wind" or the energy of one's mind; and *bindu,* "seed" or "drop," the essence of mind, the point of constellation of one's awareness. "Bindu is the quintessence secreted within the body. As is said, 'Mind consciousness rides the horse of prana on the pathways of the nadis. The bindu is mind's nourishment.' "[1]

Kalu Rinpoche comments that "this practice is based on the principle that our body is intimately related to the *nadis, prana,* and *bindu*s that make up the material support of mind. By acting on the support of mind, one acts on mind itself. There exists indeed a reciprocal action of the mind with this subtle energy system."[2]

Sakyong Mipham Rinpoche explains that the purpose of the inner yogas is to loosen the karmic blockages in our state of being.[3] Through our experiences over countless lifetimes, our energy pathways—the ways we experience our energy—have literally become tied into knots. These knots are found within the energetic interior of our psychic system. They are problematic because they bind us in a state of ignorance, distort everything we experience, and lock up our wisdom. To put the matter in psychological language, the pain and shocks that we have experienced over our samsaric history have been buried in us, impeding our ability to experience in a free and open manner; until those traumas are resolved, the wisdom they conceal will remain unavailable. Through the inner yogas, we begin to untie the knots and to work through, in a direct and rapid manner, the deep karma they hold.

In Tibetan tradition, the practice of the inner yogas is considered essential for anyone engaged in meditation as a lifelong discipline. This is because, for most of us, there comes a time when, owing to these energetic blockages, we are unable to proceed further in our practice. At this point, it becomes necessary to work directly to untie and resolve the karmic knots through inner yoga. Only through this process can we come to the full experience of mahamudra or dzokchen, our inherent nature in its complete and unobstructed form.

The idea of chakras may be explained approximately as follows. Human beings typically enter into various states of awareness and, although we are not usually aware of it, these states are associated with different regions of our body. For example, when we are overcome with very strong love, tenderness, or yearning, we experience particularly intense energy in the area of our heart. When we speak, our awareness is focused in our throats. When we are preoccupied with thinking, our energy moves to our head. Thus, we may refer to people who are very conceptual as being "mental" or "out of touch with their bodies." When we are hungry and contemplating a tasty meal, it is our belly that is thinking; and at the moment of orgasm, our awareness may be particularly oriented to our genital area. Our usual awareness of these centers is samsaric—that is, it is filtered through the interpretive and filtering system of ego. However, in the Vajrayana teaching, as we have seen, samsara is just a "cover" for nirvana. In fact, just beneath the samsaric overlay, each of these areas embodies a vast domain of selfless awareness, a reservoir of wisdom and compassion.

It is important to realize that the samsaric cover and the enlightened wisdom uncovered in the different chakras are not purely internal but have their counterparts in the external world. In this regard, Trungpa Rinpoche remarks that "the feeling of these centers should not be particularly centralized in the physical body as such, but it should be related to their essence in the universe, in the cosmos."[4] And he adds, "There is an external chakra principle in every situation."[5] The chakras, then, represent different dimensions of enlightened wisdom. While these aspects of enlightenment are found everywhere in the external and internal worlds, their existence in the body means that they are accessible to the practitioner in a uniquely immediate and direct way.

The *chakras* are linked by various nadis, or energy pathways, that run throughout the body.[6] It is along these that consciousness travels, riding on the prana, the psychic energy or "winds." Although Buddhist tantra identifies a multitude of nadis, three are of particular importance in the practice of inner yoga: (1) The central channel, known as the *avadhuti*, which is dark blue and runs parallel to the spinal column, just in front of it; (2) the *lalana*, white in color and located on the left side of the avadhuti, close to it but not touching, corresponding to the feminine principle; and (3) the *rasana*, which is red, an equal distance on the right side, corresponding to the masculine principle. The avadhuti is said to be about the thickness of a whipcord, while the rasana and lalana are said to be about the width of an arrowshaft. One text remarks that "all three channels are hollow, straight, clear, and transparent."[7] The lower end of the Avadhuti reaches down to a place below the navel, the exact location of which varies according to tradition. Its upper end travels over the top of the head and curves down to a point between the two eyebrows. The rasana and lalana, parallel to the avadhuti, run upward, also curving over the top of the head, and lead down to the right and left nostrils respectively. On their lower ends, these two nadis join the avadhuti below the navel center.

Six chakras are of importance in the practice of Buddhist tantric yoga. Four, in particular, are of special prominence, the *nirmana-chakra*, or "transformation chakra," located at the navel; the *dharma-chakra* in the heart center; the *sambhoga-chakra*, or "enjoyment chakra," in the throat; and the *svabhavika-chakra*, or "self-existent" chakra, in the head (sometimes also called the *mahasukha-chakra*, or "great bliss" chakra). The central nadi runs through these chakras and is linked with them through branch nadis extending to them like spokes from the center of a wheel. Each chakra has different numbers of these spokes and they face either up or down. In addition, also coming into play at various points in the yogas are two additional chakras, one in the "secret center" at the bottom of the avadhuti and the other at the crown of the head.

The nadi structure of the body is extensive. The lalana and rasana feed into the avadhuti, as mentioned, below the navel. The avadhuti is connected with the nadis radiating out from it at each of the chakras. And these radiating nadis connect outward some 72,000 nadis that run throughout the body, from the toes to the top of the head. It is important to realize that these nadis are not a theoretical or abstract structure. As the tantric yogin soon discovers, the nadis are real and really are there experientially as the channels or avenues through which our awareness flows in the practice of inner yoga.

In ordinary samsaric functioning, the consciousness is scattered and dispersed. The goal of yogic practice is to collect its dispersed energies into the central channel, which corresponds to the experience of the innate buddha-mind within. Trungpa Rinpoche:

> Because of dualistic thinking, *prana* enters the *lalana* (Tib.: *rkyang.ma*) and rasana (*ro-ma*), the left and right channels. This divergence of energy in the illusory body corresponds to the mental activity that falsely distinguishes between subject and object and leads to karmically determined activity. Through yogic practice, the *prana*s can be brought into the central channel (*avadhuti; dbu.ma*), and therefore transformed into wisdom-prana. Then the mind can recognize the fundamental nature, realizing all dharmas as unborn.[8]

The practice of the inner yogas, then, is a method toward the experience of the essence of mind itself. Once one has dissolved one's blockages and obscurations through the practice of the yogas, the practitioner gains access to the wisdom mind. At that point, the inner visualization of the illusory body is dissolved and he or she can then rest in the unborn awareness itself. "Once the meditator is well established in the experience of the fundamental nature of mind, he can meditate on it directly, dissolving the nadi, prana, and bindu visualization."[9]

In a very real sense, the practice of inner yoga reverses the process that occurred at conception. At that moment, our consciousness became enclosed within the white essence (the male seed) and the red essence (the female ovum). As we developed our physical form, the masculine and feminine energies separated, the masculine coming to reside in the head chakra, the feminine coming to reside in the navel chakra, the masculine energy coursing in the rasana nadi to the right of the spine, and the feminine energy traveling in the lalana nadi to the left. It is this split that enables duality to function, and duality is the ground and sustenance of ego. Thus we maintain our sense of separate selfhood through dividing things into right and left, white and black, masculine and feminine, good and bad, activity and passivity, day and night, and all of the other dualistic categories of experience that define us as human beings.

The process of conception is not restricted to the beginning of our life but is rather the way in which ego continually re-creates itself moment after moment. Thus the inner yogas reverse the process of conception and, in so doing, reverse the continual self-creation of ego, gradually leading the practitioner to the uncreated space of dharmakaya. Through the inner yogas, we bring our dualistic consciousness from the left and right nadis to a location below the navel. Here, as mentioned, there is an opening into the central channel and one enters one's awareness into the avadhuti at this point. When our awareness goes into the central channel, we enter into the nondual state.

Of course, in the beginning, we are not aware of the subtle physiology within. Therefore, we have to visualize this "illusory body," creating a facsimile of the real thing. Through the practice, by using the visualized facsimile as a stepping stone, we are enabled to make the transition from the visualization to an experience that is natural, uncontrived, and spontaneous.

The Six Yogas[10]

In Tibetan tradition, both the Nyingma and the Sarma schools possess extensive bodies of written and oral instruction on the inner yogas, and for both the practice of these yogas forms a central and indispensable part of the Vajrayana path. Among the Nyingmapas, the inner yogas are found primarily in the eighth of the nine yanas, Anuyoga-yana.

Among the Later Translation schools, the yogas are contained principally in the so-called six yogas of Naropa. Several Sarma lamas, including Kalu Rinpoche, Trungpa Rinpoche, and Lama Thubten Yeshe, have given helpful summaries of the general meaning and function of these yogas, and so it is the Naropa practices rather than the less accessible Nyingma version that I will discuss in this chapter.

The six yogas or "six dharmas," as they are sometimes termed, were originally assembled as a group of practices by Tilopa, who had received them individually from several of his human teachers. Tilopa then passed the "six yogas" on to Naropa, who transmitted them to Marpa. They were then passed on to Milarepa and thenceforward became a critical ingredient in the Kagyü transmission and subsequently, other Sarma schools. They are considered an advanced practice and require a considerable amount of previous experience of meditation. Kalu Rinpoche remarks, "These six dharmas assume that many practices have been accomplished previously. The techniques allowing one to apply them are therefore never taught in public."[11] Trungpa Rinpoche similarly comments that the six yogas "belong to advanced practice and can only be learned through direct oral transmission from an accomplished guru."[12] In keeping with this general principle of secrecy, Tibetan teachers have generally refrained from teaching publicly on the actual methods and techniques of the six yogas. In order to be given instructions on the actual practice, an individual usually must have received the necessary initiation, committed him or herself to the accompanying samayas, and undertaken the practice.*

Kalu Rinpoche explains the six yogas of Naropa as follows: "The six

---

*Lately, some publications have spoken much more openly about the practice, including many details that were previously kept secret. See, e.g., Lama Thubten Yeshe, *The Bliss of Inner Fire,* which provides a commentary on Tsongkhapa's "Having the Three Convictions," itself a commentary on the six yogas of Naropa. Significantly, this book represents the publication of two seminars, given by the Lama to people in a retreat setting, in 1982 and 1983, shortly before he died. For initiated and serious practitioners of the six yogas, there is much in Lama Yeshe's candor, warmth, and clarity that will be helpful. It is difficult to assess what the impact on others may be.

TABLE 11.2

THE SIX YOGAS OF NAROPA

English	Sanskrit	Tibetan	Area of Body Worked With	Associated *Chakra*	State Being Worked With
inner fire	chandali	tummo	4 finger-widths below navel	nirmana-chakra	functions as basic ground of all six yogas
illusory form	mayadeha	gyulü	head, crown of the head	svabhavika-chakra	waking state
dream	svapna	milam	throat	sambhoga-chakra	dreaming state
luminosity	prabhasvara	ösel	heart	dharma-chakra	deep sleep
intermediate state	antarabhava	bardo			intermediate period between death and rebirth
ejection	samkranti	phowa			moment of death

dharmas of Naropa form a group of practices allowing one to integrate all existential situations with the path and transform them into opportunities for liberation. These situations are the state of wake, dream, deep sleep, the moment of death, and the intermediate period between death and rebirth."[13] Sometimes, the situation of sexual union is also mentioned. He continues: "Often, one makes a distinction between mahamudra seen as a path of *liberation* and the six dharmas called *path of means*. One should not see this as a separation but understand that the six dharmas are profound *means* for quick access to mahamudra."[14]

Table 11.2, drawing primarily on the introduction to the six yogas by Takpo Tashi Namgyal, a sixteenth-century Kagyü lama, defines the six yogas, providing a brief characterization of each.[15]

TUMMO

Tummo is the first of the six yogas and provides the basic ground, tools, techniques, and perspectives out of which the other five arise. Because of its unique importance, in this presentation, I will discuss tummo in some detail, providing only brief characterizations of the other five inner yogas. For readers interested in pursuing this topic further, I refer them to the works of the authors mentioned above—Trungpa Rinpoche, Kalu Rinpoche, and Lama Thubten Yeshe—and also to translations of texts on the six yogas by Chang and Mullin (see the bibliography).

At first glance, it may appear that tummo and the other five inner yogas represent rather different kinds of practice from those connected with the yidam discussed in the previous chapter. In fact, all six yogas represent a deepening of experience of the yidam that was gained through abhisheka and sadhana. We saw above that through meditation on the yidam, one identifies with the egoless state of the buddha-nature. The six yogas carry that identification further, making it more profound and more extensive and inclusive of our state of being. In yidam practice, the practitioner sees, tastes, and begins to identify with another mode of being, one defined by selfless wisdom and compassion. Now, with the six yogas, we are given tools to root out our deepest habitual patterns, which obstruct our ability to remain in the empty, luminous, and compassionate awareness that, ultimately, is the yidam.

The way in which the six yogas extend and deepen yidam practice is seen clearly in tummo. For example, tummo begins with an extended section of meditation on the yidam known as the "hollow body." Here, one visualizes oneself as the yidam who, for example, in the Kagyü tradition would normally be the female buddha Vajrayogini. One pays special attention to her empty yet apparent body. As we saw in the last chapter, the yidam has shape and form but is insubstantial, like a rainbow, the play of light, or a drawing in space. One visualizes that there is nothing solid inside that body: one could pass one's hand through it. This is who—or what—we essentially are, once our belief in our solid self is removed.

The hollow body phase of tummo makes the point, which is critical to this and the other yogas, that it is not "I" who carry out the practices, but rather the deity. This undermines any attempt to think that one is performing these yogas for oneself, out of a desire for personal gratification. In fact, the yogas literally cannot be performed by a solid ego; they can only be enacted by the deity. This provides a self-protective mechanism: as long as I am sitting there thinking that "I" am doing this, nothing much is going to happen. When I let go of this idea, then everything opens up.

The hollow body segment of tummo is followed by a section devoted to meditation on the nadis and chakras that exist within the divine body of the yidam. The "ego" body is filled with bones, blood vessels, organs, muscles, and all sorts of unmentionable substances. In this habitual body of ours, there is certainly no room for anything as subtle as the nadis and chakras. However, once we let go of the conventional version of what we are and identify with the yidam, then within her empty form there is all the room in the world. Within this, we visualize the avadhuti, lalana and rasana, along with the chakras. In the beginning, of course, this visualization is more or less forced. Later, however, we begin to discover that there is a definite and tangible experience of this inner, subtle body, and we will then correct our visualization to conform to what we are discovering.

In the Vajrayana, realization is often depicted as the understanding of appearance and emptiness, of bliss and emptiness. In this case, appearance and bliss are more or less synonymous, and enlightenment is understood as awakening to the blissful nature of experience that is apparent but insubstantial. This is an experience of boundless freedom and joy. Obviously, for most of us, ordinary appearance—what occurs in our lives—is usually far from blissful. From the Vajrayana point of view, experience taken in reference to an ego, can never be truly blissful because it is always involved in the petty and suffocating game of (ego) pleasure and pain. In tummo practice, one identifies more and more fully with the body of the yidam, with her empty and apparent quality, and thus lays the ground for the kind of selfless and unimpeded bliss, the complete freedom and joy in whatever arises, that is the goal of Vajrayana.

A third critical feature of tummo involves the practice of "vase breathing." Like the hollow body and the visualization of the nadis and chakras, this element is part of the essential foundation of all six yogas.

Through the instructions of one's teacher, one is shown how to breathe in, hold one's breath in the lower part of the belly, and finally exhale. This process is accompanied by various visualizations. The vase breath sounds simple but is subtle and requires a great deal of practice. Our breathing, like everything else we do, is both an expression and a support of our basic ego fixation. The way we breathe, how we let the air in and where we bring it, how we hold it, and how we breathe out all serve to maintain the restricted awareness necessary to our belief in a solid self. Through the vase breath, we learn how to breathe all over again. We learn the open and unrestricted, yet formed and contained, breathing of the yidam. Through the vase breath, we begin to discover that "breath" involves far more than simply physical air entering our lungs. On a more subtle level, it is inseparable from our basic "psychic" (in the sense of mental and emotional) energy. Various yogic postures, also considered highly secret, are used to enable the breathing process to be extended until it permeates the entire body and to open areas of blockage.

Needless to say, the vase breath, along with its supporting physical exercises, stirs up a lot of energy, brings to light previously repressed thoughts and emotions, and confronts us with elements of experience that may be difficult, unpleasant, and painful. Therefore it is critical that it be performed with care, discipline, and gentleness, and also under the guidance of a teacher well experienced in the practice. If the vase breath and associated disciplines are performed improperly, one can find oneself falling into extreme mental states such as depression or despair, and one can make oneself physically and/or psychically ill. Even with the best expert guidance it is a tricky road to follow, and one is continually veering off in one errant direction or another. When you undertake this practice even under the best of circumstances, the challenges make it obvious why it has been felt important to keep the precise nature of the techniques secret from non-initiates. In addition, it is also clear why the six yogas are considered an advanced practice. The practitioner needs to have spent a great deal of time on the meditation cushion, so to speak, have become familiar with the various dimensions of his or her mind, and have developed the basic mental stability to handle the vivid ups and downs that the six yogas bring.

The meditation on the hollow body, the visualization of the nadis and chakras, the vase breathing, and physical yogic exercises are all considered as preparations to the main tummo practice that now follows. Once these preliminaries have been carried out to the point that one is familiar and relaxed with them, one undertakes various kinds of visualizations that center around the motif of "inner fire," the meaning of *tummo* or its Sanskrit equivalent, *chandali*. These all work with the basic heat, the life force, which is our innermost nature. They aim to bring that basic energy, which we normally repress into unconsciousness because of the pain of its intensity—into awareness and to make a conscious and intentional relationship with it. When we do so, it is seen to be nothing other than the fire of our own inherent wisdom, a fire that calls forth into awareness our ignorance, our other obscurations, and our karmic blockages, and then burns them as fuel in its intense and relentless fire. Through the practice, the body—and now we are talking about the subtle body, which is the basis of our physical egoic one—is cleaned, clarified, and rendered an immaculate vessel. At this point, we realize that our body is nothing other than that of the yidam and that our basic state of being is inseparable from hers. Now we are open to the yidam's experience of reality as bliss-emptiness, in other words, to the way in which we, at the deepest level of our being, already experience "things as they are." It is within such a vessel that the experience of the formless practices, mahamudra or dzokchen, can most easily reach their fulfillment. In this respect, Trungpa Rinpoche remarks that tummo is "an inner burning that arouses the universal flame that burns away all conceptualized notions of whatever kind, totally consuming them."[16] The realization of bliss inseparable from emptiness that is the goal of tummo, as well as the specific perspectives and techniques developed through the practice, now can provide, as mentioned, the foundation for the other five inner yogas.

The fire of tummo is also said to have the physical effect of raising the body temperature of the practitioner. In other words, the inner heat of tummo is not just mental. Even the beginning practitioner can feel the physical sensation of the inner heat generated through the practice. In the case of Milarepa and the "cotton-clad" yogins who have followed his tradition and continue to do so, living and meditating in the Himalayas, the practice of tummo renders possible living in frigid mountain caves in the middle of winter with no heat and no other clothing than a thin cotton garment. Alexandra David-Néel writes about tummo practitioners she heard of who abandoned even the cotton robe and lived naked in mountainous retreat year round, sometimes for life.[17]

Many people in the West have heard accounts of how the tummo accomplishment of Tibetan yogins is tested. David-Néel's firsthand account provides a vivid and not inaccurate picture:

> Sometimes, a kind of examination concludes the training of the *tumo* students. Upon a frosty winter night, those who think themselves capable of victoriously enduring the test are led to the shore of a river or a lake. If all the streams are frozen in the region, a hole is made in the ice. A moonlight night, with a hard wind blowing, is chosen. Such nights are not rare in Tibet during the winter months.
>
> The neophytes sit on the ground, cross-legged and naked. Sheets are dipped in the icy water, each man wraps himself in one of them and must dry it on his body. As soon as the sheet has become dry, it is again dipped in water and placed on the novice's body to be dried as before. The operation goes on in that way until daybreak. Then he who has dried the largest number of sheets is acknowledged the winner of the competition.
>
> It is said that some dry as many as forty sheets in one night. One should perhaps make large allowances for exaggeration, or perhaps for the size of the sheets, which in some cases may have become so small as to be almost symbolical. Yet I have seen some *repas* [cotton-clad ones] dry a number of pieces of cloth the size of a large shawl.[18]

Kalu Rinpoche summarizes both the spiritual and physical effects of tummo:

The beneficial effects of *tumo* are on two planes. First, *tumo* provides beneficial heat to the body. This is why one often speaks of yogins like Milarepa who, even lost in the mountains and in the middle of winter, only wore a thin garment of cotton. Mentally, this heat is associated with a sensation of happiness that, in itself, opens up to the experience of emptiness so that the practitioner finally attains realization of mahamudra, bliss, emptiness, and nonconcept.[19]

It would be hard to overestimate the great importance of tummo in Tibetan Buddhism. According to Lama Thubten Yeshe, tummo is the ultimate meditation practice.

Even if you could stay in samadhi meditation twenty-four hours a day for twenty days, Milarepa would say to you, "That means nothing! It does not compare to my inner fire meditation." This is how he responded to Gampopa at their first meeting after Gampopa had described his meditation experience. There must have been a reason for Milarepa to say this. He was not just making propaganda, exaggerating the power of inner fire. He had no partiality and had given up all worldly competition. Milarepa was simply saying that even remaining for many days in a deep, undisturbed samadhi meditation is nothing when compared to inner fire meditation. Inner fire is incomparable.[20]

The Lama remarks further that tummo is the most basic and powerful of all Vajrayana methods, for it opens the way to realization in all of the various tantric disciplines:

Inner fire [tummo] is like the main door leading into a complex of hundreds of treasure houses. All the facilities for magnetizing realizations are there. Since it penetrates the very center of the universe of the body, it is incredibly sensitive in producing realizations. In fact, the superstitious, conceptualizing mind cannot count the realizations brought by inner fire. It is the secret key that opens you to *all* realizations.[21]

The great importance of tummo is illustrated, again, by the life of Milarepa. Dudjom Rinpoche reminds us of Milarepa's first attempts to clear his enormous karmic debt through the practice of dharma. Initially, he sought out a certain dzokchen teacher and requested teachings. The master gave Mila the instructions he requested, but when he tried to practice them, owing to his evil deeds and karmic blockages, he was not able to attain understanding. Only through the path of tummo was Milarepa able to purify these obscurations. As Dudjom Rinpoche summarizes this story:

> When the venerable Milarepa first received the Mental Class [or "mind section"] of the Great Perfection from Nup Khalungpa he could not become equipoised in awareness itself, and for the time being the doctrine and the individual seemed to go their own ways. Finally on the basis of the venerable Marpa of Lhodrak's [teaching of the] inner heat, he attained accomplishment on the path of the Great Perfection, whereby all thoughts, all things are exhausted. This can be demonstrated by one of his own songs of indestructible reality, in which he says:
>
> > Stabbed in front by the Great Perfection,
> > Stabbed in the back by the Great Seal [Mahamudra],
> > I vomit the blood of instruction.[22]

THE ILLUSORY BODY

The other five of the six yogas of Naropa, as mentioned, take their foundation on the tummo. In fact, when one is pursuing the practice of the illusory body and the other yogas, one is generally advised to spend one third to one half of each meditation session in tummo, only moving on to the specific yoga one is practicing when that foundation has been well established in the practice session.

Kalu Rinpoche epitomizes the practice of the illusory body:

> Right now, we believe that the world is real. We believe that "I" and "other" really exist, and that all experiences of happiness

and suffering are also real. This notion of the reality of all manifestation is strongly anchored in us. What is called *illusory body* consists, on the other hand, of looking at all phenomena as a magical creation, a mirage, the reflection of the moon on water, or as a rainbow.[23]

In the practice of the illusory body, through a variety of techniques that are provided, one meditates on all conventional reality as a mere illusion, like a mirage, a dream, a shadow, and so on. Tashi Namgyal summarizes:

> All things [dharmas] in Samsara and Nirvana are devoid of self-nature and thus illusory. But the clinging, confusions, discriminating thoughts of sentient beings make things appear to be real. To clear away this clinging and confusion, one should observe the void nature of all dharmas and learn the truth about maya [illusion]. . . . Through the practice of the Illusory-Body . . . these clingings and confusions will be gradually cleared away. . . . As a result, the Samsaric *prana*s, *nadi*s, and *bindu*s are purified and the human body is transformed into the rainbow-like Illusory Body of Buddhahood.[24]

DREAM YOGA

The concept of the dream has many levels of meaning in Buddhism. On one level, it refers to the dreams that we have while sleeping, which seem so real to the dreamer yet which, in our normal waking state, are recognized to be unreal. On another level, "dream" indicates our everyday waking state, which seems so unimpeachable in its reality to our waking consciousness and yet, upon deeper investigation, turns out to be yet another kind of dream. On a still deeper level, dreams point to the nature of all experience in having shape and color but being ultimately transparent and unreal. To say that all reality is a dream exactly explains the meaning of emptiness: things appear but are empty of substance, definition, and permanence, and provide no ground, handhold, or nourishment for the "I."

Dream yoga involves working with one's waking and sleeping dreams to develop clarity and awareness and, in so doing, to discover the dream-like quality of all our experience.

Kalu Rinpoche describes some of the extended benefits of dream yoga:

> Instructions provided for the practice of dream allow us first to recognize, during the dream itself, that we are actually in the process of dreaming and to become conscious that anything appearing in the dream is only the dynamics of mind lacking physical reality. From there, the practitioner can increase control of the dream by voluntarily creating phenomena in the dream, multiplying them, or travelling within the dream. For example, the practitioner can go to pure lands like the Land of Bliss, meet Buddhas, or produce all kinds of miracles. Those who obtain perfect mastery of the dream can enlarge it to the waking world. Recognizing that the waking state is not fundamentally different from the dream state gives them the capacity to create miracles.[25]

Trungpa Rinpoche explains how the awakening through dream yoga can impact one's ordinary experience. Usually, in our everyday waking life, we are constantly dreaming.

> [This] is the dreams that we have all the time in our lives, the fantasies and real experiences of our life during the day, the fantasies and the thought processes that make our life like it is happening in Disneyland. The search for entertainment is an important aspect of the dream activity. If you realize the dream as dream, then there is no entertainment. . . .
>
> If we realize dream as dream, the whole approach to life becomes less businesslike, but at the same time very practical. Relating with friends, relatives, the business world, enemies—all these experiences become more real. . . . The point of this yoga is to free oneself from the Disneylandlike quality, which is our regular life, and replace that with dream experience, which

is real life. From that point of view, if one could live completely in the dream world, that would be much more real and pragmatic and efficient and complete than the so-called nondream world.[26]

The purpose of dream yoga, then, is to realize the nature of all reality as appearance/emptiness. In this sense, it is similar to the practice of the illusory body and is considered a support of the illusory body practice and supplementary to it. In fact, one of the main purposes of dream yoga is to provide further tools to realize the illusory body both in this life and in the bardo state after death. Tashi Namgyal concludes:

> The combined practice of these two Yogas can lead one to purify the habitual-thoughts of Samsara, to realize that all things are manifestations of the mind, and that mind is devoid of self-entity, like dreams; to know that both Samsara and Nirvana are unreal mirages, and that they bind nothing and liberate nothing; to cleanse oneself of all the crude and subtle, pure and impure attachments; and finally to unfold the magic-like Sambhoga-kaya of Buddhahood.[27]

CLEAR LIGHT

The actual practice of clear light is closely related to that of dream yoga and is connected with deep sleep. Kalu Rinpoche:

> When we fall into deep sleep, without dreams, we are in total darkness, with no consciousness of what happens. The practice of the clear light allows that, during deep sleep, either at the moment when one has just fallen asleep or in the periods alternating with dreams, ignorance is replaced by knowledge and the mind dwells in a state of openness and clarity.[28]

Tashi Namgyal:

> So, by the practice of this Light Yoga, Samsaric clingings and discriminations will be purified and the Self-Illuminating Wis-

dom realized. With the Wisdom Fire of the Innate Light, one can destroy all impure habitual thoughts . . . One will then attain the perfect Dharmakaya and Rupakaya, and until the end of Samsara he can, without the slightest effort, help all sentient beings in a countless number of ways.[29]

Through the clear light practice, the practitioner comes to realize the openness and transparency of all existence. Usually, we feel that there is light and there are shadows; there is the real and the unreal; there is truth and there is falsehood. Through the practice of clear light, however, one sees that every experience has its own particular clarity, integrity, and finality. Shadows have as much "beingness" as light; the experience of unreality is as vivid and "real" as the experience of supposed reality. Trungpa Rinpoche: "Luminosity, *ösel* in Tibetan, [is] all-pervading luminosity. There is nothing at all that is regarded as a dark corner, an area of mystery, anymore. The whole thing is seen as open, brilliant, as things as they really are. There are no mysterious corners left."[30]

The Bardo

Through training in the bardo practice, which rests on the development of the illusory body, one gains the ability to not be fooled by the apparent reality of the illusions in the after-death state, but to see them as they are. The detailed practices of the bardo yoga are described in chapter 14, so need not be discussed here. Through the bardo practices, one is enabled to find one's way to attain liberation or rebirth in a pure land. Kalu Rinpoche:

> After death, during the period called the bardo of becoming, a multitude of phenomena appear that, while being productions of the mind only, are not recognized as such. The deceased person does not know in fact that he or she is in the bardo, and passes through all kinds of pleasant and unpleasant experiences. Even if the person understands that he or she is dead, this discovery plunges him or her into such anguish and fear that the

person falls again into a state of unconsciousness. The person who has practiced the instructions contained in the dharma of the bardo immediately recognizes being in the bardo and from then on applies the methods allowing him or her to be completely liberated. Even if this person cannot apply the methods, the capacity is present to freely move in the bardo and to go to the Land of Bliss or to another pure land. Instructions of the bardo open up many possibilities.[31]

PHOWA, OR EJECTION

The six yogas can bring about realization in this life and also represent training for the time of death. Tummo, as the ground of the other five yogas, purifies our state of being so that we no longer identify with what is conditioned and mortal. The practices of illusory body and dream yoga enable us to see the apparent-yet-unreal nature of phenomenal manifestation, the form that we will have in the after-death state. The final three yogas relate specifically to death and dying. As we shall see in chapter 14, the practice of clear light trains us to identify with the ground luminosity, the dharmakaya, at the moment of death, thereby attaining liberation. If we are not sufficiently skilled in this, the practice of bardo yoga develops the ability to identify with the illusory body, the apparent-yet-empty form of the yidam, through which we may attain the sambhogakaya in the after-death state and thus attain liberation.

Lama Tashi Namgyal says that for yogins proficient in the clear light practice or illusory body, the yoga of ejection is not necessary, but for those who have not yet reached the advanced stages, it is extremely important. Through ejection, we are able to direct the consciousness at the time of death so that it may attain rebirth in a pure realm or at least a favorable human incarnation. As we shall see below, phowa may also be carried out for another person, by someone with the appropriate training and experience. In the context of the six yogas, however, one learns how to perform the phowa for oneself at the moment of death. Kalu Rinpoche:

The verb *powa* in Tibetan carries the idea of leaving one place for another. For example, it is used to mean *moving*. In the case of the six dharmas, it is related to a technique used at the moment of death, which allows one to leave the six realms that compose samsara and go to a land of pure manifestation as the Land of Bliss. The person knowing how to apply this meditation can go where he or she wants by directing his or her thought at the right moment to one of the pure lands.[32]

Trungpa Rinpoche explains how the practice of phowa is even possible. "Since you do not believe in physical existence as a solid thing that you can take refuge in, you can switch out of such a belief into nonbelief, transfer your consciousness into open space, a space which has nothing to do with the fixed notion of 'me and mine' and 'that and this' at all."[33]

You are capable of making your consciousness step outside of your body when the time comes. This again means cutting through a lot of possessiveness toward one's body, particularly the desire for possessions and entertainment. One has to have the power to remove clingings. You can step out in the middle of your meal; before you finish your sentence, you can step out. You don't have a chance to finish your pun or to finish your dessert. You have to leave things behind, which can be very scary and very unsatisfying.[34]

SOME CONCLUSIONS

Meditation Experiences

Tibetan tradition points to three sorts of experience in particular that are likely to arise through intensive Vajrayana practice. These are bliss (*dewa*), clarity (*selwa*), and nonthought (*mi tokpa*). *Dewa* refers to the experience of the appearances of the world, the forms of the world, as inherently blissful in nature. Most of what we experience so often seems to be problematic—the first noble truth. But sometimes in our practice, the wall of ego cracks, and through it we perceive that, in fact, what arises in the world is filled with bliss. Clarity refers to the utter "isness" of our experience. Things are absolutely what they are, just what they are, and their statement of themselves is brilliant, clear, and free from taint or imperfection. Nonthought is the experience of the mind when it has come to an utter and complete halt. Sometimes we are thinking; sometimes we are not thinking, but even here we may be thinking that we are not thinking. Moreover, under the surface there is always the bubbling of the alaya, with little carrots, onions, potato chunks, and peas of thoughts appearing and disappearing. But occasionally, the mind simply comes to an absolute, dead halt, and there is nothing going on whatsoever.

These experiences are called *nyam*, temporary meditation experiences. They arise in accord with karmic cause and effect. They are a result of practice. But they are not the goal, merely markers along the way. It is interesting the way in which such experiences accelerate the ripening of karma. For example, when a young practitioner has an experience such as this, he or she may want desperately to hang on to it. For a moment, one found oneself standing beyond the boundaries of ego—the light, the clarity, and the freedom were overwhelming. So now, by way of the intense contrast, one may feel appalled by the prospect of returning to one's ordinary, claustrophobic ego and long to repeat the meditation experience. One wants to be that kind of a person and desperately wants to reexperience that relief, which one identifies with enlightenment.

Inevitably, then, the ego itself is getting involved in trying to repeat the experience, to force it. Of course this never works, and we can spend hours, days, or weeks in retreat trying to recapture the moment of freedom that came, as it always must, unsought. We want to recapture the "sanity" we felt, but really now we are trying to repeat an experience remembered as pleasurable and gratifying, the same old samsaric game.

At this point, an important distinction needs to be made. Of course, memories of past spiritual experiences play an important, positive role on the path, inspiring us, helping us maintain correct view, generating confidence in what we are doing, and leading us back to our practice.

These would all be understood as reflections of our deeper nature, not as primarily ego-oriented. The mark of ego's involvement, however, is a grasping and clinging to one's memory and the aggressive attempt to force reality to conform to it. It is also reflected in a rigid state of mind that is driven by ambition and can no longer relate openly to the ambiguity and pain of the present moment. Ironically, only when we let go of all grasping toward our memory is the space opened for fresh insight to arise.

At the lower levels of the ordinary practitioner, then, the nyam or temporary meditation experiences tend to force the ego out of hiding—they show us how limited life is within the "I," and reveal the spiritual materialism of the ego, how it will try to co-opt spiritual experience for its own ends. This is painful, but it is also helpful in keeping us grounded and on track. It is a hard fact that the Vajrayana involves so much self-confrontation and at such a deep level. The instruction always given in this situation is, don't make too much out of the ups and downs, and stay with the practice.

The trick here—and it is a challenge that every Vajrayana practitioner faces—is to stay with the journey. There is a temptation, when we feel inundated by the chaos of the ride, to indulge in emotional upheavals, become numb, or give up. When our neurosis is blatantly in our face—particularly as Western practitioners—we may feel that we have made a mistake of some kind. We may go looking for absolution. Or we may feel that the practice is "not working" and stop meditating. Either one of these represents a "wrong view." It is precisely because the practice *is* working and our karma *is* ripening so quickly that we find ourselves sailing in a very choppy sea. The antidote in such a situation is to stick with our practice. Emphasize emptiness, resting in open awareness, until the howl of the wind dies down a bit. Then hoist the sail again and get on with the voyage.

There come times when we are really lost. The tantric journey has proceeded to such a point that we have lost our bearings. We don't know who we are; we don't know where we are; and we don't know what we think. Our meditation may occasionally bring us peace, but even that does not answer our questions.

At this point, we need to turn to the antidote that underlies all others, and this is the remedy of devotion. In a previous chapter, the importance of devotion on the tantric path was noted. Now we come to the point where it is not only important but essential. Without devotion, we could not find the way through the darkness that surrounds us.

But what is devotion at this point? It is calling on the gurus from afar. It is calling on the buddhas and bodhisattvas of the ten directions; on the masters of one's lineage; on one's own guru, whether alive or passed beyond.

Devotion is an acknowledgment of helplessness and of trust. It involves the recognition that we have run out of personal resources; that we have lost our way; that we do not know where we are, what is wrong, or what to do. Calling for help is also an expression of trust—the innate human trust that our call will be heard.

It might seem strange to bring up devotion at this point, so well along the path. Isn't devotion something mainly for the beginning, when we are getting started with our practice? In fact, devotion is the most subtle and sophisticated attitude that a person can have toward reality. It is a recognition of the truth of egolessness, that on some level we—as egos—are nothing and have nothing to say for ourselves. The further one progresses along the path, the more intense and wholehearted one's devotion becomes. The further one goes, the more devotion becomes the primary way to make the journey.

But isn't devotion an expression of theism, of finding power and reality outside of oneself, the opposite of what Buddhism is supposed to be? Devotion is looking for an answer outside of the "I," the ego. The answer is ultimately within us, yes. But, as we have seen, while we are on the path, we "discover" the buddha-nature in projected form, apparently outside of us, particularly in our teachers and spiritual friends.

So powerful is genuine devotion that once we fully acknowledge that we have lost the thread and all hope of finding the way, the answer is already there.

The Unfolding Path

In Tibet, ngöndro and sadhana practice, and the practices of inner yoga, were all typically carried out in retreat. In that context, the practitioner might hope to complete the ngöndro in perhaps three to six months. After completing it, one would then be authorized to receive the main abhishekas of the lineage to which one belongs, as well as additional empowerments suggested by one's teacher. In the Karma Kagyü lineage, the ngöndro is typically followed by the Vajrayogini abhisheka. After finishing the requisite number of recitations of the Vajrayogini mantra, one is able to receive the Chakrasamvara abhisheka and to carry out its sadhana practice. The practitioner may subsequently receive other abhishekas and pursue other cycles of practice such as the inner yogas or the formless meditation of mahamudra or dzokchen. Sometimes, new practices will require performance of another ngöndro or preliminary set of practices.

This itinerary may sound somewhat complex and intimidating. However, since the practice is carried out over a period of decades, each stage of practice resembles one of a few major sights seen on a very long journey. In the Western context, the ngöndro may take a year or two to complete, if one mixes daily practice with periodic solitary or group retreats. When doing prostrations for several months on a daily basis, the practice enters one's state of being and becomes part of who one is. It is similar when practicing Vajrayogini for five or ten years. During the many thousands of hours spent visualizing oneself and one's world as the yidam, there is ample opportunity to explore the practice in an extensive and intimate way, through many ups and downs and varied experiences of life.

It is also important to realize that each additional practice that may be undertaken, such as other yidam meditations, the inner yogas, or mahamudra or dzokchen (discussed below), are not so much something new as an extension of what one is already doing. The basic principles and processes are all contained in the simplest sadhana. In fact, the whole panoply of Vajrayana practices, from prostrations through the formless meditations of resting in the nature of mind, can all be seen as part of the same and single transformative way that is the Vajrayana. At stake here in every case is one's own insubstantiality and the increasing edge and energy presented by life, all within the universal realm of nonexistence and the sacredness of what is.

As one progresses along the path, the unworkability of samsaric states of mind and samsaric pursuits closes in like a circle of fire drawing ever nearer. Opportunities to surrender to the situation, to the futility of one's own struggling, become more frequent. And the invitations to relate to the world just as it presents itself in this moment rather than from some stronghold of strategizing become more intense and unavoidable.

In traditional Tibet, and in the modern West, different styles of carrying out *yidam* practice have evolved. As mentioned, some people may receive a series of abhishekas, each time performing the minimum requisite number of mantras required, while others may choose to carry out the practice of one yidam for the rest of their lives, forgoing other abhishekas and practices. One person may learn best from meeting and identifying with several different yidams. Another may be able to attain the most profound realization through fully exploring the practices of one. Again, some people may place more stress on the development stage of whatever practice they are doing, while others will place more emphasis on the completion stage. The precise path taken as well as the particular configuration of practices followed at any given point depends upon one's character and inclinations, and also upon one's abilities and needs at any given time.

It is also important to realize that the ngöndro and other practices are not something carried out only on the meditation cushion in situations of formal practice. At each stage of one's Vajrayana journey, one is enjoined to practice "twenty-four hours a day." An important part of the instructions include how to hold one's mind and how to regard the world when moving through daily life, engaged in ordinary activities.

One is enjoined to maintain "sacred outlook," not forgetting that fundamentally one is the deity and the environment his or her celestial palace.

The teaching on sacred outlook is illustrated by the following example. One day in the early 1980s, a number of members of the Nālandā Translation Committee were meeting in Denver, Colorado, with Khenpo Sherap Palden and his brother Khenpo Tsewang Döngyal. We were reading a text on visualization, and at one point Khenpo Palden pointed out the window to the panorama of the Rocky Mountains to the west. "What are those things over there?" he asked. We thought he was just asking what mountains they were and responded, "Those are the Rocky Mountains." The Khenpo replied, "That is just what you *think*. A person with sacred outlook would see those as the divine mandala of Chakrasamvara."

The fruition of Vajrayana is an extraordinary perception of the world and an extraordinary way of being in it. Tulku Urgyen remarks that through meditation, one progressively dissolves inner fixation on the appearance of things:

> The more this inner fixation dissolves, the more our inner feeling of solidity vanishes, until finally it becomes as Götsangpa Gönpo Dorje sang, as included in the *Rain of Wisdom*:
>
>> Appearances are an insubstantial play.
>> All the relative forms of this magical trickery
>> Are wide open and penetrable,
>> Like the rock behind my back.

At that point, he leaned back into the solid rock and made an exact imprint of his head and back. Milarepa could fly and move freely through solid rock. It is not that such yogis are miracle workers; they have simply realized the original nature of things as insubstantial. This becomes increasingly evident as the inner fixation on solidity is allowed to dissolve.

The more we train in the awakened state, in letting go of fixation, the more the outer world will be seen as it really is—an insubstantial play of illusions. That is why the great masters who attained accomplishment could walk on water, pass through solid rock and remain unharmed by flames. Padmasambhava was burned at the stake several times, but remained unscorched. The outer elements are only deluded perceptions. No one else created them but us; thus, when our inner fixation caves in, their falsehood also collapses. All appearances are insubstantial like smoke and mist. Superficially they do appear, but only as the magical play of delusion.[35]

PART THREE

Meeting the Essence of Mind

12

Mahamudra

THE GREAT SYMBOL

IN THE NEW TRANSLATION TRADITIONS, MAHAMUDRA (*chaggya chenpo*), the "great symbol" or "great seal," represents the culmination and fulfillment of all practices.[1] It is understood as the essence of the buddhas of the three times (past, present, and future) and the quintessential message of all the sutras and tantras. Tibetan Buddhism describes three somewhat distinct bodies of mahamudra teaching. First is Sutra mahamudra, as expressed in the third turning of the wheel of dharma, notably the *Uttara-tantra* (see chapter 5 above and *Indestructible Truth*, chapter 16). Through this body of teachings, one attains mahamudra by practicing the six paramitas and making the long journey to buddhahood through the five paths and the ten bhumis. Second is Tantra mahamudra, in which mahamudra stands as the essential purpose and end point of the yidam practices of the various *Anuttarayoga tantras* of the New Translation schools. Third and finally is Essence mahamudra, which refers to a self-contained body of instructions on looking directly at the nature of mind.

The Sanskrit term *mudra* means "symbol" or "seal," while *maha* means "great" or "transcendent." Mudra refers to the expressive quality of reality when seen from a realized standpoint. *Maha* means "great," but not in a comparative sense. It refers to emptiness and indicates that the expressiveness of mudra is utterly beyond limitation, comparison, or measure. In the realization of mahamudra, each phenomenon stands as a proclamation of the inseparability of form (*mudra*) and emptiness (*maha*). The form-aspect of each phenomenon is the fact that it appears vividly; the emptiness-aspect is that it is beyond concept and imagination or projection.

In mahamudra, things are symbols, but not in the ordinary sense of pointing to something beyond or outside of themselves. Phenomena are symbols of themselves—they appear, but not as emissaries of anything else. In ordinary experience, perceptions are always referred to some concept or other, to provide the "real" meaning or significance of that perception. We always assume that there is something "behind" or underlying phenomena. In mahamudra, however, things are proclamations of themselves: each phenomenon is stamped and sealed with the brilliant and final reality of itself, and each speaks for itself and itself only, in a complete, unobstructed, and definitive way.

Trungpa Rinpoche provides the following analogy of mahamudra.

[It] has been compared to the experience of a young child visiting a colorful temple. He sees all kinds of magnificent decorations, displays, rich colors, vividness of all kinds. But this child has no preconception or any concept whatsoever about where to begin to analyze. Everything is overwhelming, quite in its own right. So the child does not become frightened by this vivid scenery and at the same time does not know how to appreciate it. It is quite different from a child walking into a playroom full of toys, where his attention is caught by a particular toy and he runs right over and starts playing with it. A temple, a highly decorated, colorful temple, is so harmonious in its own right that the child has no way of introducing his fascination from one particular standpoint. The experience is all-pervasive. At the same time, it is perhaps somewhat overwhelmingly pleasurable.[2]

The experience of mahamudra, then, represents a further step in relation to the experience of emptiness described in the second turning. In the second turning, one realizes that one's samsaric experience of the world is nothing other than illusory and dreamlike projection, having nothing to do with reality. Trungpa Rinpoche explains: "Having had all the illusions and hallucinations removed by the experience of *shunyata*, there is a sense of extraordinary clarity. That clarity is called Mahamudra. . . ."

In the second-turning understanding, emptiness can function as a kind of end point for all experience. In this sense, it becomes an extremely subtle reference point against which one's experience is measured. Trungpa Rinpoche:

> In the case of *shunyata*, there is still a sense of needing a nursing process for that experience; it is not only that the sitting practice of meditation is required, but there is a sense of needing a registrar to record your experience in a memory bank. The very idea of emptiness is an experience, even though you may not have an experienc*er* as such, since the whole thing is totally open and nondualistic.

Yet, from the viewpoint of mahamudra, that very idea of emptiness itself becomes problematic.

> But even the very sense of nonduality is a faint stain, a very subtle, transparent stain. On the *shunyata* level, that stain is regarded as an adornment, like putting a varnish over well-finished wood. It is supposed to protect the wood from further stains of dirt or grease, to keep it looking fresh and new, to preserve the newness of this well-finished wood. But in the long run, that clear varnish becomes a factor that ages the new look of this fresh wood. It turns yellow and begins slowly to crumble, and scratches begin to show much more in it than they would in the original wood. So the nonduality becomes a problem in the *shunyata* experience. In the experience of Mahamudra, even the notion of nonduality is not applied, or is not necessary."[3]

The mahamudra teaching first appears in India among the eighty-four mahasiddhas. In their hagiographies, songs, and commentaries, mahamudra is described as the realization they attained as the fruition of their meditation practice. In the Indian Vajrayana, there were primarily two different ways in which the mahamudra teachings were practiced, and both are found among the siddhas. On the one hand, deriving perhaps from the practice lineage of the Prajnaparamita with which they are sometimes connected, these teachings—as "Essence mahamudra"—represent a tradition of "formless meditation" that seeks to know and actualize the naked state of awareness itself. Tradition holds the Indian siddha Saraha to have been a primary holder of these formless or Essence mahamudra teachings. On the other hand, the mahamudra—as "Tantra mahamudra"—is seen as the final state of immaculate awareness that the siddha attains as the fruition of the form tantra practices of the anuttarayoga lineages. What is cultivated through the development and perfection stages is seen, in fact, as nothing other than the awareness of mahamudra itself.

These two ways of practicing mahamudra were flourishing in India at the time of the later spreading of Buddhism to Tibet, or during the eleventh-thirteenth centuries CE. They made their way to Tibet during the later spreading through several lineages. The Tibetan founder of the Kagyü lineage, Marpa the Translator, received the Essence mahamudra teachings from the Indian siddha Maitripa, while he received the Tantra mahamudra traditions of the anuttarayoga tantra principally from Naropa. Marpa also received from his guru the "inner practices" of the six yogas of Naropa, which clarify, stabilize, and enhance the experience of mahamudra. Marpa transmitted these various mahamudra lineages to his disciple Milarepa, who carried out both the anuttarayoga tantric practices (both yidam and inner yoga) and the Essence mahamudra meditations throughout his life in retreat. Milarepa passed these mahamudra lineages to his principal disciples Rechungpa and Gampopa, and this latter combined the Vajrayana lineages he received from Milarepa with the conventional Mahayana orientation of his Kadam training. One of Gampopa's special contributions was, taking his lead from the sutra mahamudra teachings found in the *Uttara-tantra Shastra*, to introduce many of his students to mahamudra practice without first requiring tantric empowerments (abhishekas) and practice. From Gampopa and other lineage forebears, the mahamudra teachings were carried down through successive Kagyü masters to the present day. The mahamudra teachings also came from the Indian siddha Virupa to Tibet through the scholar-traveler Drogmi, founder of the Sakya school. Today, they are practiced by all three New Translation schools—Sakya,

Kagyü, and Geluk. The dzokchen of the Nyingma school is parallel and in many ways identical to the mahamudra traditions. In addition, many Nyingma lamas study with mahamudra teachers from the New Translation lineages.*

GROUND MAHAMUDRA

Mahamudra is traditionally discussed in terms of the threefold logic of ground or foundation, path, and fruition. Thrangu Rinpoche summarizes:

> Of these three, the *foundation* [of mahamudra] has to do with the nature of things as they are, the nature of truth. . . . The *path* of Mahamudra is meditation and what arises in meditation, that is, experience. Finally, the *fruition* of that experience arising in one's being is ultimately realizing that the Buddha is not outside of oneself, but within one. One's mind is the state of Buddha.[4]

> [The Buddha Nature] is called the *ground* or foundation Mahamudra, meaning that we have it already. But because it is not yet actualized, then we need the *path* Mahamudra. Based on the

---

*Thrangu Rinpoche remarks that there are three somewhat different ways of talking about mahamudra: Rangtong Madhyamaka, Shentong Madhyamaka, and the practice tradition of the Vajrayana. The Madhyamaka Rangtong school emphasizes the concept of *dharmadhatu*. The principal nature of mahamudra is emptiness, and this is called dharmadhatu, or the realm of reality. The Madhyamaka Shentong school, on the other hand, focuses on the aspect of awareness (Skt. *jnana*) and emphasizes the concept of *tathagatagarbha,* literally "essence of the tathagatas" (buddhas), often called buddha-nature or buddha essence. However, Thrangu Rinpoche says, "in meaning . . . these two concepts are essentially the same." He then tells us that the Vajrayana way of speaking places the emphasis on the pointing-out of the nature of mind, which is called mahamudra. This way of speaking, too, is no different from the sutra presentations. "The mind's essence is basically the same as the Madhyamaka concepts of the sutra tradition. That is why Rangjung Dorje said that this 'madhyamika' and this 'Mahamudra' apply to the same thing." (Thrangu Rinpoche, *The Song of Lodro Thaye,* 23.)

path, what one already possesses can be actualized, and that's called *fruition* Mahamudra.[5]

Thrangu Rinpoche provides the following analogy of ground, path, and fruition mahamudra. Suppose there is a gold treasure buried in the ground. It remains there pure and unaffected by the dirt surrounding it, but still hidden from sight. Many years later, a poor man comes and builds his hut upon it. He lives in that hut, hardly having food to eat or clothes on his back. He lives there day after day, year after year, stricken with terrible poverty, not realizing that just under his floor there lies a treasure of inestimable worth. One day, a clairvoyant comes along and tells the man that he need only remove a little dirt to find wealth that will fulfill all his dreams. The man digs in the earth, finding and taking possession of the gold.

> Similarly we say we have the nature of Mahamudra, but we don't know it. The Buddha comes along and says that we are Mahamudra and all we have to do is find it. The ground Mahamudra is the gold right underneath our feet. The poor man's effort to scrape away a little dirt to get at it is like the path Mahamudra. If we don't make some effort, then we can't get the gold. Fruition Mahamudra is like when the poor man finds the gold and completely casts away his poverty.[6]

The ground mahamudra, reality as it is, can be looked at either internally or externally. Internally, it is our own inherent nature as wisdom and emptiness; externally, it is appearances that arise without self-nature as expressions of wisdom. As we have seen, these two ways of speaking do not refer to two separate and distinct experiences. In fact, the experience of ground mahamudra precedes the process of dichotomizing reality into subject and object. It would be more correct to regard ground mahamudra as internal and as external, as two "gates" through which we can pass into the primordial experience. As mentioned, the experience of buddha-nature *is* appearance empty of attribution, and the experience of phenomena as pure appearance *is* the experience of buddha-nature. Thus the mahamudra experience is nondual. To speak of appearances and buddha-nature as if they were separate is merely an accommodation to our false, dualistic way of looking at the world.

"Ground mahamudra" is the buddha-nature that is the foundation of all our experience. It is the perfect state of awareness that pervades all sentient beings but is covered over by inessential defilements. Thrangu Rinpoche comments that "this buddha-nature, our innermost being, is of the nature of the three kayas of a buddha, the emptiness of the dharmakaya; the radiance of the sambhogakaya; and the energy of manifestation of the nirmanakaya. These three are present as the natural state of Mahamudra."[7] It is hard for us to imagine that such truth, clarity, and power actually lie within us, just underneath the neurotic overlay of our conventional but confused personalities, yet they do.

This enlightened essence of all sentient beings is, as we saw, *empty* of any concepts that could be applied to it, yet *not empty* of its own identity as luminous, unobstructed awareness with inseparable buddha qualities. In relation to ground mahamudra, Thrangu Rinpoche explains, "In the Buddhist tradition, the goal of practice is to attain the state of a Buddha. But this state is not newly attained. . . . Shakyamuni Buddha demonstrated that we already have this quality. Therefore, in Mahamudra this is called the ground or foundation Mahamudra, meaning [that] we have it already."[8]

Ground mahamudra, then, exists in two ways: the way it is and the way it is confused. "The way it is" refers to the fact that we are mahamudra. In the analogy, it is the vast and supremely valuable treasure. "The way it is confused" refers to the fact that we have not recognized our being as mahamudra. In the analogy, it is the fact that the poor man lives in his little hut, remaining in poverty because he does not realize the gold existing right beneath his floor.

Ground mahamudra is emptiness understood in the manner of the third turning of the wheel of dharma. It is empty of any substantial reality, but not empty of the qualities inseparable from it. Thrangu Rinpoche: "From the point of view of Madhyamaka the true state of phenomena is emptiness. But everything is not just empty because there is also a clear or luminous aspect to it, which we call awareness or *jnana*. That is why we talk about the indivisibility or union of space and awareness. This union of space and awareness is the view of ground Mahamudra."[9]

Thus it is said that ground mahamudra is unobstructed and manifests everything. Thrangu Rinpoche:

> Although the essence of Mahamudra is non-existent, at the same time its manifestation is completely unobstructed. For instance, we can say our mind is empty because when we look for it, it is nowhere to be found. However, when we don't look, it manifests everything. It is completely unobstructed in its nature. In the same way, Mahamudra does not actually exist as an object. It is dharmadhatu, but from the luminosity aspect it is unobstructed and can manifest in any way whatsoever. It can manifest as awareness on the level of Buddha or manifest as consciousness on the level of ordinary beings. It arises unimpeded as all positive or negative manifestation.[10]

This ultimate emptiness which is mahamudra is "unoriginated" and beyond causes and conditions: "Mahamudra also did not originate as a new phenomenon and it did not result from any cause and it is not changed by any external conditions. Mahamudra has existed from the beginning of time and is present in all beings and the essence of Mahamudra never changes. It is unborn and unchangeable and immutable." Like the gold in the story of the poor man, the mahamudra never changes whether it is covered with conceptual dirt or completely cleansed of all debris. Thus, "the Mahamudra in the state of bewilderment of samsara is not any worse [than] or any different from Mahamudra [in its realized state]. When it is recognized through the yogi's meditation, it also is not any better. . . ."[11]

As the ground, then, mahamudra provides the basis of both confusion and clarity. In and of itself, it is an open and unobstructed state of awareness. However, sentient beings lay conceptual defilements onto this open state and freeze it into dualistic experience of "I" and "other." Thrangu Rinpoche:

> Mahamudra is the foundation of everything, the foundation of
> all confusion and bewilderment, as well as the foundation of

liberation. Mahamudra is the foundation of confusion in samsara, because in samsara one's confusion is taking place in the
space of Mahamudra. Similarly one's liberation in nirvana is
taking place in the space of Mahamudra. So Mahamudra is the
ground of everything. . . .[12]

In *Cutting Through Spiritual Materialism*, Trungpa Rinpoche explains
how the ground mahamudra, or what he calls "the basic ground," is
misconceived and frozen by ego into the apparent duality of conventional thinking:

> Fundamentally there is just open space, the basic ground, what
> we really are. Our most fundamental state of mind, before the
> creation of ego, is such that there is basic openness, basic free-
> dom, a spacious quality; and we have now and have always had
> this openness.
>
> Take, for example, our every day lives and thought patterns.
> When we see an object, in the first instant there is a sudden
> perception which has no logic or conceptualization at all; we
> just perceive the thing in the open ground. Then immediately
> we panic and begin to rush about trying to add something to it,
> either trying to find a name for it or trying to find pigeon-holes
> in which we could locate and categorize it. Gradually things
> develop from there. . . .[13]

The initial point, then, is an experience of space belonging to no one. In
fact, one may call it "experience" only in a metaphorical sense, because
it precedes the arising of the media of samsaric cognition, namely the
five skandhas. This is, in Trungpa Rinpoche's words, "primordial intelligence connected with space and openness" that is within us, without
beginning or end. "There is always primordial intelligence connected
with the space and openness. *Vidya* means 'intelligence' in Sanskrit—
precision, sharpness, sharpness with space, sharpness with room in
which to put things, exchange things." Trungpa Rinpoche describes the
arising of ego from this primordial openness:

It is like a spacious hall where there is room to dance about, where there is no danger of knocking things over or tripping over things, for there is completely open space. We are this space, we are one with it, with vidya, intelligence and openness.

But if we are this all the time, where did the confusion come from, where has the space gone, what has happened? Nothing has happened as a matter of fact. We just became too active in that space. Because it is spacious, it brings inspiration to dance about; but our dance became a bit too active, we began to spin more than was necessary to express the space. At this point we became self-conscious, conscious that "I" am dancing in the space.

At such a point, space is no longer space as such. It becomes solid. Instead of being one with the space, we feel solid space as a separate entity, as tangible. This is the first experience of duality—space and I, I am dancing in this space, and this spaciousness is a solid, separate thing. Duality means "space and I," rather than being completely one with the space.[14]

In Trungpa Rinpoche's more technical *Glimpses of Abhidharma*, he gives a slightly different view of the same process. The basic ground, the mahamudra, does not depend on relative situations at all.

It is natural being which just is. Energies appear out of this basic ground and those energies are the source of the development of relative situations. Sparks of duality, intensity and sharpness, flashes of wisdom and knowledge—all sorts of things come out of the basic ground. So the basic ground is the source of confusion and also the source of liberation. Both liberation and confusion are that energy which happens constantly, which sparks out and then goes back to its basic nature, like clouds (as Milarepa described it) emerging from and disappearing back into the sky.

How is it, then, that ego arises? It arises, he says, "when the energy which flashes out of the basic ground brings about a sort of blinding effect, bewilderment."

That bewilderment becomes the eighth consciousness ["ground" consciousness], the basic ground for ego. . . . Dr. [Herbert] Guenther calls it "bewilderment-errancy." It is the error that comes out of being bewildered—a kind of panic. If the energy were to go along with its own process of speed, there would be no panic.

It is like driving a car fast; if you go along with the speed, you are able to maneuver accordingly. But if you suddenly panic with the thought that you have been going too fast without realizing it, you jam on the brakes and probably have an accident. Something suddenly freezes and brings the bewilderment of not knowing how to conduct the situation. Then actually the situation takes you over. Rather than just being completely one with the projection, the projection takes you over. Then the unexpected power of the projection comes back as your own doing, which creates extremely powerful and impressive bewilderment. That bewilderment acts as the basic ground, the secondary basic ground of ego, away from the primordial basic ground [= mahamudra].[15]

PATH MAHAMUDRA I: MAHAMUDRA SHAMATHA AND VIPASHYANA

"Path mahamudra" represents the various practices and methods of meditation given in the Vajrayana tradition for the realization of mahamudra. As mentioned above, these are twofold: on the one hand, meditation on the various yidam and inner yoga practices of the anuttarayoga tantras; on the other, the direct, formless mahamudra instructions on resting in naked awareness.

On the Vajrayana path, what is the difference between the tantric form and the formless practices of mahamudra? In the form practices, as we saw in chapter 10, one follows a specific itinerary beginning with the various ngöndro, or preliminary practices. One then meets mahamudra in the "pointing-out instructions" given by one's guru. Subsequently, one receives abhisheka, or empowerment, and encounters mahamudra again in the fourth abhisheka. Following empowerment, one undertakes the practice, or sadhana, of the yidam, the personal deity in whose cycle abhisheka was received. In this practice, one becomes further acquainted with mahamudra in the realization of the essence of the deities as appearance-emptiness and in formless meditation of the stage of completion. In the formless tradition of mahamudra, "Essence mahamudra," one engages directly in practices of abandoning discursive thinking and resting the mind in the clear, luminous awareness that is mahamudra.

The simplicity and apparent ease of the "formless" approach to mahamudra raises the question of why a practitioner would ever want to follow the more complex and seemingly more taxing "form" path. Whether one follows primarily Tantra mahamudra or Essence mahamudra has as much to do with one's own karma as it does with any conscious, personal preference. If a person can sit down and, with relative ease, rest his or her mind in the natural state for extended periods of time, then this is a person for whom the Essence practice may, in and of itself, be sufficient. In this case, once the guru has pointed out the nature of mind, the disciple is subsequently able to rest in that. Tulku Urgyen Rinpoche tells us that this was, in fact, the case with his guru, Samten Gyatso, who once told his disciple, "At a young age I was introduced to the mind essence. Since then until now, I have not had any great problems at all in sustaining the view; as a matter of fact, there does not seem to be any difference between day and night."[16]

However, for most of us, strong mental obstacles arise if we try to carry out mahamudra (or dzokchen), without first engaging in a substantial amount of yidam practice. This is so because formless practice is considered quite difficult, and the "form" practices much easier of access. Most people who try to enter the formless practices without sufficient preparation find themselves plagued with discursive thinking, daydreaming, and "spacing out." They may even sit on their meditation cushion, thinking that they are not thinking; they may have the continuous thought that they are practicing Essence mahamudra and be most pleased to be engaging such an advanced cycle of teachings. However, these very thoughts themselves can act as subtle obstacles that prevent very much from happening.

The yidam practices, by contrast, provide a variety of means of working with one's discursive mind—liturgies that are performed, visualizations that are carried out, mantras that are recited, and so on. Through this, the relative truth of one's karmic situation is directly worked on, creating a more favorable environment for formless practice. Karmic obstacles are burned up and some of the extraneous baggage we have been carrying around is jettisoned. At a certain point, the formless mahamudra practices become accessible. In traditional language, then, yidam practice is said to purify defilements, remove obstacles, and accumulate merit, all resulting in greater access to the more direct path of formless practice. Even having gained the ability to rest our minds in the natural state, at various points our access to that state may be impeded by external life circumstances or the arising of disturbances within. When this occurs, then one is grateful to be able to return to the more form-oriented practices and the purification that results from them.

Why is it so difficult for most people simply to rest in the ground mahamudra, the buddha-nature? The mind essence is so simple and stark that we cannot stay with it. From ego's point of view, it is "nothing" and "empty" and provides no sources of entertainment or comfort. We willfully depart from this state, generating wave upon wave of discursive thought. Thrangu Rinpoche explains:

> One could meditate directly on Mahamudra from the beginning with diligence and attain Buddhahood. But it has been discovered that most of us need a tremendous amount of effort to do that and lose enthusiasm just doing the same thing all the time. So various skillful methods were devised to help us along in our Mahamudra practice.
>
> It is like having a big meal of plain rice with nothing on it. We can eat it once, but we can't keep eating it. We need to put a little salt and some soy sauce [on it]; then we are able to eat more and keep on eating rice. If we just eat plain rice, we lose

our appetite when faced with a huge bowl of rice. So the yidam practices were developed as a skillful means to develop the mental faculties to focus the mind, to clarify the mind, and to develop the sharpness of mind. These methods help us maintain our diligence in the practice of Mahamudra.

These yidam practices are divided into the creation stage (Skt., utpattikrama) and the completion stage (Skt., sampannakrama). In the creation stage, the mind becomes very clear, very focused and free from distraction. The completion stage of yidam practice is not different from Mahamudra.[17]

The mahamudra path of form or tantric yidam practices, along with their associated inner yogas, were described in the previous two chapters. The present discussion of path mahamudra focuses on the "formless" mahamudra practices that are relatively standard throughout the New Translation schools.[18] As an example, we may epitomize the instructions given by Wangchuk Dorje, the seventh Karmapa, in a series of texts he composed on mahamudra practice.[19] In his teaching, Wangchuk Dorje divides mahamudra meditation into two overarching categories, mahamudra shamatha and mahamudra vipashyana. The practices grouped under mahamudra shamatha aim to bring the mind to a state of stillness. In mahamudra vipashyana, within the state of stillness, one recognizes the nature of mind itself.

Mahamudra Shamatha

Mahamudra shamatha contains instructions on how to sit properly in meditation posture, outlined in the so-called seven points of Vairochana. In one version of these, (1) one should sit cross-legged, in lotus posture; (2) place the hands in a comfortable posture, such as held together below the navel; (3) straighten the spine like an arrow; (4) adjust the shoulders back and align evenly; (5) bend the neck slightly forward to press the throat; (6) place the tongue gently against the roof of the mouth; and (7) sit with eyes neither wide open nor shut tight, but gazing ahead with a loose focus. The posture that one takes in meditation is important, particularly in retreat, where awareness opens in such an unprecedented and dramatic way. As retreatants over the centuries have discovered, maintaining good posture in retreat practice has a direct and immediately perceivable impact on the meditator's state of mind. Good posture enhances the clarity and power of awareness, while poor posture encourages discursiveness and mental confusion.

Wangchuk Dorje next instructs the practitioner to engage the practice of quieting the mind by focusing attention in the shamatha style. This focusing may be on an object—for example, a visual object such as a stick, a pebble, or the flame of a butter lamp. Or one may focus on another sensory object such as a sound, a smell, a taste, or a tactile sensation. The breath is suggested as an especially useful object to take as the focus of shamatha. As we saw in chapter 4, the shamatha practice consists of placing attention on the object that one has chosen and maintaining focus on that object. When discursive thoughts arise and pull one away from the practice, one gently but surely brings the attention back to the object of meditation. Sometimes the discursive distractions are gross thoughts and fantasies, but they may also be extremely subtle, such as the thought that we are meditating or that things are peaceful.

In addition to practicing shamatha by focusing on an object, one may also focus on no object whatsoever. In this kind of shamatha, the eyes are open and one gazes straight ahead into space, directing one's mind to nothing at all. When the mind drifts into discursiveness, one brings the attention back to the emptiness of no object. The mahamudra shamatha teachings also include specific instructions on how to work with a mind that is agitated, overly energized, and inundated with mental contents, or with a mind that is dull, without energy, and sunken. These instructions are ordinarily given by the meditation teacher as the need arises.

Through this process of mahamudra shamatha, one progresses through various stages of settling the mind. A series of three analogies suggests the nature of the journey. At first, one's mind is like a steep mountain waterfall, with thoughts cascading roughly one upon the other in a never-ending torrent. As one progresses in shamatha, one's mind next becomes like a mighty river, wherein thoughts occur but are more even and slow. Finally, through the practice, the mind becomes like a vast, still ocean in which thoughts appear only as ripples on the surface and then subside of their own accord.

Mahamudra Vipashyana

In his teaching, Wangchuk Dorje gives ten separate contemplations that are to be used to disclose the wisdom mind within: five practices of "looking at" and five of "pointing out" the nature of mind. All of these assume that some stillness has been cultivated through mahamudra shamatha practice. I give here the briefest description of each, to suggest the nature of mahamudra meditation. Those wishing to enter retreat to carry out these practices will find the actual retreat instructions of their meditation teacher quite detailed and extensive. In retreat practice, the following ten contemplations are usually assigned specific time periods. Thus, in a year-long retreat, one might spend one month on each practice. The final two months might be spent reviewing each of the ten, dividing the sixty days into ten sections of six days each.

PRACTICES OF LOOKING AT THE NATURE OF MIND

1. *Looking at the settled mind.* One looks at the state of stillness over and over. When thoughts arise, one returns again and again to contemplate that stillness. One may ask oneself certain questions to provoke awareness, such as "What is its nature? Is it a thing? Is it perfectly still? Is it completely empty? Is it clear? Is it bright?"

2. *Looking at the moving or thinking mind.* One looks at the arising, existence, and disappearance of thoughts. One tries to see a thought as it abruptly appears out of the stillness. One may ask questions such as, "How does it arise? Where does it come from? Where does it dwell? Where does it disappear to? What is its nature?"

3. *Looking at the mind reflecting appearances.* One looks at the way in which external appearances—the phenomena of the sense percep-

tions—occur in experience. A visual object is usually taken as subject, such as a tree, a mountain, a vase, or whatever may be available. One looks at the object, then looks again, to try to see how it is that appearances arise in the mind. What is their nature? How do they arise, dwell, and then disappear? Do they arise as already interpreted, or is their initial appearance otherwise?

4. *Looking at the mind in relation to the body.* One inspects the relation of mind and body. What is the mind? What is the body? Is the body just our concept or thought of it? Or is the body our sensations? If the body is sensations, then what relation do these have to our mental image of the body? One investigates these questions.

5. *Looking at the settled and moving minds together.* One looks at the stillness of settled mind and at the thoughts that arise in the moving mind. When the mind is still, one looks at that; when the mind is in motion, one looks at that. One looks to see whether these two modes of the mind are the same or different. If they are the same, what is that sameness? If they are different, what is their difference?

PRACTICES OF POINTING OUT THE NATURE OF MIND

Having looked in each of these ways, one now looks again at each but this time asks oneself over and over, "What is it? What is it?" One is attempting to recognize and realize the exact nature of settled mind (6), moving or thinking mind (7), mind reflecting appearances (8), the relation of body and mind (9), and settled and thinking mind together (10).

Conclusion

None of the above investigations have an end point. They are practices for looking more and more closely and deeply at our experience, seeking to find within its subtlety what is ultimately and truly there. None of the questions asked in the exercises can receive definitive answers. The point of the questions is not to be answered, but to provoke us to actually look at our experience. Even if in one meditation session we have the experience of having "gotten it," of having seen the answer to a question, in the next the memory of this experience will become an obstacle, because we will *think* that we know. This *thinking*, of course, covers over and hides the very facticity of what we are seeking. In each meditation session, indeed in each moment, we need to begin the contemplation afresh and ask our questions all over again. Insight is not something that we can obtain and then carry around with us like a possession. It is always fresh, always momentary, and continually needs to be rediscovered. The moment there is the thought of having attained insight, it has been covered by that very thought and we need to look all over again.

Tibetans usually advise against reading books on Essence mahamudra prior to carrying out the actual practice. This is why my own description is brief and no more than suggestive. The danger of reading about the practice is great, particularly for Westerners, who live in a culture where thoughts and concepts are taken as real, where our concepts parade around as reality itself. For anyone, but particularly for Westerners, reading about mahamudra practices can give us the impression that we understand them, that we "know" what they are pointing to. This *thought* can serve as a further covering over the buddha-nature and make one lazy, bored, and unmotivated. This is why many Tibetan meditation teachers have, at best, mixed feelings about the translation and publication of mahamudra (and dzokchen) meditation manuals.

The formless practices of mahamudra shamatha and vipashyana serve one in meditation from the very beginning of practice to the time of attainment of realization. In the early stages of practice, we may spend most of our time distracted by thoughts, returning to the natural state only infrequently. When we are not sitting on the cushion, the natural state may seem remote indeed. As we progress, we may find ourselves able to contact the wisdom mind in our meditation more frequently, and we may be able to return to it sometimes when we are not sitting. For a highly attained person, distractions are transparent and fleeting, and only serve as springboards back to the basic state, whether he or she is meditating or going about daily life.

PATH MAHAMUDRA II: THE FOUR YOGAS OF MAHAMUDRA

Through the practice of mahamudra, one progresses through various stages of attainment, which are classified according to the well-known "four yogas of mahamudra": the yoga of one-pointedness, the yoga of simplicity, the yoga of one taste, and the yoga of nonmeditation. These are briefly summarized by Lama Tashi Wangyal as follows:

> To rest in shamatha is the stage of one-pointedness;
> To terminate assumptions is the stage of simplicity;
> To transcend the duality of accepting and abandoning is the
> stage of one-taste;
> To perfect experiences is the stage of non-meditation.[20]

This arrangement of the four yogas presents the path comprehensively, beginning with one's initial mahamudra practice and continuing up until the culmination of "the yoga of nonmeditation," which is the attainment of realization.

The Yoga of One-Pointedness

Gampopa says that the yoga of one-pointedness involves "a lucid, unceasing, momentary awareness."[21] This stage is traditionally correlated with attaining a high level in the practice of shamatha, using practices like those mentioned in the preceding description of mahamudra shamatha. There are three stages to this yoga: in the lower, the meditator develops one-pointed shamatha; in the middle, he or she can rest in shamatha one-pointedness for as long as desired; and in the greater, the meditation experiences of bliss, clarity, and nonthought that arise from the practice of shamatha continually accompany one's meditation.[22] Rangdrol Rinpoche remarks that although the focus in this yoga is on shamatha, for those with mature vipashyana experience it will involve a shamatha that already includes vipashyana.[23]

The Yoga of Simplicity

Gampopa remarks that the yoga of simplicity is "understanding the essential state of that awareness [of one-pointedness] as nonarising [emptiness], which transcends conceptual modes of reality and unreality."[24]

Attainment of the fruition of the yoga of one-pointedness leads naturally to the yoga of simplicity. Having become fully one-pointed, in this yoga one sees that the state of mind developed through the previous yoga is empty: it is free of any conceptual overlay whatsoever, even the categories of existence and nonexistence. In this sense, things are seen in the most simple, unadorned way possible, just as they are. They are seen as mere appearances without any attribution of "essence" or "self-nature" added on.

Rangdrol Rinpoche says that in this yoga, "You will realize correctly that the natural state of your mind-essence is free from the extremes of arising, dwelling, and ceasing. During the ensuing understanding, you are liberated when, having embraced that state with mindfulness, it turns into the state of meditation."[25] In the lower simplicity, one retains some fixation on emptiness; in the middle, one realizes that one's thoughts are empty; and in the greater simplicity one realizes that both the inner world of thoughts and the outer world are equally empty.

The Yoga of One Taste

Gampopa says that the yoga of one taste is "understanding diverse appearances as being one, from the standpoint of their intrinsic nature."[26]
Je Phagdru says:

> By meditating on the one taste of all things,
> The meditator will cognize the one taste of all these things.
> The diversity of appearances and nonappearances,
> Mind and emptiness, emptiness and non-emptiness,
> Are all of one taste, undifferentiable in their intrinsic
>   emptiness.
> Understanding and lack of understanding are of one taste;

Meditation and nonmeditation are nondifferentiable;
Meditation and absence of meditation are unified into one
    taste;
Discrimination and lack of discrimination are one taste
In the expanse of reality.[27]

Fully realizing the yoga of simplicity leads one naturally to the yoga
of one taste. This occurs because when one fully experiences the empty
yet apparent quality of phenomena, their emptiness means that they
have no nature, no essence that one can latch on to. They provide no
nourishment or reference point for ego. Yet they have some manner of
appearing, some energy or vividness. Still, from ego's viewpoint, the
emptiness means that they have no interest or importance. It is in this
sense that they have only one taste, the taste of something that is actually
not anything. It is the taste of the *isness* of things, which, because they
have no essence or substance, always taste the same. One simply has
appearance without reference point, even those of subject and object,
mind and appearance, samsara and nirvana, and so on.

Prior to the development of one taste, one naturally attends to the
many flavors within one's world, seeking pleasure and avoiding pain.
Within one taste, pain and pleasure are replaced by the sameness of all
phenomena. In one taste, the ego is faced with a boredom of cosmic
proportions, wherein nothing stands out, nothing comes forward, everything just *is* in a kind of empty and meaningless way. From ego's point
of view, it is as if the entire world of sense pleasures has been frozen
forever, or drained of its life and reduced to a carcass.

If the experience of one taste is so devastating, why would anyone
want to pursue it? The answer may be found by referring back to the
basic notions of wisdom and compassion. In terms of wisdom, throughout his or her Buddhist journey, the practitioner has been motivated by
the inspiration to know the ultimate nature of reality. In one taste, the
nature of things just as they are finally comes into view. In spite of the
bleak prospect this presents for ego, one taste represents a breakthrough
to freedom. The enormous amount of energy required to judge things
and reduce them to concepts is no longer necessary. In one taste, every-

thing can be fully and exactly as it is, with no interference on the part of ego.

In terms of compassion, as long as we are preoccupied with maintaining ourselves and preserving our version of things, we cannot help but be prejudicial in relation to others. When we are compelled to make reality convenient and comfortable for ourselves, we cannot see others truly, we ignore their welfare, and we confuse them and cause them harm. In one taste, we reach the point where we abandon the project of our own survival, and this releases the boundless compassion within.

As in the case of the yogas of one-pointedness and simplicity, one taste also has three grades. The lesser one taste still involves some attachment to the experience of one taste. In the medium level, the meditator realizes that mind and appearance are inseparable, so that he or she is no longer fixating on "an experience" that is experienced as one taste by an experiencer. In the greater one taste, one expands the experience of phenomena limitlessly: "By the power of the multiplicity of all phenomena appearing as one taste, the expansion of the greater expression of wisdom [one attains] the realization of one taste itself manifesting as multiplicity."[28]

The yoga of one-pointedness and the yoga of simplicity are both developed on the meditation cushion. In the yoga of one taste however, meditation is mixed with postmeditation, such that the practitioner ripens this awareness both in meditation sessions and after having arisen from meditation, going about daily life.

The Yoga of Nonmeditation

Gampopa tells us, finally, that the yoga of nonmeditation is "an unceasing realization of the union of appearance and its intrinsic emptiness."[29]

Je Phagdru says:

> By perfecting this [nonmeditation] stage
> The meditator attains naked, unsupported awareness.
> This nondiscriminatory awareness is the meditation!
> By transcending the duality of meditation and meditator,

External and internal realities,
The meditating awareness dissolves itself
Into its luminous clarity.
Transcending the intellect,
It is without the duality of meditation and post-meditation.
Such is the quintessence of mind.[30]

The yoga of nonmeditation arises naturally within the attainment of one taste. Once one has realized that all experiences whatever, whether of samsara or nirvana, have no essential nature and abide in the experience of one taste, then whether one is meditating or moving about in the world, all things appear in the same way. This being the case, the mind has no possibility of departing from the true nature of experience. Not departing, there is no need to return. Therefore, meditating or not meditating is no longer a meaningful distinction.

In the yoga of nonmeditation, various distinctions that have been supporting the meditator up until now dissolve. Rangdrol Rinpoche remarks: "When, after this, you have perfected one taste, dualistic experiences, such as deliberately meditating or not meditating, being distracted or undistracted, are purified, and you are liberated into the great, primordial state in which all experiences are meditation."[31]

In the lesser level of nonmeditation, there is a slight tendency to return to some formal meditation technique. In the medium level, "the continuity of day and night becomes a single great meditation state."[32] In the greater nonmeditation, when the final veils are shed,

the luminosity of mother [reality itself] and child [the meditator's awareness] mingle together, and everything ripens into an all-encompassing expanse of wisdom, the single sphere of dharmakaya. This, the greater nonmeditation, also called perfect and complete buddhahood, is the arrival at the ultimate fruition.[33]

FRUITION MAHAMUDRA

The yoga of nonmeditation, then, brings one to the fruition of the path. Fruition mahamudra, the culmination and fulfillment of the practices, is known as the enlightenment of all the buddhas. Thrangu Rinpoche summarizes the relation of fruition mahamudra to ground and path:

> Fruition Mahamudra is the actualization of the Mahamudra experience. As an ordinary person we are not aware of our own true nature, the Mahamudra of ground. Then, through the teachings of the Buddha and the teachings of our own root lama, we are introduced to the nature and we learn that it exists and we have it within ourselves. But it is not enough to simply know that it exists, we need to have the realization brought about by meditation, which is the path Mahamudra. When the path is actualized, then we have fruition Mahamudra.[34]

In fruition mahamudra, we realize our identity as the three kayas. We come to see that our basic nature was never anything more or less than the three bodies of a buddha.

Dharmakaya. In fruition mahamudra, it is seen that all phenomena and mind itself are without any reality that can be named or thought about. In this sense, they are fundamentally empty of any relative essence, identity, or own-being. This emptiness is dharmakaya.

Sambhogakaya. When the term "emptiness" is used in the third turning of the wheel and in the mahamudra teachings, it does not mean—as we have seen—absolute nonexistence. It does not mean empty as in an empty room or an empty sky, devoid of everything. Emptiness in terms of complete nothingness means that there is nothing there to change and nothing to take place. Thrangu Rinpoche explains:

> However, when we use *empty* in terms of the nature of mind, it means this essence is essentially empty of anything substantial and yet it has a certain potential, a certain radiance. Radiance is the potential and is the aspect of appearing, rather than the aspect of being empty. Then its essence is empty but it has the potential or radiance or energy coming from the essence [which] takes the form of clarity or luminosity. This clarity or luminosity (Tib. salwa) is the nature of the Sambhogakaya.[35]

Nirmanakaya. Thrangu Rinpoche:

> This luminosity has a certain power or energy to it. It is like a wild animal. It is very powerful and there is nothing that it can't do with its power, its force. This force can manifest as all the varied phenomena of the world and there is no way of blocking or impeding it. This quality, this energy or force, is termed Nirmanakaya.[36]

Thrangu Rinpoche gives a further explanation of the relation of the three kayas in mahamudra realization:

> The Dharmakaya has all qualities of enlightenment already present as a foundation; all qualities are completely perfect already, but no one can perceive them because there is no form.
>
> The further perfection of all happiness or bliss, the Sambhogakaya, manifests out of the Dharmakaya, but ordinary people don't perceive it either. So there is a further manifestation, an actual emanated body, that anybody can perceive. . . .
>
> The energy or force of Nirmanakaya manifests on an impure level actually as confused (i.e., not true) appearances. All the appearances that ordinary beings perceive are perceived in a confused or ignorant way. The pure aspect of the Nirmanakaya is the buddha activity that is constantly taking place for all sentient beings.[37]

The fruition of mahamudra, then, is resting in the vast emptiness of dharmakaya, in which there is no coming or going, no arising or ceasing, in which all things appear exactly as they are. This vast expanse is alive with potency and potentiality, the sambhogakaya. As for the nirmanakaya, this potency or potentiality has great and transformational impact on ordinary beings. Trungpa Rinpoche comments on the inseparability of the three kayas in the realization of mahamudra: "To experience mahamudra is to realize that the literal truth [nirmanakaya], the symbolic truth [sambhogakaya], and the absolute truth [dharmakaya] are actually one thing, that they take place on one dot, one spot. One experiences reality as the great symbol which stands for itself."[38]

SOME ASPECTS OF MAHAMUDRA EXPERIENCE

The third turning of the wheel of dharma declares that in emptiness, the world does not disappear. Instead, it begins to appear in a new way, empty of anything fixed and solid, but nevertheless vivid and alive. This new mode of the world experienced in mahamudra can be spoken about in a variety of ways: in terms of the vividness of phenomena; as complete ordinariness; and as the nakedness of raw experience. The mahamudra experience is also spoken of as indestructible, youthful, and fresh, and the nature of Great Bliss. In mahamudra, one experiences the world as filled with import. Mahamudra is the essence of "crazy wisdom" and is identified as coemergent wisdom.

The Vividness of Phenomena

In ordinary perception, things are limited only because of what we think of them and how we evaluate them. Our conceptual overlay is so thick, in fact, that our perceptions are usually dull, gray, and lifeless in comparison to how they originally and primordially arise in our experience. In mahamudra, conceptual limitations have been dissolved and each phenomenon, each perception, can appear exactly as it is, in all its fullness, uniqueness, and power. This can be an experience of great vividness. Trungpa Rinpoche remarks, "Mahamudra is vividness, vividness to such an extent that it does not require a watcher or commentator; or for that matter it does not require meditative absorption."[39] "It is just a pure, straightforward expression of the world of sight and smell and touchable objects as a self-existing mandala of experience. There is no inhibition at all. Things are seen precisely, beautifully, without any fear of launching into them."[40]

Mahamudra as Complete Ordinariness

One usually thinks of the spiritual journey as moving higher and higher, until we attain fulfillment that is extraordinary in the extreme, the highest of the high. However, as mentioned, the experience of mahamudra represents the fulfillment of a journey downward, from our lofty ideas about the ultimate to the raw truth and reality of our lives, to the most basic, unadorned experience of what life is. Mahamudra, then, is the experience of the most ordinary of the ordinary. Trungpa Rinpoche:

> The only thing that confuses us and prevents us from realizing this experience is its ordinariness. . . . In that way, Mahamudra is self-secret because of its ordinariness. Ordinariness becomes its own camouflage, so to speak. It has also been said that Mahamudra cannot be expressed, that even the Buddha's tongue is numb when it comes to describing Mahamudra. And it's true. How much can you say about ordinary things?[41]

Mahamudra as Ultimate Nakedness

Not only is the experience of mahamudra most ordinary, as we have seen, it is not necessarily pleasant, at least from ego's point of view. If we have glimpses of mahamudra, as well as finding them liberating, we may find them irritatingly naked. Trungpa Rinpoche explains:

> The experience of mahamudra is also somewhat irritating, or even highly irritating, because of its sharpness and precision. The energies around you—textures, colors, different states of mind, relationships—are all very vivid and precise. They are all so naked and so much right in front of you, without any padding, without any walls between you and that. That nakedness is overwhelming.[42]

Mahamudra as Inescapable

The mahamudra experience is so raw, its vividness is so penetrating, that one wants to run away from it. Trungpa Rinpoche:

> You look for privacy of some kind—privacy from yourself. The world is so true and naked and sharp and precise and colorful

that it's extraordinarily irritating. . . . Let alone when other people approach you. You think you can avoid them, run away from them physically, put a notice on your door, or take a trip to an unknown corner of the world. You might try to dissociate yourself from the familiar world, run away from your home ground, disconnect your telephone.

You can do all kinds of things of that nature, but when the world begins to become you and all these perceptions are yours and are very precise and very obviously right in front of you, you can't run away from it. The process of running away creates further sharpness, and if you really try to run away from these phenomena, they begin to mock you, laugh at you. The chairs and tables and rugs and paintings on the wall and your books, the sounds you hear in your head, begin to mock you.

Even if you try to tear your body apart, still something follows you. You can't get away from it. . . . You begin to feel you are just a live brain with no tissue around it, exposed on a winter morning to the cold air. It's so penetrating, irritating, and so sharp.[43]

Youthfulness

The vividness or "isness" of the mahamudra experience may also be described in terms of youthfulness and freshness. In ordinary ego experience, things are taken for granted and viewed as familiar, repetitive, and boring. Trungpa Rinpoche says:

The eternally youthful quality of the Mahamudra experience is one of its outstanding qualities. It is eternally youthful because there is no sense of repetition, no sense of wearing out of interest because of familiarity. Every experience is like a new, fresh experience. So it is childlike, innocent and childlike. The child has never even seen its body—such a brand-new world.[44]

The Mahamudra experience of clarity and sharpness allows us to develop a new attitude in which things are never taken for

288

granted, in which every moment is a new experience. With that sense of sacredness, of well-being, one begins to rediscover the universe.[45]

The theme of youthfulness is prominent in the biographies of the eighty-four siddhas. Some are said, in their realized state, to take on the qualities of small children, playing delightedly in the constant wonder of the world. It is often said that a realized practitioner takes on the qualities of a person in the prime of youthful beauty. Tantipa, for example, was a tailor who, in old age, was consigned to a small hut in the back garden of his house, while his sons and daughters-in-law managed the family business. After meeting the siddha Jalandharapa and receiving initiation from him, Tantipa practiced the *Hevajra Tantra* and attained realization. One night, one of the daughters-in-law came to Tantipa's hut to bring him food. Inside the hut, she saw a brilliant light surrounded by fifteen maidens. They were wearing garments such as are not found in the human realm and holding aloft offerings in their hands. And she saw that a great feast has been set out. The next morning, the family returned en masse and, when Tantipa emerged from his hut, they saw that his body had been transformed into that of a sixteen-year-old youth, of great beauty and splendor.[46] The theme of the child-like nature of realized people appears also among the great masters of Tibetan Buddhism. For example, in later life, Jigme Lingpa was known as a person of a childlike nature and observed, "My perceptions have become like those of a baby. I even enjoy playing with children."[47] In contemporary times, this motif was prominent in the life of Kalu Rinpoche. As one of his disciples reports, Kalu Rinpoche often manifested the appearance of a small child.

He could be curious, naughty, playful, questioning, or struck with wonder. One of the first stories I heard before meeting him was of his having gotten lost in a huge department store in downtown Vancouver. Those who had accompanied him searched every floor and every department for the then-66-year-old unilingual Tibetan man in monk's robes. They eventually found him sitting on the floor at play center with children in the toy department. During that first visit to the West (1971–72), he played on the stairs of his first meditation center with a "Slinky" and in his room with a laugh box. He amused himself with toys all his life—hand puppets, wind-up dolls, masks. During his last few years, he added to the headaches of his personal secretary, Lama Gyaltsen, by insisting that the toys he collected in foreign countries be added to their already mountainous baggage, to be stored back home in the monastery, where they remained until his reincarnation was recognized.[48]

Mahamudra as Great Bliss

Sometimes the experience of mahamudra is described in terms of pleasure or bliss. In ordinary pleasure, one attempts to sate oneself with whatever is considered positive and confirming for the "self." This is not really true pleasure but rather a kind of dull and ignorant comfort arising from the positive implications of the experience for the ego. Great bliss, by contrast, is the enjoyment of—one might better say "joy" in—the nakedness of what is. The rawness of sense perceptions, experienced without coverings or filters—although from ego's point of view excruciatingly intense and therefore perhaps painful—is, when taken from the point of view of non-ego, in and of itself the nature of pure joy. In enjoying sense experiences, one identifies with them to the point that there is no longer even an enjoyer.

> On the Mahamudra level, pleasure does not take place through the pores of your skin, but pleasure takes place on your very *flesh* without skin. You become the bliss rather than enjoying the bliss. You are the embodiment of bliss. . . . One doesn't even have to go so far as to try to enjoy pleasure, but pleasure becomes self-existing bliss.
>
> We are talking about pleasure in the sense that everything can be included. There is a sense of reality involved in pleasure. There is a sense of truth in it. [In mahamudra] it is nonesuch, nothing better. It's self-existingly great, not in a comparative sense. As it is, great and dynamic.[49]

The bliss of Mahamudra is not so much great pleasure, but it is the experience of tremendous spaciousness, freedom from imprisonment, which comes from seeing through the duality of existence and realizing that the essence of truth, the essence of space, is available on this very spot. The freedom of Mahamudra is measureless, unspeakable, fathomless. Such fathomless space and complete freedom produce tremendous joy. This type of joy is not conditioned by even the experience of freedom itself; it is self-born, innate.[50]

Mahamudra as the Communicative Power of Being

In mahamudra, we begin to feel our existence in its most basic and ordinary state. Doing this, we begin to realize that there is energy, intelligence, and direction in our most ordinary experience as humans. We begin to find messages coming through our experience, and these provide illumination, guidance, and help.

In our habitual mode, we fixate on the conceptual overlay of what we experience. Suppose there is a certain visible feature of our landscape that we pass by each day, for example, a tree. The very first time we saw it, perhaps, something fresh registered simply because it had been previously unknown to us. However, for most of us, each subsequent time we see that tree, we do not really look at it, because we view it as something known and predictable.

But then suppose we actually begin to pay attention to that tree, to open our senses to it in a meditative way. Suppose we attend to how it actually appears to our perception. We soon begin to discover that each time that tree, which we thought we knew, appears within our field of awareness, it does so in a distinctive fashion. In terms of our actual experience, it is, in fact, never the same tree, but arrives one day moody, another bursting with life, another sad and contemplative, another exhibiting great flair, another heralding an approaching storm. Even these qualifications are crude and finally inaccurate, because they reduce the tree to other quantities. In fact, that tree will speak in a way that is utterly fresh, unprecedented, and surprising. Moreover, it will reveal to us the quality of that particular moment of our life. It will reveal "what is" at that moment, telling us who we are and what our life means, just then.

In a similar manner, perceptions, feelings, and emotions arise in our experience. In the experience of mahamudra, they are seen not as something already known but rather as fresh irruptions of reality, unprecedented and beyond the reach of our concepts and judgments. Each is a revelation, appearing at just that moment. Each revelation shows us the ground of actual experience that we are standing on right then. And each has implications for the path, for it contains "messages that push us into situations in which we can work on ourselves. We are being pushed into that basic situation."[51]

Trungpa Rinpoche: "So Mahamudra has to do with learning to work with the cosmic message, the basic message in our life situation, which is also teaching."

> We do not have to relate to teaching only in the religious context. We also have to read the symbolism connected with our life situation. What we live, where we live, how we live—all these living situations also have a basic message that we can read, that we can work with. . . . If you are speeding, you get a ticket. If you are driving too slow, you get a honk from behind. A red light means danger; a green light means go; an amber light means get ready to go or stop. If you try to cheat on your karmic debts, the tax authorities are going to get after you. There are numerous manifestations of all kinds. . . . From this point of view, [mahamudra] means openness to the messages that are coming across to us. Acknowledging them, respecting them.[52]

Mahamudra as the Magic of What Is

Mahamudra reveals the natural order and rightness of reality at just this moment. It reveals the magic of what is.

> The magic is simplicity. Winter gets cold, summer gets warm. Everything in every situation has a little magic. If we forget to

eat, we get hungry. There is a causal aspect, which is the truth. So in this case, the sacredness is a matter of truth, of the obviousness of the whole thing.

This has nothing particular to do with how things happen to be *made*, but rather how they *are*. There's no reference to the past in vajrayana, no concern with the case history of things, or with chronology. The concern is with what is. When we look at things as they are on a very simple, ordinary level, we find that they are fantastically, obviously true, frighteningly true. Because of their quality of being true and obvious, things are sacred and worth respecting. This kind of truth reveals falsity automatically. If we are slightly off the point, we get hit or pushed or pulled. We get constant reminders, constant help. It's that kind of sacredness.[53]

13

Dzokchen: The Great Perfection

IN THE NYINGMA OR ANCIENT SCHOOL, DZOKCHEN—
the "great perfection"—represents the culmination of the Buddhist path
and the ultimate and final teaching of the Buddha. In this respect, dzokchen plays the same role in Nyingma tradition that mahamudra fulfills
in the New Translation schools. Given this equivalent function, it is
not surprising that mahamudra and dzokchen share many of the same
perspectives, meditation practices, and fruitions. In fact, many of the
differences one finds between them are more apparent than real, and
may be traced back to the different historical periods in India in which
they arose and to their somewhat distinct histories in Tibet. Because
of the considerable overlap between mahamudra and dzokchen, in
this chapter I intend to indicate briefly where the two converge, and
give most of my attention to the particularly distinctive features of
dzokchen.

Dzokchen is the teaching, practice, and realization of atiyoga, the last
and highest of the nine yanas of the Nyingma lineage. In the Nyingma
perspective, dzokchen represents the pinnacle of human spiritual development. Trungpa Rinpoche provides the following analogy for dzokchen as the culmination of the tantric path.

> The tantric journey is like walking along a winding mountain
> path. Dangers, obstacles, and problems occur constantly. There
> are wild animals, earthquakes, landslides, all kinds of things,
> but still we continue on our journey and we are able to go be-
> yond the obstacles. When we finally get to the summit of the

mountain, we do not celebrate our victory. Instead of planting our national flag on the summit of the mountain, we look down again and see a vast perspective of mountains, rivers, meadows, woods, jungles, and plains. Once we are on the summit of the mountain, we begin to look down, and we feel attracted toward the panoramic quality of what we see. . . .[1]

In the Nyingma tradition, the celestial buddha Samantabhadra is regarded as the ultimate embodiment of buddhahood. Tulku Urgyen Rinpoche explains the transmission of dzokchen, beginning from Samantabhadra, to the gods of the heavenly realms:

Dzokchen is regarded as the primary teaching of the celestial Buddha Samantabhadra, the ultimate embodiment of buddhahood. . . . Before the Dzokchen teachings arrived in our human world, they were propagated through the Gyawa Gong-gyu, the mind transmission of the victorious ones, in the three divine [or heavenly] realms: first in Akanishtha, then in Tushita, and lastly in the Realm of the Thirty-three Gods, the world of Indra and his thirty-two vassal kings located on the summit of Mount Sumeru.[2]

The dzokchen teaching, then, originated at the pinnacle of reality from Samantabhadra and, from there, was transmitted to spiritual beings of a high level, through progressively more and more tangible and human-like realms. From the realm of the thirty-three, the lowest "heaven," it was transmitted by a celestial buddha known as Vajrasattva, the adamantine being, to the first human guru of the Vajrayana, Garab Dorje, who lived sometime prior to the eighth century. Garab Dorje was worthy to be the human progenitor of dzokchen owing to his unusual acuity: "At the very instant of having mind nature pointed out, [he] became a fully enlightened buddha without having undergone any training whatsoever."[3] Nyingma tradition records that Garab Dorje received 6,400,000 verses of dzokchen teaching in Uddiyana, known in Tibetan tradition as the "tantric country." Since Vajrasattva is considered a celestial form of Shakyamuni Buddha and inseparable from him,

FIGURE 13.1 *Samantabhadra (Kuntuzangpo in Tibetan), with consort.*

it is understood that the dzokchen teachings are part of Shakyamuni's legacy.[4] Garab Dorje transmitted the dzokchen to various Indian masters, including his principal disciple Manjushrimitra. From this master's principal disciple Shri Simha, the lineage passed to Padmasambhava, Vimalamitra, Jnanasutra, and Vairochana. As we saw above, Padmasambhava provided for the continuation in our world of the dzokchen and other Vajrayana teachings in two ways. First, he left a lineage of transmission, Kama, from human teacher to disciple, that continues unbroken to the present day. Second, he and Yeshe Tsogyal concealed various spiritual treasures, terma, that were the objects of ongoing discovery in subsequent times by *tertöns*, "revealers of spiritual treasures."

THE GROUND, PATH, AND FRUITION OF DZOKCHEN

Ground

Dzokchen tradition takes the most ordinary and common reality of our human existence as its basis, and this accounts for its simple, blunt, almost primitive approach. Namkhai Norbu comments:

> The teachings are based on the principle of our actual human condition. We have a physical body with all its various limits: each day we have to eat, work, rest, and so on. This is our reality, and we can't ignore it.
>
> The Dzokchen teachings are neither a philosophy, nor a religious doctrine, nor a cultural tradition. Understanding the message of the teachings means discovering one's own true condition, stripped of all the self-deceptions and falsifications which the mind creates. The very meaning of the Tibetan term Dzokchen, "Great Perfection," refers to the true primordial state of every individual and not to any transcendent reality.[5]

Why is our ordinary human condition, in its naked, unadorned primordiality, worthy of becoming the basis of the dzokchen? The reason is that ultimately we are not the impure and flawed beings that conventional thinking assumes we are. Nor is the world a defiled, imperfect reality as is commonly thought. Things appear to us as imperfect because of what we think about them. Apart from our thinking, our actual condition and the condition of the world is one of primordial enlightenment. "Primordial enlightenment" means that the essential nature of ourselves and our world is ultimate wisdom; moreover, this wisdom never had any beginning nor will it ever have an end. It has existed since time immemorial.

Enlightenment, therefore, is not something that remains to be attained. It is already in a state of attainment in us from the very beginning. The only task that remains is for us to wake up to the fact of the primordial enlightenment that is our natural condition. In this perspective, then, nothing need be done. In fact, all of our doing, our mental judgments, separations, discriminations, and evaluations, and all the actions of body and speech that derive from them, are nothing but ways of avoiding our primordial enlightenment. All that remains for us to do is to realize that there is, literally, nothing to do.

Only when we cease the "doing" of ego on every level can the natural enlightenment of the cosmos show itself as already present. The "doing" comprises all the various thoughts and activities of the spiritual path. It also includes even the most subtle sense of an experiencer who is enjoying the experience of egolessness, as it evolves through the eight yanas and culminates in anuyoga. Thus the "nondoing" required in dzokchen covers every inch of the terrain of ego, up to the most subtle levels of spiritual materialism of the buddha-dharma. It is in this sense that dzokchen is the final yana.

The perspective of dzokchen, then, emphasizes primordial enlightenment of the "mind." It speaks of ultimate awakening as the recognition of "mind itself," by which is meant the untrammeled awareness of the natural state, the "buddha-mind." This "mind," obviously, is not the ordinary mind of dualistic awareness, the consciousness or "subject" pole of the subject-object dichotomy. In dzokchen, this ultimate "mind" translates the Tibetan term *rikpa*, "intelligence" or "naked awareness." This rikpa is the dharmakaya. It is the flash of awareness that precedes the split into dualistic consciousness of myself, my mind, and the other, the object. It is the first instant of each moment of perception, described by Trungpa Rinpoche in the previous chapter, that occurs outside of the I-other framework of the skandhas. If this moment is not "mind" in the ordinary dualistic sense, then why call it mind at all? This is done in order to make clear that this moment is not nothing, not pure vacuity, but clear, brilliant, and cognizant.

Path

Dzokchen actualizes this view through great stress on practice. Like Ch'an and Zen, it places little stock in study, textual knowledge, or philosophy in and of themselves.* Namkhai Norbu: "In Dzogchen no importance at all is attached to philosophical opinions and convictions. The way of seeing in Dzogchen is not based on intellectual knowledge, but on an awareness of the individual's own true condition."[6] Thus it is that "when a master teaches Dzokchen, he or she is trying to transmit a state of knowledge. The aim of the master is to awaken the student, opening that individual's consciousness to the primordial state. The master will not say, 'Follow my rules and obey my precepts!' He will say, 'Open your inner eye and observe yourself. Stop seeking an external lamp to enlighten you from the outside, but light your own inner lamp.' "[7]

In its fullest perspective, the path of dzokchen is viewed in the larger context of the nine-yana journey of the Nyingma school. This nine-yana path culminating in dzokchen can be understood as a more and more complete understanding of emptiness. Tulku Urgyen remarks, "The vital point of the view in each of the nine vehicles is nothing other than emptiness. Each vehicle attempts to experience this empty nature of things and apply it in practice, in what each maintains is a

*At the same time, of course, particularly in recent centuries, the Nyingma lineage has maintained a strong tradition of monastic learning and includes in its history a number of extraordinarily learned and accomplished scholars, from Longchenpa down to the Ri-me master Jamgon Mipham Rinpoche.

flawless and correct fashion."[8] In this context, then, why are there nine yanas and why are they understood to be arranged in a hierarchical fashion? As far as the realization of emptiness is concerned, what makes each one an advance upon the previous one? Tulku Urgyen explains that "from the Hinayana on up, the concept of what mind actually is becomes increasingly refined and subtle."[9] As one practices Hinayana, Mahayana, and the various Vajrayana levels, one gains a more and more profound and vast understanding of just what is meant by emptiness.

This progressively fuller understanding that occurs through the nine-yana journey can equally be described as the deeper and more complete realization of buddha-nature. Viewed in this light, says Tulku Urgyen,

> What is most important concerning the view is to recognize buddha nature. . . . In the first eight of the nine yanas—the vehicles for shravakas, pratyekabuddhas, and bodhisattvas; the three outer tantras of Kriya, Upa, and Yoga; and Mahayoga and Anu Yoga—progressively deeper notions of buddha nature are kept in mind as the point of reference. In these vehicles the viewer, or observer of buddha nature, is called mindfulness or watchfulness, in the sense of keeping constant guard on buddha nature, like a herdsman keeping watch over his cattle. So in these vehicles there are, then, two things: buddha nature and the constant attention, the "not forgetting" it. Buddha nature should first be recognized, then sustained continuously without any distraction. When watchfulness is distracted from buddha nature, the practitioner is no different from an ordinary person. This is the general principle of the first eight vehicles.[10]

The "view" of yana number nine, dzokchen, represents yet another step in which all conceptual "ideas" of the buddha-nature are abandoned and one not only meets it face to face but identifies with it. Thus it is that "this buddha nature is precisely what is practiced in each of the nine vehicles, but exactly how it is put into practice differs, because there is a refinement of understanding that becomes progressively more subtle through the vehicles."[11]

The dzokchen path is divided into the two overarching categories of trekchö, "cutting through," and thögal, "passing over the summit" or "direct crossing." Trekchö involves cutting through discursive thought at every level so that, at the end, nothing but the illumined, nondual buddha-nature remains. Thögal addresses what reality is like from the point of view of the nondual awareness, in other words, how reality manifests itself when one is resting in the primordial nature.

In addition, the dzokchen journey is sometimes also spoken of as containing either three or four stages. When divided into three, it includes: (1) mind section (*sem-de*), (2) space section (*long-de*), and (3) oral instruction section (*me-ngag de*). These represent a full presentation of the dzokchen teachings, with trekchö treated in the mind and space divisions, and part of the oral instruction section, and thögal treated in the balance of the secret instruction section. The division of the dzokchen teachings into these three categories goes back to an early time. When divided into four, the first three are the same as above, while the fourth includes the "innermost unexcelled section," sometimes called the essential heart section, representing a later terma that brings together the three sections and distills them into their quintessential form. In relation to these four, Tulku Urgyen comments:

> There is the outer Mind Section, which is like the body. There is the inner Space Section, which is like the heart, and the secret Instruction Section, which is like the veins within the heart. Finally there is the innermost Unexcelled Section, which is like the life-energy inside the heart, the pure essence of the life-force. What is the difference between these four sections, since all four are Dzogchen? The outer Mind Section of Dzogchen emphasizes the cognizant quality of mind, while the inner Space Section emphasizes its empty quality, and the secret Instruction Section emphasizes the unity of the two. The innermost Unexcelled Section teaches everything—ground, path and fruition, as well as Trekchö and Togal.[12]

Fruition

The fruition of dzokchen is full realization of the enlightenment within. In practical terms, it involves the ability to rest in the innate state and not depart from it. Far from a state of dullness, lethargy, or apathy—as indeed it might seem from ego's standpoint—one rests in the natural state, or as the natural state, that is vivid, vibrant, and dynamic. The buddhas rest in the natural state and, as expressions of it, remain in that world, interact with others, teach the dharma, and express their compassion to sentient beings in myriad ways. Yet none of this is done based on conscious intention. It all unfolds as buddha activity that is always unpremeditated, spontaneous, and perfectly apt to the situation. The fruition of dzokchen produces men and women of extraordinary sanctity, compassion, and ability.

Among these, perhaps most notable are those who attain the "rainbow body." Tulku Urgyen explains: "The chief disciples of Padmasambhava and Vimalamitra are known as the 'king and twenty-five disciples.'"

> They all attained rainbow body, the dissolution of the physical body at death into a state of rainbow light. Such practitioners leave behind only their hair and fingernails. . . . Among the three kayas, sambhogakaya manifests visually in the form of rainbow light. So, attaining a rainbow body in this lifetime means to be directly awakened in the state of enlightenment of sambhogakaya. . . . There has been an unceasing occurrence of practitioners departing from this world in the rainbow body up until the present day. . . . So this is not just an old tale from the past, but something that has continued to the present day.[13]

THE RELATION OF DZOKCHEN TO MAHAMUDRA

What is the relationship of dzokchen to mahamudra and the Greater Madhyamaka of the third turning? In the Nyingma perspective, sometimes mahamudra is seen as the ground, Greater Madhyamaka as the path, and dzokchen as the fruition.[14] Mahamudra shows us the ground of buddha-nature, Greater Madhyamaka provides important path perspectives, and dzokchen represents the full and final attainment. This simple threefold scheme illustrates how close these three traditions are seen to be, that they are in fact all working with the same basic reality, the buddha-nature. In other words, they imply the same realization, but approach it from different angles.

In previous chapters, we have discussed Sutra mahamudra (the Greater Madhyamaka of the third turning), Tantra mahamudra (the anuttarayoga practices), and Essence mahamudra, the formless practices that lay bare the nature of ultimate awareness itself. As mentioned, Tantra mahamudra corresponds to the seventh and eighth yanas, mahayogayana and anuyogayana of the Nyingma school, which include practices of liturgy and visualization analogous to anuttarayoga tantra as well as the inner yogas. Essence mahamudra corresponds to dzokchen itself. And, according to Tulku Urgyen, Sutra mahamudra correlates with the view of trekchö. Tulku Urgyen summarizes these relationships:

> Within the Mahamudra system there is Sutra Mahamudra, Tantra Mahamudra, and Essence Mahamudra. Sutra Mahamudra is the same as the Mahayana system describing progressive stages through the five paths and ten bhumis. That definitely differs from Dzogchen, and therefore it is not simply called Mahamudra, but Sutra Mahamudra. Tantra Mahamudra corresponds to Maha Yoga and Anu Yoga, in which you utilize the "wisdom of example" [visualization practices] to arrive at the "wisdom of meaning" [mind itself]. Essence Mahamudra is the same as Dzogchen, except that it doesn't include Togal. The Great Madhyamika of the Definitive meaning is no different from the Dzogchen view of Trekchö."[15]

Thus the trekchö of dzokchen contains practices that are often similar to the mahamudra practices mentioned above and, generally, to the Essence mahamudra methods of the schools of the later spreading. In both, the "view" emphasizes laying bare the ultimate state of awareness that exists within. Both speak of the buddha-nature, the dharmakaya, the clear-light mind, and so on that, once cleansed of adventitious defilements, becomes the realization of the buddhas. Both are traditions of formless meditation that sometimes come as the culmination of form practices and sometimes stand on their own. Like the mahamudra, the dzokchen path begins with pointing-out instructions given by the root guru to the disciple. The actual techniques of "formless" meditation in dzokchen are often similar and sometimes identical with the ten mahamudra practices mentioned above. Finally, there is a fairly wide consensus among lamas of both the Old and New Translation schools that the end state of dzokchen and of mahamudra are not different from one another. Dzokchen and mahamudra do differ significantly in one respect: as Tulku Urgyen mentions, within the mahamudra tradition, there is no direct correlation to the all-important dzokchen teaching of thögal.

ASPECTS OF DZOKCHEN PRACTICE

Pointing-out Instructions

In dzokchen, particular emphasis is placed on taking the fruition of enlightenment, the dharmakaya, as the basis of the path. Tulku Urgyen remarks:

> There are three different approaches to actually applying Vajrayana in practice: taking the ground as path, taking the path as path, and taking the fruition as path. These three approaches can be understood by using the analogy of a gardener or farmer. Taking the ground or cause as path is like tilling the soil and sowing seeds. Taking the path as path is like weeding, watering, fertilizing and coaxing crops forth. Taking the fruition as path is the attitude of simply picking the ripened fruit or the fully bloomed flowers. To do this [latter], to take the complete result, the state of enlightenment itself, as the path, is the approach of Dzogchen. This summarizes the intent of the Great Perfection.[16]

How is the complete result taken as the path? As in the case of mahamudra, in dzokchen, this occurs through pointing-out instructions. When the inherent mind is introduced by the guru and when the disciple recognizes it, then this provides a critical reference point from that moment onward. Tulku Urgyen says, "According to Dzogchen or Mahamudra, when nondual awareness has been genuinely pointed out and correctly recognized, it is like the flawless dharmakaya placed directly in the palm of your hand."[17] Why? Because once one has experienced the nature of mind in the pointing out, it is like having the dharmakaya before one, guiding one's journey. Tulku Urgyen:

> Enlightenment is possible when a qualified master meets a worthy, receptive disciple who possesses the highest capacity, or transmits, or points out, the unmistaken essence of mind so that it is recognized. It can indeed be pointed out; it can indeed be recognized; and it can indeed be trained in. If the student practices for thirteen years, he or she can unquestionably attain complete enlightenment.[18]

Dzokchen Meditation: The Role of Shamatha and Vipashyana

What is the nature of meditation in dzokchen? Tulku Urgyen remarks that it is a deeper version of the same practices of shamatha and vipashyana that are known in the lower yanas.

> Each vehicle, beginning with the shravaka yana, has its own particular view, meditation and conduct. Each has the same aim, to understand emptiness; and each employs practices called shamatha and vipashyana. On the Mahayana level, the ultimate shamatha and vipashyana is called "the shamatha and vipashyana that delights the tathagatas." Though the same names are used, their depth is much superior to the shamatha and vipashyana employed in the shravaka system. Every vehicle, beginning with the shravaka yana, practices shamatha and vipashyana, so don't think that at the level of Dzogchen these two are ignored or left out.[19]

How, then, do shamatha and vipashyana manifest in dzokchen? "On the Ati level, the innate stability in rikpa, the nondual state of awareness, is the shamatha aspect, while the awake or cognizant quality is the vipashyana aspect. Our basic nature, also called awareness wisdom or cognizant wakefulness, is resolved or recognized through shamatha and vipashyana. To cite a famous statement, 'Awakened mind is the unity of shamatha and vipashyana.' "

> The principle we must understand here is stated like this: "Same word, superior meaning." Shamatha and vipashyana are ultimately indivisible. Both are naturally included and practiced in Ati Yoga. The extraordinary shamatha here is to resolve and rest in the true emptiness itself. We do not merely get the idea of emptiness; in actuality, in direct experience, we resolve emptiness and rest naturally in that state. Naturally resting is the genuine shamatha of not creating anything artificial whatsoever, of simply remaining in the experience of emptiness. And vipashyana means not to deviate or depart from that state.[20]

Shamatha and vipashyana, in the lower yanas, still involve some sense of something pursued or sought. There is still some idea that one is looking to realize and hence concept is involved in the practice. Tulku Urgyen notes:

> Only in the Essence Mahamudra and Dzogchen systems is emptiness left without fabrication. In Dzogchen, from the very first, emptiness is resolved without any need to manufacture it. It emphasizes stripping awareness to its naked state, and not clinging to emptiness in any way whatsoever. The true and authentic vipashyana is the empty and cognizant nature of mind.[21]

Working with Negative Emotions

As we have seen, Vajrayana Buddhism takes a particular approach to the kleshas, the "defilements" or negative emotions such as passion, aggression, ignorance, pride, and jealousy. As noted, these defilements are not rejected but are seen in a more positive light in their relation to wisdom. As ground, the kleshas are viewed as egoic responses to the vast and open experience of buddha-nature; as path, the kleshas are brought in various ways into one's meditation practice; and as fruition, they are seen as essentially nothing other than expressions of wisdom. As in other Vajrayana lineages, but in a distinct and characteristic way, in the practice of dzokchen strong emotions and neurotic upheavals are not rejected as "bad." Tulku Urgyen explains:

> During the Age of Strife [our present era], it seems as though people are seldom amiable; rather, they are always trying to outdo one another. This fundamental competitiveness has given rise to the name Age of Strife. But this is exactly the reason that Vajrayana is so applicable to the present era. The stronger and more forceful the disturbing emotions are, the greater the potential for recognizing our original wakefulness. . . . It is a fact that at the very moment we are strongly caught up in thought forms or in the surging waves of an emotion, of anger for instance, it is much easier to recognize the naked state of awareness. This of course is not the case when one has trained in a very tranquil, placid state of meditation where there are no thoughts and negative emotions. Then, due to what is called the "soft pleasure," it is actually much more difficult to recognize the true state of nondual mind. . . . Conversely, experiencing great despair, great fear, and intense worry can be a much stronger support for practice.[22]

The Quintessence of Dzokchen Practice: The Three Words That Strike to the Heart

Garab Dorje, as we saw, was the first human being to propagate dzokchen, in its initial, vast revelation comprising some 6,400,000 verses. As a way to epitomize this extensive array of teachings, Garab Dorje, after his death conferred on Manjushrimitra a highly condensed text, a set of three verses describing the view, practice, and result of dzokchen. The view, he said, is to recognize one's own nature; the practice is to decide on one point, namely that nature; and the result is to gain confidence in liberation. In the nineteenth century, the great Nyingma siddha Paltrül Rinpoche wrote a commentary on these three verses that has become famous and well loved among dzokchen practitioners. The verses and commentary provide a convenient overview of dzokchen practice. The following summary draws on the text and commentary themselves, as well as on Tulku Urgyen's helpful discussion.

VIEW: RECOGNIZE YOUR ESSENTIAL NATURE

What is this nature? It is "empty cognizance suffused with awareness."[23] It is empty of essence, meaning that it cannot be conceptualized. Yet it is not nothing, but is inseparable from cognizance or awareness and permeated by it. This nature is thus not like the black, empty space of nothingness, but rather like space drenched with sunlight, alive, brilliant, yet empty of any *thing*.

This rikpa, this emptiness suffused with awareness, is our essential nature. It is the state of "mind" or "experience" that is most fundamental to our very being and that underlies our normal consciousness. This is the "nature" that has always been the core of our being, from beginningless time, and will remain so through the timelessness of perfect enlightenment. This nature or rikpa is the "basic ground," to use Trungpa Rinpoche's phrase. As we saw above, each moment of experience begins with open, unbounded "space" in which there is no "self." This is the rikpa. Our self-conscious ego reacts with fear to primordial awareness, erecting the boundaries of our familiar "I," thus re-creating itself in each moment. Yet the underlying rikpa cannot be entirely shut out or denied, and it continually gnaws at the fringes of our ordinary consciousness.

Fundamentally, our experience is nondual. The apparent duality of "self" and "other" is a manufactured set of reference points that arises as a panic-response to the uncertainty, openness, and groundlessness of the "basic ground" of primordial awareness. This apparent duality is unreal in the sense that it is nothing more than an ignoring of the essential condition, an ignoring that takes place through solidifying the "no-thing-ness" of the inherent nature into concepts of duality and then clinging to them as if they were real.

In some very real sense, then, the buddha-nature is the ground of all reality. All living beings and all the worlds that ever have been or could be originate from the essential, unfabricated buddha-nature. All phenomena whatever arise from the buddha-mind. Thus Tulku Urgyen remarks, "Buddha nature, itself, is the very basis or source from which all worlds and all living beings originate. Whatever appears and exists comes from it. . . . This is the universal ground from which everything arises."[24]

That the buddha-nature is viewed as the basis of living beings may make sense, but how can it also be seen as the basis of all worlds and phenomena? The *Dashabhumika Sutra*, an important sutra for the third turning of the wheel of dharma, states that "all the three worlds are nothing but awareness (*chitta*)." The three worlds represent one of the classical ways of categorizing the entirety of the possibilities of samsaric existence: the lower gods, jealous gods, humans, animals, hungry ghosts, and hell beings all inhabit the realm of desire; the higher gods dwell in the form and formless realms. The *Dashabhumika Sutra* is saying that all of these myriad worlds are nothing but erroneous solidifications of the essential, nondual state. All of samsara is nothing other than a conceptual overlay on our basic, enlightened nature.* The idea of "beings" and "worlds" only arises once one has retreated from the openness of the basic ground.

It would be a mistake, then, to interpret Tulku Urgyen's statement that the buddha-nature is the source of all beings and all worlds in a cosmological sense, as if it were some kind of "primal substance" such as one finds in theistic schools. The ideas of a "basic substance" or some kind of existing primal phenomenon are both abstract conceptualizations very far removed from what is being pointed to here. Tulku Urgyen:

---

*Within Tibetan Buddhism, this statement is often understood as implying the substantialism of a "mind" that "truly exists." However, such an interpretation has the limitation of not bringing out the deepest level of the sutra's meaning.

We should understand that [the buddha-nature] does not fall into any category, such as an entity that exists or does not exist. The claim that buddha nature is a "thing" that exists, is incorrect. It is not a concrete thing with distinguishable characteristics; instead, it is wide open and indefinable, like space. However, you cannot claim that it is nonexistent, that there is not any buddha nature, because this nature is the very basis or source of everything that appears and exists. So the buddha nature does not fall into any category of being or not being. Neither does it fit into the category called "beyond being or not being"; it is beyond that formulation as well.[25]

Not only is the buddha-nature the ground of all reality; it is the only thing that is real. *The essential nature is all there is. There is no other reality than this.* The meaning of this is explained by recalling the third-turning doctrine of the three natures discussed briefly in chapter 5. The *imaginary nature*, the apparent world of "I" and "other" as existing realities, is a false conceptualization, overlaid on our experience and completely unreal. The *dependent nature*, which arises in dependence on causes and conditions, possesses no more than a relative reality; it is not real in the ultimate sense of having an abiding essence or definitive character. Only the completely perfected nature, the ultimate, nondual awareness of the buddha-nature, is real, in the sense of being unborn, unabiding, and unceasing, and the foundation of all.

The buddha-nature is described as the unity of experience (or appearance) and emptiness or the unity of awareness and emptiness. What does this mean? Tulku Urgyen:

Right now, visual forms, sounds and smells and so on are all present in our experience. If buddha nature were nonexistent, then there could be no such experiences taking place. But if we say buddha nature does exist, then what is it that experiences? Can you pinpoint it? You can't because it's empty of all identity, right? Thus there is no confining these two—perceiving and being empty. While perceiving, buddha nature is empty of a perceiver; while being empty, there is still experience. Search for the perceiver; there is no "thing" to find. There is no barrier between the two. If it were one or the other there should either be a concrete perceiver who always remains, or an absolute void. Instead, at the same time vivid perception takes place, that which perceives is totally empty. This is called the unity of experience and emptiness, or the unity of awareness and emptiness. The fact of experience eliminates the extreme of nothingness, while the fact that it is empty eliminates the extreme of concrete existence.[26]

Don't we agree that there is experience? This basis for experience is the cognizant quality. Can these two aspects—empty in essence and cognizant by nature—be separated? If not, that means they are a unity. This unity is what we should recognize when recognizing our buddha nature. To see this fact is what Garab Dorje meant when he said, "Recognize your own nature."[27]

Tulku Urgyen cites the traditional analogy of space to illustrate the buddha-nature.

Buddha nature is said to resemble space. Can we say that space exists? Can we say that it doesn't? We cannot, because space itself does not comply with any such ideas. Concepts made about space are merely concepts. Space, in itself, is beyond any ideas we can hold about it. Buddha nature is like this. If you say that space exists, can you define it as a concrete existent entity? But to say there is no space is incorrect, because space is what accommodates everything—the world and beings. And if we think space is that which is beyond being and not being, that is not really space, it is just our concept of it.[28]

In contrast to the previous eight yanas, in dzokchen the "view" is not a conceptually held belief of any kind. It is rather the *view* in the specific sense of the direct experience of the buddha-nature. As Tulku Urgyen explains, "The special quality of Dzogchen is the view that is totally free from any ideas whatsoever. This view is called *the view of fruition*, meaning it is utterly devoid of any conceptual formulations."[29] The "view" of dzokchen, then, is the direct, nonconceptual recognition of the ultimate awareness within. This takes place initially through pointing out and then, as we saw, this becomes the "way back" to reconnecting with that basic reality. "So, the first point of Garab Dorje's is to recognize our own nature and to acknowledge how this nature is, not as our conceptual version of it, but in actuality."[30]

MEDITATION: "DECIDE ON ONE POINT"

Garab Dorje's second statement is "decide on one point," having to do with meditation.

Having received pointing-out instructions in the "view," it is essential that one carry out the practice of meditation, connecting with the view and training to rest in it. If one thinks that simply receiving the transmission is enough and that one does not have to practice diligently, then this would be a serious mistake. In that case, the pointing out becomes merely another spiritual credential that we have accumulated, rather than the beginning point of a life of practice on the road to realization. If one does not carry the pointing-out instructions into meditation, one will simply return to the world of solid, discursive thought and relate to the pointing out as nothing more than an additional concept among many others. Then one will remain bound in samsara and, as Paltrül Rinpoche says, will be no different from ordinary people.

Meditation is nothing other than resting in the "view" of buddha-nature. How does one rest in the essential nature? Since the natural state is not a "thing," there can be no question of putting our mind to it. There is no question of knowing the buddha-nature as something "other" and then gearing ourselves up to rest in it. Therefore, in meditation, there is nothing to manufacture and nothing to attain. Any technique becomes a distraction. The only thing to do is to abstain from doing anything. In the not-doing of anything, the buddha-nature is laid bare, and to the extent that we refrain from any doing, we rest in its empty-luminous cognizance. Meditation at this level, then, is abandoning all efforts of conceptual contrivance, progressively stripping away all of our avenues of departure from the natural state.

> We call this training "meditation," but it is not an act of meditating in the common sense of the word. There is no emptying the mind essence by trying to maintain an artificially imposed vacant state. Why? Because mind essence is already empty. Similarly, we do not need to make this empty essence cognizant; it is already cognizant. All you have to do is leave it as it is. In fact, there is nothing whatsoever to do, so we cannot even call this an act of meditating.[31]

Thus it is that meditation is a matter of tuning in to the naturally existing meditation of the buddha-nature, rather than creating or concocting anything. Paltrül Rinpoche tells us that when meditating, one needs to realize the practice as an ever-flowing process of the buddha-nature that goes on without beginning or end. If the mind is still, that is the essence of dharmakaya. If the mind is active in thoughts, they are the spontaneous energy of wisdom. If one sees things in this way, whatever arises in one's mind—whether passion, aggression, delusion, pain, or pleasure—is recognized as the dharmata. This is true meditation.

As one practices, the three experiences of bliss, luminosity, and non-thought, discussed in chapter 11, will arise. These arise as great happiness, tremendous brilliance and clarity, or the complete absence of discursiveness. Although these three are signs of progress on the path, as mentioned, they are just temporary experiences. However, owing to their vividness and power, one may attempt to cling to them, thinking, "This is a sign of realization," and try to repeat the experiences in one's meditation. When these three arise, as we saw, one must dispel any thoughts and judgments about them, and any attempt to repeat them, returning to the naked face of the buddha-mind within.

One should carry out this practice in sitting meditation. It is also critical that it be carried into one's daily life. Whether in formal meditation or in ordinary daily activities, one should maintain the meditation of resting in the rikpa.

What does it mean to "decide on one point"? One should recognize that the primordial nature is nothing other than the dharmakaya of the buddhas, the essence of reality, the self-nature of the dharmata, the origin of all beings and all worlds, the fourth abhisheka, the heart instruction of all the tantras, and the essential teaching of the siddhas of India and Tibet. The meditator needs to have the great confidence that this is the case. If one feels that one must seek teachings outside, this is like the elephant tender who leaves his elephant in his tent while he goes outside to try to find an elephant. Therefore, says Paltrül Rinpoche, one must be decisive in the practice. One must know one's essential nature as the dharmakaya and then extend that awareness through meditation. It is this that forms the second of the three vajra points.

Result: Gain Confidence in Liberation

One must gain confidence in liberation. Such confidence, again, is not a conceptual attitude or belief. It is actually resting in the natural state, such that all mental activity is self-liberated. Tulku Urgyen describes three stages in the liberation of thoughts:

1. Recognize the thought as it arises. When thought is recognized in this way, it is liberated simultaneously with its arising. This is like the vanishing of a drawing made on water. This is at a beginning stage of practice.

2. One can become more and more familiar with this through practice. When the practitioner gains an immediate recognition of buddha-nature, then no further technique is needed. The moment a thought begins to move, it liberates itself. This is like a snake tied in a knot, which uncoils itself. This second stage shows increasing stability in the practice.

3. "Finally, the third analogy of the liberation of thoughts is described as being like a thief entering an empty house. This is called stability or perfection in training. A thief entering an empty house does not gain anything, and the house does not lose anything. All thought activity is naturally liberated without any harm or benefit whatsoever. That is the meaning of gaining confidence in liberation."[32]

One's confidence is ultimately realizing the essential nature as the three buddha kayas. How is this so? The buddha-nature's absence of self-nature, its emptiness of a conceptualizable essence, is the dharma-kaya. Its cognizance or clarity is the sambhogakaya; and the fact that its capacity "is suffused with self-existing awareness" is the nirmanakaya.[33]

> Our essence, nature and capacity are the dharmakaya, sambho-gakaya and nirmanakaya. They are also the three vajras—the vajra body, speech and mind of all the buddhas—which we are supposed to achieve. This real and authentic state is, in itself, empty, which is dharmakaya. Its cognizant quality, isn't that sambhogakaya? Its unconfined unity, isn't that nirmanakaya? This indivisible identity of the three kayas is called the "essence body," svabhavikakaya. So, in this way, don't you have the three kayas right in the palm of your own hand?[34]

Knowing this to be so is "gaining confidence in liberation," the third vajra point.

Conclusion

The journey of dzokchen, then, begins with recognizing the rikpa, leads through the training in resting in the rikpa, and culminates in the attainment of stability in the rikpa. Recognition of the rikpa is initially gained through pointing out and is thenceforward repeated in meditation practice throughout the day. "When the recognition lasts continuously throughout the day, we have reached the level of a bodhisattva. When it lasts uninterruptedly, day and night, we have attained buddhahood."[35]

The training thus involves developing greater and greater "familiarization" with the recognition.

> One sign of having trained in *rigpa*, the awakened state, is simply that conceptual thinking, which is the opposite of *rigpa*, grows less and less. The gap between thoughts grows longer and occurs more and more frequently. The state of unfabricated awareness, what the tantras call "the continuous instant of non-

fabrication," becomes more and more prolonged. The continuity of *rigpa* is not something we have to deliberately maintain. It should occur spontaneously through having grown more familiar with it. Once we become accustomed to the genuine state of unfabricated *rigpa*, it will automatically start to last longer and longer.[36]

Stability occurs when one can maintain nondistraction from the natural state. "By simply allowing the expression of thought activity to naturally subside, again and again, the moments of genuine *rigpa* automatically and naturally begin to last longer. When there are no thoughts whatsoever, then you are a buddha. At that point the thought-free state is effortless, as well as the ability to benefit all beings."[37]

When this moment of nondistraction lasts unceasingly, day and night, what will that be like? When the three poisons are obliterated and the qualities of wakefulness become fully manifest, will we be ordinary human beings or divine? A single candle-flame can set the whole mountainside ablaze. Imagine what it would be like when our present experience of the wide-awake moment free from thought becomes unceasing. Is there anything more divine than possessing all the wisdom qualities and being utterly free from the three poisons?[38]

TREKCHÖ AND THÖGAL

The two great phases of dzokchen practice are, as noted, trekchö, "cutting through," and thögal, "leaping across instantaneously." These two represent the dzokchen way of addressing "emptiness" on the one hand and "manifestation" or "what remains in emptiness" on the other. Trekchö refers to cutting through the last vestiges of ego. In thögal, one works with the manifestion that remains. Tulku Urgyen comments that while trekchö is the empty aspect, thögal is the manifest aspect.[39] Trekchö, then, relates to the wisdom of enlightenment, while thögal relates to its skillful-means. Through trekchö, one brings the wisdom of emptiness to its apogee; through thögal, one is able to actualize all the different aspects of enlightenment in a single lifetime. On the relation of trekchö and thögal, Trungpa Rinpoche remarks that trekchö and thögal are both completely effortless and formless. In addition, they are always linked with one another and entirely interdependent, although in any given practice a meditation will incline more toward one than the other.[40]

Trekchö

In trekchö, one brings to fruition the ability to rest in emptiness, free of concept. One realizes *the basic purity of everything*, that things are utterly and primordially free of any conceptual limitation or impurity.[41] In relation to trekchö, Sogyal Rinpoche comments, "*Trekchö* means cutting through delusion with fierce, direct thoroughness. Essentially delusion is cut through with irresistible force of the view of Rigpa, like a knife cleaving through butter. . . . The whole fantastical edifice of delusion collapses, as if you were blasting its keystone away. Delusion is cut through, and the primordial purity and natural simplicity of the nature of mind is laid bare."[42] Trungpa Rinpoche explains: "Trekcho is the 'sudden path,' achieving realization of the alaya [the basic ground, rikpa] without going through the six paramitas. It emphasizes prajna [transcendental knowledge] and the stillness of meditation and its nature is 'nowness.' It is the negative aspect of nirvana at its highest level . . . In it, one's being becomes the formless meditation itself. Mahamudra is a form of Trekcho."[43] Thus, as we saw, the practice of trekchö is in most ways identical with the mahamudra practice described earlier and need not be repeated here.

Thögal

In thögal, one explores and comes to realize the spontaneous self-perfection of everything. Having realized the aspect of emptiness, one encounters manifestation, "what remains," on more and more subtle levels. Through the practice, phenomena appear particularly in spontanteous visual appearances, and one explores in that direction, letting go on more and more profound levels. Sogyal Rinpoche: "Only when the master has determined that you have a thorough grounding in the practice of Trekchö will he or she introduce you to the advanced practice of Togal."

> The Togal practitioner works directly with the Clear Light that dwells inherently, "spontaneously present," within all phenomena, using specific and exceptionally powerful exercises to reveal it within him or herself. . . . Togal has a quality of instantaneousness, of immediate realization. Instead of traveling over a range of mountains to reach a distant peak, the Togal approach would be to leap there in one bound. The effect of Togal is to enable a person to actualize all the different aspects of enlightenment within themselves in one lifetime.[44]

Trungpa Rinpoche remarks that thögal is the ultimate path within Buddhism and, indeed, the highest attainment that is possible to human beings. It involves seeing the entire universe as meaning (*jnana*) and symbol (*kaya*), and realizing that the two are identical. It emphasizes upaya, or skillful means (in contrast to trekchö, which empahsizes prajna, or wisdom), and luminosity (while trekchö lays the stress on emptiness). In Rinpoche's words, thögal is just "beingness," with no duality of subject and object. It emphasizes the positive aspect of nirvana at its ultimate level (again in contrast to trekchö, which represents a via negativa). As the final stage of atiyoga, it represents more a result or fruition than a practice. In thögal, one realizes the identity of the external light (kaya) and the internal light (jnana), discovering their connection with the five buddhas, the five lights, and the five wisdoms (jnanas).[45]

The Bardo Retreat

The practice of thögal is typically carried out in strict seclusion, in the seven-week bardo retreat known as *yangti*, "beyond ati," in other words beyond the ninth yana, atiyoga, "one of the most highly advanced and dangerous forms of practice in Tibetan Buddhism."[46] It is held that through practicing the bardo retreat, one attains the rainbow body, which arises as the natural result of the identification of mind (jnana) and body (kaya).

In the bardo retreat, one follows a course of meditation that simulates the experiences of death and the after-death state. (See chapter 14.) The retreat itself is carried out in complete darkness, and because it is considered dangerous, facilities for it were found at only a few places in Tibet. Only those considered sufficiently well prepared both physically and mentally are authorized to carry out the retreat. The very real peril to the practitioner is one of psychosis, of dissociating from ordinary reality.[47] A variety of methods and practices are known and employed to bring practitioners "back" when such a psychotic break occurs.

A practitioner aspiring to perform yangti yoga needs to be at a most advanced stage of practice and spiritual maturity. Having been accepted for the retreat, he or she then undergoes months of preparation. Even then, one is allowed to enter the retreat only after clear evidence of mental and physical readiness. The retreat cell is specially designed so that all light can be gradually reduced until it is completely dark. The practitioner is taken to the cell and then, over the period of a week, the light is gradually excluded until he or she is in total darkness. Trungpa Rinpoche, who carried out this retreat as part of his training prior to leaving Tibet in 1959, remarks that at first the meditator feels depressed and anxious. In time, however, he becomes accustomed to the absence of light.

Each day, someone visits the retreatant to give meditation instruction and counsel. It is interesting that the instructions are the same as those provided to a dying person. Trungpa Rinpoche remarks that, as the retreat progresses, the daily visits are critically important, for without them the meditator would completely lose touch with ordinary reality.

In contrast to other types of tantric meditation, in the bardo retreat no active visualizations are involved in the practice. Instead, the mental imagery associated with death appears spontaneously. An example is provided by the appearance of wrathful wisdom eyes:

> The central place of the peaceful tathagatas is in the heart, so you see the different types of eyes in your heart; and the principle of the wrathful divinities is centralized in the brain, so you see certain types of eyes gazing at each other within your brain. These are not ordinary visualizations, but they arise out of the possibility of insanity and of losing ground altogether to the dharmata principle.[48]

Trungpa Rinpoche describes the evolving experience of the retreat. At a certain point, the dualistic notions of light and dark fall away, and everything is seen in a blue light. The meditator's projections appear as the five buddhas (lower), the five buddha lights (medium), or the five buddha wisdoms (higher). Rinpoche comments that one usually sees the blue light first, then light of one color, then another, following the course of how one broke away from the alaya in the first place.[49]

The experiences of the five buddhas manifest not in terms of physical or visual reality but in terms of energy having the qualities of earth, water, fire, air, and space. Trungpa Rinpoche explains:

> We are not talking about ordinary substances, the gross level of the elements, but of subtle elements. From the perceiver's point of view, perceiving the five tathagatas in visions is not vision and not perception, not quite experience. It is not vision, because if you have vision you have to look, and looking is in itself an extraverted way of separating yourself from the vision. You cannot perceive, because once you begin to perceive you are introducing that experience into your system, which means again a dualistic style of relationship. You cannot even know it, because as long as there is a watcher to tell you that these are your experiences, you are still separating those energies away from you.[50]

In characterizing the experience of the five buddha energies, Rinpoche remarks, "It flashes on and off; sometimes you experience it, and sometimes you do not experience it, but you are in it, so there is a journey between dharmakaya and luminosity."[51]

Through the bardo retreat, one is approaching an experience of space that is utterly beyond any interference or involvement by the human person, completely unorganized and undomesticated in any sense. It is totally naked, free-form, and unconditioned. It is naked because it contains not even the most subtle dualistic filter of subject and object. It is free-form because there are no concepts or categories to provide shape or interpretation. And it is unconditioned because it stands alone, not based on causes and conditions or leading to results, simply "as it is," without any reference to past or future. It is outside of time.

This description suggests the danger to the meditator. Out of the anxiety of the "free-fall" of the retreat, one may seek ground in what arises, becoming fascinated by the colored figures, the mental imagery, and the visions that one sees, and begin to fixate, magnify, and indulge in them. According to Tibetan tradition, this kind of fascination can lead to the withdrawal from reality mentioned above. In this case, one mentally creates a world of one's own and physically enters into a state of suspended animation in which one remains for years, decades, or even centuries.[52] Tenzin Wangyal, who carried out a bardo retreat in the Bön context, provides the following illuminating comments:

> I had heard stories and jokes about the problems people encountered while doing dark retreat, in which practitioners had visions they were sure were real. . . . In everyday life, external appearances deflect us from our thoughts, but in the dark retreat, there are no diversions of this kind, so that it becomes much easier to be disturbed, even to the point of madness, by our own mind-created visions. In the dark retreat, there is a situation of "sensory deprivation," so that when thoughts or visions arise in the absence of external reality testing devices, we take them to be true and follow them, basing entire other chains of thoughts on them. In this case it is very easy to become 'submerged' in our own mind-created fantasies, entirely convinced of their "reality."[53]

As the meditation proceeds, one passes through the bardo stages, described below in chapter 14. The meditation lasts for a nominal period of seven weeks, but it may in fact vary, depending upon the person. About the fifth week, a kind of breakthrough typically occurs. Trungpa Rinpoche:

> Generally around the fifth week there comes a basic understanding of the five tathagatas, and these visions actually happen, not in terms of art at all. One is not exactly aware of their presence, but an abstract quality begins to develop, purely based on energy. When energy becomes independent, complete energy, it begins to look at itself and perceive itself, which transcends the ordinary idea of perception. It is as though you walk because you know you do not need any support; you walk unconsciously. It is that kind of independent energy without any self-consciousness, which is not at all phantasy—but then again, at the same time, one never knows.[54]

At the end of the meditation the light is gradually readmitted, until after a week the windows are completely uncovered and the meditator may leave the cell.

The purpose of the bardo retreat, like other forms of tantric meditation, is to enable the practitioner to touch the primordial reality that precedes the formation of the personality. It enables one to "know" the energies that circulate in the ocean of being, as they are before we structure them through our perception, slot them into recognizable quantities, and filter them through the mechanism of conceptual interpretation. Moreover, one not only touches these energies and knows them, but much more profoundly recognizes them as the ultimate truth of one's own being and existence. This is, of course, a reality that is utterly free of any notion or movement of "I" or ego. What makes the bardo retreat so unique within Tibetan Buddhism is that its methods are incomparably powerful and effective, and it is able to bring this level of realization about so quickly—that is, for those who are sufficiently prepared and survive it rigors.

THE RAINBOW BODY

The ultimate fruition of the practice of thögal is the attainment of the rainbow body (*ja lü*), a body of pure energy. When a realized dzokchen practitioner is about to die, his or her physical body gradually dissolves into light. In such cases, the physical body vanishes, shrinking in size until only the hair and nails remain, as indicators of the process that has occurred.[55] Each element of the body (earth, water, fire, air, space) dissolves into the corresponding energy or colored light from which it originally arose. The attainment of the rainbow body means that the person has moved from the physical or nirmanakaya realm of existence to the sambhogakaya, in which there is the appearance of energy, light, and form, but no physical matter. Having attained this, one no longer undergoes the process of death and rebirth. This attainment of the rainbow body is typically accompanied by strange phenomena of lights and rainbows, marking the nonphysical state into which the practitioner is moving.

The rainbow body was an attainment known among the great Vajrayana masters of India. Tulku Urgyen remarks, "Of the 84 mahasiddhas of India, not a single one died leaving a corpse behind."[56] All of the great dzokchen masters, beginning with Garab Dorje, Manjushrimitra, Shri Simha, and Jnanasutra, attained the rainbow body. Similarly, the chief disciples of Pamasambhava and Vimalamitra also attained rainbow bodies. Tulku Urgyen comments that "from these practitioners onward, for many, many generations, like the unceasing flow of a river, numerous disciples also left in a rainbow body."[57] In contemporary times, there have been numerous examples of this attainment. Tulku Urgyen provides the following account of a recent occurrence:

[The person] took rainbow body in the cow shed of one of my gurus' mother's household. This event was witnessed by several people. Jamgon Kongrul the Second told me this story, so I definitely feel it is true. Jamgon Kongtrul's brother, a very tall and handsome man, was present at the time.

It happened like this. An elderly nun came through their

village on pilgrimage. When she saw the wealthy household, she asked for a place where she could make a short retreat. They offered her one of their vacant cow sheds. She told them, "I want to use it for a week to make a strict retreat. I want the door sealed up. Please pile stones against the door because I don't want any disturbance." Since they were used to sponsoring practitioners, they agreed and no one thought twice about it. They said, "Sure, you can have it your way." They didn't know who was going to look after her and bring her food; they thought she had already made arrangements.

After three days, some strange phenomena began to occur. Scintillating, swirling light-rays of different colors were seeping out of the holes and cracks of the cow shed's stone wall. Light was shining out from under the room; while outside the shed, spheres of light moved rapidly about. The people of the house wondered, "What's going on here? Who's looking after the old woman? Who's bringing her food?" They asked their servants. The servants thought someone else was giving her food, but actually no one was. They decided she must have been cooking for herself, but Jamgon Kongtrul's brother asked, "Is there any place to cook inside?" The servants said, "No, no. There is no fireplace or anything." So they wondered, "What is she eating? Does she have any water? What are these lights all about?"

Finally, they decided to take a look. They removed the pile of stones and pried open the door; they saw that the body of the nun had fallen to pieces. Her hands were lying in one place and her feet were lying in another; her limbs were no longer connected to the body, but lay scattered in pieces. From the ends of the bones, swirls of rainbow light were coiling out as the body continued to fall apart. The observers asked each other, "What is this? It looks like she's dead!" One person had the presence of mind to say, "Let's leave her alone. It looks like something unusual is happening here. She asked for seven days of solitude so let's do as she asked." And saying that, they sealed the shed up again.

When they returned after the seventh day and opened the shed, the rainbow lights had vanished. Not a drop of blood, nor flesh, nor bones could be found anywhere. Only the nails from the fingers and toes remained lying there very neatly, along with a hank of hair. This event most definitely happened.[58]

Tulku Urgyen continues: "Even after the Chinese arrived, two or three people in Golok attained rainbow body."

Nyoshul Khen Rinpoche, who is very careful about such stories, went to Tibet and through many different sources tracked down the names and places of these people. He is keeping all the details very precisely. Two of these people attained rainbow body. The third person was being beaten by the Chinese when suddenly he started to levitate upwards until they could not reach him. He went higher and higher until he vanished. This is a type of celestial accomplishment. So, it's definitely true that even these days people do attain rainbow body, and that there are still practitioners who attain accomplishment.[59]

PART FOUR

Tantric Applications

14

Lessons in Mortality

Death and Dying in Tantric Practice

The subject of death and dying occupies a central place within Tibetan Buddhism. This centrality derives from the fact that in Buddhism, and particularly in Tibetan tradition, death and life are not seen as opposed realities or even as separate from one another. To live is to experience death continuously; there is no such thing as life without the constant presence and reality of death. Death is, moreover, the key to life. Without an open and confident relation to death, one cannot live a full and meaningful life. Death is, in fact, the portal to life, and if we know how to die properly, then we are able to live fully and completely. In a very real sense, Tibetan Buddhism is about nothing more or less than learning the practice of dying in order to live in a true and authentic way.

The teachings on the process of dying, physical death, and the aftermath of death are found in an extensive body of literature preserved in Tibetan. This literature includes instructions on how to prepare for the moment of death, how to die, descriptions of the process of death, practices to be done by the dying as well as by those attending him or her, rituals to be carried out for the deceased, methods of divining the time of death, teachings on how to avoid untimely death, and so on. At the forefront of this literature is a text known in translation in the English-speaking world as the *Tibetan Book of the Dead*.[1] Its Tibetan title, the *Bardo Thödröl*, "Liberation by Hearing While In Between (Two States)," suggests more closely the function of the text: during the forty-nine days assigned to the period in the bardo between death and rebirth, the *Bardo Thödröl* is read to the deceased and describes both the geography of the journey through the bardo as well as the opportunities for liberation that are present therein.

DEATH IN THE MIDST OF LIFE

In the Abhidharma teachings of the first turning of the wheel of dharma, the impermanent nature of human experience is examined in detail.[2] According to these teachings, our conscious life is discontinuous, composed of one discrete moment after another, in unending succession. Each moment of experience arises, endures, and disappears. The apparent continuity of our conscious life is an illusion: we hang onto the belief in our continuity and ignore the ever-present data of discontinuity. This succession of individual moments of experience is habitually taken as an unbroken continuum that we label as "I" or "self." However, meditation reveals that at the death of each moment there is a gap, a discontinuity, before the arising of the next. It is this gap that is known in Tibetan Buddhism as *bardo*, the "in-between state."

In the first-turning teachings, the nature of the gap between moments is not really explored or discussed. Attention is rather focused on the content of the experiential moments (the *dharmas*), the pattern according to which they interact (*karma*), and the process by which a belief in a substantial "I" is generated (the five *skandhas*). However, the Abhidharma presentation leaves hanging a critical question: what is the nature of this gap, this "bardo," between the death of one moment and the birth of another? This question is explored in Vajrayana Buddhism and the answer that is found becomes the basis of Tibetan thought and practice surrounding death.

Vajrayana Buddhism, following the third turning of the wheel of dharma, understands this gap as disclosing the buddha-nature, in this book variously termed rikpa, the "basic ground," or the alaya, discussed in chapter 12. It is this same gap that is called rikpa in the Nyingma tradition and mahamudra among the Sarma or New Translation schools. The Vajrayana examines the nature of this gap and its relation to the dualistic consciousness of ego. In chapter 12 we followed Trungpa Rinpoche's description of the basic ground: "Fundamentally there is just open space, the basic ground, what we really are. Our most fundamental state of mind, before the creation of ego, is such that there is basic openness, basic freedom, a spacious quality; and we have now and have always had this openness."[3] This basic ground (alaya) is the primordial intelligence, "the open space belonging to no one."

In his teaching on bardo, Trungpa Rinpoche provides the following additional clarification. The alaya or basic ground is the origin of samsara and nirvana, and underlies both the ordinary phenomenal world and the three bodies of an enlightened buddha. Since the basic ground is more fundamental than either samsara or nirvana, it does not incline toward either, yet it has within it the living, creative energy of dharma, manifesting as wisdom and compassion.[4]

Within this situation, how has our ego consciousness come to be? As we saw in chapter 12, the energy of the basic ground became so intense that a splitting off occurred, and through the process of ignoring the alaya, self-consciousness developed. Through the ignoring of the alaya, a second, negative alaya develops, the *alaya-vijnana* or "storehouse consciousness" which serves as the ground of ego and in which karmic seeds are stored.[5]

The process of our alienation from the basic ground or alaya thus begins with the defilement or klesha of ignorance; from there it proceeds on to the other kleshas. As Trungpa Rinpoche describes the process, the energy that breaks away from the alaya becomes ignorance (*avidya*). This is the first bulwark of ego, and from it springs fear when one senses one's alienation from the basic ground and that one is an individual and alone. In order to cope with this fear, pride arises and the ego becomes fully developed. The existence of pride requires a defense against others, and from this arises a paranoid attitude toward others, in which one tries to fortify oneself in relation to them and to make gains at their expense. In order to further fortify one's situation, desire arises, and one tries to accumulate all those things that will further the project of ego aggrandizement. Finally, hatred arises as aggression against anything that calls one's ego fortification into question or threatens it in any way.[6]

This process of evolution is of course only an imaginary one. In fact, the basic ground does not change nor does anything really ever occur. Trungpa Rinpoche likens the evolution of the kleshas and the creation of the alaya-vijnana from the basic ground to the changing of water into ice. When water becomes ice, it does not lose its basic character as water, nor does it mean that there is any deficiency in the water. The water is always the actual reality, although it has a different appearance. In a similar fashion, as we have seen, the five buddha wisdoms, through the machinations of ego, take on the form of the kleshas, ignorance and so on. However, although they appear as kleshas, their underlying reality is the five wisdoms. They are the essential nature of the kleshas, and once the confusion of ego is dissolved, they appear in all their clarity and compassion.[7]

Trungpa Rinpoche stresses that one should not think that this occurred at some time in the past and then is over and done with. It is not something that occurred a long time ago, once and for all, as if the personality with its kleshas were born at some time in the past and then existed in solid form since then. Quite to the contrary, the generation of the kleshas from the enlightened wisdoms is something that occurs continually. At each moment, the kleshas arise from the alaya based on its overly powerful creative energy, and they dissolve back when that moment ceases. However, this is the most subtle of all psychological processes, and we are usually completely unaware that it is happening.[8]

In other words, we constantly experience impermanence, dissolution, and discontinuity—albeit subliminally, without being fully conscious of it. In each moment, we experience the death of the beloved "self" that we are continually struggling to maintain, and it is this continuous process of dissolution that produces the subtle sense of anxiety that, at some level, runs like a continuous thread through our lives. *In this specific and concrete sense, then, the experience of death is fundamental to our very being.*

On some level, no matter how hard we may insist upon our own personal existence, solidity, and continuity, we suspect the opposite. We are subconsciously aware that our fanatical belief in the existence of our "self" is a fabrication, a hoax. But like the person caught in a lie who may shout louder to drown out the truth, the more we sense our nonexistence, the more effort we apply to convincing ourselves and others of the opposite. We continually use the word "I" in our thinking and our conversation, precisely because no such thing is given in experience. Over time, each of us has developed an extraordinarily big and complicated "I" that we use to cover over and avoid the basic ground, the buddha-nature. This "I," which may become quite monstrous, is the sum total of our habit patterns in thinking, speaking, and acting in relation to ourselves, others, and our environment.

We humans are haunted by death. According to Buddhism, we are haunted because we already know what death is, experiencing it every moment as we do. Our death is something that we are constantly opposing, and we do so by ignoring and denying it. And because we are so used to this battle, if only subliminally, we have become adept at fending off awareness of it and pretending that things are otherwise.

THE PAINFUL BARDO OF DYING

The Tibetan word *bardo* (Skt. *antarabhava*) literally means "in between." It is commonly taken to refer to the after-death state, the in-between state of one's consciousness after death and prior to reincarnation and birth in another form. However, as mentioned, more fundamentally, bardo refers to an aspect of the dynamics of each moment of experience. Trungpa Rinpoche comments that it is the "nowness" in every moment of time and that to understand it is to understand the development of consciousness.[9] In other words, bardo is the moment of abiding in the "nowhere" of the basic ground prior to the re-creation of ourselves that occurs continually.

More specifically, Tibetan tradition talks about six bardos that are particular applications of bardo experience. These include the natural bardo of this life; the painful bardo of dying; the luminous bardo of dharmata; the karmic bardo of becoming; the bardo of dream; and the bardo of meditation. How are these six specific bardos related to the general meaning of *bardo* just described? Trungpa Rinpoche explains that when we are talking about one or another of the six bardos, bardo in the more generic sense is always present, underlying and common to the specific bardos. The general meaning is that of the continual dissolution into and the evolution from the basic ground or the alaya, a process that goes on all the time without stopping and of which the specific bardos of sleep, the waking state, and so on, are just particular modalities.[10] In relation to this general, generic meaning of *bardo*, Lama Tashi Namgyal comments, "All manifestations of this world are, in fact, those of Bardo, and all Samsaric existences are those of Bardo. . . . In both the sleep and waking states, one should think that all he sees, hears, touches, and acts upon is in the state of Bardo."[11]

Four of the six bardos are particularly important for understanding death and dying. These are summarized by Sogyal Rinpoche:

1. The *natural bardo of this life* spans the entire period between birth and death. Ordinarily, this may seem more than just a bardo, a transition. But if we think about it, it will become clear that, compared with the enormous length and duration of our karmic history, the time we spend in this life is in fact relatively short. The teachings tell us emphatically that the bardo of this life is the only, and therefore the best, time to prepare for death: developing familiarity with the teachings on death and stabilizing the practice to get us ready for dying.

2. The *painful bardo of dying* lasts from the beginning of the death process right up until the end of what is known as the "inner respiration." This, in turn, culminates in the dawning of the nature of mind, what we call the "ground luminosity," at the moment of death.

3. *The luminous bardo of dharmata* encompasses the after-death experience of the radiance of the nature of mind, the luminosity or "clear light," which manifests as sound, color, and light.

4. The *karmic bardo of becoming* is what we generally call the bardo or intermediate state, which lasts from the end of the bardo of dharmata right up until the moment we take on a new birth.[12]

Two other bardos are important in Tibetan tradition, the bardo of dream (the bardo experienced during the dream state) and the bardo of meditation.

The death of an ordinary person is simply a special case of the discontinuity that we experience in each moment of our lives. In ordinary life, when a moment of consciousness ceases, it is immediately followed by another moment of consciousness, arising in our present body. At the moment of death, however, after the last moment of consciousness of this present life ceases, it does not arise again in our present body. Instead, the consciousness relinquishes the body and is reborn in the after-death state.

Why do people die when they do? Why does consciousness continually re-arise in a certain body throughout the course of a lifetime and then, suddenly one day and at one moment, no longer arise in that body? After consciousness ceases in one moment, "rebirth consciousness" seeks reembodiment in the next moment. For samsaric people like ourselves, it always seeks the familiar reembodiment of our current physical body and will continue to "reincarnate" in this body as long as it can. When the karma of a certain person's life is used up or in the event of untimely death, the body no longer can sustain life. In this case, it is no longer a fit base or support for consciousness, which is thus forced to depart.

What is the actual process of death? In Tibetan tradition, one dies in two stages, an "outer dissolution" followed by an "inner dissolution."

The Outer Dissolution

As death approaches, the body gradually and progressively loses its physical senses as well as the four material elements that sustained it during life: earth, water, fire, and air. As we begin to die, the functioning of our senses begins to deteriorate. We may notice that when others speak, we hear sounds but can no longer recognize what is being said. Likewise, we may have visual impressions but are unable to make any sense out of them. Further, we may have some experience of scents, tastes, or sensations of touch but find ourselves unable to process or understand them.

Following the deterioration of the functioning of our senses, the elements begin to dissolve.[13] The earth element is the first to dissolve, causing the body to feel heavy and weighed down. We feel totally without energy and unable to make the least effort to hold ourselves up in any way. We may feel pressed down by a huge weight. Any physical effort, even that of opening and closing our eyes, becomes impossible. Physical signs of this stage include a fading, pallid complexion, sunken cheeks, and dark stains on the teeth. As the earth element dissolves, the corresponding skandha, that of form, dissolves along with it. Mentally, we are agitated and delirious, and sink into drowsiness. A "secret sign" or internal image accompanies each phase of dissolution. In the case of the earth element, the sign is the vision of a shimmering mirage.

During the previous stage, the earth element was dissolving into the element that immediately supports it, the water element. Now, in the next stage, the water element begins to dissolve, this time into the fire element. One begins to lose control of bodily fluids. Our nose runs, we dribble, the eyes may discharge, and we may become incontinent. At the same time, we begin to feel the water element receding, and we feel our eyes dry in their sockets, our lips drawn and bloodless, and our mouth and throat sticky and clogged. Our nostrils cave in and we become very thirsty. As the water element dissolves, the second skandha of feeling, corresponding with it, also begins to fade away. At this stage, mentally one feels "hazy, frustrated, irritable, and nervous."[14] The secret sign of this stage is "a vision of a haze with swirling wisps of smoke."[15]

Next the fire element begins to dissolve into the air element. The dissolution of the element of fire is marked by the ebbing of all warmth from our bodies. From the extremities all warmth recedes, inward toward our heart. Our breath is cold. We can no longer take any food or drink, and cannot digest anything. Along with the fire element, the corresponding skandha of perception also dissolves. Mentally, "our mind swings alternately between clarity and confusion. . . . It becomes more and more difficult to perceive anything outside of us as sound and sight are confused." The secret sign is of "shimmering red sparks dancing above an open fire, like fireflies."[16]

Now the air element begins to dissolve into space. One's breathing becomes more and more difficult. We have difficulty getting a breath and cannot hold the air when we do. We pant and labor to breathe. Our in-breaths are strained and short; our out-breaths become longer. There are long gaps after our out-breath until our next in-breath. As the air element fades, the corresponding skandha, that of formation, also dissolves. Our mind now becomes "bewildered, unaware of the outside world. Everything becomes a blur. Our last feeling of contact with our physical environment is slipping away."[17] Depending on whether the preponderate karma from our life is negative or positive, we will have negative or positive hallucinations and visions. The secret sign accompanying this stage is "vision of a flaming torch or lamp, with a red glow."[18]

The dying person's energy is now in the process of final withdrawal into the heart center. As it completes this process, the breathing slows. Finally, after several long out-breaths, the breathing suddenly ceases. There is now a slight warmth in the heart center. All vital signs have disappeared. This is the point at which modern medical science would pronounce the person "dead."

The Inner Dissolution

However, from the viewpoint of Tibetan tradition, death has not yet occurred, for a kind of "internal respiration" is still continuing. A further, internal stage in the dying process is about to happen. After the dying person's vital signs have disappeared, Sogyal Rinpoche says, "Tibetan masters talk of an internal process that still continues. The time between the end of the breathing and the cessation of the 'inner respiration' is said to be approximately 'the length of time it takes to eat a meal,' roughly twenty minutes. But nothing is certain, and this whole process may take place very quickly."[19] In the case of a violent, unexpected death, both inner and outer dissolution can occur in a moment.

In the inner dissolution, one's gross and subtle thought states and emotions dissolve. Sogyal Rinpoche comments:

It is if we are returning to our original state; everything dissolves, as body and mind are unraveled. The three "poisons"—anger, desire, and ignorance—all die, which means that all the negative emotions, the root of samsara, actually cease, and then there is a gap . . . And where does this process take us? To the primordial ground of the nature of mind, in all its purity and natural simplicity. Now everything that obscured it is removed, and our true nature is revealed."[20]

The internal dissolution can be understood in terms of the subtle body. In the internal dissolution the essence of the father (a white drop located in the head or crown chakra) and the essence of the mother (a red drop residing four finger-widths below the navel) come together in the heart center. When the red and white essences meet together at the heart, the consciousness is enclosed between them. Trungpa Rinpoche comments, "One feels trapped between the red and the white bindus, and as they approach [the heart center] the feeling of duality begins to vanish and the fear of annihilation is experienced, because one is returning . . . to the origin, the alaya."[21]

The inner dissolution thus mirrors in reverse the process of initial conception of a child mentioned in chapter 11. To review, in conception, the two seeds of male and female appear as the father's sperm, the white essence, and the mother's ovum, the red essence. These unite to form the fetus, and as the fetus begins to develop, the red and white essences separate; the father's comes to reside in the head and the mother's in the navel. This separation of "male" and "female" elements in the subtle body remains throughout life and provides the ground and the dynamic tension through which duality and manifestation become possible. Now, in the final, inner dissolution, this process is reversed, with the white "male" and red "female" elements joining together in the heart center of the dying person.

The Dawning of Ground Luminosity

Lama Tashi Namgyal:

> When the different elements have dissolved, one after another, the element of prana will finally dissolve into the consciousness at the Heart Center. Then the white [bindu] in the Head Center will descend, the red [bindu] in the Navel Center will rise, and the two will join in the Heart. When the red and white [bindus]

has completely merged, the Light of Death [the ground luminosity] will appear.[22]

This appearance of the ground luminosity marks the end of the process of inner dissolution and the culmination of the painful bardo of dying: for Tibetan tradition, it is the actual moment of death itself. In ground luminosity one is thus face to face with one's original nature. It is the luminous, vast expanse of dharmakaya, the experience of rikpa in Nyingma terms, or mahamudra in the New Translation schools. It is nothing other than our own inherent wakefulness, appearing like a pure and empty sky.

In relation to the ground luminosity, Chökyi Nyima explains, "What remains when all of these [samsaric] thought states have ceased is simply the unconstructed nature of mind called *dharmakaya*. . . . It dawns like a clear and cloudless sky. This ground luminosity is referred to as . . . the mind of the Buddha Samantabhadra, the wisdom beyond intellect or simply basic wakefulness."[23] "In Dzogchen terminology, this is the naked awareness itself. The Mahamudra teachings name this state 'ordinary mind.' . . . According to Madhyamika, it is ultimate truth devoid of constructs."[24]

As the dharmakaya, "in essence the ground luminosity is empty, but its nature is said to be luminous, which in this context means cognizant." It is this true emptiness as the indivisibility of emptiness and cognizance, not merely emptiness as a pure absence, that is perceived in the ground luminosity: "this actual true emptiness is directly and nakedly present" at this time.[25] "Because fixation on sense objects is absent, our innate wakefulness is able to manifest nakedly. This state of not fixating on anything whatsoever is wakefulness free from arising, dwelling and ceasing; yet, all things can be cognized. It is not a total blackout but an experience of the natural wisdom beyond words. . . ."[26] Chökyi Nyima explains further: "It is the unity of emptiness and cognizance, the unity of *prajna* and *upaya*, and has no concrete existence because in essence it is primordially pure. Nonetheless, at the same time, it is not nonexistent because the five wisdoms as well as numerous other qualities are spontaneously present."[27]

Chökyi Nyima asks, "Why is the ground luminosity experienced at this time?"

> It is simply because all sentient beings already possess an en-
> lightened essence, the *sugatagarbha* [buddha-nature]. This es-
> sence is present and permeates anyone who has mind, just as oil
> completely permeates any sesame seed. . . . So why don't we
> recognize [the sugatagarbha, dharmakaya] if it is present in our-
> selves as our true nature? We do not recognize it because our
> nature is obscured. . . . We wallow in delusion, mistaking what
> is impermanent to be permanent and holding that which is un-
> true to be true. These delusions perpetuate our wandering
> through the realms of samsaric experience. However, the end
> of the dissolution stages . . . is like a momentary lifting of the
> veil of delusion, leaving all obscurations temporarily yet totally
> absent. At this time the ground wisdom is vividly present; the
> natural state of Mahamudra is revealed bare and naked.[28]

For a trained practitioner, the dawning of ground luminosity at the
moment of death provides, in Sogyal Rinpoche's words, "*the* great opportunity for liberation."[29] In this case, the "child luminosity," which is
the ability to rest in the nature of mind developed during the practitioner's lifetime, is able to meet and merge with the "mother luminosity," which is the ground luminosity or dharmakaya itself. However,
"only if we have really been introduced to the nature of our mind, our
rigpa, and only if we have established and stabilized it through meditation and integrated it into our life, does the moment of death offer a
real opportunity for liberation."[30]

For an ordinary person, the experience of ground luminosity flashes
by in an instant and is not even noticed. Chökyi Nyima says, "Ordinary
people do not recognize this experience when it dawns upon them. Instead, old habitual tendencies reappear and carry them away into patterns of conceptual thinking. Thus they return to the state of
conditioned existence."[31]

In this case, the individual falls into a state of unconsciousness and
remains there for up to about three and a half days. At the end of this

period, the consciousness leaves the body and is immediately reborn in the after-death state, known as the bardo of dharmata, to be discussed presently. Sogyal Rinpoche:

> Even though the Ground Luminosity presents itself naturally to us all, most of us are totally unprepared for its sheer immensity, the vast and subtle depth of its naked simplicity. The majority of us will simply have no means of recognizing it, because we have not made ourselves familiar with ways of recognizing it in life. What happens, then, is that we tend to react instinctively with all our past fears, habits, and conditioning, all our old reflexes. Though the negative emotions may have died for the luminosity to appear, the habits of lifetimes still remain, hidden in the background of our ordinary mind. Though all our confusion dies in death, instead of surrendering and opening to the luminosity, in our fear and ignorance we withdraw and instinctively hold onto our grasping. This is what obstructs us from truly using this powerful moment as an opportunity for liberation.[32]

For a trained practitioner, at the appearance of ground luminosity at the moment of death, there are two avenues for attaining liberation, one associated with dzokchen practice (or its equivalent in mahamudra), the other with the tantric yogas discussed in chapter 11.

THE APPROACH OF DZOKCHEN: TREKCHÖ

In dzokchen, it is the practice of trekchö, in particular, that trains one in the recognition of ground luminosity. Here one uses the various trekchö techniques of cutting through dualistic thoughts and perceptions of all kinds, which leads to the revelation of the ground, the dharmakaya. The dzokchen practice, having enabled the meditator to return to the alaya in life, is now equally applicable in death, enabling the meditator, in the dying process, to identify more and more fully with the rikpa. Sogyal Rinpoche: "As everything that obscures the nature of mind is dying, the clarity of Rigpa slowly begins to appear and increase. The whole process becomes a development of the state of luminosity."[33]

THE APPROACH OF THE TANTRIC YOGAS

The second method of attaining rikpa at this time involves the practice of the inner yogas. As we saw above, through tantric yoga practiced during one's lifetime, one has explored the internal, subtle body of channels (nadis), psychic centers (chakras), and energies (pranas). One has become proficient in moving one's awareness through the various pathways and foci of experience. In particular, through the practice of tummo, one has been able to simulate the dissolution process that occurs at death, bringing together the red female and white male elements. He or she has trained in resting in the natural state that results from the union of the two. When one is actually in the throes of the death process, as the white "male" and red "female" essence move toward the heart center, the tantric practitioner is able to be aware of this process, follow it, and identify with it. When male and female seeds meet in the heart center and the ground luminosity of the dharmakaya arises, the yogin is able to rest in the natural state, as he or she has done during life, and thereby attain liberation.

For both dzokchen (or mahamudra) practitioners and those meditating primarily on the yidam, the ability to attain enlightenment with the arising of ground luminosity is determined by the extent to which he or she has learned to rest in the natural state during life. Sogyal Rinpoche: "When the Ground Luminosity dawns, the crucial issue will be how much we have been able to rest in the nature of mind, how much we have been able to unite our absolute nature and our everyday life, and how much we have been able to purify our ordinary condition into the state of primordial purity."[34] "As the ground luminosity dawns at death, an experienced practitioner will maintain full awareness and merge with it, thereby attaining liberation."[35] Chökyi Nyima adds:

> Practitioners who have received the pointing-out instruction
> and made it their personal experience during this lifetime will

at death, due to the power of that practice, be able to recognize their natural face, the primordial state of ground luminosity, and be liberated. *The Mirror of Mindfulness* describes this recognition: "They meet as old friends, or like a river flowing into the ocean." At that point, all that is left is dharmadhatu—space that is totally free from mental constructs yet naturally endowed with cognizant wakefulness.[36]

If a person does not recognize the ground luminosity at the moment of death, his or her consciousness will exit from the body and he or she will be reborn in the next bardo, the after-death state known as the bardo of dharmata.

THE BARDO OF DHARMATA

While the ground luminosity represents the dawning of the dharmakaya, ultimate emptiness, the arising of the bardo of dharmata represents the appearance of the sambhogakaya. In reference to this, Chökyi Nyima remarks, "A distinction should be made here between the dharmakaya luminosity [of the ground luminosity] and the sambhogakaya luminosity [of the bardo of dharmata]. If we do not recognize dharmakaya or ground luminosity at the close of the bardo of dying, the luminous bardo of dharmata offers us a second chance to attain liberation through the appearance of sambhogakaya luminosity."[37]

In the bardo of dharmata, Sogyal Rinpoche writes, "now gradually the sun of dharmata begins to rise in all its splendor, illuminating the contours of the land in all directions. The natural radiance of Rigpa manifests spontaneously and blazes out as energy and light."[38] The experience of ground luminosity is all-pervading space of dharmakaya, the ultimate emptiness and purity of mind. The experience of the dharmata is that of the luminous radiance of mind of the sambhogakaya. "Just as the sun rising in that clear and empty sky, the luminous appearance of the bardo of dharmata [sambhogakaya] will all arise from the all-pervading space of the ground luminosity [dharmakaya]. The name we give to this display of sound, light, and color is 'spontaneous presence,' for it is always and inherently present within the expanse of 'primordial purity,' which is its ground."[39] In the bardo of dharmata, then, the mind is unfolding, gradually becoming more and more manifest. "For it is through this dimension of light and energy that mind unfolds from its purest state, the Ground Luminosity, toward its manifestation as form in the next bardo, the bardo of becoming."[40]

As in the case of the dawning of the ground luminosity, so for the bardo of dharmata, Tibetan tradition describes two ways in which the yogin can attain liberation, and these are prepared for by two different sorts of training: (1) the dzokchen practice of thögal and (2) the practice of meditation on the yidam.

THE PRACTICE OF THÖGAL

According to Sogyal Rinpoche, the bardo of dharmata has four distinct phases, each of which offers additional opportunities for liberation.[41] These particular teachings are found in the dzokchen tantras and more specifically in the instructions on the practice of luminosity in thögal (see chapter 13). Just as the practice of trekchö enabled the practitioner to recognize the ground luminosity, so through practicing and attaining realization in thögal, the meditator is able to recognize the stages of dharmata and attain liberation. These four stages of the bardo of dharmata include:

1. Luminosity experienced as a landscape of light that occurs when "space dissolves into luminosity." If one realizes this as the spontaneous display of rikpa, one will attain liberation at this point.

2. If not, the next phase occurs, "luminosity dissolving into union." Here mandalas of peaceful and wrathful deities occur, filling all of space. "The brilliant light they emanate is blinding and dazzling, the sound is tremendous, like the roaring of a thousand thunderclaps, and the rays and beams of light are like lasers, piercing everything." Here appear the forty-two peaceful and fifty-eight wrathful deities described in the *Tibetan Book of the Dead*. If one recognizes this display of rikpa, liberation is attained. Otherwise, one reacts with fear and panic, and the next phase arises.

Figure 14.1 *Peaceful Deities as described in the* Tibetan Book of the Dead.

3. This is called "union dissolving into wisdom." Here one sees the buddha-wisdoms in their naked form as displays of light, except for the karma family wisdom, all-accomplishing wisdom, that will be fulfilled only at full buddhahood. If one can rest here in this manifestation of rikpa, liberation is attained.

4. If not, the final phase of the bardo of dharmata appears, "wisdom dissolving into spontaneous presence." Within the state of primordial purity, all-encompassing space, the five pure realms of the buddhas appear above and below them, the six realms of existence. The limitless-

ness of this vision is utterly beyond our ordinary imagination. Every possibility is presented: from wisdom and liberation, to confusion and rebirth. If one is able to see this as the display of rikpa, one attains liberation.

Within dzokchen, then, it is the practice of thögal that prepares one for recognition of the rikpa in the bardo of dharmata. Sogyal Rinpoche says, "An accomplished Togal practitioner who has perfected and stabilized the luminosity of the nature of mind has already come to a direct knowledge in his or her life of the very same manifestations that will emerge in the bardo of dharmata."[42]

YIDAM PRACTICE

A second kind of training for recognition in the bardo of dharmata is available for the person who has trained primarily in yidam practice. For such a meditator, this kind of training occurs in the development phase, in which one visualizes the yidam as the essence of oneself and of the pure appearance of phenomena. Through yidam visualization one is able to recognize and connect with the pure enlightened energy, the naked wisdoms, that manifest as the sambhogakaya realm of the bardo of dharmata. The basic principle of yidam practice is, as noted, to see whatever arises as the yidam. In the bardo of dharmata, when the various displays of rikpa occur, one will be able to see these as the sacred presence of the yidam and, thereby, to attain liberation. Sogyal Rinpoche explains:

> Instead of perceiving the appearances of the dharmata as external phenomena, the Tantric practitioners will relate them to their yidam practice, and unite and merge with the appearances. Since in their practice they have recognized the yidam as the natural radiance of the enlightened mind, they are able to view the appearances with this recognition, and let them arise as the deity. With this pure perception, a practitioner recognizes whatever appears in the bardo as none other than the display of the yidam. Then, through the power of his practice and the blessing

of the deity, he or she will gain liberation in the bardo of dhar-mata.[43]

Thus it is that, as Sogyal Rinpoche explains, "If you have the stability to recognize these manifestations as the 'self-radiance' of your own Rigpa, you will be liberated."

> But without the experience of Togal [or tantric] practice, you will be unable to look at the visions of the deities, which are "as bright as the sun." Instead, as a result of the habitual tendencies of your previous lives, your gaze will be drawn downward to the six realms. It is *those* that you will recognize and which will lure you again into delusion.[44]

THE BARDO OF BIRTH OR BECOMING

The experience of death, for most people, will involve simply "blacking out" and remaining in an unconscious state until they find themselves in the bardo of birth, propelled by the winds of karma toward a new rebirth. For ordinary people, the experience of the ground luminosity and the bardo of dharmata will both flash by so quickly that there is no registering or recognition whatever. In this situation, according to Sogyal Rinpoche, "the first thing we are aware of is 'as if the sky and earth were separating again.' We suddenly awaken into the intermediate state that lies between death and a new rebirth. This is called the bardo of becoming, the *sipa* bardo, and is the third bardo of death."[45] This bardo begins from this reawakening until one enters the womb of the next life.

> Now we can see exactly how, after the dawning of the Ground Luminosity and the bardo of dharmata, samsara actually arises as a result of two successive failures to recognize the essential nature of mind. In the first, the Ground Luminosity, the ground of the nature of mind, is not recognized; if it had been, liberation would have been attained. In the second, the energy of the nature of mind manifests, and a second chance for liberation

presents itself; if that is not recognized, arising negative emotions start to solidify into different false perceptions, which together go on to create the realms we call samsara, and which imprison us in the cycle of birth and death.[46]

Rather than recognizing the radiant displays as manifestations of rikpa, one sees them as irritating, painful, and terrifying. Now all of our karmic seeds and habitual tendencies are reawakened, and we look for comfort, familiarity, and security. Rather than looking up to the pure lands of the buddhas, one looks down to the soft, dull, comforting light of the six realms. By "reacting" to the brilliant wisdom lights of the five wisdoms, by attempting to centralize and maintain ourselves in the face of them, we begin to re-create our samsaric world.

During the bardo of birth, one exists in a mental body that corresponds to one's physical body in the previous life, except that this mental body is without defect and in the prime of young adulthood. The mental body possesses all the senses, and its awareness is said to be seven times more acute than in life. This mental body also possesses clairvoyance and clairaudience, and can move effortlessly and instantaneously anywhere it wishes to go. In its journeys, it can see and converse momentarily with other beings in this bardo who have previously died. Beings in this bardo can still feel hunger, and are attracted to human beings who may be able to help them. Sogyal Rinpoche remarks, "The mental body lives off odors and derives nourishment from burnt offerings, but it can only benefit from offerings dedicated specially in its name."[47]

During this bardo, we initially do not realize that we are dead. We linger in the vicinity of our previous home and seek interaction with our family and loved ones. However, no matter how we may try to get the living to notice us, they do not respond. We become aware that we do not cast a shadow in the sun or leave footprints when walking in the sand. If our attachment to our previous life is particularly strong, then we may remain around our home and family for a long time. Sometimes a person can hover around his or her previous situation for weeks, months, or even years, unable to move on to a new birth. In this case, the being becomes a ghost or spirit.

In the bardo of birth, we relive all the experiences of our past life. Every detail, no matter how minute, is reviewed. We revisit all the places of our previous existence, including, "the masters say, 'where we did no more than spit on the ground.'" Now "all the negative karma of previous lives is returning, in a fiercely concentrated and deranging way. Our restless, solitary wandering through the bardo world is as frantic as a nightmare, and just as in a dream, we believe we have a physical body and that we really exist. Yet all the experiences of this bardo arise only from our mind, created by our karma and habits returning. . . ."[48]

Another important feature of the bardo of birth is the "life review." Here, every virtuous or evil deed that we have ever committed, however small or large, is brought before us. Here we experience accountability for everything we have done in our previous life. There is no escape from the thoughts, words, and actions of the past, for each of them has left a karmic imprint upon our mind. The particular balance of virtuous and nonvirtuous actions will, along with our inheritance of unripened karma from earlier lifetimes, determine the realm and condition of our birth in our impending reincarnation. Sometimes the texts describe two beings, one white who proclaims our good deeds and another black who announces our evil actions. Yet, at the same time, it is ultimately ourselves who are the judge and jury of our own karma. As Sogyal Rinpoche says, "Ultimately, all judgment takes place within our own mind. We are the judge and the judged."[49]

Even in the bardo of birth, there are possibilities of attaining liberation. For example, if one can call to mind the guru or yidam or one's spiritual practice, this can provide an opportunity for liberation. If one has become accustomed to calling upon the guru or spiritual guide at moments of confusion, distress, or suffering, one may be able to do so now. "If you are able to invoke them fervently with one-pointed devotion, and with all your heart, then through the power of their blessing, your mind will be liberated into the space of their wisdom mind."[50]

Otherwise, one proceeds onward, coming closer and closer to the moment of reincarnation. One finds oneself yearning for the familiarity, security, and comfort of a material body and a concrete situation. Thus it is that we find ourselves attracted to one or another of the six realms, and seek reembodiment there. Trungpa Rinpoche remarks, "One becomes aware of friends, houses, children, animals, etc., offering help and security, and by becoming attracted towards them and in trying to escape from the terrifying mental imagery that one sees, one loses the memory of one's former physical body and inclines towards a future life in one of the six lokas [realms]."[51] The particular realm that one is most attracted to will be the one in most congruity with one's habitual patterns and thought forms.

Trungpa Rinpoche continues: "The six lokas themselves are mental projections, and are formed according to our own emotional reactions."

> For example, our own projection of pleasure becomes the deva-loka, our own projection of hatred, the hells, and so on. The particular kind of hell experienced depends upon the form of one's hatred. Thus the six lokas are like dreams, and the hells like nightmares. However, the hells and heavens differ from an ordinary dream in that since there is no physical body to act as an anchor, one gets caught up in one's own projection and the situation becomes completely real and vivid, and the intensity so great as to constitute a virtually timeless moment of pain or pleasure, which corresponds to those vast lengths of time for which life in these worlds is said to last. The "nowness" of the moment of one's birth in the loka to which one has been attracted is the bardo of birth.[52]

THE BARDO OF LIFE

Tibetan tradition mentions forty-nine days as the typical amount of time that one will spend in the bardo of birth. However, as Sogyal Rinpoche points out, these "days" do not correspond to their conventional counterparts, and the actual time period will vary depending on the karmic situation of the individual. If one has been unable to attain liberation in the course of the bardo of dying, the bardo of dharmata, or the bardo of birth, one will find oneself drawn helplessly toward a new incarnation in one of the six realms. If the balance of karma is sufficiently positive, one will head toward the fortunate birth of the human realm. In this case, looking for a familiar situation for rebirth, one will be seeking a father and mother who can provide a karmic situation corresponding to one's propensities. This means that the genetic, psychological, and social karma of the prospective parents will provide the kind of physical body and mental conditioning most in keeping with one's karmic configuration at the last moment of the previous life. When seeing such prospective parents engaged in intercourse, one has strong reactions—if headed to a male rebirth, strong attraction to the mother and antipathy to the father; if a female birth, strong attraction to the father and antipathy to the mother. When the mother's ovum, the father's sperm, and the consciousness seeking rebirth all come together, then the mother conceives and the bardo being has found a new birth. This marks the end of the bardo of birth and the beginning of the bardo of life.

ASSISTANCE TO THE DYING AND THE DEAD

The process of dying is, of course, the loneliest of journeys. As the Buddhist teachings say, we are born alone and we die alone. Nevertheless, in the Tibetan perspective, the community of the living can be of tremendous assistance to the dying and to those in the bardos after death. Trungpa Rinpoche commented that, within the traditional context, one of the most important tasks of a lama has always been working with the dying, and it is a responsibility that is taken most seriously.

This may seem strange, particularly in light of the Buddhist insistence on individual responsibility and on the need for each of us to be, as the Buddha advises in an early sutra, a "lamp unto oneself, relying on oneself alone."[53]

In Tibetan societies, however, death, like life, is a community affair and a community responsibility. Human beings are closely connected with one another through the ties of karma. How each of us acts affects the others around us, both near and far, for good or for ill. Much of

Tibetan Buddhism is concerned to acknowledge the karma linking people and to have us act in such a way that our behavior generates positive karma and avoids negative karma for ourselves and others.

We cannot make the spiritual journey for someone else, but we can either put obstacles in their way or help them begin to move again when they become bogged down or stuck. Think of the child who has received only harshness, with no love or acceptance from his or her parents, and of the difficulties created on all levels. On the other hand, we can all think of someone who appeared in our lives at a period of crisis and, through kindness and selflessness, helped us to survive and move on.

There is no reason why our ability to help others while they are alive should not extend to them not only when they are dying but also when they have passed over into the bardos of the after-death state. In Tibetan perspective, death is a most important transition, the equal of birth itself. Moreover, dying and death are not automatic processes that can simply be left alone to take care of themselves; they are times of tremendous openness, sensitivity, and potential impact on the future journey of the individual. For this reason, Tibetan Buddhism not only describes the realities of death and dying, as we have seen in this chapter, but also provides many methods both for finding in death the deep lessons it has to teach and for helping the dying person to enter as fully as possible into the truths laid bare at death.

For example, the more the dying person's consciousness is open, attentive, and unafraid, the greater the possibility that he or she will be able to recognize the ground luminosity or the dharmata. If liberation does not occur, as we saw, the consciousness will be drawn to a new incarnation that corresponds to the karmic configuration at the moment of death. In this light, it is clear why, in Tibetan tradition, it is held that the atmosphere surrounding the dying person is critically important. If the atmosphere is filled with fear, confusion, and aggression, we are inflicting the greatest harm on the dying person. If, by contrast, it is peaceful, settled, even joyous, the dying person will be immeasurably helped.[54]

Perhaps the most important Tibetan practice connected with death is that of *phowa*, or "ejection of consciousness" or "transference," as it is sometimes called." This practice directs the exiting of consciousness at the moment of death so that full realization, rebirth in a pure realm, or at least a positive human birth can be achieved. As we saw in chapter 11, phowa is a yogic practice, one of the six yogas of Naropa, that the accomplished yogin can perform for him- or herself at the moment of death. Much more commonly, however, phowa is performed for another person at death. This must be done by someone—usually a lama—who has been trained in the practice. Chagdud Rinpoche explains:

> This practice is done at the moment of death or soon after to transfer the dead person's consciousness from the bardo—the intermediate state between one birth and another—to a realm of pure awareness such as the pureland of the Buddha Amitabha. There is no suffering in the purelands and beings are able to accomplish the path to full enlightenment blissfully, without obstacles. If transference cannot be made into a pureland, then at least it can be used to avert great suffering and to direct rebirth as a well-born human or in other high realms of existence.[55]

Sogyal Rinpoche describes the phowa performed at the death of one Lama Tseten, a teacher of some accomplishment. At the time of this occurrence, Sogyal Rinpoche was a young boy and was traveling with the great master Jamyang Khyentse, his guru, and that master's entourage. When Lama Tseten had become seriously ill, the party halted and set up camp. Sogyal Rinpoche was sitting with the lama when he seemed to pass away peacefully. Jamyang Khyentse was immediately summoned and, coming quickly through the tent door, sat down beside Lama Tseten's body. Sogyal Rinpoche:

> Transfixed, I watched what happened next, and if I hadn't seen it myself I would never have believed it. *Lama Tseten came back to life.* Then my master sat by his side and took him through the phowa, the practice for guiding the consciousness at the moment before death. There are many ways of doing this practice, and

the one he used then culminated with the master uttering the syllable "A" three times. As my master declared the first "A," we could hear Lama Tseten accompanying him quite audibly. The second time his voice was less distinct, and the third time it was silent; he had gone.[56]

Chagdud Tulku Rinpoche recounts the admonitions and instructions he received on phowa in his own education under his teacher, Lama Atse; in so doing he provides insight into the training and perspective of the lamas who perform the rite.

> Lama Atse taught me p'howa, transference of consciousness. . . . Tibetans rely on their lamas to do p'howa for their deceased relatives, and when a family member dies, many offerings are made to generate merit and ensure that transference is accomplished. Actually, p'howa is a relatively easy practice to learn and accomplish for oneself, but requires considerable power and skill to accomplish for someone else. In training me, Lama Atse stressed strong visualization, but he emphasized pure motivation more. 'Think of the dead person. Remember that he has lost everything he held dear including his own body, that he is being blown about helplessly with no place to sit, no food to eat and no one to rely on but you to release him from the turbulence of the bardo or the possibility of a difficult rebirth. Think about the relatives who have lost their loved one. What they can do is very limited. Their hope is in you. Meditate from the depth of your love and compassion, and concentrate on the accomplishment of transference. Otherwise, you will fail the dead, you will fail the living, and you will fail yourself by breaking your commitment to them.'[57]

A second key practice in the death and dying process revolves around the *Tibetan Book of the Dead*. Commonly, when a person is dying, his or her guru, a lama close to the family, or another local lama will be notified. After the death has occurred, various rituals will be performed to facilitate the journey and rebirth of the deceased. Among the most important of these is the reading aloud of the *Tibetan Book of the Dead.* Owing to the supernormal abilities ascribed to the consciousness in the bardo, it is believed that the deceased can hear the reading and profit from the instructions given in the text. These instructions chronicle the process that the dying are going through, remind them that all the fearful experiences of the bardo are expressions of their own minds, and urge them to remember their practice, recognize their yidam, call upon their guru, and turn the mind to the spiritual power and truth that they were exposed to while alive. The reading of the *Tibetan Book of the Dead* typically goes on for the forty-nine days during which the deceased is believed to reside in the bardo of birth.

A third important practice that is commonly done for the dead is the *nedren* and *changchok,* which bring about purification of the deceased and the guiding of consciousness to a better rebirth. This ritual is performed close to death but no later than forty-nine days following death. Sogyal Rinpoche: "If the corpse is not present, the consciousness of the deceased is summoned into an effigy or card bearing their likeness and name, or even a photograph."[58] The deceased person's self-conscious, samsaric identity is thus concentrated in the effigy. In the ritual, his or her consciousness is purified of defilements, his or her karma is cleansed, some teaching occurs, and transmission into the nature of mind is given. Following this, a phowa is performed and the consciousness is directed toward a pure land. Finally, the corpse or representation is burned, marking the dead person's abandonment of the old, outworn identity and his or her freedom to move toward realization.

CONCLUSION

In the face of all these rituals and especially those to help the already deceased, Western Buddhists naturally find themselves confronted with a large array of questions. For example, are the dead really conscious and aware? Does their after-death situation correspond to the bardo as described in the texts? Do the deceased actually see and experience what is being performed on their behalf? Do the liturgies performed by the living for them have any benefit?

As a way of addressing these questions—which, while perhaps best left unanswered, certainly need to be thought about—I would like to report an incident that happened in my own community many years ago.[59] At the time, the event in question certainly captured my own attention and has remained provocative for me ever since.

In the mid 1980s, I was leading a meditation program at Rocky Mountain Shambhala Center, high up in the mountains near Red Feather Lakes, a tiny, remote village in northern Colorado. Adjoining the main property, was a small parcel with some buildings on it owned by the Girl Scouts but rented out by RMSC, and it was in this facility that the program was occurring. One night, a participant heard someone wailing in a high, sharp-pitched, mournful voice. On subsequent nights, others heard this same desolate cry.

A woman who worked at RMSC said it wasn't unusual to hear this sound and that people had been hearing such cries for some years. She then told the story of a little girl, perhaps ten years old, who had been killed here a number of years before. She had been climbing on some rocks that tower up just behind the camp. Her parents had been battling each other for years. The family, in disarray, was disintegrating. The girl's parents had finally decided to divorce, so they sent her away for the summer to remove her from the situation. She was beside herself with anxiety, loneliness, and fear.

One day, the girl fell from the rocks and was gravely injured. She was brought into a cabin nearby, and laid down in a small, unused room. It was here that she died, before emergency help could arrive from Fort Collins, down the mountain and a long drive away. After this tragedy, use of the camp by the Girl Scouts tapered off. There were even thoughts of selling the place.

Chögyam Trungpa Rinpoche was informed of the story and, in fact, for some time had been hearing reports of the mournful cries from RMSC staff members. He said that the cries were probably those of a hungry ghost who, because of her unresolved feelings toward her family and her tormented state of mind when she died, was stranded, unable to move on to a new birth. Unable to let go of her old life, which was inaccessible to her, she hung around the place she had died, literally caught between worlds.

Rinpoche suggested a *sukhavati* ceremony, similar to the nedren and changchok ceremony just described. The sukhavati is a Tibetan Buddhist funeral service performed for the recently deceased to ease their suffering and confusion in the after-death state and, through the collective intentions of the community, to open the way toward a favorable rebirth. It may also be performed to help a hungry ghost, such as the girl in this account, who had gotten stranded in the bardo and who, through attachment and unresolved karma, could not move forward.

Those of us participating in the retreat, most of whom had been Buddhists for many years, all more or less arrived at the conclusion, without hardly any explicit discussion, that now was time to perform the sukhavati. One of my friends, well acquainted with the story, took me into the cabin and into the bedroom where the little girl had died. The air of sadness and grief in the room was very heavy, almost unbearable. I sat on the bunk with my friend, just feeling the atmosphere and, for a long time, neither of us could speak.

I asked another senior practitioner to lead the ritual, a woman who had lead sukhavati ceremonies before. I attended, glad to be an observer. I had my doubts. In fact, I thought, "Well, maybe this is real and maybe it's a collective fantasy. Who knows?" So I sat there, with these uncertainties hanging there and also, because of them, paying close attention to see what I might find out.

At a certain moment in the ceremony, the officiant snaps his or her fingers to release the trapped ghost. When the woman leading the ceremony snapped her fingers, I saw a being rush off to the east, in a bolt of light, and a sudden sense of joy and relief filled the room. Startled and taken completely by surprise, I knew without thinking that this was the little girl, off to a new birth and a new life.

Prior to that moment, I had tended to think of the concept of the hungry ghost primarily as a Tibetan method of elucidating the doctrine of karma or a way of illustrating aspects of human psychology. However, from that moment onward, I have more or less known that this notion has much more to it than that. Now I have some understanding of the Tibetan conviction that such ceremonies are ways of connecting with beings in other realms of existence and allowing us to use our unique human situation to help them. I see now why Tibetans are so resistant when Western Buddhists question the legitimacy of such rituals and wonder whether it might not be better to jettison them along with beliefs in "other realms."

After our performance of the sukhavati, the air of sadness that hung over the room where the little girl had died dissipated completely. The mournful cries were no longer heard at night. People at RMSC stopped talking about the tragedy. The Girl Scouts began using the camp more frequently and a new board decided against selling the property. The people who subsequently came to manage the facility did not seem to be familiar with the incident of the little girl's death.

But then the karma took another turn, as it will, and recently the Girl Scouts sold the property to RMSC. Now it is part of the permanent RMSC complex, with renovations and new meditation facilities having been built. As I write this, forty new practitioners are engaged in a month long meditation intensive, exploring the further reaches of their minds, on the very spot where the little girl died.

As this and the more classical examples previously mentioned illustrate, in Tibetan Buddhism the human community is intimately involved in the processes of dying and death. This is seen not only as a benefit for the dying and the dead, but also as an offering of assistance to the living. Why? Because the dying have at least as much to offer those of us with the prospect of further life as we have to offer them. As the Buddhist teachings say, when we distance ourselves from death, when we ignore, cosmeticize, or reject it—whether in the moment-to-moment death of ordinary life or in physical death as the end of our lives—we render ourselves unable to live. We carry on as if we were going to live forever and, in so doing, our priorities become confused and we lose our perspective. The dying remind us that death is real, and they demonstrate for us the end that we also are going to come to sooner or later.

It is not at all surprising, therefore, that one finds Western Buddhists frequently involved as caregivers of the dying in hospitals and homes, and as hospice workers. Buddhist-oriented hospices are coming into being throughout the West, and the first prison hospice program was started by a Buddhist inmate. In the West, when Buddhists are involved with someone dying, great attention is given to the atmosphere around the dying person. In addition to providing physical and emotional assistance, family and friends will come to meditate with the dying person. They will also typically carry out the tonglen meditation, inviting to themselves whatever fear, confusion, or pain the dying person may be feeling, and projecting a sense of well-being and goodness toward that person. Coming into such a situation, one often feels peace, warmth, clarity, and even confidence, quite a contrast to the depressing, confused, and conflicted atmosphere that so often surrounds the dying in many modern environments. Thus it is that death and dying are not only unavoidable parts of life, but the very essence of the Buddhist teachings: that only through understanding, accepting, and integrating impermanence, discontinuity, and death do we have any hope of leading a true, genuine, and joyful life.

15
Bodhisattvas in the World
TÜLKUS, REINCARNATE LAMAS

ONE OF THE MOST STRIKING AND UNUSUAL, AND ALSO IMportant, aspects of Tibetan Buddhism is the tradition of the reincarnate lamas or *tülkus*.[1] In the most common usage of the term, a tülku is a person who has been identified as the reincarnation of a specific former holy person. While this definition may seem simple enough, as we shall see, the tülku phenomenon is actually subtle and complex, and appears in many different forms. Within Tibetan Buddhism, tülkus were found as the primary spiritual leaders in all of the Tibetan schools and subsects, in every monastery of any standing, and in every locale. The purpose of the present discussion is to examine something of the history, theory, and practice of this most important aspect of Tibetan Buddhism.

The term *tülku* translates the Sanskrit word *nirmanakaya,* which may be glossed as "pure physical body." Most fundamentally, *nirmanakaya* refers to the human body of Shakyamuni and all other fully enlightened, world-redeeming buddhas. In that context, it indicates a being who has incarnated into this human realm and, having attained full enlightenment, remains here to teach others. The buddha as nirmanakaya, then, although living in this world, is beyond stain and defilement of any kind and is guided in life solely by wisdom and compassion for others.

In Tibet, the term *tülku* retains its basic meaning of a "pure incarnation" but is expanded. Tibetan tradition identifies three major types of tülkus or nirmanakayas, all of which are found in one form or another in Indian antecedents: (1) Fully enlightened buddhas; (2) other human beings who similarly manifest realization—including, in the present context, those understood as tülkus in Tibet; and (3) "created objects," sacred art such as statues, thangkas, stupas (Buddhist reliquaries), and other creations that, once consecrated, transmit the power of enlightenment.

The first type of tülku needs no explanation, while the second forms the primary subject of this and the next chapter. The third type of pure incarnation, the empowered religious object, functions as a transmitter of the realization of the buddhas, in terms of both wisdom and compassion. The wisdom aspect is found in the clarity, charged atmosphere, and power that one often feels, for example, in the precincts of stupas, particularly the most sacred ones. The Ven. Thrangu Rinpoche provides an illustration of the compassion aspect of this type of tülku. In the district from which he came in Tibet, there is a particular stupa famed for its ability to take on human suffering. Whenever an outbreak of smallpox would surface in the region, one morning residents would awake to find the white exterior of the stupa covered with black circular "poxes" and, more or less simultaneous with this appearance, the infection would disappear.

In Tibet, as mentioned, the term *tülku* most commonly refers to people who, though not world-redeeming buddhas, nevertheless are thought to embody the qualities of spiritual realization. While theoretically a person can be a tülku in this sense without necessarily being identified with a previous master, in actual practice any person judged a tülku is seen as the reincarnation of some particular previous realized person. Employed in this way, the term is used in Tibet in two somewhat different contexts, one more general, the second more specific.

First, in a general sense, it is applied to any person of realization who is felt to be a reincarnation of a certain holy person, even if he or she lived many centuries before. Thus the tertöns are generally understood to be reincarnations of one or another of Padmasambhava's primary disciples. Sometimes, a master is seen as the incarnation of several earlier saints. In recent times, the Ri-me master Jamgön Kongtrül the Great was considered a reincarnation of the great translator of the earlier spreading, Vairochana and, further back, of the Buddha's beloved attendant Ananda.[2] His contemporary Jamyang Khyentse Wangpo was known as the incarnation of, among others, both of Milarepa's primary disciples, Gampopa and Rechungpa.[3] Jigme Lingpa, whose life was discussed in chapter 3, was, in Dudjom Rinpoche's words, "the combined emanation of the great pandita Vimalamitra, the religious king Trisong Detsen, and Gyelse Larje [grandson of King Ralpachen]."[4]

Developing out of this general meaning of the term *tülku* is a second, more specific usage. Here it refers to the identification of a person, usually as a small child, as the reincarnation of a particular recently deceased lama. In traditional Tibet, whatever that previous person's religious and institutional affiliation—and usually it was with a specific monastery (*gompa*), often as its abbot—the newly recognized tülku would be reinstalled in the same position. Thenceforward he or she— for women were also recognized as tülkus, though far less frequently than men—would be understood as the "rebirth" of the person who had previously held that seat and would take up again the work of teaching and administration interrupted by the previous incarnation's death. In the past number of centuries, most abbatial seats in Tibetan monasteries were held by tülkus, and the prestige of the various gompas depended to a considerable extent on the stature of the tülku who resided and taught there. This second, more specific, institutional meaning of tülku applied to a wide variety of people at various levels of realization. Some tülkus might be considered quite realized, but others might be understood as much more ordinary. It is this more specific usage, namely the tülku phenomenon as it provides the foundation of institutionalized Buddhism in Tibet, that is the subject of this and the next chapter.

This second, institutional meaning of tülku can be understood as a specific application of the more general meaning of reincarnation. In addition, in many cases, the general and more specific meanings are operative at the same time. In fact, many of those recognized as the incarnation of an immediately preceding master and reinstalled in his or her seat are also, at the same time, identified as the incarnations of masters who may have lived previously. For example, Karma Pakshi, understood to be the second incarnation in the Karmapa lineage, is also remembered as the incarnation of Garab Dorje's disciple, Toktsewa.[5]

Rangjung Dorje, the third in the Karmapa lineage, is similarly identified as an emanation of Vimalamitra.[6] Jigme Lingpa, incarnation of the
three earlier masters mentioned above, was also seen as the immediate
rebirth of Rikdzin Chöje Lingpa.[7] The Tibetan tülku tradition possesses
both theoretical and practical dimensions. On the one hand, basing itself
on Indian bodhisattva doctrine, a body of Tibetan thought explains
what a tülku is and how the repeated, intentional reincarnation of an
accomplished person is possible. On the other hand, a rich oral and
written tradition describes the actual practice of the tülku tradition,
including its many variations and diverse faces. Both theoretical and
practical aspects imply one another. The theory, at least to some extent,
inspires and explains the practice; and the practice—in some sense always fresh and ahead of the theory—continually calls for new ways of
thinking about tülkus and for revisions in the theoretical framework.
The present chapter reviews some of the theory surrounding the tülku
tradition, while the next chapter summarizes the more important aspects of the practice.

THE BACKGROUND OF THE TÜLKU TRADITION

When one looks at other Buddhist traditions in the world, it sometimes
appears that the tülku tradition is a relatively late, purely Tibetan phenomenon, having little to do with classical Indian Buddhism. In fact,
the tülku tradition has many roots in its Buddhist past and is much
more closely related to early and later Indian developments than might
appear at first glance.

The foundations of the tülku phenomenon are established in earliest
Buddhism. In traditions reflected in the Pali canon, for example, Shakyamuni Buddha is understood as having been a bodhisattva who, on his
journey to full enlightenment, was reborn over and over, working for
the benefit of others. On this journey, he is depicted as taking intentional rebirth, talking about his various former incarnations, and even
remembering specific people, places, and events of those former lives.
These motifs provide the essence of the tülku ideal. While in the early

tradition the bodhisattva concept is applied only to Shakyamuni Buddha and other buddhas,* enlightenment is presented as something that ordinary human beings can attain. In other words, those who are not buddhas can purify their incarnation by carrying out spiritual practice and attaining realization. Thus in the early tradition, there are ordinary people who attain enlightenment, the basic notion of the Tibetan tülku. They also identify and recollect former rebirths.†

In Mahayana Buddhism, as we have seen, the way of the bodhisattva became an ideal for all. In the classical literature, we are told that bodhisattvas are not all the same in their spiritual development but reflect many different levels of realization. These are most commonly divided into the "ten bhumis," or stages of awakening. In the context of the tülku tradition, it is particularly interesting that, according to the *Dashabhumika Sutra*, as a bodhisattva progresses through the bhumis, he acquires the power to consciously and intentionally choose the situation of his rebirth in terms of time, place, family, and so on. This power, along with other abilities and miracles associated with high-level bodhisattvas, is a central feature of the tülku tradition. The power to choose one's rebirth, for example, explains how a person of attainment can die and then find his way back to a locale and family where he can be recognized and reinstalled in his previous seat.

Within Vajrayana Buddhism in India, the siddhas are understood as high-level bodhisattvas. As such, these human saints, as reflected in their biographies, are understood to have attained many of the powers and abilities of the bodhisattvas of the upper bhumis. The Indian siddhas, then, represent human beings who embody the exalted state of being of

---

*All currently living human beings, however saintly they may be, are striving for the more limited enlightenment as arhants, which does not imply the wisdom and compassion of the bodhisattva ideal.
†For example, in the *Theragatha* and *Therigatha* and among other early Buddhist texts, enlightened disciples of the Buddha are credited with having attained the same enlightenment as their master. While the term *nirmanakaya* was probably never applied to such saints, they were certainly understood as living within samsara but as having once and for all transcended its defilements. This idea that others beside the Buddha can attain this state is obviously the ground of the Tibetan tülku tradition.

highly developed bodhisattvas. Since the siddhas are understood as actual people, they provide a bridge between the more theoretical bhumi literature of the Mahayana and the tradition of human tülkus in Tibet.

One can see this in the *Lives of the Eighty-four Siddhas*, where certain siddhas exhibit power over rebirth and other abilities and powers of the accomplished bodhisattvas. For example, the siddha Sakara is conceived among wonders; miraculous dreams come to his mother; he seems to be practicing meditation in the womb, pointing to his prior attainment; his birth is accompanied by miracles; and so on. These are all themes one finds among the later Tibetan tülkus. Again reminiscent of the Tibetan tülku tradition, in the biographies of Padmasambhava, one finds the idea of a realized being—in this case the enlightened buddha Amitabha—taking conscious and deliberate rebirth in a particular time, place, and family, in order to help others. Within the Indian Mahayana and Vajrayana, bodhisattvas appear in a diverse manner, as monastics, yogins, and laypeople. Particularly among the eighty-four siddhas, high-level bodhisattvas live in the world, and many of them are kings and queens and hold political power. Again, these themes are definitive of the later Tibetan tülku tradition. Thus it appears that much of the configuration of the tülku tradition was in place within the Indian context, both in the theoretical Mahayana literature and the biographies of the Indian siddhas.

In addition to the Indian strands that flow into the formation of the tülku tradition, there are indigenous Tibetan features as well. For example, the accounts of the early Tibetan dynasties speak of the "heavenly" origin of the first Tibetan kings. These beings had lived in the sky—that is, they had essentially "celestial" identities—and came to earth to rule by way of a "sky-cord." They were thus in some sense "on loan" from another, higher realm. This tradition of rulers who come from a spiritually more powerful place to render assistance on this earthly plane undoubtedly nourished the later tülku tradition in some fundamental ways. For example, the bodhisattva ideal did not necessarily put the buddha-to-be in positions of political power, and important Indian Mahayana texts like Shantideva's *Bodhicharyavatara* certainly reflect an ideal of extreme renunciation. However, the legends of the early kings show that in the Tibetan mind, great spiritual power is not incompatible with political authority. In fact, in the indigenous Tibetan perspective, they can and should go together, for it is precisely spiritual power and integrity that make a person fit to rule. This idea is reflected in the tülku tradition, for here it is precisely the person held to be most spiritually gifted who is chosen to rule, whether over a single monastery, a group of monasteries, a lineage, or even, as sometimes happened, an entire geographical region.

Westerners sometimes react with ambivalence to the political affiliations of Tibetan teachers and the social and political hierarchies over which they preside. We need to realize that such a reaction reflects our culture's belief that corruption inevitably results if church and state are not kept separate. This assumption is, it seems to me, not unconnected with the deep Western assumption of "original sin." This fundamental Western idea, although having explicitly disappeared from the "secular" discourse of modern mass culture, is certainly still a powerfully functioning archetype: in modern, Western culture most people find it literally impossible to conceive of people who might be above self-interest.

THE ORIGINS OF THE TÜLKU TRADITION IN TIBET

Precursors

The tülku idea—of high bodhisattvas taking conscious reincarnation and reappearing on earth to help others—is found among the Nyingma accounts of the early spreading. As mentioned, the twenty-five enlightened disciples of Padmasambhava were charged with taking intentional reincarnation at specific times and places, remembering their former births and the locations of spiritual treasures (terma) hidden by their master and discovering them and bringing them to light. Thus among the account of the early spreading, one finds the idea of bodhisattvas taking rebirth to continue the work of their previous incarnation, remembering their previous lifetime, and carrying specific memories of that former birth.

The biographies of Machik Labdrönma, whose dates (1031–1124) place her before the genesis of the tülku tradition in Tibet, depict her as recounting to her disciples her past lives as an Indian yogin. She also claimed to be the reincarnation of two women who played key roles in the earlier spreading of Buddhism in Tibet, Yeshe Tsogyal and the Indian saint Sukhasiddhi. In Machik, then, we find the motifs of a realized person taking rebirth to continue the propagation of dharma of her previous incarnations, explicit memories of those previous incarnations, and "self-recognition" of her status as a tülku, a pure incarnation. In the examples of both the tertöns and Machik Labdrönma, there is no clear evidence of the presence of two other central features of the later classical tülku tradition—rebirth closely following the death of the predecessor and association with institutional seats.*

The Classical Ideal

The classical form of the tülku tradition took definitive shape among the schools of the later spreading. Here the various ideas of deliberate reincarnation came together with the evolving monastic system in Tibet. Now the bodhisattva took rebirth closely following the death of a known predecessor, was identified with that person, and was reinstalled in the institutional seat of the previous incarnation.

The evolution of the classical tülku ideal occurred partly in conjunction with an attempt to strengthen the integrity and independence of the newly developing monastic system. Prior to the later spreading, despite the presence of Samye Monastery, there appears to have been no monastic system with even relative independence in Tibet. The Buddhist lineages, and such monastic establishments as there may have been, prospered through affiliation with the royal court, the landed nobility, and other powerful families. Thus Buddhism was dependent upon and more or less controlled by the concerns of these powerful laypeople. In

---

*It needs to be borne in mind, of course, that to some extent that is difficult to determine, the accounts of the early spreading themselves took shape during the period of the later spreading.

the later spreading, through the work of Atisha and others, a monastic system began to evolve within Tibet. Initially, powerful families were the supporters of the monasteries and exerted great influence over the selection of monastic leaders and the conduct of monastic affairs. The tremendous power of the laity over monastic affairs presented obvious problems, and there developed a tension between the monasteries and the powerful families for control over the Buddhist teachings.

With the rise of the tülku system during the later spreading, the balance of power shifted. Now it was the monasteries themselves that chose their new leaders, a choice made in accordance with the clairvoyance of realized masters. This meant that the powerful families, while still retaining considerable leverage, generally lost ultimate control of the governance of the monasteries and were no longer able to direct monastic affairs quite so strictly according to their own particular interests. The development of the tülku tradition, then, gave monastic culture a certain independence from outside interference, although the close mutual ties between the monastery and the laity (through the exchange of material support and dharma teachings, ritual relations, family ties to monks and nuns) meant that this independence was always relative and limited.

The genesis of the tülku idea in Tibet raises an interesting question: to what extent did the tradition first develop primarily out of a conscious intention to find a way for the monasteries to gain the upper hand in their ongoing struggle with powerful families? In other words, to what extent was its genesis primarily political? Certainly, one of the eventual outcomes of the appearance of the tülku phenomenon was just such a shift in power. But it is probably unwise to try to explain the rise of the tülkus exclusively by this one result. In fact, it was only sometime after the classical tülku practice arose among the Karma Kagyüpas that its institutional implications began to become evident. In time, Tibetan tülkus came to be the respositories not only of social, political and institutional power, but also (and perhaps more significantly) of mastery that was scholastic, ritual, and yogic. Thus the rise of the tülku as a centerpiece in Tibetan Buddhism fulfilled the need, in a relatively decentralized culture, for spiritual leaders spread throughout the country who were more or less equivalent in function, embodying in one person and one place the various dimensions of Buddhism. Most likely, then, many social, political, as well as religious and spiritual factors and needs came together to create the opening within Tibetan culture for the ancient bodhisattva ideal to take the particular shape of the tülku tradition.

The actual formation of this tradition is held to have occurred at Tsurphu Monastery among the followers of the Karmapa subsect of Tüsum Khyenpa (1110–1193), Gampopa's primary disciple. Tüsum Khyenpa had passed his transmission principally to his disciple Drogön Rechenpa, who in turn passed it on to Pomdrakpa.[8] According to Karma Thinley Rinpoche, this latter had a young student by the name of Chödzin, who had demonstrated considerable intellectual and spiritual precocity. In Rinpoche's account, when his teacher Pomdrakpa introduced Chödzin to the nature of his own mind, the young boy attained immediate recognition. It was the young Chödzin who was identified as a reincarnation of Tüsum Khyenpa.

In Karma Thinley's summary of the traditional accounts, the eight-year-old Chödzin says to Pomdrakpa, "I am Tüsum Khyenpa, the Karmapa. Because I am the teacher of your teacher, you should be showing me respect, instead of vice versa." This "self-recognition," while not the kind of identification process that was later to characterize the tülku tradition, set in place the idea that Tüsum Khyenpa had reappeared in a new birth, Chödzin, who became known as Karma Pakshi (1206–1283).

The more or less official recognition by an acknowledged master, as a third party, of a rebirth occurred only in the next generation. In Karma Thinley's account, when Rangjung Dorje, the third Karmapa, was born, his extraordinary precocity drew the attention of the famed yogin Urgyenpa (1230–1309), who had been the principal disciple of Karma Pakshi. Among other things, the young child, like Karma Pakshi, had declared himself the reincarnation of the Karmapa. When Urgyenpa met the child, his direct perception told him that this was indeed the reincarnation of his beloved master and in 1288 he publicly recognized him as such. Thus this child became known as the third Karmapa, with Tüsum Khyenpa being recognized as the first and Karma Pakshi as the second.[9]

FIGURE 15.1 *Tüsum Khyenpa, the first Karmapa. Drawing by Chris Bannigan (Namkha Tashi).*

FIGURE 15.2 *Karma Pakshi, the second Karmapa.*
Drawing by Chris Bannigan (Namkha Tashi).

By the time of Rangjung Dorje, the third Karmapa (1284–1339), most of the elements of the classical tülku tradition are in place.[10] For example, we read in his biography that, upon his birth, various extraordinary phenomena occurred and the child himself immediately showed unusual signs. As a young child, he demonstrated remarkable intellectual and spiritual understanding and, as mentioned, declared himself Karma Pakshi's reincarnation. Following official recognition by Urgyenpa, he was given the novice ordination, and formally installed as Rangjung Dorje, the third Karmapa. Following this, during the course of his youth and adolescence, he underwent rigorous training in Buddhist doctrine, meditation practice, and liturgy. At his majority, he assumed his responsibilities as abbot of Tsurphu and leader of the Karmapa subsect, performing religious, administrative, and political functions until 1339, when he predicted his own passing and shortly thereafter died. Subsequently, the line of Karmapa incarnations continued down to Rangjung Rikpe Dorje, the sixteenth Karmapa (1923–1981) and now his new incarnation, the seventeenth Karmapa, who is still in training in Asia.

The birth of the classical tülku ideal, suggested above, represented a turning point in Tibetan religious history. From a political point of view, now monasteries had some real internal control and, in time, came to manage not only their own affairs but those of the entire country. But the tülku tradition represented a turning point in other ways. Most important, it provided a way for spiritually gifted children to be identified and brought into a religious, institutional arena. Here, from a very young and impressionable age, they could be trained in the ideas, practices, and points of view most needed by a religious leader in Tibet. This represents a level of social control over the upbringing and education of children that would make most Westerners uncomfortable. And yet we probably need to judge the tradition ultimately by the results it produced.

From the time of the early Karmapas onward, the tülku tradition gradually spread throughout Tibet, eventually becoming the dominant method of succession not only among the Kagyü lineages but among the Kadam/Geluk and the Nyingma as well. It is interesting, however,

FIGURE 15.3 *Rangjung Dorje, the third Karmapa.*
Drawing by Chris Bannigan (Namkha Tashi).

that while the tülku method of succession became widespread in Tibet, not all of the Tibetan lineages chose to adopt it. As we have seen, leadership of the Sakyapas is still passed down through family lines. As the succession system has developed among the Sakyapas, there are now two main family dynasties of sorts: the Drolma Photrang and Phüntsok Photrang, which are lead respectively by the Sakya Tridzin ("throne holder of the Sakyas," who is the main leader of the lineage) and the Sakya Dagchen ("great lord of the Sakyas"). These *photrang* ("palaces") alternate generationally in terms of who is the ruler. Although the succession is thus according to family lineage, drawing on the larger, more general, noninstitutional definition discussed above, Sakya masters such as Sakya Tridzin Deshung Rinpoche are regarded as tülkus. Certainly the way the Sakyapas have applied the method of family succession, it has unquestionably produced a lineage of incomparable strength and integrity.

WHAT IS A TÜLKU?

At first glance, the concept of the tülku seems fairly straightforward. A person is born (1) who is considered a "pure incarnation" operating from a standpoint of wisdom rather than ego and (2) who is identified as the reincarnation of a previous holy person. However, there are problems with each of these two parts of the definition. First, it is not clear that all tülkus are fully realized people; in fact, Tibetan experience makes clear a wide range in the levels of attainment of people called tülkus. Second, the idea that a tülku is in all cases a literal reincarnation of a specific former person seems questionable. For example, tülkus who do not exhibit an exceptionally high level of attainment would not possess the powers to be able to select their own rebirth. On a more practical level, many people identified as tülkus claim to have no memories of their former lives or feeling of connection with the previous incarnation. Most tülkus that one talks to agree that there is spiritual validity to the tradition, but they often have many questions about how it should be understood and explained.

Trungpa Rinpoche offers some interesting perspectives. According to him, one needs to distinguish between three different sorts of tülkus. First are those who are tülkus more in name than in fact. These are ordinary people whom tradition has placed in the position of a tülku, to fulfill certain religious, social, and political functions. Such a person is not a genuine tülku in the strict sense of the word because he is not really the reincarnation of an earlier, identified saint and has no connection with that person. He has merely been chosen, in this present life, to play out the assigned role. There is no particular sense of karmic destiny associated with this level of tülku and the fact that he rather than someone else was chosen is somewhat arbitrary. This perhaps reflects a situation in which it was considered institutionally desirable to fill abbatial positions with "tülkus," thereby following accepted methods of leadership succession in Tibetan Buddhism and taking advantage of the prestige of the title and the office to the greater glory of the monastery. Trungpa Rinpoche expressed the view that, from his own viewpoint, this was a legitimate practice. He also remarked that it is "very good karma" to be selected in this way, for it inevitably accelerated one's own development a great deal.

The second type described by Trungpa Rinpoche is that of the "blessed tülku." Most of the tülkus that we are aware of in the West would be of this category. Rinpoche mentioned that some of the better known incarnation lines, including that of Trungpa Tülkus belong to this type. The "blessed tülkus" should also not be understood as being the literal reincarnation of the previous person. Then what is the relation of the previous person to the reincarnation? The previous person chooses someone who is very close to him or selects some passing bodhisattva who is still on the path. Then the previous person transfers his spiritual energy to this other individual. The energy transmitted is the spiritual force or character of the tülku and his line that the previous master himself had received from his own "predecessor." This new individual, then, is recognized as the reincarnation of the previous person. Trungpa Rinpoche remarks that blessed tülkus are people who are already somewhat advanced on the path and are for that reason chosen by the previous incarnation.

In order for a blessed tülku to be able to fulfill his calling, however, rigorous training and education are necessary.

> Such tulkus have to be raised and educated; they have to go through training and practice. . . . They have the element of realization; they have more potential of realization than just an ordinary person who has no push or encouragement and nothing injected into them. So these people have a great deal of potentiality. But they haven't quite realized it so therefore they have to go through the training and education. . . . They then begin to come up to the level of their previous incarnation because such spiritual energy has been put into them.[11]

Sometimes blessed tülkus have memories of their previous incarnation. In fact, in the next chapter, we shall consider some examples of such memories of Trungpa Rinpoche and Chagdud Tulku. But even such phenomena do not necessitate the existence of one person simply being reborn as another. In the case of a blessed tülku, how could the phenomenon of such memories be explained? Trungpa Rinpoche commented that in his case, as a blessed tülku, he felt that he was not the actual person of the tenth Trungpa. "I'm not him exactly, but I have part of his memory, part of his being, maybe."

A final question is raised concerning the blessed tülku. What happens to the previous incarnation, once he has transmitted his spiritual energy to someone else, so that that person can become the new incarnation? Where does that person go? In order to understand the answer, it is necessary to realize that, although the predecessor has passed his spiritual energy on to the one who will be the new incarnation, his original realization and spiritual energy are still with him. Trungpa Rinpoche: "Once you give energy, you don't give it away; you radiate energy but you have the same amount of energy left, exactly the same volume." Thus it is that the person who has transferred his energy to another returns to this world but in a different guise.

> Those original people also come back to this world, not as the reincarnation of themselves particularly, but anonymously, in-

cognito, so to speak. They come back as farmers or fishermen or businessmen or politicians or whatever. They don't necessarily have to come back into a Buddhist environment . . . because the teachings of enlightenment could be taught at any level. People can be helped at all kinds of levels. . . . There are possibilities of meeting such people who never heard or thought about any form of the teachings of Buddha but who somehow are realized in themselves. And in such cases some memories exist within them; they have some idea of their basic being. But there's no point in advertising that eccentricity, particularly if they're going to communicate with the ordinary world.[12]

Trungpa Rinpoche remarked that the notion of the blessed tülku may be hard for Westerners to comprehend. Why? Because we tend to believe ourselves to be one entity, one existent self, with a relatively fixed identity and solid and definite boundaries. Within this belief system, it is perhaps not possible to conceive that another person could inject a certain spiritual energy into us that would dramatically alter our direction and determine our next birth. When one is not so invested in the idea of a unitary, solid, separate ego, however, more possibilities immediately open up. One can conceive of the "person" as a center of consciousness, a vortex of awareness that is open and permeable to other energies and emotions outside of the perimeter of one's concept of "self."

The third type is what Trungpa Rinpoche calls the "direct tülku." This is a bodhisattva of a high level who takes rebirth over and over to help sentient beings. The direct tülku is understood as the actual, literal reincarnation of a previous realized master. The direct tülkus are the highest category, and in any generation there would be very few of this type. Of them Trungpa Rinpoche says:

There are some extraordinary stories about such people. When they are brought up and they are something like six years old, they're very articulate. They seem to know everything. And their parents begin to feel very inferior to their kids. Their kids seem to function much better in the world than they could.

377

> They haven't been taught reading or writing or maybe they are taught just a hint of it, but they pick it up very fast and they even correct their teachers as they go on. . . . Very little training is needed.[13]

But even in the case of the direct tülku, we should not make the assumption of a single "self" that is reborn over and over. In some cases, a direct tülku might, in his next birth, split into five separate incarnations representing his body, speech, mind, quality, and action. This was, for example, the case with Jamgön Kongtrül the Great, the renowned Ri-me scholar of the nineteenth century. Subsequent to the death of this master, five incarnations were anticipated, and several of these were identified, each becoming the source of a subsequent line of tülkus. In cases such as these, each of the five tülkus is understood to have a "direct" link to the previous incarnation, as reincarnations of his *santana*, or life stream, but in five separate forms. Trungpa Rinpoche remarked that, again, for modern Westerners, such a notion would be difficult to accept owing to our belief in the reality, unity, and solidity of our "self." In fact, Rinpoche said, we are composed of enlightened energies that are held together and maintained in a unitary stream only because of the strength of our belief in an "I." Once this is removed, many more things become possible.

The tradition makes a distinction between the purpose of the educational process as it applies to blessed tülkus and direct tülkus. For the direct tülku, education is viewed as having no basic effect on his understanding or realization. It has for its explicit purpose demonstrating the Buddhist path to his disciples and acquiring the tools he needs to carry on his work of helping others. For the blessed tülku, by contrast, the training and education are essential to his own development. The experience of learning is also said to be different for the two types of tülkus. For direct tülkus, "learning" has mainly the quality of review, as if one were refreshing oneself with something already known. For blessed tülkus, there is rather the experience that something is actually being learned and a journey is being made.

According to Trungpa Rinpoche, blessed tülkus and direct tülkus have quite different relationships to the contexts into which they are born. The blessed tülku is strongly affected by his birth situation and family. If there is heavy neurosis in his environment, he may pick this up; if he fails to receive the right kind of training, he may not develop his higher qualities. Direct tülkus, by contrast, are much more inwardly driven and much less dependent on the particular conditions of their environment. Their sense of realization is natural and spontaneous from their birth onward, and is not diminished or altered by the vagaries and inconsistencies in their environment and training. Trungpa Rinpoche: "This level of Tulku does not have the problems that might come up for ordinary Tulkus, because everything that happens in their lives is a reminder of their enlightened intelligence. Nothing can undermine them because of their enlightenment and unconditioned being, so any relative conditions that might arise are experienced as superfluous. The analogy is that the sun is never influenced by the clouds."[14] In an interview, Trungpa Rinpoche mentioned the case of a tülku of this level who had been denied much of his formal training. This unfortunate circumstance nevertheless seemed to have no diminishing effect on his ability to fully embody the bodhisattva ideals of his lineage.

FROM THEORY TO PRACTICE

When one looks at the actual Tibetan situation, the way in which tülkus appear is not nearly so tidy as this three-leveled schema might suggest. There were hundreds and even perhaps thousands of tülku lines in Tibet, reflecting different regions, schools, lineages, types of training, and specific monastic traditions. There was a considerable variety and diversity of those called tülkus. Still, Tibetans might generally agree on which tülkus are in the highest or "direct" category. But after that, there would inevitably be divergent views on the other two categories. Each lineage has it own revered teachers. Different traditions value different qualities, and what may qualify in one lineage as "high" in another might have lower ranking.

The situation is complicated by the fact that no individual tülku and no line of tülkus has a necessary and static value associated with it. At any given time, within a particular lineage and within the larger world of Tibetan Buddhism, there is a kind of official hierarchy of the different lines of tülkus. But equally important in each generation is not the assigned value but the extent to which a particular tülku lives up to the expectations of his teachers, his disciples, and his devotees, the extent to which he "proves" himself. In other words, the estimation of a tülku and his line will ultimately depend on the qualities of wisdom and compassion that the current incarnation shows, the various powers and abilities he exhibits in his teaching, and his effectiveness in helping his followers.

The stature of a tülku will undergo changes during his life, either ascending if he is a truly remarkable and selfless person, or perhaps declining if he has not been able to fulfill the expectations put upon him. Through this means, the reputation of a line of tülkus and its associated monasteries will usually undergo some shift in each generation. Sometimes, a very modest line will, through the appearance of an extraordinary incarnation, suddenly become endowed with the greatest prestige. In Tibetan Buddhism, then, there is always the "official" status of a line of tülkus or a particular incarnation, but alongside this there is the unofficial, general consensus as to who are in fact the most accomplished masters.

The theory surrounding the tülku phenomenon, then, is not a cut and dried matter, and there is no final and definitive dogma to it. In fact, for thoughtful Tibetans, it could be something of an enigma and an object of serious and ongoing reflection. Indeed, one often has the feeling that the tülku tradition could be as much a mystery to Tibetans—including even tülkus themselves—as to outsiders.

An apt illustration is provided by the Ven. Thrangu Rinpoche, recognized by Rangjung Rikpe Dorje, the sixteenth Karmapa. Thrangu Rinpoche offers a wonderfully candid glimpse of the way in which the uncertainties implicit in the tülku theory might provoke ongoing contemplation in someone considered an exemplar of the tradition. Rinpoche begins by telling us that, from his youth, he did not feel that he was really a tülku in the most literal and authentic sense. This impression led him to think deeply about how someone such as himself might come to be recognized by no less a person than the Karmapa, well known for his remarkable clairvoyance and the accuracy of his recognitions.

Rinpoche remarks on the variety of levels of attainment of the people recognized as tülkus: "Eventually, there were numerous tulkus in Tibet, some of whom had bad behavior, some who were unintelligent, which made some people wonder whether there was anything special about tulkus. [On the other hand,] the tulku may have practiced very diligently and have lead a very pure life, and so be recognized lifetime after lifetime."[15]

Then, recalling Trungpa Rinpoche's description of the blessed tülkus, Thrangu Rinpoche considers the matter of tülkus who, for one reason or another, are not reborn to continue the tülku line but go somewhere else. Rinpoche is particularly interested in how an incarnation may still be "discovered."

> His or her pupils, not knowing this, would go to the Karmapa and ask about the reincarnation, and the Karmapa couldn't say, "He hasn't come back." Instead, the Karmapa would say something like, "Well, maybe this child could be him, and it will be beneficial if you choose him." Believing the child was the tulku, the students would find him, give him training, and his practice would benefit many beings.[16]

Thrangu Rinpoche then tells us of his own experience and the understanding to which it led him:

> I am called Thrangu Tulku. When I first gave this some thought, I was perplexed. I thought, "Well, I know that I'm not Thrangu Tulku, but the Karmapa said that I was! The Karmapa knew [by clairvoyance] my father's name and mother's name, even though I was born far away, and he didn't know my family." I thought about this a lot and felt that it was all very strange. So one day I asked my *khenpo*, "I know I'm not the Thrangu Tulku, but I've been declared to be him. Why?

Perhaps the real one will turn up someday." The khenpo said that there definitely wouldn't be anybody else, but that I knew what my own mind was like, and if I was certain I wasn't a tulku, then I wasn't one!

This left me wondering, "What does all this mean?" until finally I understood. The Karmapa had given me the name of Thrangu Tulku, because it would be very beneficial for me. Otherwise, I would have either become a merchant like my father, or worked in the fields like my mother. Having been recognized as Thrangu Tulku, I became a monk, received teachings from many lamas and had the opportunity to practice the dharma. So he didn't declare me to be the Thrangu Tulku because I was the actual tulku, but in order for me to carry on the work of the Thrangu Tulkus, which is what I am now doing.[17]

Thrangu Rinpoche concludes, "So we should understand that . . . in the tulku tradition of Tibet, there are superior tulkus, inferior tulkus, and finally counterfeit tulkus like myself!" One is free, of course, to make one's own assessment of Thrangu Rinpoche's comments. For me, at any rate, the manifest learning and wisdom, as well as the selflessness and compassion of this very remarkable lama, not to speak of the humility evident in these reflections, speak convincingly of the authenticity and authority of this Thrangu Tülku. And they suggest that the Karmapa's prescience may have emerged as flawless in this case as in others.

The tülku tradition, amid its variety and its ups and downs, is perhaps best understood as an attempt to locate particular children within the culture who either possess or have an unusual potential to develop a certain quality in a high measure. What is this quality? It is the unconditioned energy of intelligence that is not ego-bound, with its insight and compassion, in other words, the inherent wakefulness or buddha-nature within. In its best and most authentic manifestations, the tülku tradition attempts not only to locate such children but to train them to as high a level as possible and put them in a position where this selfless intelligence can be made available to the rest of the culture. The facts that personal and political ambitions sometimes confused or even defeated the process, and that not every tülku was a saint, do nothing to diminish the power of the idea and the remarkable fact that, at least in many cases, the tradition was actually able to succeed in its aims.

CONCLUSION

As mentioned, the tülku phenomenon makes no sense as long as one remains within a theoretical framework that insists on the unity of the person and its substantial and indivisible existence. However, when this belief is called into question, other possibilities can be entertained. Then we can imagine a life, a mode of being, that is infinitely more expansive and responsive to this realm of reality, such as it may be, that we inhabit.

As we have seen, for Tibetan Buddhism the "real person" that we are is found not in the conditioned, "historical" individual with which most of us identify, but rather in the more timeless qualities of enlightenment that reside within. If we continue to be reborn, life after life, apparently as single, ordinary people, it is not because this is the way we really are, but because we have not yet realized our true nature and are bound to such a limited existence by our own ignorance. As we gradually come to realization of our primordial identity, then the limitations under which we currently suffer will begin to fall away. At a certain point, like others who have traveled the path before us, we will arrive at the stage of high level bodhisattvas, able to undertake conscious rebirth to assist others, to separate our energies into several discrete streams, to attain multiple rebirths, and to manifest simultaneously throughout the six realms of samsara in fulfillment of our vow to save all beings. Eventually, as the great master Asanga states in the *Bodhisattva-bhumi*, we will be able to manifest ourselves in dreams and visions, as food to the hungry and water to those who thirst, and as balm to the sick. We will become protection to the oppressed, clouds and rain in time of drought, or earth, water, fire, and wind, and anything that can bring relief to those who suffer.

The nineteenth-century Ri-me scholar Jamgön Kongtrül, speaking of the tülkus or emanations of his friend, the master Jamyang Khyentse Wangpo, summarizes this range of possibilities in an evocative passage:

> Some of these emanations have appeared simultaneously, others have appeared earlier or later during the same lifetime, but most have followed one another after the last. When we examine this list [of Khyentse's past lives], it is difficult to intellectually analyze it; however, it must be said that this is not the case of an ordinary person whose consciousness takes rebirth in a series of lives through the three worlds driven by the force of his or her own acts, i.e., a consciousness that leaves a previous body at death and enters a new womb impelled by the creative energy of previous acts. Instead, this is a case of an individual who rests in spiritually advanced states and, by the strength of his or her aspirations and compassion, surpasses the domain of single or multiple births: the magical play of his or her innate awareness reveals itself in any form whatsoever that can serve others. He or she resembles the sun, which, although one form in the sky, will appear reflected in as many containers of water as can be placed on the ground.[18]

16

Themes of a Tülku's Life

IN SPITE OF THE GREAT DIVERSITY AMONG THE EXEM-
plars of the tülku tradition, Tibetan tülkus share many things in common. Beyond the reservoir of theory summarized in the previous
chapter, there exists a body of practical cultural assumptions of how
tülkus are supposed to appear and what they are supposed to do. They
are expected to be well trained, well mannered, responsive to the laity,
and competent in fulfilling their institutional responsibilities. One looks
for them to be intelligent and compassionate people. Allowing for different emphases in the various lineages, they are also expected to be
paragons of virtue, to excel in scholastic matters, and to have meditational attainment. In general, tülkus are expected to embody the highest
ideals of their particular seat, monastery, and lineage.

There is another area of commonality among those considered tülkus, namely certain typical themes or motifs that mark their lives.
Taken together, these features provide a kind of biographical template
of the spiritually accomplished person that is more or less actualized in
each individual case. Particularly among the more prominent tülkus,
these themes are found in an exemplary way. Although no tülku will
exhibit all of these elements, and those at a more ordinary level may
show few, taken together they define the tülku ideal.*

*It is interesting the extent to which, in their general configuration, these features
recall the major moments in Buddha Shakyamuni's life. The higher the tülku, in
fact, the more likely that his or her life will exhibit a close approximation with the
biography of the Buddha. For example, the texts tells us that the Buddha's birth
was predicted well in advance of its occurrence; in Tibet, prediction of the births

The following account touches briefly on the most important themes of a tülku's life, beginning with prediction and leading up to the attainment of majority and assumption of the full responsibilities of his seat. Left out of the description here is only the death of tülkus, which will be discussed in some detail in chapter 18. The following account includes the traditional lore surrounding tülkus' lives and also descriptions of how the various elements have played out in practice and been experienced by tülkus themselves.

---

of the more prominent tülkus was common. The Buddha's conception and gestation were marked by extraordinary signs, and so are those of the higher tülkus. The Buddha's birth was attended by various wonders, and the same is true of the tülkus. As children, both the Buddha and the tülkus give evidence of remarkable talents and capacities. Both undergo rigorous training. Meditation is an important part of the education of each. And just as the Buddha attained enlightenment beneath the bodhi tree, so Tibetans look to their tülkus to gain and exemplify some measure of genuine realization. Among those tülkus who are most highly realized, one finds various powers and extraordinary abilities, paralleling and even in many respects duplicating those of the Buddha. Finally, the Buddha died in an extraordinary manner, exiting this life in a state of meditation, and so do the high tülkus.

These "themes of a tülku's life," as we may call them, as well as their correspondence with the biography of the Buddha, raise an interesting question. Why do the lives of tülkus tend to appear in this typical way? To what extent are we dealing here with the way that holy people appear within the Tibetan context, spontaneously and without deliberate interpretation? And to what extent do these themes reflect a more self-conscious attempt to bring tülkus' lives into conformity with expectations of what makes an accomplished person?

In fact, these two dimensions cannot be separated. As may become evident from our discussion in the preceding and the present chapter, the themes mentioned above reflect the depths and subtleties of Tibetan experience. This is how traditional Tibetans, without forethought, experience their saints and accomplished masters; and it is how tülkus experience their own lives. Thus it is that when one looks at the lives of tülkus, one finds unanticipated and unsought experiences in the form of dreams, visions, insights, and other extraordinary experiences surrounding the lives of the greatest tülkus.

These typical themes also reflect what people think about tülkus, including both the theorizing of scholars and the more self-conscious attempt to bring events of a tülku's life in line with the traditional expectations. It seems, then, that experience and thought about tülkus have grown up together, each informing and conditioning the other.

PREDICTION, CONCEPTION, GESTATION, AND BIRTH

Among the higher tülkus, the theme of the prediction of a reincarnation is not uncommon. This can occur in any number of ways. For example, a dream or vision may point to a rebirth that is to occur. Matthieu Ricard reports the following event from the life of Dilgo Khyentse Rinpoche:

> Some thirty years ago, while on pilgrimage in Nepal, Khyentse Rinpoche dreamed one night that he was climbing a lofty mountain. At the summit was a small temple. He entered, and inside he saw, seated side by side, his own former teachers—the three main lamas of Shechen Monastery, Shechen Gyaltsap Rinpoche, Shechen Rabjam, and Shechen Kongtrul. Khyentse Rinpoche prostrated himself before them and, singing in sorrowful verse, asked them how they had suffered in the hands of the Chinese (all three of them having perished in Chinese jails in the late fifties and early sixties). With one voice they replied, also in verse, saying, "For us birth and death are like dreams or illusions. The absolute state knows neither increase nor decline." Khyentse Rinpoche expressed his wish to join them soon in the Buddhafields, since he saw little point in remaining in a world where the teachings were vanishing fast and most teachers were but spurious imposters. At this point, Shechen Kongtrul, gazing at Khyentse Rinpoche with a piercing stare, said, "You must toil to benefit beings and perpetuate the teachings until your last breath. We, the three of us, merging into one, will come to you as a single incarnation, a helper to fulfill your aims." Soon afterward, in 1966, Khyentse Rinpoche's eldest daughter, Chime Wangmo, gave birth to a son whom the sixteenth Karmapa recognized as the incarnation of Shechen Rabjam. Shechen Rabjam Rinpoche is not only Khyentse Rinpoche's grandson but also his true spiritual heir. He was brought up by his grand-

father from the age of five and received every teaching Khyen-tse gave over twenty-five years.[1]

Sometimes a lama, before he dies, will provide indications concerning his rebirth that will facilitate recognition. For example, one of the unique features of the line of the Karmapas has been that, before death, the Karmapa would often write a letter predicting the precise details of his next birth, giving time, locale, parents, and so on. This information could then be used to locate the reincarnation once it had occurred.

The theme of prediction of rebirth also occurs in another way. Indian and Tibetan texts contain many predictions concerning the expected rebirth of highly realized people. Sometimes, once a tülku has appeared, and particularly if he has attained an extraordinary stature in his life-time, scholars will look back at their texts for predictions made about him in previous times. When reading the life stories of great tülkus, one will often find a section mentioning predictions of this person's appearance that were made perhaps centuries ago.

As mentioned in chapters 14 and 15, it is held that for realized people death need not lead to a state of unconsciousness. Similarly, awareness may be maintained throughout the process of the intermediate, post-mortem state (bardo), conception, gestation, and birth. Such awareness is commonly attributed to the highest tülkus. In this respect, Kalu Rin-poche remarks, "For the great beings who are tülkus, the process of the conception, gestation, and birth is different from that of ordinary be-ings. According to the realization of the tülku, various possibilities are envisaged."[2] These include:

1. "Awareness of the process occurring in the bardo and during conception, then absence of consciousness during the fetal devel-opment and birth";

2. "Awareness of the process occurring during conception and the fetal development, but not at birth" and

3. "Awareness with no interruption during conception, gestation, and at birth."[3]

Kalu Rinpoche continues:

> In the secret biography of the Third Karmapa, Rangjung Dorje,
> it is stated that, between the death of the Second Karmapa,
> Karmapakshi, and the birth of Rangjung Dorje, no discontinu-
> ity affected the awareness, at the moment of death, in the fol-
> lowing period, during conception, during gestation, and at birth.
> In the thangkas, Rangjung Dorje is represented sitting on a
> lotus to symbolize that he was able to be born free of the veils
> [of ignorance] that normally stain birth."[4]

When a woman becomes pregnant with a tülku, it is sometimes reported that miraculous signs accompany conception. Trungpa Rinpoche
comments of the time when his mother was pregnant with him, "That
year flowers bloomed in the neighborhood although it was still winter,
to the surprise of the inhabitants," an event that signaled the possible
imminent birth of a tülku.[5]

During the pregnancy, it is believed that the mother-to-be can have
direct awareness of the remarkable being in her womb and can feel the
auspiciousness of the birth that is about to occur. The pregnancy is often
unusually peaceful and effortless, and the mother may have extraordinary dreams and visions. It is also said that the fetus of a great tülku
can communicate with the pregnant mother. Kalu Rinpoche: "Although
a fetus cannot articulate sounds, it [happens] that the mother pregnant
with a great tülku [can] hear the latter recite a mantra, ask about her
health, and advise her to avoid situations harmful to her pregnancy."[6]
The period of gestation may also be marked by various signs and unexpected occurrences indicating the extraordinary being soon to be born.

The birth of the tülku is also often heralded by unusual circumstances. Trungpa Rinpoche says, "I was born in the cattle byre; the birth
came easily. On that day a rainbow was seen in the village, a pail supposed to contain water was unaccountably found full of milk, while
several of my mother's relations dreamt that a lama was visiting their
tents."[7]

The present Dalai Lama's birth was similarly surrounded by various signs and portents. In his own words:

> There is a widespread superstition in Tibet that before a high incarnate lama is reborn, the district where he is born will suffer. For four years before I was born, the crops had failed in Taktser either through hail storms when the corn was ripe, or through drought when it was young, and the village people had been saying that an incarnation must be going to be born among them. And my own family especially had fallen on hard times. Several of our horses and cattle, which were among our few valuable possessions, had died, and my father could not discover any reason. And in the few months before I was born, my father himself had been badly ill and unable to get out of bed. Yet on the morning of my birth, he got up feeling perfect well. . . . My mother remembers being annoyed at this and accusing him of having stayed in bed through laziness, but he declared that he was cured.[8]

DISCOVERY, RECOGNITION, AND ENTHRONMENT

When an important teacher dies, his disciples and followers turn their attention to the task of finding his next incarnation. Usually, this actual search will not begin before a minimum of a few years, giving time for the infant to have reached early childhood.

Sometimes, as in the case of the Karmapas mentioned above, the previous master has left a letter or other indication of where his next birth will be. This indication would typically point to the general locale, the neighborhood, the house, and the family of his next birth. Ideally, these directions would be specific enough to enable a search party to locate the new tülku.

If the teacher did not give directions for finding his reincarnation, sometimes a vision with indications would appear to a high lama. Chagdud Tulku reports that his mother became pregnant by his father, Karto Tulku, a Geluk monk with whom she had had a tryst.

> Soon after, a sealed letter arrived for my mother from Dzog-chen Rinpoche, a lama respected throughout Tibet. He wrote, "In your womb there is a great tulku who will be known as Thubtan Geleg Palzang. Take special care, keep very clear and eat only the purest food for the full term of your pregnancy. . . . A second letter arrived from Karto Tulku, which accurately foretold many events in the life of his child in my mother's womb. My mother took these letters to heart and was very careful during her pregnancy.[9]

At other times, the disciples of the deceased teacher would look for assistance to a master known for his abilities to identify tülkus. Chagdud Tulku describes the approach of the great Nyingma Lama Jamyang Khyentse Chökyi Lodrös. He used "an extraordinary process that only very great lamas can accomplish reliably. Through the appearances that arose in his meditation, he was able to see the physical and personality traits of each of the tülkus and give precise details as to how to find them."[10] Among the great lamas, the Karmapas are particularly known for being very gifted in finding new incarnations, especially when the Karmapa is in his youth. In recent times, the sixteenth Karmapa, Rikpe Dorje, performed this function in relation to tülkus not only of the Kagyü but of other lineages as well. An attendant of the sixteenth Karmapa gave a firsthand account of what happened when His Holiness had been asked to help locate a new incarnation: "His Holiness might be eating lunch or talking with someone, and he would suddenly and urgently ask for his secretary. He would then begin dictating very rapidly, as if he were watching some scenario unfold in his mind, reporting images and other indications of the whereabouts of the new tulku." The Karma Kagyü line of the Situ Rinpoches is similarly known for exceptional abilities in discovering new incarnations.

Trungpa Rinpoche's discovery shows how this process could work. When the tenth Trungpa died, his followers sent a message to the Karmapa, asking him if he had any indications on where the reincarnation would be found. "They begged him to let them know at once should he obtain a vision, . . . for the monks of Surmang [the seat of the Trungpa incarnations] were feeling lost without their abbot and were eager that his reincarnation should be found without delay."[11]

A vision had in fact come to Gyalwa Karmapa, who dictated a letter to his private secretary, saying that the reincarnation of the tenth Trungpa Tulku has been born in a village five days' journey northwards from Surmang. Its name sounds like two words Ge and De; there is a family there with two children; the son is the reincarnation. It all sounded rather vague; however, the secretary and the monks of the Dudtsitil Monastery at Surmang were preparing to go in search of the new abbot when a second sealed letter was received at the monastery. Rolpa-dorje, the regent abbot of Dudtsitil, called a meeting, opened the letter and read it to the assembled monks. It said that Gyalwa Karmapa had had a second and much clearer vision: "The door of the family's dwelling faces south; they own a big red dog. The father's name is Yeshe-dargye and the mother's Chung and Tzo; the son who is nearly a year old is Trungpa Tulku."[12]

Once indications were received of the new incarnation's whereabouts, a search party would typically be sent out to locate him. Usually the party would travel incognito and seek to interview the family and suspected tülku without being recognized. Again, Trungpa Rinpoche's autobiography illustrates this process. A party of monks from Surmang located the nomad settlement specified in the Karmapa's vision. "In one tent they found a baby boy who had a sister and, as had been written in Gyalwa Karmapa's letter, the entrance faced south and there was a red dog." The mother's name corresponded to the Karmapa's vision, although strangely the father's did not.

Yet they looked closely at the baby, for as soon as he had seen them in the distance he waved his little hand and broke into smiles as they came in. So the monks felt that this must be the child and gave him the gifts which Gyalwa Karmapa had sent, the sacred protective cord and the traditional scarf; this latter the baby took and hung around the monk's neck in the pre-scribed way, as if he had already been taught what was the right thing to do: delighted, the monks picked me up, for that baby was myself, and I tried to talk. The following day the monks made a further search in another part of the village and then returned to say goodbye. As they made prostration before me, I placed my hand on their heads as if I knew that I should give them my blessing, then the monks were certain that I was the incarnation of the tenth Trungpa.[13]

Subsequent discussion turned up the fact that Trungpa Rinpoche's actual father was a man with the name given in the Karmapa's vision and that his mother was now married to another man. The news was taken to the Gyalwa Karmapa, who was certain that the eleventh Trungpa Tülku had been found.

When we read traditional accounts of the recognition of tülkus, it sometimes appears that this is a strictly "top down" process, that a great lama has a vision or other indications and, based on those, the new incarnation is found. The recent discovery of the reincarnation of Kalu Rinpoche is interesting because it shows how the recognition of a rein-carnation could entail a broader, more inclusive, and more organic proc-ess, involving the disciples and friends of the previous master, other lamas, and only finally coming to the attention of those high lamas charged with making recognitions official. In this instance, it was the actual disciples of Kalu Rinpoche who played the critical role, making the discovery and becoming convinced that a particular child was the new incarnation. Later, the official recognition followed, but more as a confirmation of what had occurred on a much more informal and con-sensual level.

The child in question was born to Drolkar and her husband, Lama Gyaltsen, the personal secretary of the late Kalu Rinpoche for some forty years. This baby, so it is reported, was remarkably happy, virtually never crying, but smiling and laughing continuously. In time, a close Western disciple, an international corporate lawyer with his own family,

FIGURE 16.1 *Ven. Chögyam Trungpa Rinpoche.*

became convinced that the young baby was the rebirth of Kalu Rinpoche and, just on his own, treated him as such. Soon Chadral Rinpoche, the previous Kalu Rinpoche's close friend, expressed the opinion publicly that this was, in fact, the new Kalu Rinpoche. Later, Situ Rinpoche, part of whose responsibilities include recognizing new incarnations, visited the child and expressed privately that he felt this was Kalu Rinpoche's rebirth and wished to ask the Dalai Lama for confirmation.

The Dalai Lama responded promptly with a firm affirmation that, yes, this was indeed Kalu Rinpoche's tülku.[14]

When it was believed that the new incarnation had been located, he would then be put through a series of tests to further authenticate and prove his legitimacy. In Trungpa Rinpoche's case, at eighteen months, he along with his mother and stepfather were invited to Surmang monastery, the seat of the Trungpa Tülkus.

> A few days later I was put through a test; pairs of several objects were put before me, and in each case I picked out the one that had belonged to the tenth Trungpa Tulku; among them were two walking sticks and two rosaries; also, names were written on small pieces of paper and when I was asked which piece had his name on it, I chose the right one. Now the monks were certain that I was the incarnation, so a letter was sent to Gyalwa Karmapa telling him the results of the examination and inviting him to officiate at my enthronement ceremony.[15]

The discovery of the reincarnation of the Dalai Lamas was somewhat more complex and formalized, reflecting their unique importance in Tibet. After the death of the thirteenth Dalai Lama, for example, a regent was appointed in Lhasa. Then the state oracles and learned lamas were consulted as the first step in the process of finding the new incarnation. Any unusual signs were duly noted, and it was observed that a number of strange events and omens pointed to the northeast. In 1935, in accordance with custom, the regent went to the sacred lake of Lhamoi Latso, about ninety miles southeast of Lhasa. It is believed that visions of the future can be seen when one meditates upon the waters of this lake, and indications of a new Dalai Lama are traditionally sought there. Meditating in that place, the regent did have visions, including the appearance of a monastery with roofs of jade green and gold and a house with turquoise tiles. The next year, delegations of high lamas and dignitaries were sent out all over Tibet to search for the place revealed in the regent's vision. When a delegation from Sera monastery in Lhasa came to the present Dalai Lama's region, they noted the green and golden roofs of Kumbum monastery and, upon entering his village of Taktser, noticed a house with turquoise tiles. In the Dalai Lama's words, "their leader asked if the family living in the house had any children and was told that they had a boy who was nearly two years old."[16]

When the young boy met the lama who was leader of the delegation, although the entire party was disguised and the leader was dressed as the party's servant, the boy asked to sit in the lama's lap. "The lama was disguised in a cloak which was lined with lambskin, but round his neck he was wearing a rosary which had belonged to the thirteenth Dalai Lama. The little boy seemed to recognize the rosary, and he asked to be given it. The lama promised to give it to him if he could guess who he was, and the boy replied that he was Sera-aga, which meant, in the local dialect, 'a lama of Sera.'" The young boy was also able to identify by name members of the search party. When it came time for the delegation to leave early next morning—and they had still not revealed their identity—in the Dalai Lama's words, "The boy got out of his bed and insisted that he wanted to go with them. I was that boy."[17] The boy was later put through the same kind of tests mentioned above. Being presented with a series of pairs of objects, only one of which belonged to the previous Dalai Lama, in each case he selected the right one. Although through these and other indications, the delegation and leaders in Lhasa were convinced they had found the authentic reincarnation, it took two additional years of difficult negotiations with local Chinese officials—for the Dalai Lama's village was located in a part of Tibet under Chinese control—before the new incarnation could be brought to Lhasa to be enthroned and established in his former seat.

The recognition of a new tülku did not only depend upon such formal and elaborate procedures as just described. In addition, there was often an important intuitive element, and this could take precedence over the more traditional, technical apparatus of signs, divinations, and tests. Tulku Urgyen Rinpoche told me that often a realized master who had known a certain person in his previous birth could identify the reincarnation simply by looking at him—he would see the very same qualities and aspects in the baby as had marked the personality of the previous incarnation. Nor was it only the older member of a previous

FIGURE 16.2 *H. H. Tenzing Gyatso, fourteenth Dalai Lama.*
(Photograph by Clive Arrowsmith.)

friendship who would have the experience of recognition. Dilgo Khyentse Rinpoche provides this account of a meeting, entailing mutual recognition, that occurred when he was still a small child:

> I was taken to see Kunsang Dechen Dorje, a highly accomplished master. He said, "This child and I have known each other before," and asked me, "Do you know me?"
> "Do you know him?" repeated my father.
> "Yes, I know him," I said, a bit scared.
> Kunzang Dechen Dorje said, "For many previous lives we have had a connection. I am going to give him a fine present." He had a rare and cherished collection of cups. Gold, silver, and other possessions were of no interest to him, but he treasured his cups. He said to his wife, "Bring my box of cups," and presented me with an exquisite cup, which he filled with raisins.[18]

Khyentse Rinpoche also met other highly attained lamas who similarly could see the qualities of his predecessor in him. He reports, for example, "When Dzongsar Khyentse Chökyi Lodrö had first spoken to Gyaltsap Rinpoche about me, he had said, 'I have met this child before and I feel strongly that he is an incarnation of Jamyang Khyentse Wangpo. Please take care of him, and I will do whatever I can to serve him.'"[19]

The feeling of familiarity that sometimes arose when meeting the incarnation of a well-known and loved teacher could be extraordinarily intense. Matthieu Ricard provides the following account of Dilgo Khyentse Rinpoche's first meeting of Dzongsar Khyentse Rinpoche, born in 1961, the reincarnation of Khyentse Chökyi Lodrö, one of Dilgo Khyentse's primary gurus:

> When the young incarnation was recognized and invited to Sikkim to be enthroned, Khyentse Rinpoche went down to the Sikkim-India border to welcome him. During the few hours' drive back up to Gangtok, Sikkim's capital, Khyentse Rinpoche held the boy on his lap and shed tears all the way. Some other people on the journey later asked him if this apparent sadness was not

due to forebodings about the young incarnation's future. But he explained that his tears had been tears of joy and devotion, for during those few hours he had been seeing not the young boy but the former Khyentse Chökyi Lodrö as if in reality.[20]

The selection of the authentic rebirth and this person's proper training were obviously a matter of great importance to the disciples and devotees of the previous incarnation. Trungpa Rinpoche says that recognition and training were also a matter of great importance to the tülku himself, for the high tülkus' very well-being could depend upon them.

While Dilgo Khyentse Rinpoche was still very young, a number of important lamas informed his father that his son was a reincarnation. This news did not please his father, who had already had another son similarly recognized over his objections. On one occasion his father was advised, "You should look after this child very carefully because he must be an incarnate lama." Khyentse Rinpoche recalls: "My father said nothing. But when we came back to our lodgings, he declared, 'The lamas won't let me keep this son, but I'm not going to let him become a lama. We have a large family, an estate, and much land to look after. I want him to stay a layman so that he can take care of it all.' "[21]

His father was subsequently informed by two different masters that serious obstacles would arise for the young boy if he were not made a monk and allowed to fulfill his destiny. Rinpoche remembers:

> That same year I was burnt by the soup. Summer on our estate was the busiest time of the agricultural year, during which we employed many workers. To feed them all, huge quantities of soup were cooked in an enormous cauldron. One day, playing with my brother, I fell into the cauldron of boiling soup. The lower half of my body was so badly scalded that I was bedridden for many months, seriously ill despite the many long-life prayers that my family recited for me.
>
> My father asked me in desperation, "What ceremonies do you think will help you get better? If there's anything that can save your life, we must do it!"
>
> What I wanted most was to become a monk, so I replied, "It

FIGURE 16.3 *H. H. Dilgo Khyentse Rinpoche. (Photograph by Matthieu Ricard.)*

would help if I could wear monk's robes." My father gave his word, and quickly got some robes made. When I had them laid over me in bed, I felt overjoyed. I also had placed on my pillow a bell and ritual hand drum.

The very next day I asked Lama Ösel to come and shave my head. I was told that a few of our old retainers wept that day, lamenting, "Now the last Dilgo son has taken vows, that's the end of the family line." But I was so happy that soon my health improved, and the risk of untimely death receded. I was then ten years old.[22]

If parents or relatives remained unwilling to yield to the destiny of the new tülku, more serious consequences could result. Trungpa Rinpoche remarks:

> I met a local king in the neighborhood next to mine. He had five sons, one of whom was an incarnate lama. The father did not want to let him go because he didn't want him to face the hardships [of a tülku's life], such as harsh treatment by the tutors and so on. He held him back and kept him at home and eventually he married. And he went completely insane. People had to restrain him to keep him from jumping out of windows. Somehow something begins to fuse when you don't meet that particular kind of karmic demand from higher authorities, so to speak, and you just turn back into a vegetable.[23]

Elsewhere, in relation to this same situation, he remarks, "This is an example of what often occurs in Tibet among incarnate lamas who have for any reason abandoned their vocation: some have died suddenly, while others seem to lose their purpose in life and become mentally deranged, or else their whole personality changes."[24]

Once the young tülku is located and his identity is confirmed, he is then typically brought to the monastery of his predecessor and enthroned as the new incarnation. The enthronement is a formal and often highly charged ritual. Dilgo Khyentse Rinpoche describes his own enthronement as one of the five incarnations of the nineteenth-century master Jamyang Khyentse Wangpo, which occurred in the hermitage of Gyaltsap Rinpoche, his root guru, high on the mountain above Shechen monastery. Gyaltsap Rinpoche presided over the ceremony.

> On the morning of the enthronement I climbed up the path to the hermitage. Inside, a large throne had been set up. Shechen

Kongtrul, who was still very young then, was holding incense, and Shechen Gyaltsap was dressed in his finest clothes. They told me to sit on the throne. Only a few people were present in the room. They chanted verses describing the sacred qualities of the time and place of a teaching, of the teacher, of what he teaches, and of those who receive his teaching.[25]

The heart of the enthronement liturgy involves presenting the young tülku with gifts of sacred objects belonging to his immediate predecessor and other great lamas. Khyentse Rinpoche was given artifacts once belonging to his predecessor Jamyang Khyentse Wangpo and also to Mipham Rinpoche, the great Nyingma Ri-me master, who had taken a great interest in Khyentse Rinpoche when he was a baby, made predictions about him, and given him important blessings.

Gyaltsap Rinpoche . . . made me precious gifts symbolic of the body, speech, mind, qualities, and activity of the Buddhas. As symbol of body, he gave me images of Buddha Shakyamuni that had belonged to Mipham Rinpoche and Jamyang Khyentse Wangpo. As symbol of speech, he gave me many volumes of their writings. As symbol of mind, he gave me the vajra and the bell that Mipham Rinpoche had used throughout his life. As symbol of qualities, he gave me all the articles necessary for giving empowerments. Finally, as symbol of activity, he gave me Mipham Rinpoche's seal.[26]

Finally, the ceremony concludes with a declaration of the new, official identity of the young child:

Then [Gyaltsap Rinpoche] presented me with a written document, which said: "Today I take the son of the Dilgo family and recognize him as the re-embodiment of Jamyang Khyentse Wangpo. I name him Gyurme Thekchog Tenpai Gyaltsen, Immutable Victory Banner of the Supreme Vehicle. I entrust him with the teachings of the great masters of the past. Now, if I die I have no regret."[27]

MEMORIES OF THE PREVIOUS INCARNATION

Although most Tibetans accepted the legitimacy of the tülku principle, in each individual case there were bound to be doubts and questions, and, given how human affairs operate, these would certainly not be put entirely to rest by official recognition. "Has the reincarnation been found correctly? Is this really the right person?"

Such questions might be resolved by the tülku's own demonstrations of connections with his previous incarnation, which might occur later and independently of the tests and rituals surrounding "recognition." Chagdud Tulku reports an incident from his own life when he was in his midteens, after he had finished his first three-year retreat. At this time, he had come to Chagdud Gompa, the seat of his previous incarnation, and was receiving visitors. All at once, a man whom Chagdud Tulku had never met strode into his room unannounced.

> As soon as I saw him, I said fiercely, "Dzug Tsering, why have you come here? You had no faith in me in my last life and you have no faith in me now. And since I have no need to pass some test of yours, you can leave." Suddenly I seized a charcoal brazier and for a moment it seemed as if I would fling it at him. Instead, with a jerk of the brazier, I spilled out the burning coals over my own head. As the coals tumbled down my robes, everyone leapt up to gather them and were amazed that there were no burns or scorch marks.[28]

It turned out that Dzug Tsering had been the brother-in-law of the previous Chagdud Tulku, Chagdud Tanpai Gyaltsan, and had harbored animosity against him. As Tsering had approached the room of the new incarnation, he had boasted, "If this is really the tulku of Tanpai Gyaltsan, he will know me. If he doesn't know, he is only a fraud." Chagdud Tulku comments, "After our encounter everyone agreed that all auspicious signs were present and there was no doubt of my being the incarnation of Chagdud Tanpai Gyaltsan."[29]

Young tülkus, particularly before they reach adolescence, may also have memories of their previous life. Trungpa Rinpoche comments that

FIGURE 16.4 *Ven. Chagdud Tulku Rinpoche.*

such memories are generally told to one's teacher but not made public. In his case, he was forbidden to tell anyone besides his tutor about them. Rinpoche tells of two incidents that were more public:

> There was a place where the tenth Trungpa died, some local lord's house. He died in the house and there was a particular place where his bedroom and the shrine were. . . . I visited there.

404

People were busy organizing my welcome party outside and I was helped off my horse and walked in. Nobody was leading me. Traditionally there's somebody to lead you, with incense, but somehow this wasn't organized. I had to walk over because there were a lot of people waiting and it was getting rather late. As soon as I walked through the door I knew exactly where to go and I knew where the room was. My attendant, who had never been to the house before, followed me. All the doors were closed and he said, "Well, maybe we should get somebody." I said, "Let's find out first," and "How about here?" And we went on that way and found the room. It was exactly the same place as when the tenth Trungpa arrived; it was arranged exactly the same way.[30]

On another occasion, Trungpa Rinpoche was on his way to visit a particular nomad camp for the first time.

We were lost in the rain and mist. . . . There's a certain fork of the road you are supposed to take. Everybody was completely bewildered and cold and [on edge], and everybody was hungry. The monk in charge of discipline with his loud voice was really getting hungry and whenever he got hungry he got mad. Everybody was completely down. And they began to curse the people who had invited us to this strange place.

I wasn't quite sure but I thought I knew the whole way. I thought everybody knew it, you know. Then suddenly I clicked that nobody knew about this, but somehow I had some memory about having been here. . . . As far as I could remember I had never been there in this body, so to speak. There was usually a [person] who rode on a white horse who was supposed to lead the procession or journey. And then there was [someone] with flags, and then a guy who carried the umbrella behind me. And then the rest of the people were supposed to follow after me; everything was set as to who comes next. And although the whole thing was very miserable, the ceremony still continued.

I said I would like to break the rule and maybe I should go

with the guy with the white horse. My attendant didn't know what to do, "maybe we shouldn't tell anybody. Okay. Well, we should do it." And I said, "Don't tell anybody," and we broke the rule. I rode with the guy with the white horse at the head of our procession. And I said, "Well, let's go this way. Go this way and then there's going to be a pass. Then we are going to pass another village, which is not the place we are looking for. We are going to pass the next one, which is not our village either. There's a bridge on the other side. And beyond that, seemingly hidden in a sort of dimple in the meadow (you can't see it until you get to it), you can see their village setup, the smoke going up and everything." We arrived there. And actually I expected that somebody would be surprised about that. But nobody said anything at all.[31]

TRAINING

The training of young tülkus becomes a focus of energy and attention on the part of everyone involved, including lineage leaders, monastic officials, other monks of the monastery, family, and other members of the lay community. In order for the young tülku to step into the shoes of his predecessor and fulfill the heavy duties and responsibilities of his position, a most demanding training is required. The education the tülku will receive is generally strenuous, lengthy, and many-faceted. It is typically composed of several main areas: decorum, reading and penmanship, memorization and study of sacred texts, scholastic debate, teaching, painting and the composition of poetry, meditation, ritual, and administration. Although these are the main areas of training for most tülkus, as mentioned, in the different traditions, subtraditions, lineages, and individual monasteries the educational process varies both in the emphasis that is placed on each area and in the contents of each.

After their recognition, most tülkus will live as monks in the monastic seat of their predecessor. This is particularly true of the New Translation schools, with their strong monastic and celibate emphasis.

However, this is not invariably the case. While monastic institutions have played an important role in the Nyingma tradition during the past few centuries, many accomplished Nyingmapas, both men and women—in the original Nyingma style—will marry not just as a matter of social convenience but as a spiritual practice. It is not uncommon for a yogin to be advised by his guru, "Now it is time for you to bring your practice into the world by marrying and having a family." When a lama does marry, his family becomes a container and seat for his teachings, and children recognized as tülkus may be brought up and trained in the family. Chagdud Tulku's mother and stepfather were both accomplished practitioners. After his recognition, Chagdud Tulku, though obviously expected to fulfill his connections to Chagdud monastery, continued to live with his parents and to study and practice under their direction. His mother, in particular, who was a respected spiritual adept, took a strong hand in seeing to the quality of her tülku son's education.

From the very beginning of the training of a tülku, which may be while he is still a small child, there is a strong emphasis on discipline. He is taught how to sit, eat, handle himself in ritual, receive and bless visitors, and so on. This typically means having to forgo the normal spontaneous enjoyments of being a child and being required to sit for long periods of time, on one's throne, behaving in a strictly prescribed manner. Something of the kind of demands this placed on the small child is gleaned from A. Waddell's account of a nineteenth-century visitor to Tibet, the British envoy, Captain Turner. This gentleman had the opportunity to meet the newly recognized Panchen Lama, then eighteen months old, at the monastery of Terpaling. Turner, representing the British government, was brought before the child, who was sitting on a throne, with his mother and father to one side. Having been informed that although the child was unable to speak, he could understand, Turner made a speech, conveying his government's sorrow at the passing of the previous Panchen Lama, its joy at the finding of the new incarnation, its hope for good future relations, and so on.

> The infant looked steadfastly at the British envoy, with the appearance of much attention, and nodded with repeated but slow

motions of the head, as though he understood every word. He was silent and sedate, his whole attention was directed to the envoy, and he conducted himself with astonishing dignity and decorum. He was one of the handsomest children Captain Turner had ever seen, and he grew up to be an able and devout ruler, delighting the Tibetans with his presence for many years, and dying at a good old age.[32]

At the same time, it is clear that the rigorous requirements placed upon one so small could be experienced as difficult and painful. The continual demand to conform to rather stringent conventions of behavior, the hours of memorization and study, and the loneliness of a small boy not permitted to play with other children are all themes often mentioned by tülkus who have written about their lives. The separation from their mothers was, in particular, a most painful experience. During the time when the child was very young, his mother would typically reside outside the monastery and make daily visits. However, a day would come when the child was still quite small that his mother would no longer be part of his ongoing monastic life.

Trungpa Rinpoche, recognized and brought to the monastery at the age of eighteen months, began his studies in earnest at the age of five. He tells us:

> At this time, my mother's visits became less frequent; to begin with she only came to see me every other day, then every third, after which her visits became more and more spaced out, until after a fortnight without seeing her, she came to tell me that she was going back to Dekyil; I missed her as only a small boy can.[33]

The Dalai Lama makes the interesting comment that "most of my boyhood was spent in the company of grown-up men, and there must inevitably be something lacking in a childhood without the constant company of one's mother and other children."[34]

Once in the monastic environment, the young tülku begins his training in scholarship, meditation, ritual, and the other topics that he must master in order to fulfill his role. In this environment, the tülku's primary companions are elder monks who are responsible for his training, and in this the Dalai Lama's experience is typical. The fact that the young tülku is separated from the usual pleasures and pursuits of childhood leaves him with little choice but to focus his attention upon his studies. Initially, his tutors may be gentle and kind, bringing him through his first years in the monastery with patience and tolerance. As he approaches puberty, however, and his training must begin in earnest, the discipline and demand of his teachers gradually increase. Both the Dalai Lama and Trungpa Rinpoche report that the relaxed and spacious attitude of their initial mentors was soon replaced by teachers who were stern, tough, and demanding.

Chagdud Tulku, who as a Nyingma tülku was trained in the home of his family, gives us a glimpse of what it was like for a small boy to undergo education in that environment.

> [From the age of four], for the next seven years, until I went into three-year retreat at the age of eleven, my life would alternate between periods of strict discipline in which my every move would be under the surveillance of my tutors and interludes in which my suppressed energy would explode. Throughout, I had many visions, many clairvoyant experiences, many extraordinary dreams, and within these, I sometimes had glimpses of absolute open awareness. My mother and my teachers took note of these as indications of special abilities I had developed in previous lifetimes, but they never wavered from their intention that I should go through the rigors of Buddhist training in this lifetime [for] only through effort would I reestablish the effortless realization I had attained previously.[35]

Study of the sacred texts and their various philosophical viewpoints forms an important ingredient in a young tülku's training. In Tibet, some real mastery of the texts is considered critical to a tülku's ability to understand the teaching, succeed in his meditation practice, and be able to lead and teach others. Consequently, considerable time and energy is typically put into this dimension of the tülku's training, although the style and emphasis vary from school to school. In the traditions that put more focus on scholarly understanding the emphasis will be greater, while for those stressing meditational development it will be correspondingly less. The young tülku begins his textual and philosophical study with lessons in reading and writing.

The Dalai Lama, for example, began his studies at the age of six, by learning the letters of the Tibetan alphabet and beginning to read simple texts. Each day, he would also memorize a verse from the scriptures and read from them for another hour. By the time he was eight, he was studying grammar and spelling, and reading his books morning and evening, memorizing larger and larger sections. When he reached the age of twelve, he began his training in dialectical discussion or debate, the method through which mastery of the inner reasoning of the sacred texts is attained in the Geluk school. In the following years, the Dalai Lama progressed through a curriculum, the topics of which were fairly standard in the training of tülkus: the Prajnaparamita, Vinaya, Logic, Abhidharma, Chittamatra (Yogachara), and the various schools of the Madhyamaka, culminating in the Prasangika. Within these general topics, he studied particularly those works of specific importance to his Geluk training, while tülkus being schooled in other lineages would read the writings considered definitive in their own schools.

In the Geluk tradition, study of the sacred texts aimed toward passing a series of examinations leading to the advanced degree of Geshe in one of its grades. The comprehensive path to this supreme goal was considered to include five elements. First, children would learn reading and penmanship by imitating their teacher. Second, they would gradually embark on the memorization of the scriptures. This process only trained their memory but over time provided them with an extensive knowledge of the major topics and viewpoints contained in the sacred texts. This proved invaluable as they continued their studies, engaged in debate, and began teaching. The third area of education was known as "teaching from experience." This would involve using analogies, imagery, and stories drawn from ordinary life situations to illustrate and give life to the Buddhist teachings. This approach made doctrinal points in a way that would never be forgotten and would provide a body of oral teachings that the young tülku could then pass on to his own students when he reached his majority. The fourth area involved contemplation, in the evening reflecting upon what one had learned in the course of the day. Finally, the fifth area was formal debate. In relation to the Dalai Lama's education, Goodman remarks that this involved

> highly stylized dialectical debating between students or between students and teachers. Since he had no companions, Kundun [the Dalai Lama] was provided with seven tutorial assistants, scholars known as *tsenchaps*—one from each of the monastic colleges within Drepung, Sera, and Ganden—who would help him prepare for examinations in Buddhist logic, metaphysics, and dialectics through a demanding series of debating sessions that dealt in ever-finer philosophical questions as he progressed in his studies.[36]

An essential area of training for young tülkus, particularly those of the Nyingma and Kagyü lineages, was meditation. Chagdud Rinpoche's training began at the age of four. One day, at his mother's invitation, a nun arrived to teach him how to meditate.

> She gave me no instructions regarding what to contemplate or how to hold my mind, but she was an expert in enforcing proper meditation posture. She made me sit with my back absolutely straight and rigid, my legs crossed and my feet resting soles-up on my thighs, my hands on my knees, my chin tucked in and my tongue curled back to the roof of my mouth. Some days she made me close my eyes, and if I opened them, she thumped me on the forehead and said, "Meditate." Some days my eyes had to be open in an immovable gaze. If I dozed, she thumped me, "Meditate." This went on from the moment I awoke until bedtime, for weeks or perhaps months. In the excruciating pain and boredom, I lost track of time.[37]

Chagdud Tulku's story shows the way in which, among the Nyingmapas, study and meditation are interwoven. After some period of time, the nun departed and another tutor took over, Lama Tse Gon, the family treasurer who was a kindly and well-loved teacher. Under his tutelage, Chagdud Tulku studied scriptures and meditated for a portion of each day. Various empowerments and training in ritual were also included in the curriculum. When Lama Tse Gon left for an extended absence, Rinpoche's mother saw to it that he was replaced by another tutor, Lama Wanga, "one of the most formidable lamas in the Tenp'hel Gonpa region."[38] Under Lama Wanga, Chagdud Tulku would arise in the morning, practice meditation, study texts, and memorize passages. When mistakes were made, the young tülku was pinched sharply on his thigh.

> Every afternoon, Lama Wanga rolled up his little carpet, tucked it under his arm and walked with me to a high meadow. When we reached our spot, he unrolled the carpet for me to sit on while he sat on the ground. The view overlooked the monastery, and it seemed we could gaze out across the whole world. We never chatted, but instead sustained an unbroken chain of mantra recitation, accompanied by the monotonous click-click of his prayer wheel revolving. In the evening we would be served more tsampa and tea, and then we would continue to sit and practice until bedtime.[39]

Eventually, after three months, the beloved Lama Tse Gon returned, but Chagdud Tulku comments that in the period with Lama Wanga he had learned more than in the previous several years. During this period and afterward, alongside his studies and meditation, Chagdud Tulku met and received empowerments and instructions from the seniormost lamas in his region, thus immeasurably enriching his training.

At the age of eleven, Chagdud Tulku entered his first three-year retreat. He was rather young to be attempting such an undertaking, but as such retreats were offered in that place only every three years, his mother did not want him to have to wait until the next cycle. The schedule was demanding: rising at three or four in the morning, breakfast, ritual and meditation, lunch, ritual and meditation, dinner, ritual and meditation, bed. As Rinpoche tells it, during this time he did not fully understand why he was practicing and generally had a hard time of it. Sometimes he felt inspired and connected, at other times it seemed boring and he went through it by rote. Early on in the retreat, news came that his mother had died. This had a profound effect on the young boy and deepened his practice experience. During this retreat, Chagdud Tulku had the opportunity to study with some outstanding masters. He mentions particularly one practitioner named Lama Atse, who "brought extraordinary qualities to my retreat. He was a siddha, meaning that he had a direct realization of absolute truth. Almost daily, Lama Atse stopped somewhere in the *puja* to explain its inner meaning to me, and a vast understanding began to unfold."[40] By the end of this first three-year retreat, Chagdud Rinpoche had attained a profoundly deepened connection with his practice, and many experiences and visions unfolded. He was fourteen years old.

Chagdud Rinpoche's training continued after his three-year retreat. He went on with his studies and received teaching from a number of great masters, including Dilgo Khyentse Rinpoche and Jamgön Kongtrül of Sechen, both accomplished yogins and renowned teachers. Nevertheless, his path was not smooth, and a series of regional and inter-family disputes led Chagdud Tulku to abandon his monastic training for several years in favor of a career in Tibetan medicine. This too was a critical learning experience and led him back once again to the heart of his Buddhist education. In his mid-twenties, he undertook a second three-year retreat, realizing that the dilemmas of life can be answered only by the dharma of full realization. This time he practiced the dzokchen path in order to purify his mind and make himself worthy of the highest teachings. From this point forward in his life, until forced to leave Tibet in the late 1950s, Chagdud Tulku spent much of his time meditating and carrying out retreats of various lengths, exploring the rich heritage of practices of his lineage and the larger Buddhist world of Tibet.

THE PROCESS OF MATURATION

There is an important maturation process that occurs within the tülku's training. At first, he is completely at the mercy of his tutors, going through the difficult course of training. As he grows up, he gradually incorporates and integrates the various facets of his education. Finally, what he has been taught becomes his own, he is no longer reliant on his tutors and is able to act with responsibility and independence.

Trungpa Rinpoche reflects on these themes in his own upbringing and in so doing provides a glimpse into a tülku's own experience of growing up. His education began when he was brought to the Surmang monasteries at the age of eighteen months. At that time, he began to be trained in the matter of proper decorum—how to sit, hold his hands, receive visitors and bless them, eat his meals, and so on. This training, he commented, made the point from the earliest of ages that his life was not his private concern and that a great deal was expected of him.

As he grew older, the demands increased. To discipline in behavior and decorum were gradually added schooling in reading, writing, memorizing, chanting, performance of ceremonies and rituals, and other skills. Virtually his entire life was given over to this strict and rather uncompromising training. He comments that virtually the only time he was allowed to be alone and not watched over was when he went to the privy. He was never allowed to play as a child. "It was highly discouraged. You could only do that if you could steal time, without them seeing it. My second tutor was a strict one. When his nephew died, he had to attend to that situation. It meant that he had to be away for ten days and I had a great time."[41]

Trungpa Rinpoche sometimes mentioned the harshness of his tutors. When asked if he felt this was essential to tülkus' training, he replied: "Not the harshness. In the early days, my journey was still uphill. I think that was because my tutor was very critical and would get very frustrated and demanding. I don't think that helped particularly. The strictness is perhaps necessary, but not the neurosis that went along with it. You could be strict without that."[42]

Meeting and studying with realized teachers can make a great impact on the young tülku. As Trungpa Rinpoche grew older, his understanding of the Buddhist teachings and practices matured. As this occurred, he noticed that there seemed to be some discrepancies between what his tutors were teaching him and what they themselves seemed to have realized and incorporated into their own persons. Thus it came as a great relief when he met masters who seemed to fully embody the teachings.

> At the age of nine, I met Jamgon Kongtrul [of Sechen] and [Dilgo] Khyentse Rinpoche. Up to then my tutors told me to sit up and behave like a good tulku and I actually felt somewhat silly. I felt that in a certain way I had been trained in how to be a charlatan. They couldn't actually do what they were asking me to do, and they said do a better version of this. My tutor was always like that. When my handwriting went beyond his instruction, he would bring all kinds of samples of good handwriting and I would have to copy that. And if I couldn't do it, he would punish me. And so sitting up properly felt as if one were fooling oneself. I felt funny and almost guilty.
>
> That changed when I met Khyentse Rinpoche and Jamgon Kongtrul and saw how they behaved. I saw that they embodied the forms of the tradition and did so with tremendous genuineness. I saw that I could emulate that. And then actually without my tutors telling me very much, I just simply did it. Realizing other, real people were doing it fully was tremendously encouraging to me, and that encouragement has continued since then.[43]

Through Khyentse Rinpoche and Jamgön Kongtrül, Trungpa Rinpoche came to feel a more and more complete identity with his lineage.

> Their example was very important. When you have someone to emulate, it makes a tremendous difference. You begin to feel that you can legitimately join in with the rest of the lineage. And then you can imagine further what the previous lineage figures would be like. And at that point you feel that you are entering into a world and there is no sense of aloneness at all.

As Rinpoche grew still older, the moment came when he began to be a teacher in his own right.

> When this happened, it was quite a shock for me. On one particular occasion, I was asked to give just a small teaching on the

four reminders. It was at a very early stage, and it was the first lecture that I gave. Our staff people and monks were there, and also some others. As I gave the lecture, I came out with all these things. After the lecture, the others left and just our monks were there. And there was a very heavy silence in the room. I wondered if I had done something wrong. They were so awestruck. And actually that was a turning point. After that my tutor became very respectful of me and even somewhat fearful.[44]

At a certain point in the tülku's training, the heavy-handed monitoring of the tutor ceases, and the tülku realizes that he is now his own master. Trungpa Rinpoche comments on this moment in his own life:

On the day [my tutor] left, I realized that I could do anything I liked. But I couldn't find anything to do. In fact, I became more strict with myself. Everyone had expected that with his departure, I would run around and misbehave and they were actually quite afraid of that. They were completely surprised at what happened. It's like training in riding. At a certain point you move from the lunge line to free riding and you just carry on as before.[45]

As he approaches maturity, there is also a definite sense of loneliness that the tülku feels, separated from others as he is by his identity and his training. Trungpa Rinpoche:

The loneliness part of it, of being left by yourself, comes much later when you have actually achieved emulating your teachers fully and then they are somewhere else and you can't ask them a question. You have to figure it out by yourself.[46]

Trungpa Rinpoche said that beyond the specific forms and procedures of his education, two additional factors helped him find his way: first, the awareness that he had developed through his meditative training and, second, the needs and expectations of others.

You have the form and then you also begin to feel the environment. There are lots of different kinds of environment and they begin to affect you internally, particularly when the sitting practice is introduced to you, from that point forward. And there is also help that comes from the people who want to study with you and learn from you, and from your work with them.[47]

The kind of training that tülkus underwent, particularly beginning at such a young age, meant that their sense of identity was almost entirely shaped by their religious environment. From the moment they were recognized, they were told, "You are a bodhisattva. The purpose of your life is to help others. There is no room for selfishness or unkindness here. Your predecessor was a realized master who helped countless suffering beings. You must aspire to emulate his greatness and your training is for this purpose." At the same time, the tülku was definitively separated from his family. He typically received little sense of identity from his birth parents and formed his own sense of himself entirely from the bodhisattva ideal and model of his predecessor that were daily presented to him and from the culture of his monastic environment.

This kind of upbringing raises some fascinating questions. What would be the impact of being told daily from early childhood that one was a compassionate bodhisattva whose only purpose in life was to help others? What if one's training continually reinforced that ideal? Suppose that the models held up were masters presented as selfless and realized; how would this affect the formation of the personality? If one were taught that the sense of an "I" that must be served and protected is not real but a construct, how would that affect a person's sense of self? If trained to consider others first, and to believe that acting in one's own self-serving interests is *not the thing to do*, how would this affect the way one came to understand oneself and to relate with others?

We have reviewed the Buddhist teachings that the self-referential ego is not a reality but an inculcated ideology; that people behave selfishly because they believe in the existence of self and believe that self assertion is the way to maintain it. But if such a belief is not reinforced, if there is conviction in selfless wisdom and compassion as the core of one's identity, it is likely to provide a very different orientation to the world. In Buddhist terms, would it not open the way for the natural altruism of the buddha-nature to manifest itself in kindness and concern for others? The tülku tradition, for all of its ups and downs and sidetracks, aimed to bring about such a result and, through the prestige and central role of the tülkus, to make this result available to society at large.

CONCLUSION

In spite of its dominance in traditional Tibet, the tülku tradition was a fragile phenomenon, dependent on many factors for its survival. Some of the more important of these included the following:

1. *General ideological consensus.* The basic Buddhist beliefs in the nonexistence of the "self" as an ultimate reality obviously provided the background to the tülku tradition. Because the "self" or ego is seen as an empty idea, the ground is cleared for the tülkus to act in ways that do not confirm or aggrandize some supposed "individuality." The belief in the supreme value of selfless service to others is similarly a necessary foundation. Within the Tibetan context, tülkus are seen as not "out for themselves," and their entire training and behavior are geared to reflect this fundamental altruism. This is not to say that the more ordinary human motivations of selfishness and use of power for one's own aggrandizement were unknown among the tülkus, but rather that the traditional Buddhist teachings provided a counterpoint and check against such tendencies. Without this kind of consensus of belief, there would be no ground for the tülku tradition to stand on.

2. *Cultural consensus concerning the validity of the tülku ideal.* In order for the tülku tradition to work, there also needed to be a cultural consensus concerning the authenticity of the ideal and its importance within the culture as a whole. Two groups, in particular, needed to feel the strength and health of this consensus: the families who produced recognized tülkus and the monastic institutions that trained them.

In Tibet, it was customary to send one of one's children to be a monk or, less frequently, a nun. Social recognition and approbation came back to the family who had thus given a child to the monastic life. Within this climate, the recognition of a child as a tülku was generally welcomed as an extremely auspicious event, as it brought considerable prestige to the family and offered the child unique opportunities. Nevertheless, as we have seen, it was not uncommon for families who gave up their sons to the tülku training to have mixed feelings, for everyone was well aware of the long and difficult educational process he was about to enter. In addition, as we have seen in the case of Khyentse Rinpoche, the loss of working members of a family and of heirs could generate considerable strain.

The cultural consensus was also critical for the monastic establishments that undertook the training of young tülkus. A tremendous amount of human resources was devoted to this process. There was always at least one adult tutor supervising the process, and usually more were involved, with attendants and other assistants. Senior teachers of a lineage typically put a great deal of time and energy into the training of tülkus as well.

3. *The rigors of the training.* We have had a glimpse of the level of rigor implied by the training of tülkus. Whether in study or in meditation, extraordinarily high demands were made on them from infancy through their late teens, when most assumed their adult responsibilities. By then, the discipline was so ingrained that it continued to define the tülku's life. We have seen how small children were under the requirements of their training from early in the morning until late at night. The young trainees were pushed far beyond what would be considered reasonable in modern culture.

4. *Isolation.* This training included a considerable degree of isolation. In Tibet, tülkus spent most of their time with their tutors and mentors, in the monastery or in retreat. Prohibited from playing with other children, they were in particular kept apart from the distractions and amusements of the social world outside of the monastic environment.

5. *Social investment in the tülku's accomplishments and effectiveness.* People in the tülku's immediate environment, his teachers, disciples, and devotees, all felt a great stake in his reputation, defined by his accomplishments in scholarship and meditation, and in his integrity and effectiveness as a leader. This meant that the tülku was always under close

scrutiny, from the moment he was brought to the monastery as a young child to the moment of his death and even after. He was, in a real sense, expected to meet the highest standards set for him, and everyone in his environment participated, in one way or another, in the ongoing evaluation that was made of him.

6. *The tülku's own estimation of the tradition.* When young tülkus are under the thumb of their tutors, so to speak, their own appreciation of their education clearly would go up and down. As mature individuals, however, their support of the authenticity, importance, and effectiveness of the tradition was a key element in its ongoing health.

7. *A hierarchical view of human society.* The tülku tradition is, in a very real sense, elitist. Certain children, believed to be more spiritually gifted and capable than others, are chosen. Their superiority is articulated in their being identified with a saint from the previous generation. Then they are given a training that is not available to others in the culture. As adults, they are revered as saints who are seen as spiritually "above" most others.

Each of these factors contributes essential elements to the tülku tradition. Together, they form an organic whole. If any of them is missing, the balance of the tradition is thrown off. For example, the hierarchical view of human society in Tibet meant that the tülkus were, to a large extent, revered as saints. Whenever someone came into their presence, it was the universal convention to do three prostrations to them. How is it that this kind of reverence did not lead to pernicious effects? In our modern world, we are all aware of the pitfalls of "fame" and adulation and the fact that they can result all too easily in self-satisfaction, arrogance, and lack of sympathy for others. Yet among tülkus trained in the classical Tibetan system, one often finds a remarkable degree of humbleness, self-deprecation, and genuine concern for others. The tülkus one meets generally don't seem to be overly impressed by their own stature. One may ask, how has this humility come about? To say that the tülkus "were just born that way" is not satisfactory because Tibetans themselves hold that the painful course of the training is essential to what a tülku becomes. A more reasonable answer is that such humility is due to other features of the tradition that provided a counterbalance to the reverence tülkus experienced. These other factors would have been both ideological (the foundation of a belief in the negative effects of belief in a "self" and an insistence on altruism) and practical (the demanding nature of the training).

In a similar way, the cultural investment in the tülku's identity as a selfless bodhisattva would have put brakes on the development of feelings of self-importance. Unkind words or actions, exhibitions of scholarly weakness or other falling short of expectation would typically have been noticed and required response. If one were young, the matter would be dealt with by tutors; if one were older, by teachers or peers. A tülku's failings—if excessive and unaddressed—would impact his reputation and that of his monastery. Apart from other undesirable impacts is the economic one: donations to unvirtuous people do not produce much positive merit. In these and other similar ways, it seems that while affirming the tülku's inner gifts and while putting him through a very high degree of training, the tülku system was able to do so without encouraging undue or harmful self-importance. This is certainly not to say that there were not inflated and self-serving people among the ranks of the tülkus, but rather that the tradition itself contained certain restraints and discouragements against such a development.

The tülku tradition is obviously central to Tibetan Buddhism. It has been perhaps the single most important factor in shaping the classical Tibetan Buddhist configuration and in facilitating its longevity and its spiritual authenticity and vitality. Without leaders like the tülkus, trained in the traditional way, it is hard to imagine what Tibetan Buddhism would be like. The continuation of the tradition in something like its classical form is certainly on the minds of Tibetan teachers in exile. Efforts are being made to find ways to continue to identify and train tülkus both in greater Asia and in the West.

It is clear, however, that the challenges to maintaining the tülku tradition in exile are steep. In particular, of the seven factors mentioned above, in the exile situation not one of them exists in its traditional form. For example, (1) In the modern cultural context, the values of personal happiness and fulfillment have obviously become rampant, and younger Tibetans living in exile—whether tülkus or others—are probably far more influenced by these values than one might expect. The ideas of nonself and the service of others are certainly still taught and accepted; however, the impact of a modern world in which the existence of a solid self lies at the basis of all social, political, and economic life cannot be underestimated.

(2) Among Tibetans in exile, there is a diminishing cultural consensus regarding the importance of the tülku system. Parents are less willing to give up their children identified as tülkus, and monasteries in exile have fewer resources to train them. Moreover, among the younger generation of Tibetans, the religious way of life altogether has less prestige and is in competition with the promise of modern education and prosperity. In the West, where tülkus have begun to be identified among North American and European children, the situation is obviously even more mixed. The case of one American child identified as a tülku is typical. His mother had been amenable to having him learn about Buddhism and receive some training. His father, on the other hand, had no interest in Buddhism or sympathy with the idea of his son being the reincarnation of a Tibetan lama. The child, whom I met, was highly intelligent and remarkably alert, but he had no cultural context to respond to, and was rather blasé about his recognition.

(3) Some of the most important Tibetan monasteries have been recreated in Asia, usually in India and Nepal, and monastic establishments also exist in Sikkim and Bhutan—locales that are culturally Tibetan. In these various places, there are tülkus in residence, undergoing their training. However, the situation in exile provides unique obstacles. For one thing, the conditions are harsh. The climate, particularly in India where most of these monasteries are located, is inhospitable to the highland constitution of Tibetans, and sickness and chronic illness are common. The economic resources in most monasteries in exile are severely strained—this means crowded housing, low-grade food, limited medical resources, and so on. Within the monasteries, the traditional scholarly education is provided, but it is often truncated or interrupted. Opportunities for long retreats are limited, and many tülkus have little chance to do them. Within the various multiyear monastic training programs that exist for tülkus, the attrition rate is high; out of a given starting

class, all too often only a small percentage may actually complete the program. Yet a thorough scholarly and meditative training would seem essential to the tülku's identity. Imagine a tülku who was not particularly well educated in the texts or doctrines and who had little meditative training to speak of. How could a person in this situation be expected to carry Tibetan Buddhism forward as before?

(4) Tibetan monasteries in exile are often located in urban or other populated areas, and the surrounding population is not only not usually Buddhist, but embodies values and distractions that pull tülkus away from their training. The "bright lights" of the modern, urban world provide a very real alternative to the monastic way. Once a tülku in training has learned to read and write, and has received some education, it is all to easy to decide that the monastic way is just too hard, and to be dazzled and attracted by the promise of greater happiness and personal fulfillment elsewhere.

(5) For Tibetans living in exile, most of their time and energy is expended trying to survive in an environment that is usually neither Buddhist nor Tibetan. Moreover, to make their way in this world, and to prepare their children for its challenges, Tibetans are increasingly looking to modern education and vocational training. Within this context, the kind of study and practice taking place in the monasteries, and particularly the training being received by tülkus, must at times seem somewhat peripheral to what is really needed. Certainly, the monastery along with its ideals and its inhabitants, can no longer be the exclusive focus of a community that it once was. In spite of these factors, the older generation of Tibetans usually maintains great devotion to the old ways, veneration for their lamas, and a desire to preserve the tradition in as strong a form as possible. But, as mentioned, the younger generation is growing up in an entirely different world, where a good secular education and a good job clearly seem necessary if one is going to survive. Not having been brought up in the Tibetan world of their parents or grandparents, as Tibetan traditions becomes weakened or slip away, the young people are often not particularly aware that anything important is happening.

(6) Contemporary Tibetan teachers have expressed concerns and

doubts over the future of the tülku tradition. Given the kinds of obstacles and pressures mentioned above, it is indeed hard to see how the tradition could survive in anything like its classical form. At times, the Dalai Lama has raised questions as to whether there will be future incarnations of his line. When Trungpa Rinpoche was asked in 1974 if there would be any more Trungpa Tülkus, he replied, "I don't think so." Other lamas have expressed the same view. Yet a new incarnation of the Trungpa Tülku has been recognized, and it is hard to imagine that after the present Dalai Lama there will be no more. Still, even if another incarnation may be expected, the Dalai Lama has become such a prominent political figure in the world arena, it is hard to see how any future Dalai Lama could be as trained and prepared as the previous incarnations have been.

(7) In the West, we live in a world that—while increasingly rigidly stratified into a hierarchy of rich and poor—espouses a social ideology that is "anti-elitist" and "democratic." This ideology of "equality" is obviously a powerful and entrenched cover for what is actually the case. As such, it has become a virtual dogma among many liberal-minded people that any hierarchy is automatically suspect because it confers greater power on some at the expense of others. It also militates against any attempt to select certain people as more gifted and promising than others and to give them special, privileged training.

One of the major obstacles facing the tülku tradition today, and indeed Tibetan Buddhism as a whole, is the fact that most tülkus were male and that the institutional tradition was almost entirely controlled by men. In a world where women increasingly want and expect the same opportunities as men, Tibetan Buddhism faces an important question: is it willing to respond positively to the desire on the part of women for education and training in the various Buddhist disciplines, both scholarly and meditative, and to their interest in occupying positions of leadership? In the face of a question such as this, older Tibetans, both men and women, may well reply that women were just as important in maintaining Tibetan tradition as men, though in different roles; that men and women worked together to maintain the dharma; and that in every generation, there were a considerable number of women identified as realized people and teachers in their own right. While this is true, it is not an adequate response to the modern situation, and basic changes are called for, to reflect the growing education, visibility, and power of women in the modern world.

As Tibetan Buddhism evolves in Asia and the West, it does appear that it is beginning to address the change in gender roles and expectations. Tibetan teachers in the West accept both men and women students equally, and the scholarly and meditative training is also available to both in equal measure. Senior Western women are increasingly coming to occupy positions of leadership in the Western adaptations of Tibetan Buddhism, as translators, scholars, meditation teachers, and administrators. One anticipates that the younger generation of Tibetan women will not be far behind them.

17

The Practice of Retreat

THE VAJRAYANA GIVES TIBETAN BUDDHISM ITS BASIC character and provides its overarching orientation. In addition, it plays a central role in the daily life of monks and nuns who live in institutionalized contexts: the tantras and their commentaries are studied, tantric liturgies are practiced by the assembled community, and the color and iconography of the Vajrayana pantheon fill the walls of assembly halls and temples. Nevertheless, in spite of its cultural and institutional importance, throughout Tibetan history, the core Vajrayana practices have always been carried out in retreat. This approach follows the ancient traditions of the Indian siddhas, most of whom attained realization through extensive retreat practice.

In the preceding pages and in my book *Indestructible Truth*, many examples have been cited illustrating the importance of retreat practice within the Indian Buddhist meditative traditions and in Tibetan Buddhism. Figures as diverse as the Buddha, Nagarjuna, Asanga, Padmasambhava, Tilopa, Milarepa, and Rechungpa, as well as the most important teachers of all of the major contemplative schools of Tibetan Buddhism, particularly of the Kagyü and Nyingma lineages, spent substantial periods of their lives in retreat.

Although often not highlighted in Western books on Tibetan Buddhism, retreat practice is central to the entire tradition. On a practical level, most Vajrayana practices, including those of the yidam, inner yogas, and mahamudra and dzokchen, originated in retreat contexts in India and were designed to be carried out in seclusion. Seen from another angle, retreat practice is critical because it provides the most direct and effective way to attain personal realization of the teachings that one has received. A month of retreat can bring about a maturation of practice and understanding that might take many years of daily meditation while living an ordinary life. When one can spend a matter of years in retreat, ripening can occur that is generally not possible at all within the limitations of life "in the world."

Retreat practice in Tibetan Buddhism is carried out within the perspective and commitments of the Mahayana. In order for one's practice to bear fruit, it is considered essential that the primary motivation for entering retreat be the assistance of sentient beings. The purpose of retreat, then, is to cultivate wisdom and compassion, and to develop the two accumulations of merit and wisdom, so that when returning to the world (in this life or any other), one will be that much more able to be of genuine benefit to others.

It may be recalled that in the Vajrayana there are three phases in the tantric journey to awakening. In the first, one prepares for and gains initiation into the Vajrayana. In the second, one meditates upon what has been received, cultivating the buddha-nature through yidam practice, the inner yogas, and the essence practices of mahamudra and dzokchen. And, in the third, realization is attained, wherein one does not waver from the natural state whether meditating on one's cushion or moving about in the mundane activities of ordinary life. Retreat addresses the second phase, in which one cultivates familiarity with the buddha-nature through the various Vajrayana methods.

Daily meditation is an important discipline for Buddhists living "in the world," but generally this practice has a somewhat different purpose and effect when compared with that of retreat. Daily meditation brings the mind back into balance; it helps us digest the sharp points and chaos of experience; and it unlocks our sanity, warmth, and creativity so that we can live our lives more clearly and effectively. However, in the ordinary activities of daily life, our minds are usually in a state of continual distraction. The sheer volume of thinking, social demands, and physical activity seemingly required by ordinary life tends to inhibit attempts to look at the depths and subtleties of our experience.

Retreat offers quite a different environment, one of utter simplicity, solitude, and silence. In retreat, we find that over a period of days and weeks our mind slows down, we are able to practice with increased clarity and focus, and the more hidden and subtle dimensions of the mind begin to reveal themselves.

The Vajrayana practitioner is in retreat to develop the ability to rest in the deepest, awakened level of the mind. However, the path to this noble goal is long and arduous, and considerable commitment is required. At first, we are aware only of our distraction. In time, we begin to glimpse moments of deeper, natural awareness. Through sustained practice, we begin to be able to rest briefly in the nature. As the practice evolves, these periods of resting become more and more extended and a kind of stabilization occurs. Ultimately, resting in the nature of mind does not preclude mental, verbal, and physical activity and, as stability increases, these activities can occur without interrupting awareness. However, in order to attain this level of maturity, usually a great deal of practice in the drastic environment of retreat is required. When some measure of realization has been attained, then one leaves the retreat experience behind and returns to the world, expressing his or her attainment in the various activities of ordinary life.

THE PHYSICAL ENVIRONMENT

Retreat Places

In India, retreat locations were quite varied—an isolated part of the jungle, a remote ravine, a desert region, an uninhabited island in the middle of a river or lake, or an inaccessible place in the mountains. In Tibet, mountainous as it is, retreats were typically carried out in mountain locales, removed from the villages. Ideally, one looked for a relatively inaccessible cave that offered protection from the elements, was dry inside, and had a spring of water within easy access. Preferred were caves small enough to have the closed-in feeling of a room, and often retreatants built a wall across the mouth of their cave with a small entrance, to provide a further buffer against the intense Tibetan cold and winds, as well as wild animals. In addition to caves, retreats were also sometimes carried out in small huts built in the forest or on a mountainside, in an isolated place. Sometimes, meditators took vows to live out of doors for periods of time, practicing in the open in high fields, on the flanks of hills, or on mountaintops and, like the great nineteenth-century Ri-me master Paltrül Rinpoche, sleeping in ditches or hollows at night.

Certain kinds of retreats were also carried out in charnel grounds, the places where corpses were taken, hacked apart, and left for vultures and wild animals to consume. In Tibet, these places were removed from population centers and were considered dangerous and inauspicious because of their association with death, the wild animals that prowled there, and the demons and malevolent spirits that were believed to haunt them. The tradition of practicing in charnel grounds derives from the Indian siddhas who, as we saw, often lived, meditated, and taught their disciples in cremation grounds. The chö (cutting-through) practices, associated with Machik Labdrönma and now found in all of the lineages, were specifically charnel-ground practices. In chö, one makes an offering of one's body to the various spirits and demons inhabiting the place, as an act of kindness to them, in order to overcome the attachment to "I" or self. Nyoshul Khenpo recalls his own experience of this practice: "I practiced the tantric Prajnaparamita sadhanas called Chod [chö] or Cutting Ego, meditating all night in terrifying cemeteries and charnel grounds, offering my body to the hungry ghosts and karmic creditors."[1]

In Tibet, monasteries often maintained retreat sites for the use of members of the monastic community. Dilgo Khyentse Rinpoche provides the following description of the retreat facilities attached to Shechen monastery in East Tibet, the seat of his root teacher, Shechen Gyaltsap Rinpoche (1871–1926):

> Gyaltsap Rinpoche's hermitage was perched on the spur of the mountainside about forty-five minutes' walk above Shechen Monastery. The path up to this beautiful spot was quite steep, and slippery during the rainy season. From the window you could see the monastery and the river down below in the valley,

framed all around by mountains snow-covered for most of the year. Just below the hermitage was a platform among juniper bushes, ideal for sitting quietly on sunny days. Lower down was a small cave called the Cave of Luminous Great Bliss, in which Gyaltsap Rinpoche had spent some months in retreat. Above the hermitage were more caves; in one, sacred images seemed to have formed spontaneously in the rock face. Halfway down towards the monastery was Shechen's main retreat center, where nearly twenty monks at a time would practice the traditional three-year, three-month, and three-day retreat.[2]

If the retreatant was affiliated with a monastery, he or she would typically occupy a cave or hut maintained by the monastery and have food and other necessities provided. If the retreatant was on his own, he was typically responsible for finding a suitable location and arranging for material support. In such a case, he would locate an isolated cave where the retreat could be carried out. Certain caves and certain areas were well known as good retreat places, but new locations could always be found among the endless mountain tracts. It sometimes happened that yogins searching for good places to practice would come upon caves that had been used hundreds of years prior but had long since been abandoned and forgotten. It was common for yogins to meditate in a certain cave for a number of months or years and then wander abroad to find another cave in which to practice.

Individual retreatants were often entirely on their own, with no one keeping track of them or even knowing where they were. Even to people they met when they wandered for alms, they might not reveal their identities or exactly where they were currently in retreat. Even if a certain yogi was known to be practicing in a certain area, his or her exact whereabouts might be unknown. If he ran out of food, injured himself, became ill, or was attacked by thieves, he would often have no recourse. The isolation of the individual retreatant was often accentuated by the fact that, because of heavy snows and other extreme weather conditions, it was common for retreat locations to be cut off and inaccessible for many months of the year. Milarepa, for example, during much of his meditative career, pursued his aspiration for enlightenment in solitary retreat, without institutional affiliation or support and without protection from anyone, much of the time cloistered and more or less imprisoned by the heavy snows and the bitter cold and winds of winter. The life of the solitary, wandering retreatant was a chancy and dangerous one, and it is not surprising that when a son or daughter chose this way of life, it was often difficult for families to accept. However, in spite of its rigors, it remained attractive for those with strong spiritual aspirations, for the potential benefits were priceless.

Food in Retreats

A retreat required not only a suitable location but also sufficient food. Since most retreats were carried out far from towns and villages and might be entirely cut off for months out of the year, a store of food adequate for the retreat period was critical. In some cases, this food might be supplied by a patron who agreed to provide for the retreatant's needs for a certain period of time. When this was wanting, one might—as Milarepa sometimes did—come out of retreat for a period in the summer to go alms gathering among the villages. The food collected—perhaps barley, tea, dried meat, cheese, and butter—would then serve as the provisions for the ensuing months. Retreatants might make use of whatever scanty resources occurred naturally near their retreat site. Milarepa, for example, used to make broth from the nettles that grew near his cave, and, for him, this was one of his principal forms of nourishment. Even when food had been collected, however, this was no guarantee of adequate provisions. Perhaps the retreatant did not bring enough, perhaps animals got into it, it spoiled, or thieves plundered the stores. Given these variables, it is not surprising that undernourishment and periodic semistarvation were common experiences of people in Tibet who engaged in extensive retreat practice.

Something of the importance, difficulties, and worries of ensuring adequate food are seen in the life of Milarepa. When Mila was about to go into retreat, a patron assisted him.

> He gave me a sack of barley flour and some excellent dried meat. I withdrew to a good cave on the hill behind my house to

meditate. As I was sparing with my provisions, my body began to weaken. Nevertheless, I was able to withstand several months of ardent meditation. When my provisions were exhausted and I had nothing left to eat, I felt I could not hold out much longer. I thought, "I will beg for meat from the herdsmen in the highlands and for grain from the farmers in the valley. By carefully rationing my food, I will be able to continue my meditation." And so I went to beg from the herdsmen.[3]

On another occasion Milarepa was engaged in a three-year retreat at White Rock cave and had made a vow, for the duration, not to descend to an inhabited place. He had acquired several sacks of meal.

Each year I consumed one of my sacks of meal. And if I had had nothing else to sustain me, it would have been the end of my life. When men of the world, having found one-tenth of an ounce of gold, rejoice over it and then lose it, they despair. But that cannot be compared to dying without having attained Enlightenment. For a life which leads to Enlightenment is more precious than a billion worlds filled with gold. I thought, "What shall I do? It is better to die than to break my vow. I shall not go down to the village. I will not break my vow. But since it is for a religious aim, I must find just enough food to sustain my life."

I went out in front of the White Rock cave where the sun was warm and the water excellent. Here were many nettles—an open place with a distant view. Joyfully, I stayed there. Sustaining myself with nettles, I continued my meditation. Because I had no clothes on my body and no other nourishment whatever, my body, covered with grayish hair, became like a skeleton and my skin turned the color of nettles.[4]

Milarepa, like other yogins, was not averse to adequate food, but often it came down to a choice of continuing in retreat in accordance with his vows, or leaving and seeking food. Sometimes it happened, though, that food came to Milarepa. On one occasion, a group of hunters happened on Mila's cave and, moved by the example of his renunciation and practice, left him with a large supply of meat and other provisions. He rejoiced in the food and immediately began to feel its beneficial effects.

> "What good luck," I said to myself joyfully. "Now I can eat like a human being." After I had eaten cooked meat, my body began to feel tranquil bliss. My health improved, my sensitivity was keener, and my practice was strengthened. I experienced a blissful state of emptiness as never before.[5]

THE CONFIGURATIONS OF RETREAT

Inspiration for Entering Retreat

Throughout Tibetan Buddhism, as mentioned, it was assumed that in order to attain full realization of the Buddhist teachings, it was necessary to enter solitary retreat and spend significant amounts of time meditating in that context. Particularly among the Nyingma and Kagyü lineages, retreat practice extending over at least several years was a critical part of the training offered. In the other schools, it depended more on individual inclination and inspiration.

Among monks and nuns, it was often the case that one entered into the retreatant way after coming to a painful recognition of the limitations of the monastic life. For example, Tilopa and Naropa, the Indian progenitors of the Kagyü, both originally monks, came to a dead end in their development and were only able to find a way through by abandoning their robes and pursuing the solitary way of the yogin. Similarly, Gampopa sought out Milarepa because he could see that only by intensive training in meditation would he gain full understanding. Exiting the monastic way in Tibet was not always easy, owing to the web of family, social, and institutional expectations that might surround the monk. Interesting in this regard is the example of the Kagyü monk

Tsangnyön Heruka, who came to find that way of life suffocating. In order to extricate himself from the situation, he feigned insanity, talking and laughing incoherently, and finally gravely insulted a rich and powerful donor, after which his community was relieved to be rid of him. From then on, he followed the example of Milarepa, taking up the life of a yogin, roaming the mountains and living and meditating in remote caves.[6]

Sometimes it was other kinds of crises that pushed individuals toward the retreatant way. Padmasambhava, for example, was branded a criminal and exiled from his father's kingdom; only then did he enter into retreat, practicing for many years in cremation grounds. Virupa, the Sakya progenitor, entered the retreatant way after being forcibly expelled from his monastery for apparent infractions of the monastic rules. And Milarepa's disciple Rechungpa, as a young boy, came to live and practice under his master after brutal treatment by his family.

It is often the death of one's guru that crystallizes one's inspiration and intention to devote oneself to a life of retreat. For example, when Chagdud Tulku's mother—also his spiritual teacher—died, the profound shock caused him to appreciate meditation practice much more deeply and inspired him in his retreat practice from then on. Similarly, Dilgo Khyentse Rinpoche recalls his feelings upon hearing the news of the death of his root guru, Gyaltsap Rinpoche, and the profound impact it had on him. Previously, Khyentse Rinpoche had spent some five years with his teacher, living not in the master's monastery itself, but in his hermitage just described.

> Sometime later, I went to Kyangma Ritrö, where Khenpo Thubga lived. There was no monastery or other buildings there, only tents. It was there, at the age of fifteen, that I learned in a letter from my father that Gyaltsap Rinpoche had died. For a moment my mind went blank. Then, suddenly, the memory of my teacher arose so strongly in my mind that I was overwhelmed and wept. That day I felt as if my heart had been torn from my chest. I went back to Denkhok and started a period of retreat in the mountains that would last for thirteen years.[7]

Retreat Vows

Not a part of the physical context of retreat, but important to its role as a container for the practice are retreat vows. It was common for those entering retreat to take vows involving a commitment to remain there for a specified period of time. In Tibet, retreats typically varied in length from a few weeks, to several years, up to a life retreat in which one vowed to remain until death. Whatever the length, retreatants would typically take a vow to remain for the intended length. When Milarepa left one of his retreats prematurely to journey to his home and seek out his mother, Marpa chastised him, expressing the traditional view: "My son, why have you so suddenly broken the strict seclusion of your retreat? It might engender inner obstacles and open the way for Mara. Go back and remain in your solitude."[8] These and many other examples in the lives of Milarepa and other retreatants show how important retreat vows were considered and how seriously they were taken.

This leads to the natural question of why such vows were considered so important. In the Buddhist understanding of vows, once they are made, they are binding; if kept, they accelerate the path to enlightenment, but if broken, they bring all kinds of obstacles and misfortunes. One may mention another, more immediately tangible factor. When a person is in retreat, his or her mind opens to new, previously undiscovered depths. With this comes a more intense experience of one's obstacles as well as wisdom and sanity. Particularly in the intensive retreat environment, the meditator acutely realizes the wildness of the steed of mind. There are times when the steed seems to be getting away or when the ride becomes very rough indeed. And sometimes the ride may be very painful. At such times, the thought may arise, "Anything would be easier than this, even samsara. I'm leaving!" It is, ironically, often right at such a point that one verges on a breakthrough. At such moments of intensity, it is imperative to not yield to the impulse to bolt. The retreat vow is a powerful reminder of the importance of sticking with the practice and fulfilling one's original intention in entering retreat.

Group Retreats

Individual retreats have been the staple of Tibetan Buddhism. In Tibet, group retreats were also common, where a small number of students would live in retreat with their teacher, receiving instructions and carrying out the associated practices. Milarepa exemplifies this pattern later in his life, when disciples began to make their way to his retreat locations and take up residence in nearby caves, in order to study with him. When Rechungpa was still a child, he happened to encounter Milarepa, was inspired by him, and went to stay where he was living with his yogi disciples.

It should not be thought that group retreats were necessarily very much easier than individual ones. An example of just how challenging group retreats could be is seen in the life of Longchen Rabjam, the great Nyingma master, who trained under Rigdzin Kumaradza. The following story, quoted in *Indestructible Truth*, is indicative of the retreatant way in Tibet. It was Rigdzin Kumaradza's practice to teach his disciples in remote locations in the mountains.

> While he was studying with Rigdzin Kumaradza, Longchen Rabjam lived under circumstances of severe deprivation. In order to combat his attachment to material things, it was Rigdzin Kumaradza's practice to keep moving from place to place instead of settling at one location and getting attached to it. In nine months he and his disciples moved their camp nine times, causing great hardship to Longchen Rabjam and every one else. Just as soon as he got his simple life settled in a temporary shelter, usually a cave, which would protect him from rain and cold, the time would come to move again. He had very little food and only one ragged bag to use as both mattress and blanket to protect himself from the extremely cold winter. It was under these circumstances that Longchen Rabjam obtained the most rare and precious teachings of the tantras and instructions of the three cycles of Dzogpa Chenpo.[9]

In spite of its inevitable deprivations and hardships, the retreatant way could be experienced as an uplifted and joyful period in one's life.

In this regard, Nyoshul Khenpo recalls his own retreat practice with other disciples under his guru:

> During another period of intensive practice I lived for a time like a wild animal in the forest, uninhibitedly practicing *rushen*, the Dzogchen preliminary practices, with several other yogis under the guidance of my guru. I still remember what that was like, living freely and uninhibitedly, beyond all conceptual restraints and social conventions—just like the mahasiddhas of old! It was a wonderful period of spiritual practice.[10]

LIFE IN RETREAT

When practitioners in traditional Tibet entered into retreat, it was with the expectation that they faced a life of considerable physical hardship. Indeed, many considered it an essential part of the retreatant way that they willingly took on its difficulty and insecurity. Something of this may be gleaned from the following interchange between the great Tibetan yogin Shabkar (1781–1851) and his main teacher, Ngakyi Wangpo (1736–1807). Prior to entering retreat, Shabkar had been paying a visit to his guru, whom he called "the precious Dharma King." The evening before Shabkar's departure, his guru dug through a big bag, normally used for medicine, and pulled out money and white scarves that were inside. He then said, "Tonight, now that no one is around, I shall say farewell to my son." Shabkar then continues the account:

> He then gave me nine sang of silver and twenty white scarves— long ones and short ones—and told me, "Take these, and buy provisions." I took them in my hands, but I kept only two white scarves for the sake of our auspicious connection, and offered the rest back to him, saying, "If I had any possessions, I would make a large offering to repay your kindness, but I don't have sufficient merit for that. So, of all the gifts you have given me I shall only accept a token, to make an auspicious connection.
>
> "The life-stories of the sages tell how they received pith in-

structions from their gurus and then went into solitary retreat. Giving up all thoughts of this life, they continuously visualized their guru on the crowns of their heads, and kept his pith instructions in their hearts. They took with them into retreat nothing more than a staff and a small book to remind them of the teaching. There is no mention of them taking gold, silver or valuables. Following their worthy examples, giving up all concern for the affairs of this life, I will go to the mountains without any silver or gold."[11]

Shabkar is then inspired to set off for his retreat, with no possessions and no knowledge of how he will survive.

Something of the physical hardship entailed by a life in retreat is illustrated by the story of the Ri-me master Jigme Gyalwe Nyugu, a disciple of Jigme Lingpa and guru of Paltrül Rinpoche.[12] As a disciple of Jigme Lingpa, he would receive teachings from his guru and then practice these in retreat until he attained some understanding. He would then return to his guru for more instruction. Gyalwe Nyugu often stayed in caves as an anonymous practitioner with no assistants or attendants and no patrons. So harsh were the conditions under which he lived that he was frequently afflicted with various physical ailments. On one occasion, descending from his mountain retreat, weak and sick, he collapsed. As Lama Surya Das recounts the story:

> He thought, "I'm accomplished, but now I cannot benefit beings. I'm just going to die here alone in this wilderness, but that's all right." Then he prayed wholeheartedly to Jigme Lingpa to be able to fulfill the aims and aspirations of others and himself. Eventually two fierce savages with feathers in their hair appeared carrying some maize and meat. They gave him food, and after a few days he regained his strength. Then he continued on until reaching some villages where he could find shelter.[13]

When he finally reached his guru Jigme Lingpa, the master informed him that he had been saved by the two dharma protectors of that locale, Tsari.

Jigme Gyalwe Nyugu was originally from Kham, in East Tibet, but for many years had been receiving teachings and practicing in Central Tibet. After he had attained realization, his guru sent him back to Kham and directed him to meditate on a certain mountain by the name of Tramolung, in a remote region. In Surya Das's words,

> He had left Kham so long ago that no one recognized him or knew of him. He was alone, carrying his bag on his shoulder, when he arrived at the mountain in the north of Derge. It was totally uninhabited, with neither people nor animals, with sparse vegetation. The nomads took herds there in the summer, but they lived further north, at lower altitudes the rest of the year.
>
> The nomads were leaving when he arrived. He had no supplies or shelter, but he followed his guru's order and stayed in a cave he happened to discover. Living conditions were extremely harsh, but he decided he would rather die there than fail to fulfill his omniscient guru's wishes. And so he subsisted, meditating most of the time and foraging for whatever grass and shrubs might be found palatable.
>
> After several months, a group of travelers on horseback passed by. One of them, a man dressed in white, riding a white horse, called to Gyalwai Nyugu and said, "What are you doing there? You are supposed to follow your guru's prophecy by dwelling up *there*!" And he pointed to a cold, desolate place even higher up the windswept mountainside, where there was no shelter or wildlife.[14]

Gyalwe Nyugu knew that this person was a dharma protector whose dictum could not be ignored, and so he immediately moved to the spot indicated and took up his residence there on the open and exposed mountain slope. He stayed in that place for twenty-one years, practicing under the harshest of conditions. In the beginning of his time there, he almost died from the great hardships he endured.

Eventually, people came to learn of him and began to make offerings in the way of provisions. One donor gave Gyalwe Nyugu a heavy felt blanket, which he propped up with sticks to make into a shelter. As his fame spread, more and more disciples came to request teachings and to practice under his guidance. Eventually, hundreds of yogis gathered around Gyalwe Nyugu on this high mountain slope, living in makeshift tents and tiny huts.

Rigorous as life in retreat might be, it was a wonderfully self-contained existence and one with its own rhythm, beauties, and fulfillments. Khyentse Rinpoche describes his own experience over many years of retreat practice:

> I practiced from the early hours before dawn until noon, and from afternoon late into the night. At midday, I read from my books, reciting the texts aloud to learn them by heart. I stayed in a cave at Cliff Hermitage for seven years, at White Grove for three years, and in other caves and huts for a few months at a time, surrounded by thick forests and snow mountains.
>
> Not far from the Padampa caves was a cottage, where my brother Shedrup and two attendants made food. My cave had no door, and small bears used to come and snuffle around the entrance. But they were unable to climb the ladder into the cave. Outside in the forest lived foxes and all sorts of birds. There were leopards not very far away, too; they caught a small dog I had with me. A cuckoo lived nearby, and he was my alarm clock. As soon as I heard him, around three o'clock in the morning, I would get up and start a session of meditation. At five o'clock I made myself some tea, which meant that I had no need to see anyone until lunchtime. In the evening, I would let the fire go out slowly so that next morning the embers were still hot enough to be stoked up again. I could revive the fire and boil tea in my one big pot without getting up from my seat, just by leaning forward. . . . The cave was quite roomy—high enough to stand up in without hitting my head on the roof—but slightly damp. Like most caves, it was cool in summer and retained some warmth in winter.
>
> I sat all the time in a four-sided wooden box, occasionally

stretching my legs out. Shedrup, my elder brother, was my retreat teacher, and he told me that unless I sometimes took a walk outside I might end up quite deranged; but I felt not the slightest wish to go out. Shedrup was practicing, too, in partial retreat in a hut nearby.

Many small birds ventured into my cave. If I put some butter on the tip of my finger, they would come and peck at it. I also shared the cave with two mice. I fed them with barley flour, and they used to run around on my lap. Crows would carry off the offerings I put outside.

For five or six years I ate no meat. For three years, I did not speak a single word. . . . My brother Shedrup often encouraged me to compose prayers, spiritual songs, and poems, which he thought would give me practice in writing. I found it easy to write, and by the end of that period I had written about a thousand pages; but later, when we fled Tibet, it was all lost.

The cave had a very clear feeling about it, and there were no distractions. I let my hair grow and it got very long. When I practiced "inner warmth" [*tummo*] I experienced a lot of heat, and day and night for years, in spite of the very cold climate, I wore only a white shawl and a robe of raw silk. I sat on a bearskin. Outside everything was frozen and solid, but inside the cave was warm. . . . I lived in the cave at Cliff Hermitage without coming out of retreat for seven years.[15]

A WESTERN RETREATANT IN A TIBETAN CONTEXT

How feasible would it be for a Westerner to carry out a Tibetan-style retreat in Asia within a traditional Tibetan cultural context? What would it be like for Westerners to engage in this traditional practice? Quite interesting in this respect is the experience of Tenzin Palmo, an English woman who went into retreat for fourteen years in Lahoul in the Indian Himalayas, under conditions very similar to those in Tibet.

Tenzin Palmo's inspiration for becoming a mountain yogini was none other than Milarepa. When still in her teens, she had already made a connection with the Theravadin Buddhist tradition. Then, one day she read about the four schools of Tibetan Buddhism.

> When I read the word *Kagyu* it was like a voice inside me said, "You're a Kagyupa." I went to the only woman in London I knew who had any idea about Tibetan Buddhism and asked her, "What is a Kagyupa?" She said, "Have you read Milarepa?" and handed me Evans-Wentz's translation. It was such an incredible revelation, I mean my whole mind just turned around.[16]

At the age of twenty, in 1964, Tenzin Palmo found her way to India, where she taught English to tülkus. On her twenty-first birthday, she met Khamtrül Rinpoche, who became her root guru. She worked as his secretary for six years until one day he said to her, "Now it's time you went away to practice." Rinpoche sent her to Lahoul, a valley some eleven to twelve thousand feet up in the Himalayas between Manali and Ladakh, a region with which Rinpoche had close ties. This remote valley is completely cut off from the outside world by heavy snows for eight months of the year. Most of the people there are Kagyüpas. Tenzin Palmo stayed in the Kagyü monastery for five years, practicing as much as she could. Finally, she decided that she needed the more isolated environment of strict retreat. There are few caves in the area, and those that were available did not have water. After learning of Tenzin Palmo's inability to find a suitable place, a nun she was talking to remembered hearing of an isolated cave, which had water, in the upper slopes of the mountain, about an hour and a half above the monastery. The "cave" in question was actually just an overhang hollowed out as a shelter sometimes used during the summer by villagers tending cattle. It did not seem very workable as a retreat place, particularly in view of the frigid and stormy winter weather in that region and at that altitude. For these reasons, initially, the monastery down below where Tenzin Palmo had been residing and where she sought help was resistant to her idea. She remained firm, however, and eventually enlisted the help of the villagers to build up an outside wall, fashion a door and window, and pack mud on the outside to make the dwelling weatherproof. Tenzin Palmo moved in and stayed there in retreat for twelve years.

For most of the year, her cave was cut off from the rest of Lahoul by heavy snows that came early each fall and lasted well into the spring. During the summer, she would come out of retreat for a period to see her lama and to prepare for the next winter. At the end of her stay there, she remained in retreat continuously for three years. In commenting on her isolation for so much of the year, Tenzin Palmo remarks:

> This makes the mind very spacious and open with a sense of infinite time. It's not like being in retreat in a more inhabited area where you always have to stay inside, because there was somebody around. [During the eight-month winter] nobody would come because of the snow. I could sit outside and look at the mountains, look at the sky. That was very good for the mind, rather than always being inside. That's why I stayed.[17]

During these years, Tenzin Palmo mainly concentrated on one yidam meditation, that of Akshobhya, a specialty of the Kagyü. This practice was given to her by Sakya Tridzin, who, when he met her, told her that this was her yidam and gave her the necessary empowerments. Many other lamas, including the Karmapa and her own root guru, confirmed that this was indeed her yidam.

Tenzin Palmo found the retreatant way of life, with its extreme simplicity and self-containment, utterly satisfying. When asked whether she ever longed to leave retreat and return to the outside world, she replied:

> Never, never. I can honestly say that when I was in my cave, I had this very strong feeling that there was no other place in all the world that I would rather be and no other thing that I would rather be doing than what I was doing. Even when I was doing the three-year retreat [at the end], on one or two occasions when I felt a little restless, what I wanted was a nice inspiring book. I didn't want to meet anybody or talk, or do anything, I just wanted something to pep up my practice a little bit. My life

was incredibly satisfying in retreat. . . . I remember standing at
the edge of my cave, looking down over the valley, thinking,
"Well if you could go anywhere in the world, where do you
want to go?" And there was nowhere I wanted to go.[18]

What were the benefits of this extended retreat practice for Tenzin
Palmo?

I think for myself the most important thing was a sense of self-
sufficiency. When one is completely by oneself, then whatever
happens, one has to deal with it oneself. There is nothing to
distract you, you are there with your own mind, and that's it.
That teaches one, first of all, a tremendous amount about how
the mind works and also how to deal with it. Now I see how
inwardly self-sufficient I am. I do not feel involved in the emotions that arise, the feelings that arise. Whatever happens now,
I feel completely happy. There's a kind of inner freedom there
which I don't think I had when I started . . . there is this inner
peace and clarity which I didn't have when I started.[19]

Tenzin Palmo carried out her retreat practice as a nun. In an interview, she was asked whether she thought that it made any difference
whether one did retreats as a nun or a layperson. Her initial response
was that no, it does not make any difference. However, a married friend
of hers thought differently, remarking, "No, that's not true. When I am
in retreat I am thinking of my husband. I'm thinking of my property.
I'm thinking of places I'm going to go to next, and I am very much still
involved in the worldly things that are going to happen to me next and
people I'm attached to. As a nun you're not thinking about that sort of
thing."[20] Tenzin Palmo:

I realized it was true. One of the reasons you become a nun
or a monk is because it leaves you tremendously free, not only
physically but emotionally to devote yourself completely to the
Dharma. When I was in the cave I wasn't thinking about my
friends except occasionally, and then only in the sense of wish-

ing them well; it was not that I wanted to be with them. I didn't want to be with anybody. Being ordained, I didn't have to plan what I was going to do next. I was just completely where I was. The Indians used to compare being ordained to a wild swan leaving lake after lake behind without any impediment, and ideally that is how it should be.[21]

When, after fourteen years, she left retreat, Tenzin Palmo went to see His Holiness the Dalai Lama. She had not seen him since she first arrived in India, twenty-five years before. She wanted to seek his advice about starting a nunnery. She also wanted to ask about her conflict between her desire to be a hermit and the thought that perhaps there were more tangible and obvious ways to be helpful to others. The Dalai Lama's response was instructive: "Well, of course, this nunnery project is very important and you should certainly help with it, but don't think of it as a lifetime's vocation. Give it one or two years; then it is very important that you go back into retreat, because that is the way you are going to help people."

Tenzin Palmo comments, "And all my lamas have told me the same thing. That in this lifetime the way that I can really help is simply by practicing in solitude." She remarks further that her retreat practice is preparing her for the benefit to others in future lifetimes: "I feel very strongly that until I really have very strong and firm realizations, then I could spend the rest of eternity and [yet] won't be helping others. In the meantime, in this lifetime, it's very important to try to make the practice strong, otherwise in future lifetimes, who knows where one will go."[22]

There would also seem to be immediate and tangible benefits to extended retreat practice. Friends have told Tenzin Palmo how much it has meant to them that she has renounced the cycle of ordinary success and failure and devoted her life to meditation. Like many hermits before her, although much of her time may be spent in seclusion, she still encounters others in various contexts, teaches them by the peace and joy of her very state of being, instructs them in dharma, and encourages them in their own practice.

Tenzin Palmo eventually left India and returned to the West. She was looking for a place where her contemplative bent and experience could find a resting place. Subsequently, at the invitation of friends, she traveled to Spain and settled in Assisi, the birthplace of Saint Frances.

Western practitioners who hear of her experience might have the impression that carrying out a retreat in Asia would be a very good thing to do. It sounds like a nearly ideal situation, to live in a cave in the mountains, as Milarepa did, and meditate for years on end. And it certainly may seem better than trying to do retreats in the West, with its frantic and anticontemplative cultural environment. Tenzin Palmo responds by talking about the physical difficulties and obstacles she faced during her practice.

Conditions in the West would probably be much easier than my conditions in the cave. First of all the cave was not weatherproof. When it rained, it rained in and usually dripped right over my meditation seat. In the spring the snow melted, and then the whole cave was soaking wet and it took a great deal of energy trying to stop the waters rushing in. Also, because it was a very snowy place, one had to be continually clearing up the snow, which was an enormous chore. Otherwise the cave would be completely covered in snow and I could not get to the wood. In fact my mind was often distracted, so to say, by the externals, whether it was going to snow, whether it was going to rain, what to do before it happened, to be prepared.

In the West the houses are weatherproof, you don't have to care whether it's snowing or raining outside, and you have water inside. In Lahoul, although I had a spring in the summer, which meant a lot of hard work carrying water, in the winter I had to melt snow. Melting snow is quite something because a huge tin of snow gives you a tiny amount of water. Of course, there were other compensations. I mean, the tremendous vibrations of the place and simplicity of the living, so I didn't mind the hardships. It didn't get me down, but looking back, I can see how hard it was. There were times when I got completely snowed in for a week and had to tunnel my way out.[23]

The hardships of Tenzin Palmo's way of life were not without their benefit and in fact yielded profound lessons for her.

I remember one May when the undersoil had ceased to be frozen, but it was still snowing very hard. The snow was coming in and the cave was dripping in all directions and really wet; on top of that for some reason my health was not very good. I thought, "Oh dear, maybe what they say about living in caves is really true," and I was beginning to feel down. Then I thought, "But didn't the Buddha say something about Dukkha in Samsara? Why are you still looking for happiness in Samsara?" and my mind just changed round. It was like, "That's right. Samsara is Dukkha. It's OK that it's raining. It's OK that I'm sick because that's the nature of Samsara. There's nothing to worry about. If it goes well that's nice. If it doesn't go well that's also nice. It doesn't make any difference." Although it sounds quite elementary, at the time it was quite a breakthrough. Since then I have honestly never really cared about external circumstances. In that way the cave was a great teaching.[24]

RETREATS IN THE WEST

It may be difficult for us to see how the practice of retreat, in its classical form, could be transplanted into the West. Leaving job and family for months or even years at a time would seem beyond the realm of possibility for most people. Should one be interested in doing so, the financial resources that would need to be mobilized are not small. Unlike Tibetans, few Westerners could survive a long period living in an unheated cave, exposed to the vagaries of the weather, subsisting on a bag of grain and whatever plant life they could forage nearby. Even the somewhat more supported situation of Tenzin Palmo would be beyond the capabilities of most Western practitioners. Most would require warm, dry housing, a reliable supply of fresh food, means to heat their retreat facility and to cook their food, some access to medical treatment if necessary, and so on.

447

In spite of these obstacles, however, more and more Western practitioners are managing to find the time and the means of practicing meditation in retreat. In fact, retreat practice is rapidly becoming an important staple of the Western practice of Tibetan Buddhism. Serious practitioners, particularly of the Nyingma and Kagyü lineages, are well aware of the importance of retreat in their practice life, and many include some kind of solitary meditation in their annual calendar. Indeed, in order to move through the traditional itinerary of meditation practices made available by one's teachers, beginning with ngöndro, a certain amount of retreat practice would seem essential. In addition, as mentioned, many of the more advanced practices can only be carried out in retreat. In my own community, for example, it is quite common for people with families and jobs to dedicate anywhere from a week to a month or more each year to going on retreat. Although by Tibetan standards these retreats are short, a few weeks of intensive meditation on the yidam, for example, can lead one deeply into the practice. In addition, the experience of leaving one's daily life and habitual activities and engaging solely in meditation even for a few weeks can be powerfully refreshing, eye-opening, and transformative. It not only enables one to bring fresh perspectives back to one's ordinary existence, but also effects the kind of deepening of one's meditation that can be carried back into daily practice.

Increasing numbers of Western practitioners are also undertaking the traditional three-year retreat in the West. These retreats were offered to Westerners initially by Kalu Rinpoche, the late Shangpa Kagyü master. At the present time, there are a number of retreat centers in both North America and Europe where one can carry out this retreat. In this practice, one trains in the same kinds of meditations followed by tülkus in their traditional training. These include a large number of sadhanas, yoga practices, and also the formless practices.

In recent times, an important modification has occurred in this traditional retreat format. Many practitioners have found it extremely difficult to save at one time the total amount of money needed for a full three-year, three-month, three-day retreat. Also, the impact on jobs and family of such an extended absence has been found to be difficult and

FIGURE 17.1 *Ven. Kalu Rinpoche, a Kagyü meditation master and one of the most influential Tibetan lamas to have taught in the West.*

destabilizing. Given these facts, some teachers have authorized dividing the three-year retreat into segments, so that one does one year or even six months at a time, returns to job and family for a period, then does another segment. Retreatants have found it difficult to go back and forth between the world and retreat in such a manner, but also powerful and transformative in its own way. Although such modifications as these are beginning to be offered, most Westerners carrying out this retreat continue to do it in the traditional format, all in one continuous period.

As an illustration of the possibilities and experiences of doing three-year retreats in the West, I offer the following account of my friend Jenny Bondurant, who, together with her husband, Brendt, recently undertook this practice.

Jenny's Account

"In 1987 my guru, Chögyam Trungpa, died. His death brought with it a feeling of loss and also a sense of urgency to understand and follow his teachings more profoundly. Although I had been practicing meditation for many years, I felt the need for more extended meditation practice. One time he said that when one encounters the dharma, it is like going into an excellent restaurant and reading the menu. The menu is so good that one can confuse it for the real thing, and it is only when one begins to eat the meal that one realizes that the menu was only the menu. With the death of Trungpa Rinpoche, I felt that the time for accumulating was over. Two years later my husband's father died, and this brought a further sense of the transitory quality of life. It was time to start eating the meal before time ran out.

"In 1990, my husband and I attended a two-month retreat offered at Gampo Abbey, located in Cape Breton in northern Nova Scotia, in a remote area by the sea. We subsequently learned that the first three-year retreat to be offered by the Abbey would begin a year later. This was to be a traditional retreat, along the lines of the retreat that was the training ground for lamas in the Kagyü lineage. The same practices would be taught here, but the texts were being translated into English, and this would be the first time that Westerners could undertake this long retreat without first having to learn Tibetan. The retreat was to be under the direction of the Very Venerable Thrangu Rinpoche, a close dharma brother of Trungpa Rinpoche and one of the foremost teachers in the Kagyü lineage. Thrangu Rinpoche wanted to continue the style of teaching that Trungpa Rinpoche had adopted in the West, making the most profound teachings available to lay practitioners who could mix the teachings with being in the world. So instead of the traditional Tibetan three-year format, this retreat would continue for double that amount of time, with six months of each year in retreat and six months in the world.

"When my husband and I undertook the two-month retreat at Gampo Abbey, entering into the three-year retreat was the furthest thing from our minds. Two months seemed like such a long time! I had never been a particularly diligent practitioner and normally found the matter of meditation quite arduous. However, I settled down during the two months and gradually found myself longing to continue.

"At the end of the two-month retreat, it was suggested that my husband and I join the three-year retreat. Although it seemed outrageously impractical, I could not sleep with excitement, and we decided that we would work things out so that we could take part. However, when we returned to our ordinary lives, and the practical realities of our lives began to reassert themselves, we changed our minds and decided to postpone it until the following retreat, six years later. My husband returned to his work, and I was offered an excellent new job. The morning my job began, I was putting on my makeup and my husband was meditating before going to work. He came out of our shrine room and said, "I think we should go on retreat." My response was immediate: "Yes!"

"There were many apparent obstacles and many things to work out. For example, my husband's teenage son—my beloved stepson—had been spending summers with us and the rest of the year with his mother. We were able to restructure things so that for the six months of each year that we were in retreat, he stayed with his mother, and in our six-month period "in the world," he would stay with us. Finally, this and the other arrangements necessary for us to do the retreat fell into place.

"A year after our two-month retreat, we returned to Gampo Abbey and to the new three-year retreat center, built on the edge of a windswept cliff, overlooking the Gulf of Saint Lawrence. The abbey and its retreat facility were fifty miles and a world away from the nearest village, at the end of the road: a place of wild beauty with vast skies and water, shared with golden eagles, ravens, and the whales. In winter, ice floes brought in by the Labrador current cover the water from distant horizon to the shore. In spring, the ice breaks up and gives way once more to the open ocean with its waves and endless swells. Again the moods of the sea return, sometimes gentle and sometimes ferocious, and one is witness again to the life of the deep, to the birds, the leaping fish, and the huge pods of whales that swim and feed and play with their young. The retreat center is called Söpa Chöling, or Dharma Place of Patience.

"The Söpa Chöling retreat building is surrounded on three sides by a fence and on the fourth by high cliffs dropping down to the water below. For the duration of the retreat, practitioners do not go outside this boundary. There are no phone calls, and mail is delivered once every two weeks, at which time we can send out a maximum of two letters. Everyone takes temporary monastic vows for the time spent in retreat, which along with abstaining from killing, stealing, and lying, also include refraining from alcohol and sexual relations. Each participant lives alone in a small room. Practice begins at 4:00 A.M. each day and finishes at 8:00 P.M., with the schedule built—as in the classical tradition—around four meditation sessions of three to four hours in length. Times in between the sessions are given to meals, eaten alone in our rooms, and to one period of work assignments. We were to remain sitting even while sleeping—there being no beds, only a rectangular box in which we meditated— although we could lean back against the wall and stretch out our legs. Depending on which practice we were engaged in, we would be in total silence, or in "functional talking," meaning that we could talk when we needed to convey some practical information, but no unnecessary chatting was allowed.

"The retreat building has two wings—one for eight men and the other for eight women—and the two groups are mostly separate, coming together every two weeks for a day of group practice. When each six-month section of the retreat began, I would say goodbye to my husband, and the door between the two wings would close. This part was always difficult. But when I entered the door to my nine-by-nine-foot room where I would spend most of the next six months alone, there was always a feeling of profound peace, and 'coming home' on a primordial level. Six months was such a long period, so timeless. I was just there and could settle down.

"Before we entered the retreat, the schedule, the silence, sleeping in sitting posture all seemed monumentally daunting. But it very quickly became apparent that this discipline was an invitation rather than a denial, and it allowed us immense freedom to explore. I, who can't even sleep sitting up on airplanes, was in a state of panic before the retreat about sleeping sitting upright for six months. However, the first night of the retreat, with a comfortable array of support cushions, I fell asleep immediately and did not awaken until the sound of the gong roused me at 4:00 A.M. to begin practice. Sleep was not quite so deep, and as time went on, there was a sense of maintaining some thread of awareness of practice during the night, which was extremely powerful.

"At the beginning of the retreat, we all agreed that we would not tell each other about our practice experiences, in order to remove the ground for comparison. Even to hear 'I had a great practice session' when one was struggling merely to stay awake, or 'I had a really rough one' when one was experiencing great stability, would feed the flames of inadequacy, pride, or whatever our habitual states of mind were. I found this to be very helpful. With no outside reference point, I began to trust my own connection rather than trying to find the way through to what I thought was the 'right way' to proceed. How one worked with one's mind and approached one's practice was so intensely personal.

"My love of sleep and being in a dreamy kind of state was very compelling. At times I struggled, and at times I gave in. If I gave in too much, my mind just felt mushy and somewhat degraded, and if I was too rigid, I would just be uptight and engaged in struggle. Either way was quite painful, but it felt very good to explore how to work with my mind in my own way. Sometimes I would take blissful little naps in the middle of practice and awake and be totally present. In Vajrayana Buddhism, the awakened state of mind is described as a mandala, and there are different gates suitable for different types of practitioners through which to enter. For the first time in my life as a Buddhist, I felt completely empowered to explore and find my own gate rather than trying to squeeze through an entrance that didn't fit.

"I came to find the discipline, rather than being punitive, a wonderful support, and I began to discover a love of practice. As time went on, the teachings became more and more accessible, and it was like discovering the truth of the dharma from the inside rather than through the intellectual process. The aroma of the meal was beginning to permeate one's being.

"Of course a meal has many flavors. Confused emotions can arise with ferocious intensity out of a clear blue sky. I remember very peaceful and profound meditation sessions and feeling that some level of neurosis had been permanently transcended. At the end of the session, however, I would leave my room and wham! There was the situation most guaranteed to irritate me in the most immediate way.

"During each six-month retreat, we would have just one day off when there were no wake-up gongs to begin meditation and the schedule was totally open. I remember looking forward so much to this one free day, when I could sleep in. Usually I would be ready for sleep the moment the last meditation session of the day ended so that I could sleep long enough to wake up again at 4:00 A.M. to resume practice. On this occasion, on the night before 'day off,' I stayed up late, walking outside and looking at the stars in celebration and anticipation of the coming morning when I could sleep in and have a luxurious, unstructured day.

"The next morning, however, I was awakened at 4:00 A.M. by the sound of the morning gong ringing! Why? Rage! Was someone feeling so sanctimonious that they wanted us all to practice on Day Off? I was so angry that I couldn't go back to sleep, and my whole day was spent in a state of exhaustion. My mind was wild with projections, but of course it was just someone whose job it was that week to awaken the rest of us, who did not share my fixation on sleep, and who forgot in the groggy space of 4:00 A.M. that it was day off.

"Of the eight men and eight women, there was no one in charge, and so we arrived at decisions by consensus. What would have been minor and inconsequential decisions in the middle of a fast-paced, complex everyday life 'in the world' could loom large indeed in the spacious sky of retreat. At the beginning, when decisions needed to be made, I just assumed that my commonsense view would be the prevailing one, and it was with total shock that I realized that my view was not shared at all! In fact, there were usually as many divergent views as there were people involved in the deliberations. I think that the two sides, the men's and the women's, probably had a different way of working with this process. On the women's side, at the beginning, there was a lot of communication. In times of silence, this was done by notes, and the silence would be broken by the furious scratching of pen on paper. Each note could inspire the response of a further note, the mental composition of which could overtake an entire meditation session.

"I began to notice that my attempts to clarify or convince seldom had the desired result and generally caused a proliferation of more confusion and irresolution. At one point I pasted a note to myself on the inside of my door which said, 'DON'T DO IT!'—hoping it would catch me before I hurled myself off once again. Someone else had the brilliant idea, probably born of exhaustion, to post a sheet of paper that described the decision to be made, and three columns to choose between: 'Yes,' 'No,' and 'DRM.' DRM meant 'Doesn't Really Matter,' and this became the most frequently used column. There was a lot more relaxation and a lot less paper used up.

"The other alternative to a group three-year retreat, which was followed in Tibet and is also available at some centers in the West, is to practice in total solitude. There were times when I longed for this, as I believe many of us did. How wonderful to be without the irritation of one's neighbors!

"At the same time, Tibetan teachers often prefer to see their students in group retreat situations. I heard about a group of retreatants who had finished a three-year retreat with only minimal interaction with one another and had decided to continue in that mode for the rest of their lives. They were dismayed when their retreat master told them that they had to come out of solitude each day to eat their meals together. When they complained he looked at them in astonishment and said, 'How can you possibly become enlightened without other people?'

"Certainly when interacting with others our projections and neuroses are constantly in our faces, and this is considered essential grist for the mill of practice. Our defenses are thick, our self-deception is quick to arise, and our blind spots are truly blind! Without one another, we could easily remain oblivious to the tenacity of our habitual patterns, believing that in the space and solitude of practice, they had dissolved. So the interactions with others in our group retreat situation, painful though they might be, help keep one's feet on the ground and undercut the more grandiose fantasies about one's accomplishments. But apart from this rather painful benefit that we provided to one another— indeed probably inseparable from it—one found an enormous support and energy from group practice, with deep, lasting friendships and camaraderie.

"So much of the time is spent alone, and one goes through so many moods—sometimes I would sit on my cushion, rocking in silent laughter, and sometimes I would cry for hours, remembering someone's fragility, or my own. I remembered seeing my father crying after my mother died, or his face like a child's, waving goodbye as my train pulled out of the station in England, taking me back to America. I thought of my husband and my stepson, and longed to be with them. So many memories of the past, of loved ones, haunted by the times my heart was shut down. Retreat was stripping off the layers and there was so much tenderness.

"When extreme emotions arise on retreat, there is no antidote or escape as there is in ordinary life. There are no movies, novels, TV, no allies to commiserate with, or distractions of any kind. So experience is very vivid and direct. There is no way out but just to sit with whatever arises. One can't stop it or change it into something else. Being willing to let it just be is a crucial turning point. The story line is constantly spinning in order to avoid just being here. When there is a gap in the story line, there is enormous energy and fresh air.

"In a sadhana written by Trungpa Rinpoche, 'the sadhana of mahamudra,' there is a line: 'Happy and sad, all thoughts vanish into emptiness, like the imprint of a bird in the sky.' Sad thoughts can be excruciating, and happy thoughts exhilarating, but all thoughts vanish into emptiness like the track of a bird in flight. Over time, the solidity of thoughts gives way, and there is a thread that begins to permeate the various highlights, moods, and dramas of one's identity. It is coming home to utter simplicity; to what has always been there. It cannot be described because that puts it in the realm of imagination and concept rather than the primordial place from which everything arises. But by knowing that place, whatever arises from it is seen as the realm of the sacred.

"A glimpse of this, pointed out by the Guru, can be earth-shattering in profundity, but trying to grasp on to this brief experience is as ephemeral as trying to grasp onto mist. The path of meditation stabilizes and extends this glimpse. Sitting on my cushion, looking out of my window, all I could see was endless sky and water and the changing complexion of the clouds and the sea. I felt such an immense gratitude to the lineage of teachers who had mixed their minds with vast space and brought these teachings to us. I also felt a kinship with all the meditation practitioners throughout time who had dug their own ditches, climbed their own mountains, and sung songs filled with longing, joy, and devotion to their gurus for showing the way.

"The Buddhist teachings talk of discovering wisdom from within, and this is a process of shedding layers rather than attaining something that one did not already possess. The natural state of mind is intrinsically good and compassionate, and also beyond any personal sense of achievement. It just is. It can't be increased or diminished, but it can be overlooked. And in the speed of conventional life, it usually is. Growing up in a culture that emphasizes original sin as our ground, we all tend to focus on that as the basic condition of our lives. It is a subtle but enormous shift, then, to glimpse that the basis is profoundly open, sane, and vast like the ocean, and that the surface of pettiness and grasping, while extremely vivid and compelling, is in fact fleeting, transparent, and insubstantial as an ocean wave.

"I remember sitting on my meditation cushion for the last practice session before the gates opened at the end of the last six-month section of retreat that I did. My husband and I still had two six-month sessions ahead of us. I felt the exhilarating excitement of rejoining my husband and reentering the world, and at the same time a feeling that I could sit on my cushion forever. There was such profound appreciation and sense of well-being, and also the realization that this moment might never return.

"The gong rang, the gates opened, and we reentered the world. We discovered that our boy was navigating through some very difficult rapids of adolescence and needed us to stay rather than return for our next six-month session. Although this was a difficult time for all of us, there was never a question of continuing on retreat at that time. It was definitely a time to stay home and to reenter the world wholeheartedly. Our son needed stability, and it was a wonderful time for my husband and me to be with him during the remainder of his growing up.

"Up until now, between retreats, I had done various temporary jobs, but now it was clearly time to reestablish some kind of stable livelihood. With years of practice shredding any semblance of a reasonable résumé, I had no idea what to do. However, I had always been passionate about houses, and despite the dim prognosis for realtors being able to make a living during their first few years of business, I decided to become a realtor. To my surprise, my business was immediately very successful and very enjoyable. In meditation, there are practices without form and practices with very intense form. Now was the time to practice in the world with form. The phenomenal world was intense, but for the first time in my life, I felt completely at home in the world, certainly an unexpected development after so much time in retreat.

"It is almost five years since we left retreat the last time. Our son is now a wonderful young man exploring his own path in the world. It is time again for retreat. My husband and I are building a home in the mountains of Colorado, near Rocky Mountain Shambhala Center, the place where my Buddhist journey began almost twenty years ago. Thrangu Rinpoche, our preceptor for the three-year retreat, recently came and blessed our home as a place for us to continue practice, and named it Tsöndru Chöling, "Dharma Place of Exertion." It is our intention to finish the three-year retreat here and then continue with long retreats each year, interspersed with periods 'in the world,' for the rest of our lives.

"The meditative journey gradually teaches us how to ride the wild waves of mind, which are inseparable from the still, fathomless ocean depths. I see the example of my teachers—how they live effortlessly with great joy and humor, boundless compassion, and vast wisdom. I realize that being open to all sentient beings and the whole phenomenal world in this way is indeed a vast undertaking. However, this journey has been made throughout time and space by people just like us. The lineage of enlightened ones began as ordinary confused people. Milarepa had accumulated great negative karma for himself, Marpa was arrogant, and all began their journey believing in their own projections. It is a sacred path, and although it is undertaken alone, it is only possible through the enormous kindness and guidance of those who have traveled this way before. For me, retreat is the beginning of this journey, of relaxing and making friends with myself, and gaining trust and confidence that I can progress further. Enjoying the entire, vast feast of dharma is the project of many lifetimes, but beginning to enjoy the actual meal has made for a wonderful beginning."

CONCLUSION

It is true that the restrictions, disciplines, and rigors of the retreat situation are necessary to the cultivation of the abiding awareness of the buddha-mind within. Nevertheless, in Tibetan Buddhism, the classical practice of retreat is not seen as an end in itself, but rather as a method for developing an awareness that is not dependent on the physical isolation of the actual retreat situation. The goal, as we have seen, is to develop a "retreat mind" that carries over after one has returned to the world and again taken up the occupations and busyness of daily life. If one can engage in the activities of ordinary life and remain in touch with the stillness and warmth of the deeper mind, then the retreat practice has achieved its goal. Certainly, when one meets realized Tibetan teachers, one feels such an accomplishment. In fact, it is often through experiencing the extraordinary state of mind of such people, as they teach and move about their lives, that one is inspired to enter into the practice of retreat.

The teaching that the purpose of retreat is only fulfilled when one can be in the world with a "mind of retreat" is already found in the Indian tradition, in a story told about the "grandfather of the siddhas," the great master Saraha. As told in the *Lives of the Eighty-four Siddhas*,[25] Saraha was in retreat with his wife, a young woman of awakened insight. At one point, he asked her to make a radish curry. While she was preparing it, he went into an extended samadhi. The radish curry went bad, and his wife threw it out and waited. Saraha remained in samadhi for twelve years. When he finally emerged, he asked his wife, "Where is my radish curry?" She replied, "For twelve years you did not rise from your samadhi. Where did you think it would be? The spring has long since passed, and radishes are no longer in season." Saraha retorted, "Fine! Then I will go into the mountains to meditate!" His wife countered, "Mere isolation of the body is not true solitude. Removing oneself from mental concepts and judgments is the highest solitude that one can attain. Although you dwelled in samadhi for twelve years, you have obviously not been able to separate yourself from the mental concept and judgment of 'radish curry.' Since that is the case, what possible benefit could there possibly be in going into the mountains?" Upon receiving this instruction from his wife, we are told, Saraha abandoned concepts and judgments and put into practice the primordial nature. In so doing, he attained the supreme siddhi of mahamudra and was able to make himself most useful to sentient beings.[26]

This important principle that the true meaning of retreat transcends the physical retreat situation is found, again, in the life of Shabkar. One day, the yogin had crossed his retreat boundaries and was taking a walk. One of his yogin companions saw him and said, "Heh! You're supposed to be in retreat in your cave. Have you come out?" Shabkar playfully responded:

> Fortunate friend,
> Listen without distraction.
> For the yogin of the most secret Great Perfection
> There is no leaving of retreat,
> Neither is there any entering.
> In the simplicity that is beyond concepts,
> There is no crossing of boundaries.
> With all this formal entering and leaving
> One cannot really be called a retreatant.
>
> My way of doing retreat is this:
> In the retreat hut that is my own body
> Endowed with the six characteristics,
> With the three pure vows
> I sweep away the dirt—negative actions of the three doors;

In the stream of the four initiations,
I wash away all defilements.

Seated on my cushion—
The fundamental consciousness,
Coarse and subtle thoughts—
I, the yogin of awareness
That is itself brilliant and cognizant,
Remain in the retreat
That is the uncontrived natural state.

Freed from discursive thoughts,
Staying within the limits
Of naturally abiding meditation,
Fearing visitors—mental dullness and wildness—
I mark my retreat boundaries
With the poles of undistracted mindfulness. . . .

In the vastness of awareness,
Without any separation into sessions of practice,
For a yogin, practice is relaxed and at ease—
And the yogin is content. . . .

As for the duration of such a retreat:
When at death, the net of the body is finally torn apart,
And one is freed in the clear light of the dharmakaya,
One could call that "taking down the boundaries of one's
    retreat."

The virtuous practice of such life long retreat,
Beyond fixed periods,
Was the way of great yogins of the past.

Ha! Ha!
Having done no such things myself,
I've just been joking![27]

18

The Passing of a Realized Master

In Tibetan Buddhism, the passing of a realized person—called his or her *parinirvana*, or "full enlightenment"—is regarded as a sacred and telling event. The period leading up to the moment of death is often marked by various unusual events and signs. The death itself typically occurs in a prescribed way, with the teacher entering into meditation and passing away in that manner. And the atmosphere around the passing and subsequent cremation offer many opportunities for experiencing the realization of the master, the depth of his teachings, and the inspiration, commitment, and ongoing vitality of those who loved and revered him. In Tibet, the death of a master represented a confirmation of his attainment and sanctity, and was also regarded as one of his greatest teachings. Therefore, although death was a time of grief and mourning, it was at the same time an occasion for celebrating the master's person and his lineage, and praying for its continuation.

THE PASSING OF REALIZED MASTERS

When a great bodhisattva is going through the death process, because of his realization it is said that he has no particular attachment to this life. Because he is not attached to this life, the prospect of death holds no particular fear. When the sixteenth Gyalwang Karmapa, head of the Kagyü order, was in the final days of dying of cancer, Ösel Tenzin, the Regent of Trungpa Rinpoche, was sitting by his bedside. Tenzin was expressing his grief at the imminent passing of this beloved teacher who had meant so much to him. The Karmapa looked at him with compassion, stroked his head tenderly, and said, "You know, when you die, nothing happens." From the Karmapa's point of view, his own death represented no particular highlight and nothing noteworthy. It was just another moment of discontinuity, like all the others.

Tradition says, as we saw above, that the highly attained bodhisattva follows the death process, including both the outer and the inner dissolutions, in full consciousness. With willingness and awareness, he progressively lets go of his sense perceptions and his concepts. According to the classical form, as the moment of death approaches, he sits upright in meditation posture, crosses his legs, and enters into samadhi. At the moment of death, he enters the ground luminosity, the vast and liberated space of dharmakaya (see chapter 14).

Were it not for an additional factor in his karmic stream, his round of rebirths would be over. The reason is that a realized master does not possess the same motivation for taking rebirth as an ordinary, unenlightened person. Because he sees the futility of samsaric ideals and pursuits and has gained insight into the nonexistence of self, after death he is no longer driven by the winds of karma to take rebirth in one of the six realms. This means that without some intervening cause, at death his five skandhas would dissolve and his mental continuum would come to an end. Like an arhant who has abandoned samsara and realized *anatman,* or absence of self, he would disappear into the realm of reality or dharmadhatu, about which nothing can be said.

However, as a Mahayanist, the realized person has taken the bodhisattva vow. This means that he has made a commitment to be reborn over and over within the realms of samsara in order to benefit beings. The bodhisattva vow acts as a powerful force to extend indefinitely the existence of his mental continuum. The vow functions as a binding factor that holds his five skandhas together beyond the moment when realization would have been expected and dissolved them into space. Thus it is that when the master dies, his consciousness does not enter the dharmakaya for good. Instead, it dwells in the dharmakaya, awaiting the moment of his rebirth as dictated by his vows. Then the bodhisattva's consciousness is drawn downward toward samsaric beings out of mercy and love. With unbroken awareness, it is said, he enters the realm of the sambhogakaya and finally approaches the place of his new life, incarnating in the womb of his mother-to-be.

It may be asked, if the realized bodhisattva is no longer blindly driven by his or her karma to take rebirth in a particular realm, then what determines where and under what conditions that rebirth will occur? Put simply, the bodhisattva will be reborn depending upon his general and specific commitments to serve others. In Tibet, as we have seen, this meant that a realized person would not only continue to be reborn but that he or she would typically take rebirth in a dharmic region in order to continue to teach and to serve others.

Trungpa Rinpoche remarked that sometimes a bodhisattva would find himself in a situation where there were no students or where such students as there were had no interest in the dharma or in receiving teachings. In such cases—and he knew of several himself—the teacher would die at a young age. Having no personal interest in his own continuity and having no object for his compassion, he would simply pass away.

The passing of the tenth Trungpa Tülku, the predecessor of Chögyam Trungpa Rinpoche, provides an apt example of the classical tradition of the death of a realized master.[1] In 1938, in the residence of a local lord in a village within the Kham district of East Tibet, the tenth Trungpa died. The Trungpa Tülku was the spiritual and political head of the Surmang district, a political entity of about ten thousand families within the larger kingdom of Nangchen. Previously the tenth Trungpa had had indications that his life was drawing to a close. One day, for example, he had a dream that he was a young child and that his mother was wearing the style of headdress peculiar to northeastern Tibet. Later he made indirect reference to his own impending death. When a new robe was being made for him, he told his secretary that it should be a small one; on being asked why, he turned it away as a joke. In 1938, the tenth Trungpa was invited to visit one of the King of Lhatog's ministers. He accepted, replying that he might have to ask him to be one of the most important hosts of his lifetime. On the morning of the day of his arrival, the full moon day, he had commented to one of his chief attendants that he wondered what it would be like to be a baby again and to have the experiences of a small child once more. He arrived in a very happy mood but did what was for him an unusual thing: he took off his socks and overrobe and, turning to the monks, told them to prepare for a very special rite. A meal was served, but he did not feel inclined to eat and, having said the meal chant, he told them to put the food before the shrine.

After the meal, the customary closing chants were recited. Then the tenth Trungpa lay down, saying, "This is the end of action." These were his last words. Lifting himself up in meditation posture, he closed his eyes and entered into samadhi. After some time, his monks concluded that he must be in a coma, and one doctor among them, following traditional Tibetan medical practice, drew some blood and burned some herbs in an attempt to revive him. But his blood was congealed and would not flow, and it seemed as if his body had been dead for some time. It was later noted that the fifteenth Karmapa, who had recognized the tenth Trungpa when he was just a baby, had predicted that he would live until sixty-six, the precise age at which he died.

The death of the tenth Trungpa exemplifies the classical pattern of the death of realized masters in Tibet, including predictions made earlier in life, omens of impending death, the teacher's own realization of the approach of his passing, his attempts to gently prepare his close attendants, and the extraordinary manner in which he passes from this life.

THE PASSING OF HIS HOLINESS THE SIXTEENTH KARMAPA

The tradition of the way in which accomplished people die in Tibet raises some intriguing questions. What would it have been like to be present when a realized teacher passes away? What would have been one's experiences and impressions? Beyond this, to what extent is this element of Tibetan Buddhism dependent upon the traditional Tibetan

FIGURE 18.1 *H. H. the sixteenth Gyalwang Karmapa.*

context? Is it something that could translate into a Western environ-ment? And if it could, how might a Westerner experience that?

Some interesting answers to these questions are provided by the fol-lowing interview describing the passing of His Holiness Rangjung Rikpe Dorje, the sixteenth Gyalwang Karmapa, in 1981 in a cancer hospital in Zion, Illinois. The interview was conducted immediately after His Holiness' passing with Dr. Mitchell Levy, a Buddhist and physician to His Holiness in his final illness. It has an urgent, vivid quality, owing partly to the fact that it took place the afternoon Dr. Levy arrived back home in Boulder, Colorado, before he had had time to catch his first full night of sleep since His Holiness began failing. I have edited out my own questions and rearranged the text in chronological order. Otherwise the content and the words are just as they occurred in 1981.

Dr. Levy's Account

THE EARLY ILLNESS

"I first saw His Holiness in May of 1980. Now he had cancer and had come to America to get worked on and to see if he had any further cancer in his body. His cancer was on top of serious diabetes, which he had had much of his life. I was engaged as his primary physician at that time.

"When he arrived, we did a full workup on him. That was somewhat uneventful. A few things do stick out in my mind about that period. First of all, there was a thread that began here and ran through all the rest of my contact with him as physician. There was nothing other than a feeling of business as usual from His Holiness' point of view. This was just another experience, and this happened to be an experience of finding out whether his cancer was going to kill him or not. But, in a way, to him, it didn't make any difference one way or the other. You could have been talking about chicken soup.

"From this time until the moment when he died the next year, there was always this thread of basic and tremendously overwhelming presence. His warmth and the clarity of his own mind through all these experiences were unfailing. It was very simple. I would say, 'Do you have this pain or do you have that pain?' And we would get rather complex with our questions. Almost inevitably, our line of questions led to a lot of smiling on his part, and the response, 'No, no, there is nothing.' Then we would say, 'Well, how about . . . ?' and he would say, 'No,' and we would say, 'Well, how about . . . ?' and he would say, 'No.'

"We were always running into this kind of vastness of his state of mind. He was never willing to narrow things down and focus on himself. It is sort of like when you have questions about your meditation experience and you have the same feeling of just spinning your wheels. And he smiles at you. Well, the same thing would happen when we said, 'Are you in pain? Are you having discomfort after eating?' We would run into that same vast space.

"I think that that was very much a teaching situation for the medical people taking care of him. All of us, Buddhists and non-Buddhists alike, saw that there was no end point for His Holiness even in medicine, in bodily things. It wasn't, 'Yes, now you have hit upon it. That is where I have my pain.' We never got to that. So we would be frustrated and awed at the same time. The way he approaches his own death is just another tool for working with others and trying to help them. I think this was a commonly shared experience among all of us taking care of him: wonderment and also confusion about why he wasn't following what we thought he should be doing, and amazement at his warmth and concern for others, no matter what was happening to him. This was the thread that ran up until the moment he died.

"The same day we did the workup, later we went in and had a meeting with His Holiness. I started to ask him the same sort of questions, and he would keep smiling and saying no or yes to certain of them. Finally, at the end, he said to me, 'There is one thing that is very important for you to understand. If I am needed here to teach sentient beings, if I still have work to do here, then no disease will ever be able to overcome me. And if I am no longer really required to teach sentient beings, then you can tie me down, and I will not stay on this earth.' This was certainly an interesting way to get introduced to one's patient.

HONG KONG

"The second time I saw His Holiness was in Hong Kong a number of months later. The first thing that impressed me was how much more weight he had lost and how much weaker and sicker he was, and also, at the same time, how he hadn't changed at all, in terms of his presence and his warmth.

"There was still this person lying in this bed who was absolutely dying of cancer, and he looked like he could have been there for a tonsillectomy. Every time I would walk into the room, he would smile and light up, and my mind would stop. And I would think, 'Wait a minute, who is taking care of whom here? He is supposed to be sick, not me.' And I started to want to go, 'Well, uh, here's what happened to me yesterday.'

"So, instead, I would look at him and say, 'How are you today?' And he would smile and say, 'I'm okay.' And then I'd say, 'Well, are you having any pain?' And he would laugh and say, 'No. Not today.'

"This sort of became an ongoing joke of 'You have to look at me like I am sick, so go ahead and do your job. You know, and we will both pretend, that this is what is really happening.'

"This began to affect the nursing staff as well, because you have a fixed idea of what a sick, dying patient should be like, and he never would do it. He would always lie there and people would feel totally uncomfortable that they couldn't help this 'poor invalid person.' And this is the way it happened over and over again. He was just there doing what needed to be done for everybody else.

"What came out of my experiences in Hong Kong was the realization that His Holiness' state of mind was fundamentally unchangeable and that he was continually helping those around him. He was especially helping the four young tülkus [in their teens and early twenties] who were with him, the Rinpoches whom he had been training at his monastery in Sikkim since their childhood. His Holiness was helping them to accept what was going on.

"When I got to Hong Kong, I began to ask myself, 'Why is he dying now?' And I began to watch the way he dealt with the younger tülkus. He had brought up the four major Kagyü tülkus, and for some reason it turned out that they were all the same age and ready to go out now and teach in the world. He was their daddy, in some real sense, and he had brought them up to this point, and now this was another step in their education, the fact that he was dying. There was something that felt to me very right about the whole thing. To me, in many ways, he had fulfilled his life work. But this may be just my own simple-minded view.

"The younger tülkus would say to me, 'Oh, he has so much else to do, this thing and that thing.' And I would think that if he lived another fifteen years, he would start more projects, and at the end of fifteen years they would still say, 'How could he die now?' You could never imagine His Holiness retiring. And so I really felt the consistency of the whole thing: he had very much brought the tülkus up to the point where they were ready to go out into the world, and now he was exposing them to death.

"Trungpa Rinpoche said something that made sense to me, later, when the younger tülkus were having such a hard time. He said, 'Well, if we were living in Tibet, we would see death all the time. A real charnel-ground quality. Even at a young age. On the other hand, having grown up at His Holiness' monastery at Rumtek [Sikkim], and now having been exposed to the West, they are not that familiar with death.'

"And now, given that it was His Holiness himself who was dying, they were initially unable to reconcile that for themselves. And in many ways, it felt as if he were teaching them about death. I couldn't help but feel that he was letting his own death be drawn out so that they could just slowly come to grips with it and watch the process and explore it, so that they could digest it later on.

"And that is also what impressed me in my experiences with His Holiness in Zion, Illinois, where he finally died. I saw His Holiness' presence and realized how he was taking care of the tülkus. They were young, and they might have had varying degrees of realization, but still, emotionally and chronologically, in terms of living in the world, they were young. And so this was part of their own growth process.

ZION, ILLINOIS

"The third time I saw His Holiness was near Chicago, in a cancer hospital in Zion, Illinois, at the time when he died. People there—the hospital staff as well as visitors—were just completely overwhelmed by him. To appreciate this, you have to keep in mind that ICU [intensive care unit] personnel are typically quite jaded. They see death all the time, and this is their work—and the reason they are good is that they aren't too affected by it, they can 'take care of business.'

"So to see a staff like that be so overwhelmed by His Holiness' gentleness was very impressive. And that is what happened. Most of them were Christian, and none of them knew the first thing about Buddhism, but they had no hesitancy whatever in calling him His Holiness. They never once said, 'Karmapa,' it was always 'His Holiness.'

"And people, after a while, couldn't understand how he wasn't having pain or responding in the way people do in his situation. Then they began to just feel so much concern about taking care of him.

"As you know, each Karmapa is supposed to write a letter before he dies, indicating the circumstances of his next birth. The staff expressed concern about the letter. And it was so amazing to see, because, you see, everybody's concern switched from 'What are we going to do for this patient today?' and 'Did you give him his bath?' to *'Did he write his letter? Is this lineage going to continue?'*

"They had a nurse in the intensive care unit who came to me one day with tears in her eyes and said, 'I am so worried that this lineage is going to end here in this hospital.' I mean, mind you, we were in Zion, Illinois. It's a dry town. It is very traditionally Christian. So, to me, it was very moving to see how completely they were taken with His Holiness.

"The staff couldn't stop talking about his compassion and about how kind he seemed. After four or five days, the surgeon—a Filipino Christian—came up to me and he said, 'You know, every time I go in to see His Holiness, I feel like I am naked and that he sees me completely and I feel like I should cover myself up.'

"He kept saying to me, 'You know, His Holiness is not an ordinary man. He really doesn't seem like an ordinary person.' And everybody kept having that experience before his final days. Just the force of his will and his presence were so powerful, that they were completely taken with it.

"This was a continuation of what I had experienced in New York, which was that he just kept going, and whether he was in shock or eating grapes, there was some complete unchangeability about his state of mind that radiated to everybody, and no one knew how to compute it.

"His Holiness really seemed to have changed a lot of the staff of doctors and nurses. As it was, we left books for them, and beyond that, people were saying to me, 'You know, I am Christian and I don't believe in Buddhism, but I have to say that His Holiness is a very unusual person.' They said this almost apologetically, not knowing how to combine both beliefs, but so obviously and deeply touched by His Holiness.

"As the days went on, His Holiness seemed to deteriorate physically. Then he did a few things that, from what the Rinpoches were telling me, had some precedent in his life. Apparently when he was thirteen or so, when he was very ill, the doctors came to see him and said that his illness was very, very serious and that he had only a matter of hours to live, or a day at most. You have to realize that Tibetan doctors will never say something this negative as long as there is any hope. They will never say something like this until they believe that imminent death is certain. Yet His Holiness paid no attention to them, and he recovered quickly. The doctors couldn't understand how that had happened. But this was in Tibet, and it was perhaps easier for them to accept, him being His Holiness.

"But the same thing happened in Zion. One day after examining him and finding that drastic deterioration had set in, I came out and said, 'His Holiness has two hours to live, maybe three hours.' He had every symptom I have seen in that situation, and he was going downhill very rapidly. Every system was failing. He was having trouble breathing, he was vomiting up blood and coughing up blood, his blood pressure was dropping, even on blood pressure support medication.

"When you have worked with a lot of critically ill patients, you get a very definite feel when a patient is about to go. You just feel it because you see the stress their body is under, and you know that it won't be able to carry on much longer. You know they are going to collapse. And so I could just feel it.

"I said, 'We should wake him up if you feel a letter is important.'

And so I woke him up with some medication that we have that reverses some of the sleepiness.

"The tülkus said, 'Will you excuse us, now we need to talk to His Holiness in private.'

"They came out in about forty-five minutes and they said, 'Well, His Holiness said that he is not going to die yet, and he laughed at us. He laughed at us!' They said that a few times, 'He just laughed at us. And he said, 'Don't give me that pad. I am not writing any letter.'

"I walked into the room and he was sitting up in bed. Just *up*. And his eyes were wide open and the force of his will was immense, and he turned to me and said in English (of which he knew only a few phrases), 'Hello. How are you?'

"And within thirty minutes, all his vital signs got stable and to a normal level, and he stopped bleeding. I walked out after about an hour of being in the room, and one of the staff from the intensive care unit came up and he said, 'Look at my arms.' And I looked and he had goose bumps all up and down his arms. No one had ever seen anything like this in their lives. The force of his will was so strong, and he wasn't ready to die yet. I am completely convinced that he willed himself back into stability. I had never seen anything remotely resembling this, or even read or heard about such a thing.

The reaction of the young tülkus was interesting. They interpreted my telling them His Holiness was dying as me panicking. Maybe it was part of their not wanting to let His Holiness go. But I have seen enough so that I was just telling them what was going on. He was dying. I knew it. Everyone on the staff knew it. And yet, he woke up and just sat up. He literally opened his eyes and he willed himself back to health. He filled his body out with his will. Visually, I could almost see his will coming out of his body. I have never experienced anything like that. Trungpa Rinpoche later said to me, ' Now you see what is really possible.'

"It was almost as if someone had unplugged the monitors and fiddled with them and then plugged them back in, and they were normal. The blood pressure was normal. He stopped bleeding, but not from anything that we had given him; he just turned the whole process around. After that, he was healthy for another nine or ten days. He was completely stable.

"After this, it became a running joke in the hospital that we should let His Holiness write his own orders. We should just bring in the order book at the beginning of the day and say, 'What would you like us to do today?' The whole intensive care unit staff was saying, 'Well, what does he want done today?'

"Then about nine or ten days later, suddenly his blood pressure dropped precipitously, and we couldn't get it back up with drugs. I said, 'This is very bad.' I had gotten out of the habit of saying that he might die soon. I just looked at the tülkus and said, 'This is very bad, very, very bad.' And that is all I would say. And so they would lean over to His Holiness and say that Dr. Levy thinks it's very bad. And usually, he would smile.

"At this point, he was in DIC—disseminated intervascular coagulation. It means that there is so much infection that the bacteria, when they break apart, liberate something called endotoxin. The endotoxin in turn affects the clotting mechanism of the blood; it uses up all your ability to keep the blood clotted, so you start bleeding from everywhere.

"This is a more or less uniformly fatal event. And again I said, 'This is very bad.'

"I said it to His Holiness, and he sort of looked up and gave an attempt at a smile and, within two hours, not even two hours, he stopped bleeding completely. His blood pressure went back to normal, and he was sitting up in bed and talking.

"By this time, the intensive care unit almost had a chalk board, and everyone said, 'Chalk up another one for His Holiness.' It really became almost humorous. Given a patient with terminal cancer and diabetes and massive infection in his lungs, already recovering from shock, to go into gram negative shock, someone in that condition just doesn't come back, ever. And yet, here he was.

"Then the day after that, he went into what we call respiratory failure, which was that his lungs weren't working because he was so filled up with pneumonia. At this point it was clear that if we didn't intubate him, he was going to stop breathing. We did that, and so prolonged that for thirty-six hours.

"Then early on the day he actually died, we saw that his monitor had changed. The electrical impulses through his heart had altered in a way that indicated that it was starting to fail. And so we knew, the surgeons knew, that something was imminent. We didn't say anything to the Rinpoches.

"Then his heart stopped for about ten seconds. We resuscitated him, had a little trouble with his blood pressure, brought it back up, and then he was stable for about twenty-five minutes, thirty minutes, but it looked like he had had a heart attack. Then his blood pressure dropped all the way down. We couldn't get it back up at all with medication. And we kept working, giving him more medication, and then his heart stopped again.

"And so then we had to start pumping his chest and then, at that point, I knew that this was it. Because you could just see his heart dying in front of you on the monitor. But I felt that we needed to demonstrate our thoroughness as much as we could, to reassure the Rinpoches. So I kept the resuscitation going for almost forty-five minutes, much longer than I normally would have.

"Finally, I gave him two amps of intracardiac epinephrine and adrenaline and there was no response. Calcium. No response. So we stopped and this was the point at which we finally gave up. I went outside to make the call to Trungpa Rinpoche to tell him that His Holiness had died.

"After that, I came back into the room, and people were starting to leave. By this time, His Holiness had been lying there for maybe fifteen minutes, and we started to take out the NG tube, and as someone goes to pull the nasal gastric tube out of his nose, all of a sudden I look and his blood pressure is 140 over 80. And my first instinct, I shouted out, 'Who's leaning on the pressure monitor?' I mean, I was almost in a state of panic: *'Who's leaning on the pressure monitor?'* I said to myself, 'Oh, no, here we go again.' Because I knew that for pressure to go up like that, someone would have to be leaning on it with . . . well, it wouldn't be possible.

"Then a nurse almost literally screamed, 'He's got a good pulse! He's got a good pulse!'

"And one of the older Rinpoches slapped me on the back as if to say, 'This is impossible but it's happening!' His Holiness' heart rate was 80 and his blood pressure was 140 over 80, and there was this moment in that room where I thought that I was going to pass out.

"And no one said a word. There was literally a moment of 'This can't be. This can't be.' A lot had happened with His Holiness, but this was clearly the most miraculous thing I had seen. I mean that this was not just an extraordinary event. This would have been an hour after his heart had stopped and fifteen minutes after we had stopped doing anything.

"After this happened, I ran out of the room again to call Trungpa Rinpoche and tell him that His Holiness was alive again. 'I can't talk. Goodbye.'

"To me, in that room, it had the feeling that His Holiness was coming back to check one more time: could his body support his consciousness?' He had been on Valium and morphine, and that disconnected him from his body. It felt to me that, all of a sudden he realized his body had stopped working, so he came back in to see if it was workable. Just the force of his consciousness coming back started the whole thing up again—I mean, this is just my simple-minded impression, but this is what it actually felt like, in that room.

"His heart rate and blood pressure kept up for about five minutes, then just petered out. It felt as if he realized that it wasn't workable, that his body couldn't support him anymore, and he left, he died.

"Trungpa Rinpoche arrived at the hospital shortly after that, not knowing whether His Holiness was alive or not. So I had to tell him that he had died. And that was it. Those were his comebacks, which were very remarkable.

"Even in death, His Holiness did not cease to amaze the Western medical establishment. At forty-eight hours after his death, his chest was warm right above his heart. This was how it happened.

"Situ Rinpoche [one of the younger tülkus] took me into the room where His Holiness was lying. First I had to wash my hands completely and put a mask on. And Situ Rinpoche walks in and puts his robe over his mouth, as if even breathing might disturb the samadhi of His Holiness. And he took my hand, and he put my hand in the center of His Holiness' chest and then made me feel it, and it felt warm.

"And it's funny, because since I had washed my hands in cold water, my Western medical mind said, 'Well, my hands must still be a little cold.' So I warmed my hands up, and then I said to Situ Rinpoche, 'Could I feel his chest one more time?' He said, 'Sure,' and he pulled down His Holiness' robe and put my hand on his chest again. My hands were warm at this point, and his chest was warmer than my hand. To check, I moved my hand to either side of his chest, and it was cool. And then I felt again in the middle, and it was warm.

"I also pinched his skin, and it was still pliable and completely normal. Mind you, although there is some variation, certainly by thirty-six hours, the skin is just like dough. And after forty-eight hours, his skin was just like yours and mine. It was as if he weren't dead. I pinched his skin, and it went right back. The turgor was completely normal.

"Shortly after we left the room, the surgeon came out and said, 'He's warm. He's warm.' And then it became, the nursing staff was saying, 'Is he still warm?' After all that had happened, they just accepted it. As much as all that had happened might have gone against their medical training, their cultural beliefs, and their religious upbringing, by this point they had no trouble just accepting what was actually occurring.

"This is, of course, quite in keeping with traditional Tibetan experience, that realized people like His Holiness, after their respiration and heart have stopped [the outer dissolution], abide in a state of profound meditation for some time [the 'ground luminosity' that follows the inner dissolution; see chapter 14 for details], with rigor mortis not setting in during that period.

"One thing I should mention is the quality of the room where he was lying. The tülkus said, 'His Holiness is in samadhi' [i.e., resting in the dharmakaya of ground luminosity]. What people experienced in that room seemed to depend on varying levels of perception. I asked Trungpa Rinpoche about it. He said that when he walked into that room, it was as if a vacuum had sucked out all the mental obstacles.

There was no mental chatter. It was absolutely still. Everything was starkly simple and direct. He said that it was so one-pointed that there was no room for any kind of obstacle at all. And he said that it was absolutely magnificent.

"My experience wasn't quite like that. To me, the air felt thin and there was a quiet that was unsettling in a way. There was no familiarity, no background noise. It was like being in some other realm, one that was absolutely still and vast. It was just His Holiness' body in the center of the room, draped in his brocade robe, and you felt as if you didn't even want to breathe. That was my experience. It felt as if anything I did would disturb that stillness. My actions screamed at me. I mean, all of my coarseness and vulgarity just shouted at me.

"It felt as if in each movement I made toward his body, I was hacking away at something thick to get through it. And everything I did was clumsy. And, from a normal point of view, it wasn't. I was just walking. But there was an air of stillness and awareness in that room that was overpowering. I understood what Trungpa Rinpoche meant about vacuum, because it felt like that.

"After about three days, His Holiness' samadhi was still continuing. It was interesting, because the doctors and nurses were as concerned as the younger tülkus that we leave his body there and not move it until the samadhi ended. This was unusual, because ordinarily when someone dies, a hospital staff wants to get rid of the body as quickly as possible. That's just the way we do it in the West.

"After three days, the samadhi ended. You could tell because His Holiness was no longer warm, and rigor mortis finally set in. And also the atmosphere in the room changed, becoming more normal.

"We called the morticians to come pick up the body. They arrived. First of all, the whole wing smelled. They went to pick his body up, and the skin stuck to the table and the fluid dropped out, and it was as if they could never even conceive of death looking like this. And they quickly put the body down.

"I suppose that they were typical morticians, with the black overcoats, thin black ties, and the one guy who was very heavy and had a quivering lower jaw. And he went outside and said, 'Oh, oh, this is terrible. This is a terrible situation.' I was so punchy from lack of sleep, I almost burst out laughing. He said, 'Oh, this is a terrible health hazard. Why didn't we get this body before?'

"And I said, 'Well, if the nurses had told us when he died three days ago, we would have called you.' And the guy just looked at me as if I was out of my mind. And the nurses almost did this double-take, almost instinctively, 'Don't blame me,' but they realized, How absurd.

"The morticians walked away in a huff, and they put gloves and masks on and went back in the room and put him in a box. They were completely freaked out. It was an interesting learning experience for me, because I realized that they weren't really concerned with the health hazard, but rather they were really worried that they were not going to be able to embalm him and make him look good. They kept talking about how they weren't going to be able to do a good job, and 'How terrible he is going to look when we give him back to you,' and 'Now we won't be able to make him look alive.' And I had to keep reassuring them, saying that it was really all right and that we understood and not to worry. I said, 'No one is expecting you to make him look alive. We would just like you to do what you can so we can get him back to Sikkim for the funeral.' After I had said this four or five times, it put their minds at rest, but their whole take on what their job was was very interesting. Make him look good. Make him look alive.

"After that, we got ready to leave. But the entire experience had had very pronounced effects on everyone involved, especially the non-Buddhists, who were the majority of those there. Just to give one example, the assistant administrator, one of the people who had been close to these events, one night was reading in some of the books on Buddhism that someone had lent her. She came to me the next morning and said the thing that she liked about these books was that after reading them, they pretty much matched some conclusions that she had come to on her own. They really made sense to her. And so I think that people there made very powerful connections with His Holiness and Buddhism. It will be interesting to see who he brought in, even in his death.

"After His Holiness died, it's very interesting, I wanted to leave right away, that very day. Usually doctors, when death happens, get out very quickly. They're done. They've had it. But Trungpa Rinpoche asked me to stay for a while, to give the staff a sense of continuity and help them make the transition. He said it shouldn't be that when a patient is alive, the doctor is there, and when he dies, too bad, the doctor disappears and you are on your own. He said, 'Stay at least until the samadhi is over, until we move the body, until the staff are finished. Then we can all leave together.

"So that is what I did. We all left together. The tülkus, with the body, left an hour after me on a flight. And it did make a big difference. I was there every day when His Holiness was struggling with his life, and then every day after he died, until it was really finished. I was there through the samadhi. I was there to help with the body being transported. It felt right. There was this thread, just as one felt with His Holiness himself, of not reacting to one's own impulses, but keeping one's mind and heart open, and relating to others' needs and to the larger situation."

 *Conclusion*

This book and its companion volume, *Indestructible Truth*, have examined the Buddhism of Tibet as it existed in its indigenous context and is now beginning to move into the modern, technological world. The journey made in these two books has led us through traditional Tibetan cosmology; the critical role of ritual; the history of Tibetan Buddhism from its Indian ancestry, through its formative and classical periods, and down into modern times; its doctrinal and philosophical underpinnings; and its path of the three vehicles, Hinayana, Mahayana, and Vajrayana, including a detailed investigation of the tantric vehicle with its specific perspectives, ideals, practices, fulfillments, and applications. By way of bringing our journey to a close, I offer here some reflections on Tibetan Buddhism as it enters the Western environment.

During the past thirty years, Tibetan Buddhism, with the Vajrayana as its heart, has become increasingly known and practiced in the West. In this process, one may observe the steady growth of the tradition in Europe as well as North and South America, the seriousness and dedication of its practitioners, the profile of the Dalai Lama as one of the world's most respected persons, and the wide public awareness of Tibet through books, films, and the popular media. All of these suggest that Tibetan Buddhism has made a most successful initial entry into modern Western culture. This very success seems all the more remarkable when one considers traditional Tibet—geographically remote, technologically primitive, tiny in its population, poor by modern standards, militarily powerless, isolated from the modern world, and possessed of an "archaic" social and religious world view. This leads to an obvious question: how could the religion of such a marginal culture be making such a remarkable impact on the modern world? What is it about Tibetan Buddhism that Westerners have found so appealing?

Certainly, there are many features of the Tibetan outlook that Westerners find engaging. For example, the affirmation that spirituality is real and its goals attainable is heartening to many who have been brought up on "scientific materialism," which, in its more extreme expressions, denies the existence of spirituality altogether. In addition, the nonmaterialistic outlook of the tradition—that ultimate human fulfillment cannot be attained through acquisition of money, possessions, power, or fame—is refreshing in a consumeristic society where life often seems driven solely by material, social, and other forms of self-aggrandizement. Again, the teaching on buddha-nature and innate human goodness is appealing for many burdened by a cultural heritage of "original sin." Beyond this, Westerners find specific Buddhist attitudes and ideas helpful to them as they think about their lives, such as the teachings on suffering, egolessness, karma, and the importance of self-knowledge.

The Tibetan emphasis on spiritual practice and realization is also attractive in a modern context where often the religious life is reduced to doctrinal belief, conventional morality, and sectarian membership. The Tibetan stress on meditation particularly speaks to those living in a world where the focus is largely turned outward in accumulating and consuming and where peace, contentment, and inner tranquillity are rare. In addition, the emphasis on realization in the present life speaks directly to an increasingly chaotic world where the fortunes of tomorrow and next week, not to speak of the next year or the next decade, are felt as more and more uncertain. The fact that the Tibetan and particularly Vajrayana teachings present a spiritual path that can be followed "in ordinary life," amid the struggles and strains of making a living is encouraging to modern people for whom retreat from the world is not usually a realistic possibility.

It is also clear that many people see in Tibetan Buddhism an alternative to the individualism, self-absorption, and personal isolation that plague Western society. Many are frustrated and disheartened by the rampant self-centeredness and lack of concern for others endemic to modern consumeristic societies. There is something in all of us that refuses to believe that egotism is the deepest truth of the human heart. Within this context, the Buddhist affirmation that one's most basic purpose is to serve and assist others comes, surprisingly, as a relief. Along the same lines, many Western people are attracted by the emphasis on sangha and appreciate the opportunity to enter into community life primarily intended to serve the spiritual interests and maturation of its members.

There is a further reason why modern people find Tibetan Buddhism so compelling, one that is quite far-reaching in potential implications. This is the extent to which Tibetan Buddhism appears to address many of the psychological concerns and problems that preoccupy modern people.

As hardly needs to be pointed out, those of us alive today inhabit a world increasingly dominated by "psychology." Psychology, indeed, is the reigning ideology of the modern era and comprises not only specific clinical and experimental fields but also the multitude of social concerns and projects revolving around the question of who we are as human beings, why our souls or psyches are troubled, and how we can be healed. Included here are virtually all of the "human sciences," much creative expression in writing, music, dance, and the visual arts, and a great deal of popular culture as well. The culture-wide preoccupation with psychology and therapy reflect a general acknowledgment of *the* Western problem: divided hearts and minds.

Buddhism has been able to enter successfully into this discussion because it appears to address the modern psychological preoccupation directly. In this respect, the historical sequence of Buddhist traditions making their way westward is intriguing. Theravada arrived first, over a century ago, presenting a Buddhist psychology in the form of the Abhidharma analysis of the conditioned samsaric mind. Here was an Asian tradition that examined the most problematic aspects of human psychology—its unawareness, its drivenness and lust, and its destructiveness—and provided a survey of the lay of this land and how we got here. Theravadin meditation was subsequently offered, like Western psychotherapy, as a way to explore this conditioned mind and, in knowing it, to begin to find freedom. It is significant that many of the leading insight meditation teachers in the West are themselves psychologists and therapists.

Zen followed, setting forth its teaching on the practice of *zazen* as the avenue to realizing the vast mind of our original enlightenment. It is true that Western Zen does not typically refer to itself as a "Buddhist psychology," placing its primary emphasis on meditation practice rather than on analyses of the problematic "small mind" of samsara. Nevertheless, in pointing to the primordial enlightenment of our original nature, it provided a most eloquent response to the basic modern question, "Who or what am I?" And it was tantalizing in suggesting that a satisfying answer can only be found outside of the realm of words and concepts in the direct experience of *satori*, or awakening.

Tibetan Buddhism arrived in the modern world last of all, beginning in the 1960s. Like Theravada, it possessed a rich and active tradition of Abhidharma analysis. Drawing on both Sarvastivadin and Yogacharin Abhidharma thought, it presented a convincing portrait of the wayward, samsaric mind, in both its relative sickness and its relative health. And similar to Zen, in mahamudra and dzokchen, it pointed to the unborn and undying "wisdom mind" as our basic nature. As we have seen, Tibetan Buddhism holds that our essential experience is one of open space; we are, most fundamentally, awareness without boundary or limitation. However, our actual condition is that, in the midst of this unconditioned openness and in denial of it, we have frozen space, erecting solid boundaries that comprise our "I," the extensive self-concept or image that forms our samsaric "identity."

As it entered the psychological conversation, Tibetan Buddhism was thus unusual among Buddhist traditions in the way in which it presented a detailed model of mind that included both its samsaric and its enlightened aspects. As we have seen, this enabled it to demonstrate how, beginning with the unconditioned space of our primordial enlightenment, the "self" initially arises, develops, and maintains itself. And, on the basis of this analysis, it was able to show how to work with the details of our samsaric entrapment, to recover our primordial awakening. One is shown how to take the most problematic states of mind and, through applying awareness directly to them, to find the way back to the freedom and joy of the original state.

As we have seen, this revelation then enables us to return to samsara and to work with it in a different, more creative way.

This is the beginning of our true life. But what is this true life? It is the limitless existence that arises once we have surrendered our ideas, concepts, and images of who we are and what reality is like. The boundless space of ourselves continually gives birth to our true personhood, which is finally a mystery that can never be put into words or confined in any way. It is an unfolding process, and the goal of life, as seen in Buddhism, is to be in the stream of this process, holding nothing in reserve. This unfolding is creative in the deepest sense.

At this stage, we are like an eagle that, since beginningless time, has been dressed up in boots, a hat, and an overcoat, and locked in a cage on the edge of a cliff.[2] Then, one day, the door of our cage is opened and we find ourselves standing on the edge of the abyss, feeling the rush of the wind and looking into the vast, empty space before us. Hearing a call that we do not understand yet cannot resist, suddenly we spring off into the open expanse, shedding our overcoat, dropping off our boots, and casting away our hat. We spread our wings, soaring in space, riding the updrafts of the wind, enjoying the brilliant blue sky, delighting in the heat of the naked sun. As we mount upward on the currents, we taste the joys of free flight and finally enter the existence for which we were born.

Tibetan Buddhism has not particularly resisted modern attempts to style it a "psychology," but, as we have seen, in many respects it transcends most modern psychological perspectives and practices. For example, Tibetan tradition begins with the notion of the fundamental and indestructible goodness and wholesomeness (buddha-nature) of the human person, rather than with his or her pathology. Again, within the Tibetan context, a "healthy" sense of self is not the final goal but rather only a preliminary to the abandonment of any and all self-concepts whatsoever. In addition, in the Tibetan view, the problematic notion of self comprises our concepts not just of ourselves and others, but also of the entire animate and inanimate worlds, at the most subtle perceptual levels. Beyond this, what we call the "psyche" in the West is ultimately seen in Tibetan Buddhism not as a "natural" phenomenon, but rather as the play of transcendent energies, the enlightened wisdoms of the five buddhas, only mistakenly reduced to the desacralized, habitual "I." And the Tibetan methodologies and particularly the tantric ones emphasize the cultivation of direct awareness through meditation as the way to resolve blockages and obstacles.

Other broad domains of Tibetan Buddhist experience, the selfless devotion and veneration toward one's teachers and guides, seen and unseen; the invisible world of spirits, ancestors, bodhisattvas, and buddhas; the cosmos alive with wisdom and meaning; the synchronicity and final indivisibility of oneself and the outer world, of one's karma and reality itself; the miraculous and magical elements that increasingly appear as one matures—all these would seem to have no direct counterparts in typical conventional Western psychological and therapeutic models. And yet, for Tibetan Buddhism, dimensions such as these present themselves as irrefutable elements of experience as one's openness and awareness develop. More than this, they must be acknowledged and integrated in order for one to proceed toward the realization of "oneself," whatever that may turn out to be. The psychology offered by Tibetan Buddhism and particularly the Vajrayana is thus more extensive in its scope and more openly daring and demanding in its means than one typically finds in Western psychologies. And it is finally more empowering because it leads us to a place where all views are transcended and one is liberated to make the unprecedented discoveries that make up the substance of one's true life.

This should suggest that, in allowing itself to be taken as a psychology, Tibetan Buddhism has no particular intention to narrow itself down in any way. Rather, it is simply recognizing that for us modern people, it is most typically in psychological terms that we articulate the age-old questions addressed by Buddhism concerning the true nature of our "selves." In fact, in formulating the psychological problem as its central preoccupation, the modern world appears to have asked a question for which Tibetan Buddhism has a most credible and serviceable answer. How much of the Tibetan answer modern people will be able to receive, of course, remains to be seen.

Notes

INTRODUCTION

1. See Geoffrey Samuel's illuminating discussion of the relation of the geographical, social, and political aspects of Tibetan culture to the success of Vajrayana Buddhism in Tibet: *Civilized Shamans,* pp. 3–154.

CHAPTER 1. THE INDIAN PRELUDE

1. For a discussion of the Indian background of Tibetan Buddhism, see Ray, *Indestructible Truth*, chap. 3.
2. This story is told in Lama Taranatha's "Seven Special Transmissions," (*bka'.-babs.bdun.ldan*), in Tseten Dorji, *Five Historical Works of Taranatha.*
3. As we shall see below, the "three yanas" intend to describe three stages in the development of each practitioner and should not be viewed as descriptions of actual, existing historical schools. See below, chapter 4, and *Indestructible Truth*, introduction to part three.
4. For a discussion of these three lifeways, see Ray, *Buddhist Saints in India.*
5. Ibid., 251–92 and 404–16. It appears that the Mahayana arose in multiple communities more or less at the same time and that some of these communities were also lay in orientation.
6. Ratnagunasamchayagatha. An English translation by Edward Conze is titled *The Accumulation of Precious Qualities.*
7. Taranatha, *History of Buddhism in India*, 151–53.
8. Tseten Dorji, *Five Historical Works of Taranatha*, 456–58.

CHAPTER 2. HOW THE VAJRAYANA CAME TO TIBET: THE EARLY SPREADING OF THE DHARMA

1. Tulku Thondup, Buddhist Civilization in Tibet, 20.
2. Ibid., 20–21.
3. Ibid.
4. Ibid.
5. E.g., see Evans-Wentz, *Tibetan Book of the Dead*, 121 and 131–32.

Chapter 3. How the Vajrayana Came to Tibet: The Later Spreading and Beyond

1. For a discussion of the later spreading, see Ray, *Indestructible Truth*, chaps. 6 and 7.
2. For a tantric account of his life, see Robinson, *Buddha's Lions*, 60–64.
3. The Shangpa Kagyü was originally independent and only later came to be included within the Kagyü orbit. See *Indestructible Truth*, chap. 7.
4. See Geoffrey Samuel's innovative and most helpful *Civilized Shamans*, where this model of Tibetan Buddhism is developed in detail.
5. Lama Thubten Yeshe, *The Bliss of Inner Fire*, 31, 35.
6. Ibid., 34.

Chapter 4. The Vajrayana in the Context of the Three-Yana Journey

1. Sakyong Mipham Rinpoche, Vajradhatu Seminary, Red Feather Lakes, Colo., 1999.

Chapter 5. The View of Vajrayana

1. The translation quoted here is that of the Nālandā Translation Committee.

Chapter 6. Some Initial Tantric Perspectives

1. See Ray, *Indestructible Truth* for a detailed discussion of the Hinayana and Mahayana phases of the Tibetan Buddhist path.
2. For a summary of the origins and development of both the Nyingma and the New Translation school, see *Indestructible Truth*.
3. Chögyam Trungpa, *Journey without Goal*, 59.
4. Stanley Tambiah, *The Buddhist Saints of the Forest and the Cult of Amulets*, pp. 81–110.
5. Tulku Thondup, *Hidden Teachings of Tibet*, 45–46.
6. This story is told by Lama Taranatha in his *Seven Special Transmissions*, a history of Vajrayana Buddhism in India, pp. 391–92.
7. Trungpa, *Journey without Goal*, 20–21.
8. Tulku Thondup, *Buddhist Civilization in Tibet*, 14–16.
9. See Conze, *Buddhist Thought in India*, pp. 172–73.
10. Ibid.

Chapter 7. The World beyond Thought

1. Chögyam Trungpa, *Journey without Goal*, 26–27.
2. *Gerard Manley Hopkins: Poems and Prose* (London: Penguin Books, 1985), 27.

3. Trungpa, *Journey without Goal*, 78.
4. Chögyam Trungpa, *Lion's Roar,* 165.
5. Trungpa, *Journey without Goal*, 83–84.
6. Trungpa, *Lion's Roar*, 165.
7. Trungpa, *Journey without Goal*, 79.
8. Chögyam Trungpa, *Cutting Through Spiritual Materialism,* 225.
9. Recalling a line from the *Sadhana of Mahamudra*, a tantric liturgy composed by Chögyam Trungpa Rinpoche in Bhutan in 1968 (Boulder: Vajradhatu Publications, n.d.), 8.
10. Trungpa, *Journey without Goal*, 80.
11. Trungpa, *Cutting Through Spiritual Materialism,* 226.
12. Ibid., 81–82.
13. Ibid., 227.
14. Ibid., 82.
15. Ibid., 228.
16. Thanks to Giovannina Jobson for creating this chart.
17. In the alternate arrangement, Akshobhya is placed at the center of the mandala and Vairochana in the east.
18. Chögyam Trungpa, *Secret beyond Thought*, 28.
19. Ibid., 30.
20. Ibid., 166–67.

CHAPTER 8. THE VAJRA MASTER

1. Kalu Rinpoche, *Secret Buddhism*, 30.
2. Kalu Rinpoche, *Luminous Mind*, 177.
3. Chagdud Tulku, *Gates to Buddhist Practice*, 46.
4. Kalu Rinpoche, *Secret Buddhism*, 27.
5. Patrul Rinpoche, *The Words of My Perfect Teacher,* 138.
6. Tulku Urgyen Rinpoche, *Rainbow Painting*, 101.
7. Chagdud Tulku, *Gates to Buddhist Practice*, 46–47.
8. Ibid., 47.
9. Nālandā Translation Committee, *The Life of Marpa the Translator*, 10.
10. Lobsang P. Lhalungpa, *The Life of Milarepa,* 43.
11. See Ray, *Indestructible Truth*.
12. Chögyam Trungpa, *Cutting Through Spiritual Materialism*, 40.
13. Ibid., 41.
14. Kalu Rinpoche, *Luminous Mind*, 178.
15. Chögyam Trungpa, *Journey without Goal*, 59–60.
16. Ibid., 60–61.
17. Ibid., 61–62.

18. Ibid., 62.
19. Chögyam Trungpa, *Illusion's Game*, 122–23.
20. Vajra Assembly, Jan. 25, 1998.
21. Urgyen Rinpoche, *Rainbow Painting*, 92.
22. Ibid., 94.
23. Kalu Rinpoche, *Secret Buddhism*, 28–29.
24. Ibid., 28.
25. Ibid., 29.
26. The rough outline of these stages was given by Trungpa Rinpoche in a talk given in 1979 at the Vajradhatu Seminary held at Lake Louise, Alberta, Canada.
27. Chögyam Trungpa, *1979 Seminary Transcripts: Vajrayana* (Vajradhatu Publications, 1980), 21.
28. Urgyen Rinpoche, *Rainbow Painting*, 93.
29. Tenzin Palmo, "Tenzin Palmo in Conversation," 94.

CHAPTER 9. ENTERING THE VAJRAYANA PATH

1. James Robinson, *Buddha's Lions*, 122, 236–39.
2. Dzigar Kongtrül Rinpoche, Intensive Training Seminar, January 1998.
3. Sogyal Rinpoche, *The Tibetan Book of Living and Dying*, 41–42.
4. Tulku Thondup, *Masters of Meditation and Miracles*, 202.
5. Matthieu Ricard, *Journey to Enlightenment*, 34.
6. Sogyal Rinpoche, *The Tibetan Book of Living and Dying*, 42.
7. Ibid., 89.
8. Tulku Urgyen Rinpoche, *As It Is*, vol. 1 (Boudhanath, Nepal: Rangjung Yeshe Publications, 1999).
9. Ibid., 88–89.
10. Ibid., 89.
11. Ibid., 94.
12. Urgyen Rinpoche, *Rainbow Painting*, 67.
13. Ibid.
14. Janice Willis, *Diamond Light*, 103.
15. Urgyen Rinpoche, *Rainbow Painting*, 67–68.
16. Ibid., 68.

CHAPTER 10. TANTRIC PRACTICE

1. Kalu Rinpoche, *Secret Buddhism*, 114.
2. Tulku Urgyen Rinpoche, *Rainbow Painting*, 159–60.
3. Ibid., 160.
4. Ibid.

5. Ibid.
6. Ibid., 158.
7. Ibid., 163.
8. Ibid., 164.
9. Ibid.

CHAPTER 11. SUBTLETIES OF PRACTICE

1. Nālandā Translation Committee, *The Life of Marpa the Translator*, 235.
2. Kalu Rinpoche, *Secret Buddhism*, 95.
3. Vajradhatu Seminary, Red Feather Lakes, Colo., 1996.
4. Chögyam Trungpa, *Secret Beyond Thought*, 1.
5. Ibid., 12.
6. See the description given in Garma C. C. Chang, *The Six Yogas of Naropa and Teachings on Mahamudra*, 56–57.
7. Ibid., 56.
8. Nālandā Translation Committee, *The Life of Marpa the Translator*, 235.
9. Ibid.
10. The following description of the six yogas relies largely on Chang, *The Six Yogas of Naropa and Teachings on Mahamudra*.
11. Kalu Rinpoche, *Secret Buddhism*, 95.
12. Nālandā Translation Committee, *The Life of Marpa the Translator*, 235.
13. Kalu Rinpoche, *Secret Buddhism*, 95.
14. Ibid., 96.
15. Chang, *The Six Yogas of Naropa and Teachings on Mahamudra*.
16. Chögyam Trungpa, *Illusion's Game,* 51.
17. Alexandra David-Néel, *Magic and Mystery in Tibet*, 228.
18. Ibid., 227.
19. Kalu Rinpoche, *Secret Buddhism*, 95–96.
20. Lama Thubten Yeshe, *The Bliss of Inner Fire*, 24.
21. Ibid., 23.
22. Dudjom Rinpoche, *The Nyingma School of Tibetan Buddhism,* vol. 1, 922.
23. Kalu Rinpoche, *Secret Buddhism*, 96.
24. Ibid.
25. Ibid., 97.
26. Chögyam Trungpa, *Illusion's Game*, 137–38.
27. Chang, *The Six Yogas of Naropa and Teachings on Mahamudra*, 94.
28. Kalu Rinpoche, *Secret Buddhism*, 98–99.
29. Chang, *The Six Yogas of Naropa and Teachings on Mahamudra*, 101.
30. Chögyam Trungpa, *Illusion's Game*, 51.
31. Kalu Rinpoche, *Secret Buddhism*, 98–99.

32. Ibid., 99.
33. Chögyam Trungpa, *Illusion's Game*, 51.
34. Ibid.
35. Urgyen Rinpoche, *Rainbow Painting*, 176–77.

CHAPTER 12. MAHAMUDRA

1. See the helpful introduction to mahamudra by Lodro Dorje in his readers' guide to the English translation of Lama Takpo Tashi Namgyal, *Mahamudra*, pp. xliii-lxii.
2. Chögyam Trungpa, *Illusion's Game*, 117.
3. Ibid., 116.
4. Thrangu Rinpoche, *The Song of Lodro Thaye*, 19.
5. Ibid., 21. Emphasis added.
6. Ibid., 21.
7. Ibid., 66.
8. Ibid., 20–21.
9. Ibid., 21.
10. Ibid., 23–24.
11. Ibid., 23.
12. Ibid., 24.
13. Chögyam Trungpa, *Cutting Through Spiritual Materialism*, 122.
14. Ibid., 123.
15. Chögyam Trungpa, *Glimpses of Abhidharma*, 9.
16. Tulku Urgyen Rinpoche, *Rainbow Painting*, 102.
17. Thrangu Rinpoche, *The Song of Lodro Thaye*, 24.
18. See also the work of Lama Tashi Namgyal and Tsele Natsok Rangdrol.
19. Wangchuk Dorje wrote three primary texts on mahamudra: a long one, a medium-length one, and a short one. The middle-length text, published in English, is *The Mahamudra: Eliminating the Darkness of Ignorance*. Wangchuk Dorje's instructions in this text parallel his instructions in the shortest one and are similar to those given in other New Translation school texts on mahamudra practice. His long text is a detailed compendium of mahamudra practices and provides an elaboration and in-depth commentary on the material contained in the shorter works.
20. Takpo Tashi Wangyal, *Mahamudra*, 358.
21. Ibid.
22. Tsele Natsok Rangdrol, *Lamp of Mahamudra*, 38–39.
23. Ibid., 39.
24. Wangyal, *Mahamudra*, 358.
25. Rangdrol, *Lamp of Mahamudra*, 40.

26. Wangyal, *Mahamudra*, 359.
27. Ibid, 360. The original translation uses the phrase "one flavor" instead of "one taste" and "equipoise and non-equipoise" instead of "meditation and nonmeditation."
28. Rangdrol, *Lamp of Mahamudra*, 42.
29. Wangyal, *Mahamudra*, 359.
30. Ibid., 361.
31. Rangdrol, *Lamp of Mahamudra*, 44.
32. Ibid.
33. Ibid.
34. Thrangu Rinpoche, *The Song of Lodro Thaye*, 66.
35. Ibid., 68.
36. Ibid.
37. Ibid.
38. Chögyam Trungpa, *The Heart of the Buddha*, 168.
39. Chögyam Trungpa, *Illusion's Game*, 117.
40. Chögyam Trungpa, *Lion's R*oar, 192.
41. Trungpa, *Illusion's Game*, 119.
42. Ibid.
43. Ibid., 120.
44. Ibid., 118.
45. Ibid., 133–34.
46. See James Robinson, *Buddha's Lions*, 65–68.
47. Tulku Thondup, *Masters of Meditation and Miracles*, 129.
48. From the introduction by Ngawang Zangpo, in Jamgon Kongtrul Lodro Thaye, *Enthronement*, 73.
49. Trungpa, LR, 46.
50. Chögyam Trungpa, *The Heart of the Buddha*, 168–69.
51. Trungpa, LR, 163.
52. Ibid., 164.
53. Trungpa, *Illusion's Game*, 132–33.

CHAPTER 13. DZOKCHEN

1. Chögyam Trungpa, *Journey without Goal*, 133–34.
2. Tulku Urgyen Rinpoche, *Rainbow Painting*, 26.
3. Ibid., 121.
4. Ibid., 27–28.
5. Namkhai Norbu, *Dzogchen*, 23–24.
6. Ibid., 29.
7. Ibid., 28–29.

8. Urgyen Rinpoche, *Rainbow Painting*, 32.

9. Ibid.

10. Ibid., 34–35.

11. Ibid., 35.

12. Ibid., 34.

13. Ibid., 31.

14. Ibid., 33.

15. Ibid.

16. Ibid., 25–26.

17. Ibid., 41.

18. Ibid., 41.

19. Ibid., 35.

20. Ibid., 35–36.

21. Ibid., 36.

22. Ibid., 25.

23. Ibid., 50.

24. Ibid., 50–51.

25. Ibid., 51.

26. Ibid., 51–52.

27. Ibid., 52.

28. Ibid., 51.

29. Ibid., 36.

30. Ibid., 51.

31. Ibid., 81.

32. Ibid., 54.

33. Ibid., 50–51.

34. Ibid., 57.

35. Ibid., 82.

36. Ibid., 85.

37. Ibid., 80.

38. Ibid., 84.

39. Ibid., 159.

40. Chögyam Trungpa, *Nyingma Teachings on the Intermediate State*, 11.

41. See John Reynolds's helpful summary in *The Golden Letters*, 32–34.

42. Sogyal Rinpoche, *The Tibetan Book of Living and Dying*, 167.

43. Trungpa, *Nyingma Teachings on the Intermediate State*, 11.

44. Sogyal Rinpoche, *The Tibetan Book of Living and Dying*, 167.

45. Trungpa, *Nyingma Teachings on the Intermediate State,* 7.

46. Francesca Fremantle and Chögyam Trungpa, *The Tibetan Book of the Dead*, 11. See also Namkhai Norbu, *Dream Yoga and the Practice of Natural Light*, 61, 69.

47. Chögyam Trungpa, *Nyingma Teachings on the Intermediate State,* 7–8.
48. Fremantle and Trungpa, *The Tibetan Book of the Dead*, 12.
49. Trungpa, *Nyingma Teachings on the Intermediate State,* 7.
50. Fremantle and Trungpa, *The Tibetan Book of the Dead*, 11.
51. Ibid., 12.
52. See Ray, *Indestructible Truth*, chapter 11.
53. Tenzin Wangyal, *Wonders of the Natural Mind,* 11.
54. Fremantle and Trungpa, *The Tibetan Book of the Dead*, 12.
55. Trungpa, *Nyingma Teachings on the Intermediate State,* 8.
56. Urgyen Rinpoche, *Rainbow Painting*, 183.
57. Ibid., 31.
58. Ibid., 181–83.
59. Ibid., 183.

Chapter 14. Lessons in Mortality

1. See Fremantle and Trungpa, *The Tibetan Book of the Dead.* See also Evans-Wentz, for an earlier translation, and Thurman, for a more recent one.
2. Mentioned in chapter 1 of this book and discussed at length in chapter 14 of *Indestructible Truth.*
3. Chögyam Trungpa, *Cutting Through Spiritual Materialism*, 123.
4. Chögyam Trungpa, *Nyingma Teachings on the Intermediate State*, 1.
5. Ibid.
6. Ibid., 1–2.
7. Ibid., 2.
8. Ibid.
9. Ibid., 3.
10. Ibid.
11. Garma C. C. Chang, *The Six Yogas of Naropa and Teachings on Mahamudra*, 109.
12. Sogyal Rinpoche, *The Tibetan Book of Living and Dying*, 103–4.
13. In this account, I am summarizing Sogyal Rinpoche's articulate description, ibid., 251 ff.
14. Ibid., 252.
15. Ibid.
16. Ibid.
17. Ibid., 253.
18. Ibid.
19. Ibid.
20. Ibid., 255.
21. Trungpa, *Nyingma Teachings on the Intermediate State,* 5.

22. Chang, *The Six Yogas of Naropa and Teachings on Mahamudra*, 104.
23. Chökyi Nyima Rinpoche, *The Bardo Guidebook*, 114–15.
24. Ibid., 114.
25. Ibid., 115–16.
26. Ibid., 118.
27. Ibid., 117.
28. Ibid., 116.
29. Sogyal Rinpoche, *The Tibetan Book of Living and Dying*, 260.
30. Ibid., 261.
31. Chökyi Nyima, *The Bardo Guidebook*, 116–17.
32. Sogyal Rinpoche, *The Tibetan Book of Living and Dying*, 261.
33. Ibid., 255.
34. Ibid., 263.
35. Ibid., 274.
36. Chökyi Nyima, *The Bardo Guidebook*, 117.
37. Ibid., 119.
38. Sogyal Rinpoche, *The Tibetan Book of Living and Dying*, 275.
39. Ibid.
40. Ibid.
41. Ibid., 276–79.
42. Ibid., 285.
43. Ibid.
44. Ibid., 278–79.
45. Ibid., 287.
46. Ibid., 282–83.
47. Ibid., 289.
48. Ibid., 290.
49. Ibid., 292.
50. Ibid., 294.
51. Trungpa, *Nyingma Teachings on the Intermediate State*, 5.
52. Ibid., 4–5.
53. T. W. Rhys Davids (trans.), "The Mahaparinibbana Sutta," p. 38.
54. See Sogyal Rinpoche, *The Tibetan Book of Living and Dying*.
55. Chagdud Tulku, *Lord of the Dance*, 36–37.
56. Sogyal Rinpoche, *The Tibetan Book of Living and Dying*, 6.
57. Chagdud Tulku, *Lord of the Dance*, 36–37.
58. Sogyal Rinpoche, *The Tibetan Book of Living and Dying*, 306.
59. A condensed version of this story appears in Ronald L. Grimes's recent, remarkable study on ritual, *Deeply into the Bone: Re-Inventing Rites of Passage* (Berkeley: University of California Press, 2000), 252–53, with Prof. Grimes's comments, pp. 253–54.

CHAPTER 15. BODHISATTVAS IN THE WORLD

1. The following account draws on a series of articles I wrote for the *Vajradhatu Sun* (now *Shambhala Sun*) in 1980 and 1981 and also on my 1986 article "Some Aspects of the Tulku Tradition in Tibet." See bibliography for references.
2. H. H. Dudjom Rinpoche, *The Nyingma School of Tibetan Buddhism*, vol. 1, 858.
3. Jamgon Kongtrul, *Enthronement*, 23–24.
4. Ibid., 833.
5. Ibid., 922.
6. Ibid.
7. Ibid., 833.
8. Karma Thinley, *The History of the Sixteen Karmapas*, 47–52.
9. For an account of these events, see Ngawang Zangpo, in Jamgon Kongtrul, *Enthronement*, pp. 16–17. Zangpo notes that the yogi Urgyenpa had traveled widely in India prior to recognizing Rangjung Dorje. This raises some fascinating questions: was Urgyenpa exposed to an institution in India paralleling that of the Tibetan tulku, and might this have been the source of his inspiration for finding his own teacher in Rangjung Dorje? As Zangpo correctly observes, since there is so far no evidence of the Tibetan style of tulku in India, we are unable to provide any answers at this point. He suggests, however, that a close study of the extant biographies of Urgyenpa may provide some clues.
10. Ibid., 55–58.
11. Chögyam Trungpa, *1974 Seminary Transcripts: Vajrayana* (Boulder: Vajradhatu Publications, 1975), 144.
12. Ibid.
13. Ibid., 149.
14. Ibid.
15. Thrangu Rinpoche, *Treatise That Differentiates Consciousness and Wisdom*, 56.
16. Ibid.
17. Ibid., 91–92.
18. Jamgon Kongtrul, *Enthronement*, 24.

CHAPTER 16. THEMES OF A TULKU'S LIFE

1. Matthieu Ricard, *Journey to Enlightenment*, 142.
2. Kalu Rinpoche, *Secret Buddhism*, 89.
3. Ibid., 90.
4. Ibid.
5. Chögyam Trungpa, *Born in Tibet*, 25.
6. Kalu Rinpoche, *Secret Buddhism*, 90.
7. Trungpa, *Born in Tibet*, 25.

8. Dalai Lama, *My Land and My People*, 26.
9. Chagdud Tulku, *Lord of the Dance*, 13.
10. Ibid., 63.
11. *Born in Tibet*, 25.
12. Ibid., 26.
13. Ibid.
14. See Jamgon Kongtrul, *Enthronement*, 46–49.
15. Ibid., 28.
16. Dalai Lama, *My Land and My People*, 8.
17. Ibid., 9.
18. Ricard, *Journey to Enlightenment*, 14.
19. Ibid., 34.
20. Ibid., 143.
21. Ibid., 14.
22. Ibid., 14–15.
23. Chögyam Trungpa, *1974 Vajradhatu Seminary Transcripts: Vajrayana*, 149.
24. Trungpa, *Born in Tibet*, 132.
25. Ricard, *Journey to Enlightenment*, 34.
26. Ibid.
27. Ibid.
28. Chagdud Tulku, *Lord of the Dance*, 72.
29. Ibid., 73.
30. Trungpa, *1974 Vajradhatu Seminary Transcripts*, 152.
31. Ibid., 152–53.
32. A. Waddell, quoted in Ray, "Some Aspects of the Tulku Tradition in Tibet," 61.
33. Chögyam Trungpa, *Born in Tibet*, 44.
34. Dalai Lama, *My Land and My People*, 53.
35. Chagdud Tulku, *Lord of the Dance*, 20.
36. Goodman, *The Last Dalai Lama*, 108.
37. Chagdud Tulku, *Lord of the Dance*, 21.
38. Ibid., 29.
39. Ibid., 31.
40. Ibid., 58.
41. Private interview, May 4, 1980.
42. Ibid.
43. Ibid.
44. Ibid.
45. Ibid.
46. Ibid.
47. Ibid.

CHAPTER 17. THE PRACTICE OF RETREAT

1. Nyoshul Khenpo. *Natural Great Perfection*, 21.
2. Mathieu Ricard, *Journey to Enlightenment*, 33.
3. Lobsang P. Lhalungpa, *The Life of Milarepa*, 108.
4. Ibid., 118.
5. Ibid., 120.
6. See *Indestructible Truth, chap.* 9.
7. Ricard, *Journey to Enlightenment*, 34.
8. Lhalungpa, *The Life of Milarepa*, 90.
9. Tulku Thondup, *Masters of Meditation and Miracles*, 111.
10. Nyoshul Khenpo, *Natural Great Perfection*, 20–21.
11. Mathieu Ricard, *The Life of Shabkar*, 98.
12. The following account draws from the account of Lama Surya Das, found in Nyoshul Khenpo, *Natural Great Perfection*.
13. Ibid., 163–64.
14. Ibid., 164.
15. Ricard, *Journey to Enlightenment*, 40–41.
16. Tenzin Palmo, "Tenzin Palmo in Conversation," 91.
17. Ibid., 92.
18. Ibid.
19. Ibid., 93.
20. Ibid.
21. Ibid.
22. Ibid.
23. Ibid., 94.
24. Ibid.
25. See James Robinson, *Buddha's Lions*.
26. Ibid., 30.
27. Ricard, *The Life of Shabkar*, 59–61.

CHAPTER 18. THE PASSING OF A REALIZED MASTER

1. The following represents a summary of the account found in *Born in Tibet*, 23–28, with some additional details provided by Trungpa Rinpoche in an interview. It first appeared in the *Vajradhatu Sun*, June–July 1980, 5–6.
2. This imagery is adapted from a talk given by Trungpa Rinpoche in the spring of 1979 at the Vajradhatu Seminary.

Bibliography

Asanga. *Bodhisattvabhumi*. Edited by Nalinaksha Dutt. 2nd ed. Patna, India: K.P. Jayaswal Research Institute, 1978.

Bercholz, Samuel, and Kohn, Sherab Chödzin, eds. *Entering the Stream: An Introduction to the Buddha and His Teachings*. Boston: Shambhala Publications, 1993.

Chagdud Tulku. *Gates to Buddhist Practice*. Junction City, Calif.: Padma Publishing, 1993.

———. *Lord of the Dance: Autobiography of a Tibetan Lama*. Junction City, Calif.: Padma Publishing, 1992.

Chang, Garma C. C. *The Six Yogas of Naropa and Teachings on Mahamudra*. New York: University Books, 1963.

Conze, Edward. *Buddhist Thought in India*. London: George Allen and Unwin, 1962.

Dalai Lama of Tibet, H. H. *My Land and My People*. New York: Warner Books, 1997.

David-Néel, Alexandra. *Magic and Mystery in Tibet*. New Hyde Park, N.Y.: University Books, 1965.

Dorje, Tseten (ed.). *Five Historical Works of Lama Taranatha*. Arunachal Pradesh, India, 1974.

Dorje, Wangchuk (the ninth Karmapa). *The Mahamudra: Eliminating the Darkness of Ignorance*. Translated and edited by Alexander Berzin. Dharamsala: Library of Tibetan Works and Archives, 1978.

Dowman, Keith. *The Divine Madman*. London: Rider, 1980.

———. *Masters of Mahamudra*. Albany: State University of New York Press, 1985.

Dudjom Rinpoche, H. H. *The Nyingma School of Tibetan Buddhism*. 2 vols. Boston: Wisdom Publications, 1991.

Evans-Wentz, W. Y. *The Tibetan Book of the Dead*. 3rd edition. London: Oxford University Press, 1957.

Fremantle, Francesca, and Chögyam Trungpa (trans.). *The Tibetan Book of the*

Dead: The Great Liberation through Hearing in the Bardo. Boston: Shambhala Publications, 1975, 1988.

Goodman, Michael Harris. *The Last Dalai Lama: A Biography*. Boston: Shambhala Publications, 1987.

Johnston, E. H. *Ashvaghosha's Buddhacarita or Acts of the Buddha*. Delhi: Motilal Banarsidass, 1972.

Kalu Rinpoche. *Luminous Mind*. Boston: Wisdom Publications, 1997.

———. *Secret Buddhism*. San Francisco: ClearPoint Press, 1995.

Dilgo Khyentse Rinpoche. *Enlightened Courage*. Ithaca, N.Y.: Snow Lion, 1993.

———. *The Excellent Path to Enlightenment*. Ithaca, N.Y.: Snow Lion, 1996.

———. *The Wish-Fulfilling Jewel*. Boston: Shambhala Publications, 1998.

Kongtrul, Jamgon. *Creation and Completion: Essential Points of Tantric Meditation*. Translated by Sarah Harding. Boston: Wisdom Publications, 1996.

———. *The Teacher-Student Relationship*, Translated by Ron Garry. Ithaca, N.Y.: Snow Lion Publications, 1999.

Kongtrul Lodro Thaye, Jamgon. *Buddhist Ethics*. Translated and edited by the International Translation Committee founded by V.V. Kalu Rinpoche. Ithaca, N.Y.: Snow Lion Publications, 1998.

———. *Enthronement*. Translated and introduced by Ngawang Zangpo (Hugh Leslie Thompson). Ithaca, N.Y.: Snow Lion Publications, 1997.

Kunga Rinpoche, Lama, and Brian Cutillo. *Drinking the Mountain Stream: New Stories and Songs by Milarepa*. Lotsawa Publications, 1978.

———. *Miraculous Journey: New Stories and Songs by Milarepa*. Lotsawa Publications, 1986.

Lhalungpa, Lobsang P. *The Life of Milarepa*. New York: Penguin, Arkana, 1992.

Lingpa, Dudjom. *Buddhahood without Meditation: A Visionary Account Known as Refining Apparent Phenomena* (Nang-jung). Translated by Richard Barron. Junction City, Calif.: Padma Publishing, 1994.

Mackenzie, Vicki. *Cave in the Snow*. New York: Bloomsbury Publishing, 1998.

Mullin, Glen H. *Death and Dying: the Tibetan Tradition*. London: Arkana Paperbacks, 1986.

———. *Readings on the Six Yogas of Naropa*. Ithaca, N.Y.: Snow Lion, 1997.

———. *Tsongkhapa's Six Yogas of Naropa*. Ithaca, N.Y.: Snow Lion, 1996.

Nālandā Translation Committee. *The Life of Marpa the Translator*. Boston: Shambhala Publications, 1995.

Namgyal, Takpo Tashi. *Mahamudra: The Quintessence of Mind and Meditation*. Translated by Lobsang P. Lhalungpa. Boston: Shambhala Publications, 1986.

Norbu, Namkhai. *Dream Yoga and the Practice of Natural Light*. Ithaca, N.Y.: Snow Lion Publications, 1992.

———. *Dzogchen: The Self-Perfected State*. Ithaca, N.Y.: Snow Lion Publications, 1996.

———. *The Mirror: Advice on the Presence of Awareness*. Barrytown, N.Y.: Station Hill Openings, 1996.

———. *Rigbai Kujyug: The Six Vajra Verses*. Singapore: Rinchen Editions, 1990.

Norbu, Thinley. *Magic Dance*. Boston: Shambhala Publications, 1999.

Nyima Rinpoche, Chökyi. *The Bardo Guidebook*. Kathmandu: Rangjung Yeshe Publications, 1991.

———. *The Union of Mahamudra and Dzogchen*. Kathmandu: Rangjung Yeshe Publications, 1986.

Nyoshul Khenpo. *Natural Great Perfection*. Translated by Lama Surya Das. Ithaca, N.Y.: Snow Lion Publications, 1995.

Palmo, Tenzin. "Tenzin Palmo in Conversation." An interview appearing in *Cho Yang* magazine, no. 6 (published in India, n.d.), 91–98.

Patrul Rinpoche. *The Words of My Perfect Teacher*. Translated by the Padmakara Translation Group. Boston: Shambhala Publications, 1999.

Rabjam, Longchen. *The Precious Treasury of the Way of Abiding*. Junction City, Calif.: Padma Publishing, 1998.

Rangdrol, Tsele Natsok. *Lamp of Mahamudra*. Translated by Erik Pema Kunsang. Boston: Shambhala Publications, 1989.

Ratnagunasamchayagatha, edited by Akira Yuyama. Cambridge, 1976. English translation: Edward Conze (trans.), *The Accumulation of Precious Qualities* (Prajnaparamitaratnagunasamcayagatha). In *Indo-Asian Studies*, edited by Tagu Vira., part 1 (New Delhi, 1962), 126–78.

Ray, Reginald A., *Buddhist Saints in India*. New York: Oxford University Press, 1994.

———. *Indestructible Truth: The Living Spirituality of Tibetan Buddhism*. Boston: Shambhala Publications, 2000.

———. "Some Aspects of the Tulku Tradition in Tibet." *Tibet Journal* 11, no. 4 (Winter 1986): 35–69.

———. "The Tulku Tradition I: A Case in Point." *Vajradhatu Sun* (Boulder, Colo.), June-July 1980.

———. "The Tulku Tradition II: Themes of a Tulku's Life." *Vajradhatu Sun* (Boulder, Colo.), August-September 1980.

———. "The Tulku Tradition III: The First Tulku." *Vajradhatu Sun* (Boulder, Colo.), October-November 1980.

———. "The Tulku Tradition IV: From Buddha Shakyamuni to the Mahasiddhas, Part One." *Vajradhatu Sun* (Boulder, Colo.), December-January 1980–1981.

———. "The Tulku Tradition IV: From Buddha Shakyamuni to the Mahasiddhas, Part Two." *Vajradhatu Sun* (Boulder, Colo.), April-May 1981.

Reynolds, John Myrdhin, *The Golden Letters*. Ithaca, N.Y.: Snow Lion Publications, 1996.

Rhys Davids, T. W. "The Mahaparinibbana Sutta." In *Buddhist Suttas*, Sacred Books of the East, vol. 11 (1881). Reprint. Delhi: Motilal Barnasidass, 1965, pp. 1–136.

Ricard, Matthieu (trans.). *Journey to Enlightenment: The Life and World of Khyentse Rinpoche, Spiritual Teacher from Tibet*. New York: Aperture Publications, 1996.

——— (trans.). *The Life of Shabkar: The Autobiography of a Tibetan Yogin*. Albany: State University of New York Press, 1994.

Robinson, James. *Buddha's Lions: Abhayadatta's Lives of the Eighty-four Siddhas* Berkeley: Dharma Press, 1979.

Samuel, Geoffrey. *Civilized Shamans*. Washington, D.C.: Smithsonian Institution, 1993.

Snellgrove, David. *The Hevajra Tantra*. 2 vols. London: Oxford University Press, 1959.

———. *Indo-Tibetan Buddhism*. 2 vols. Boston: Shambhala Publications, 1987.

Sogyal Rinpoche. *The Tibetan Book of Living and Dying*. San Francisco: Harper San Francisco, 1992.

Stearns, Cyrus (trans.). *Hermit of Go Cliffs*. Boston: Wisdom Publications, 2000.

Stewart, Jampa Mackenzie. *The Life of Gampopa*. Ithaca, N.Y.: Snow Lion Publications, 1995.

Tambiah, Stanley. *The Buddhist Saints of the Forest and the Cult of Amulets*. Cambridge: University of Cambridge Press, 1984.

Taranatha, Lama. *bka'.'babs.bdun.ldan* (The *Seven Special Transmissions*). In Tseten Dorje (ed.), *Five Historical Works of Lama Taranatha*. Arunachal Pradesh, India, 1974, pp. 361–499.

———. *History of Buddhism in India*. Translated by Alaka Chattopadhyaya. Simla: Indian Institute of Advanced Study, 1970.

Thinley, Karma. *History of the Sixteen Karmapas*. Boulder: Prajna Press, 1980.

Thondup, Tulku. *Buddhist Civilization in Tibet*. Mahasiddha Nyingma Center, U.S.A., 1982.

———. *Hidden Teachings of Tibet*. London: Wisdom Publications, 1986.

———. *Masters of Meditation and Miracles*. Boston: Shambhala Publications, 1996.

————. *The Tantric Tradition of the Nyingmapa*. Marion, Mass.: Buddhayana, 1984.

Thrangu Rinpoche. *The Song of Lodro Thaye*. Translated by Sarah Harding. Rev ed. Boulder: Namo Buddha Seminar, 1997.

————. *Songs of Naropa*. Boudhanath & Hong Kong: Rangjung Yeshe Publications, 1997.

————. *Treatise That Differentiates Consciousness and Wisdom*. Boulder: Namo Buddha Seminar, 1996.

Thurman, Robert A. F. *The Tibetan Book of the Dead: Liberation Through Understanding in the Between*. New York: Bantam Books, 1994.

Trungpa, Chögyam. *Cutting Through Spiritual Materialism*. Boston: Shambhala Publications, 1973.

————. *The Heart of the Buddha*. Boston: Shambhala Publications, 1991.

————. *Illusion's Game*. Boston: Shambhala Publications, 1994.

————. *Journey without Goal: The Tantric Wisdom of the Buddha*. Boston: Shambhala Publications, 2000.

————. *Lion's Roar: An Introduction to Tantra*. Shambhala Publications, Boston, 1992.

————. *1974 Vajradhatu Seminary Transcripts: Vajrayana*. Halifax: Vajradhatu Publications, 1975.

————. *Nyingma Teachings on the Intermediate State* (a summary of teachings given by Chögyam Trungpa Rinpoche). Edited by Michael Hookham. London: private publication, 1971.

————. *Secret beyond Thought: The Five Chakras and the Four Karmas*. Halifax: Vajradhatu Publications, 1991.

Urgyen Rinpoche, Tulku. *Rainbow Painting*. Hong Kong: Rangjung Yeshe Publications, 1995.

————. *As It Is.* Vol. 1. Boudhanath, Nepal: Rangjung Yeshe Publications, 1999.

Wangyal, Tenzin. *Wonders of the Natural Mind: The Essence of Dzogchen in the Native Bon Tradition of Tibet*. Barrytown, N.Y.: Station Hill Press, 1993.

Willis, Janice. *Diamond Light*. New York: Simon and Schuster, 1973.

Yeshe, Lama Thubten. *The Bliss of Inner Fire: Heart Practice of the Six Yogas of Naropa*. Boston: Wisdom Publications, 1998.

————. *Introduction to Tantra: A Vision of Totality*. London: Wisdom Publications, 1987.

Credits

TEXT

The author thanks the following publishers and individuals for permission to quote material to which they control the rights:

ÉDITIONS CLAIRE LUMIÈRE for excerpts from *Secret Buddhism* by Kalu Rinpoche, published in English by Clear Point Press, P.O. Box 170658, San Francisco, CA 94117. Copyright © Éditions Claire Lumière (France).

PADMA PUBLISHING for excerpts from *Lord of the Dance: The Autobiography of a Tibetan Lama* by Chagdud Tulku (Junction City, Calif.: Padma Publishing), © 1992. Reproduced by permission of the publisher.

PADMAKARA TRANSLATION GROUP for excerpts from *Journey to Enlightenment: The Life and World of Khyentse Rinpoche, Spiritual Teacher from Tibet* (Aperture Publications, 1996).

RANGJUNG YESHE PUBLICATIONS (http://www.rangjung.com) for excerpts from *Rainbow Painting* by Tulku Urgyen Rinpoche (Hong Kong: Rangjung Yeshe Publishing, 1995).

SHAMBHALA PUBLICATIONS for excerpts from *Cutting Through Spiritual Materialism* by Chögyam Trungpa, © 1973 by Diana J. Mukpo; *Journey without Goal* by Chögyam Trungpa, © 1987 by Diana J. Mukpo; *Illusion's Game* by Chögyam Trungpa, © 1994 by Diana J. Mukpo; and *Born in Tibet* by Chögyam Trungpa, © 1995 by Diana J. Mukpo. Reprinted by arrangement with Shambhala Publications, Inc., Boston, www.shambhala.com.

VEN. THRANGU RINPOCHE and NAMO BUDDHA SEMINAR for excerpts from *Treatise That Differentiates Consciousness and Wisdom* (Boulder: Namo Buddha Seminar, 1996) by Thrangu Rinpoche, and *The Song of Lodro Thaye* by Thrangu Rinpoche, translated by Sarah Harding (Boulder: Namo Buddha Seminar, 1997). Reprinted by courtesy of Ven. Thrangu Rinpoche.

CREDITS

ILLUSTRATIONS

Slides from the Argüelles collection, The Allen Ginsberg Library, Naropa University, are reproduced courtesy of Naropa University.

Figs. 1.1, 15.1, 15.2, and 15.3, the drawings of Tilopa, Tüsum Khyenpa, Karma Pakshi, and Rangjung Dorje by Chris Bannigan (Namkha Tashi), are from *The History of the Sixteen Karmapas* by Karma Thinley, © 1980 by Norbu Publications, Toronto. Reproduced by permission.

Fig. 3.1, the drawing of Atisha by Konchok Lhadrepa, is reproduced by kind permission of the Padmakara Translation Group.

Fig. 3.12, the thangka painting of Jamgön Kongtrül Lodrö Thaye by Cynthia Moku, is reproduced by permission of the artist.

Fig. 7.2, mudra drawings from *Mystic Art of Ancient Tibet* by Blanche Christine Olschak, © 1973 by George Allen & Unwin Ltd., is reprinted by arrangement with Shambhala Publications, Inc., Boston, www.shambhala.com.

Fig. 16.2, the photograph of H. H. the fourteenth Dalai Lama by Clive Arrowsmith, is reprinted by permission of the photographer.

Fig. 16.3, the photograph of Khyentse Rinpoche by Matthieu Ricard, is reproduced by kind permission of the photographer and the Padmakara Translation Group.

Fig. 16.4, the photograph of Ven. Chagdud Tulku Rinpoche, is reproduced courtesy of Padma Publishing.

Fig. 18.1, the photograph of H. H. the sixteenth Gyalwang Karmapa, is from *Empowerment* (Vajradhatu Publications, 1976).

Index

bodhisattva vow, 67, 79, 82–83, 85, 87, 89, 205, 463–464
Bodhisattva-yana, 37 table 2.1, 57 table 3.1
bodhisattvas, 3, 25, 28, 67, 80, 95–96, 120, 166, 315, 417
  passing of, 463–464
  rebirth of, 364, 366, 367
body of unification (yuganaddha), 120–121
Bön, 4, 34
Bondurant, Jenny
  retreat account of, 449–459
Born in Tibet, 157
Boulder, Colorado, 467
Buddha, the. *See* Buddha Shakyamuni
buddha activity, 146, 302
buddha family, 132–135, 144 table 7.1
buddha-nature, 15, 18 table 1.1, 78–79, 80, 82, 90, 98, 103–107, 169, 485–486
  devotion and, 167
  in dzokchen tradition, 300, 309, 311, 312–313
  in mahamudra tradition, 266–267, 273
  in Vajrayana, 106–107, 111–112, 126–127, 130, 223, 330–333
  yidam and, 209, 238
Buddha Samantabhadra. *See* Samantabhadra
Buddha Shakyamuni, 11, 13–15, 16 fig, 1.3, 17, 18, 69, 91–92, 98–99, 116, 351
  enlightenment of, 102
  mudras of, reflected in mandala of five buddhas, 133, 136
  as nirmanakaya, 360, 364
  rebirths of, 363–364
  themes in the life of, 385–386
  and Vajrayana teachings, 117–122, 124–125, 267, 295, 297
buddha-vachana, 97, 125
Buddha Vajradhara. *See* Vajradhara
Buddhapalita, 58
Buddhism
  overview of, 3–4, 14–15

view, practice and result in, 69
See also Ch'an Buddhism; Eighteen Schools; Indian Buddhism; monastic Buddhism; Pure Land Buddhism; Theravada Buddhism; Tibetan Buddhism; Zen Buddhism

Cessation (third noble truth), 79–80, 89–90
Chadral Rinpoche, 394
Chagdud Tulku, 390–391, 403, 404 fig. 16.4, 407, 409, 411–413, 434
  on phowa, 353, 354
  on the spiritual teacher, 154, 156
chakras, 112, 231, 232–233
Chakrasamvara, 197, 210, 212 fig. 10.3
Ch'an Buddhism, 299
Charya Tantra, 57 table 3.1
charyayoga-yana, 37 table 2.1, 57 table 3.1
Chenrezig. *See* Avalokiteshvara
chö, 429
Chödzin. *See* Karma Pakshi
Chökyi Nyima
  on the bardo, 339–340, 342–343
Christ, 218
clarity (selwa), 250–251, 279, 313
clear light practice, 247–248, 249
coemergent wisdom, 286
Collection of Precious Qualities, 20
commitment, 197, 225–226, 228–229
  See also samaya
compassion, 28, 37 table 2.1, 85, 96, 103, 147, 172, 208
completion stage (sampannakrama), 222, 230, 231 table 11.1, 274
Conze, Edward, 124
"cosmic guru," 174
creation stage. *See* development stage
cremation grounds, 30–31, 123, 227, 228
Cutting Through Spiritual Materialism, 269

Dashabhumika Sutra, 309, 364
David-Néel, Alexandra, 242